CONTRIBUTORY NEGLIGENCE

CONTRIBUTORY NEGLIGENCE

SECOND EDITION

JAMES GOUDKAMP
DONAL NOLAN

OXFORD
UNIVERSITY PRESS

OXFORD
UNIVERSITY PRESS

Great Clarendon Street, Oxford, OX2 6DP,
United Kingdom

Oxford University Press is a department of the University of Oxford.
It furthers the University's objective of excellence in research, scholarship,
and education by publishing worldwide. Oxford is a registered trade mark of
Oxford University Press in the UK and in certain other countries

First Edition published in 2018
Second Edition published in 2023

Published in the United States of America by Oxford University Press
198 Madison Avenue, New York, NY 10016, United States of America

British Library Cataloguing in Publication Data
Data available

Library of Congress Control Number: 2023939359

ISBN 978–0–19–286791–9

DOI: 10.1093/oso/9780192867919.001.0001

Printed and bound by
CPI Group (UK) Ltd, Croydon, CR0 4YY

FOREWORD TO THE FIRST EDITION

One of the most important areas of legal practice is the law of negligence. Since claims in negligence—especially personal injury claims—are commonly met by defences of contributory negligence, judges and practitioners have to apply that doctrine day in and day out. In doing so, they are liable to encounter a number of difficulties.

Some of these difficulties concern questions of law. To give only a few examples, to what causes of action, other than tortious negligence, does the doctrine of contributory negligence apply? Does it apply in cases of strict liability? Is the test of contributory negligence always objective, or can it sometimes take account of the characteristics of the individual claimant? If the claimant deliberately fails to take reasonable care for his own safety, can he be described as negligent? Is it relevant that the claimant failed to take reasonable care for his own safety, if the risk to which he negligently exposed himself was not a cause of the injuries which he sustained? In what circumstances can a claimant be contributorily negligent by reason of another person's conduct? How does contributory negligence operate in a situation where the damages recoverable by the claimant are also limited by the principle in *SAAMCO* (*South Australia Asset Management Corp v York Montague Ltd* [1997] AC 191)? If contributory negligence is pleaded along with other defences, such as *volenti non fit injuria* (that the claimant voluntarily incurred the risk of injury) or *ex turpi causa non oritur actio* (illegality), how do these defences interact with one another?

Other difficulties, arising in most if not all cases of contributory negligence, concern the apportionment of responsibility between the claimant and the defendant. As judges have often remarked, this naturally depends on the circumstances of the particular case. Nevertheless, it is important that the courts should adopt a coherent approach. It is elementary justice that like cases should be treated alike, and that unlike cases should be treated differently. But consistency is only possible if the courts are provided with information about apportionments in other comparable cases, and about the salient facts of those cases. The same requirement exists when practitioners seek to settle claims by agreement: the procedure by which the great majority of claims are determined.

The present work is designed to assist practitioners and the courts to address these difficulties. Parts I and II explain, clearly and succinctly, the law relating to contributory negligence. They answer all the questions mentioned above, and many others besides. Part III contains a guide to the practice of the UK courts in relation to apportionment in the factual situations which arise most commonly in practice. In relation to each of the most common categories of case—for example, cases where child pedestrians have been knocked down by motorists, or cases where the claimant failed to wear a seat belt—statistics are given for the extent to which damages were discounted for contributory negligence, based on an analysis of all the cases decided by the courts during the past twenty years, so far as available. What emerges from these analyses is that the discounts applied by judges, in situations which arise time and time again, generally fall within a relatively narrow range. It is therefore possible to provide practice-based guidance as to the average extent to which damages are discounted in each category of case, and the general range of discounts, together with illustrations of circumstances involving a higher, or lower, discount than the average.

This concise book is the first guide since Glanville Williams's *Joint Torts and Contributory Negligence* (1951), published shortly after the passing of the Law Reform (Contributory Negligence) Act 1945 and the Law Reform (Miscellaneous Provisions) Act (Northern Ireland) 1948, both to the interpretation and effect of the legislation, and to how it is applied in practice by the courts of England and Wales, Scotland, and Northern Ireland. It will assist courts and practitioners in understanding this area of the law, and in applying a consistent approach when assessing, in the most common types of case, the extent to which damages should be reduced for contributory negligence. It is greatly to be welcomed.

The Rt Hon Lord Reed
31 August 2018

PREFACE

This work is concerned with the law of contributory negligence as it currently stands. It is a much more extensive product than the first edition, which was published in 2018. Whereas the earlier edition was strongly focused on the black-letter law, we have rebalanced things by including significantly more discussion of normative issues, both within the law of contributory negligence and regarding its interaction with other parts of (in particular) the law of torts. We have also given greater prominence to historical matters as well as to case law and literature in other common law countries. Perhaps most importantly of all, however, we have taken a much deeper dive into the contributory negligence doctrine in this jurisdiction. The upshot of the foregoing is that the book has more than doubled in length, and now provides a comprehensive account of the English law of contributory negligence. In addition to increasing significantly the breadth and depth of the coverage, we have also made major structural changes to the work.

We remain very grateful to Lord Reed for writing the foreword to the first edition, which we have reproduced. Alvin Cheung gathered the data that underpin appendix 1, while Aurora Guerrini provided significant assistance with the figures and boxplots that feature therein. Daniel Leyva likewise provided excellent research assistance in connection with the chapters on the law. We would also like to acknowledge financial support provided by the Oxford Law Faculty and Keble College. The Bodleian Law Library (by Elizabeth Wells) helped us to locate certain sources. We additionally wish to thank Oxford University Press (and especially Fay Gibbons, Andy Redman, and Matthew Williams) for supporting the new edition and for shepherding it through the production process, along with the anonymous referees for their constructive comments on our publication proposal. Finally, we acknowledge our indebtedness to Glanville Williams. Although his towering work on *Joint Torts and Contributory Negligence* was published more than seventy years ago, it is a book of such quality and timelessness that it remains essential to a proper understanding of this field today.

We have endeavoured to state the law as it stood on 11 December 2022.

James Goudkamp
Donal Nolan
Oxford
11 December 2022

CONTENTS

TABLE OF CASES

UNITED KINGDOM

AUSTRALIA

CANADA

IRELAND

NEW ZEALAND

UNITED STATES OF AMERICA

TABLE OF LEGISLATION

UNITED KINGDOM

STATUTORY INSTRUMENTS

AUSTRALIA

CANADA

EUROPEAN UNION

IRELAND

NEW ZEALAND

SINGAPORE

ABBREVIATIONS OF FREQUENTLY CITED WORKS

Burrows	A Burrows, *Remedies for Torts, Breach of Contract, and Equitable Wrongs* (4th edn, OUP 2019)
Charlesworth	M Armitage (ed), *Charlesworth & Percy on Negligence* (15th edn, Sweet & Maxwell 2022)
Clerk & Lindsell	MA Jones (ed), *Clerk & Lindsell on Torts* (23rd edn, Sweet & Maxwell 2020)
Fleming	JG Fleming, *The Law of Torts* (9th edn, Law Book Co 1998)
Goudkamp and Nolan	J Goudkamp and D Nolan, *Contributory Negligence in the Twenty-First Century* (OUP 2019)
Harder	S Harder, *Measuring Damages in the Law of Obligations: The Search for Harmonised Principles* (Hart Publishing 2010)
Luntz	H Luntz and S Harder, *Assessment of Damages for Personal Injury and Death* (5th edn, LexisNexis 2021)
McGregor	J Edelman et al, *McGregor on Damages* (21st edn, Sweet & Maxwell 2020)
Mitchell	P Mitchell, *A History of Tort Law 1900–1950* (CUP 2015)
Munkman	D Bennett, *Munkman on Employers' Liability* (17th edn, LexisNexis 2019)
Prosser	WL Prosser, *Handbook of the Law of Torts* (West Publishing 1941)
Prosser & Keeton	WP Keeton et al, *Prosser and Keeton on Torts* (5th edn, West Publishing 1984)
Todd	S Todd et al, *Todd on Torts* (8th edn, Thomson Reuters 2019)
Williams	G Williams, *Joint Torts and Contributory Negligence: A Study of Concurrent Fault in Great Britain, Ireland and the Common-Law Dominions* (Stevens & Sons 1951)
Winfield & Jolowicz	J Goudkamp and D Nolan, *Winfield & Jolowicz on Tort* (20th edn, Sweet & Maxwell 2020)
Woods and Deere	H Woods and B Deere, *Comparative Fault* (3rd edn, Clark Boardman Callaghan 1996)

1

INTRODUCTION

Contributory negligence is a failure by a claimant to take reasonable care for their own safety or interests that is causally related to the damage of which they complain. Self-regarding fault and its consequences for tortious liability 'have been central issues in the study of private law for centuries'.[1] At common law, a finding of contributory negligence defeated claims to which the contributory negligence doctrine applied. However, since 1945 (in England, Wales, and Scotland[2]) and 1948 (in Northern Ireland[3]), legislation has provided that contributory negligence does not prevent liability from arising but that the claimant's damages shall instead be reduced to such extent as the court thinks just and equitable having regard to the claimant's share in the responsibility for the damage.[4] **1.01**

In this work we seek to provide a comprehensive account of the modern English law of contributory negligence. We begin our analysis in this chapter with a discussion of the history of the doctrine, an exploration of possible justifications for it, and an evaluation of where the issue of contributory negligence belongs in the structure of tort analysis. We then proceed in the remainder of the book to consider the scope of the contributory negligence doctrine (chapter 2), the circumstances in which a finding of contributory negligence will be made (chapter 3), the apportionment exercise that follows such a finding (chapter 4), the relationship between the doctrine and related rules (chapter 5), and questions pertaining to procedure and appeals in the contributory negligence context (chapter 6). The doctrinal analysis that makes up the main body of the work is accompanied by appendices in which we report the findings of an empirical study of the discounts imposed for contributory negligence in a range of frequently recurring situations (appendix 1) and reproduce the key legislation in this area (appendices 2–5). **1.02**

In 1951, at the dawn of the age of apportionment, Glanville Williams published his towering work *Joint Torts and Contributory Negligence*.[5] That book remains by a significant margin the most important contribution to this field of enquiry in any common law jurisdiction.[6] However, while still of huge value to the modern reader—as demonstrated **1.03**

[1] EGD van Dongen and HP Verdam, 'The Development of the Concept of Contributory Negligence in English Common Law' (2016) 12 Utrecht L Rev 61, 61.

[2] Law Reform (Contributory Negligence) Act 1945.

[3] Law Reform (Miscellaneous Provisions) Act (Northern Ireland) 1948.

[4] Law Reform (Contributory Negligence) Act 1945, s 1(1).

[5] G Williams, *Joint Torts and Contributory Negligence: A Study of Concurrent Fault in Great Britain, Ireland and the Common-Law Dominions* (Stevens & Sons 1951).

[6] 'Glanville Williams['s] ... text on contributory negligence ... remains, arguably, the best analysis available today' of the law in this area: *Chae v Min* [2001] ABQB 1071, (2001) 100 Alta LR (3d) 65 [14] (Veit J).

Contributory Negligence. Second Edition. James Goudkamp and Donal Nolan, Oxford University Press.
 DOI: 10.1093/oso/9780192867919.003.0001

by the many references to it peppered throughout this volume—Williams's work is now more than seventy years old, and developments during the period since it was published mean that it can no longer be regarded as a reliable guide to the state of the law. The only other monograph on contributory negligence in English law, *Contributory Negligence in the Twenty-First Century*,[7] was written by the authors of the current volume, and published in 2019. That book was based on an empirical study of 572 first-instance decisions from across the United Kingdom decided between 2000 and 2016, as well as 129 appellate decisions handed down in the same period. Consideration was given in that work to the operation of the contributory negligence doctrine at first instance and on appeal, as well as in a range of contextual settings, including road accidents, accidents at work, and professional negligence claims. Substantial appendices set out the core data on which the book was based, including the key features of every case that was included in the study. Although we have drawn extensively on the findings reported in that work in the present volume, the aspirations of the two books are very different, and while we hope that they can fruitfully be read in parallel, there is little overlap between them.

1.04 This book is concerned with the law of contributory negligence in all parts of the United Kingdom. The relevant law is substantially uniform across the nations.[8] The law in other Commonwealth jurisdictions is for the most part founded on the same principles as English law, and the core statutory provisions are often more or less identical to those in the United Kingdom legislation. However, in some jurisdictions the law of contributory negligence has acquired distinctive features as a result of legislative intervention, while differences have inevitably emerged between common law systems as a result of divergences of judicial reasoning. As is so often the case in the law of tort, the law of contributory negligence (or 'comparative fault') in the United States has parted ways with English law in many quite fundamental respects.[9] Although the American authorities and commentary are a rich resource on which we often draw, these differences must be kept in mind when transatlantic comparisons are being made.

1.05 The material on which reliance is placed in this book (including the empirical data in appendix 1) has been gathered from judicial decisions. No attempt has been made to investigate the operation of the doctrine of contributory negligence in the settlement process, partly because several such studies already exist,[10] and partly because it is very challenging to obtain accurate and representative information regarding settlements. It is

---

[7] J Goudkamp and D Nolan, *Contributory Negligence in the Twenty-First Century* (OUP 2019).

[8] 'As one would expect, given that [the rule in] section 1(1) [of the Law Reform (Contributory Negligence) Act 1945] applies throughout the United Kingdom, the same approach has been followed in Scotland': *Jackson v Murray* [2015] UKSC 5, [2015] 2 All ER 805 [32] (Lord Reed).

[9] For a comprehensive treatment of the US law, see *Woods and Deere*.

[10] Studies of the law of contributory negligence in the context of personal injury settlements in the United Kingdom are offered in *Report of the Royal Commission on Civil Liability and Compensation for Personal Injury* (Cmnd 7054, 1978) vol 2, 163 (Table 117); D Harris et al, *Compensation and Support for Illness and Injury* (Clarendon Press 1984) 91, 111; Law Commission, *Personal Injury Compensation: How Much is Enough? A Study of the Compensation Experiences of Victims of Personal Injury Law* (Law Com No 225, 1994) 81–82. See also *Report of the National Committee of Inquiry on Compensation and Rehabilitation in Australia* (Australian Government Publishing Service 1974) vol 1, paras 129–130.

important to bear in mind that the practical significance of the doctrine in the negotiation of settlements is immense, and far outweighs its importance in cases that are litigated to judgment.[11]

A final point on the scope of the work is that no attempt is made to provide a comprehensive account of the distinctive regime of contributory negligence that applies in the case of collisions at sea, although frequent references are made to that regime for the purposes of comparison, illustration, and historical background. Detailed treatments of the rules on maritime collisions can be found in specialist texts.[12] **1.06**

Two additional preliminary points should be made. One is that the seismic nature of the changes wrought by the Law Reform (Contributory Negligence) Act 1945 cannot be over-emphasized. It is particularly important to remember when looking at the pre-1945 authorities that in those cases a finding of contributory negligence meant that the claim would fail in its entirety. This naturally disinclined the courts to make such a finding, especially where the fault of the claimant was relatively minor compared with that of the defendant. By softening the consequences of contributory negligence, the 1945 Act removed that disinclination, so that the advent of apportionment had profound implications not only for the consequences issue with which it was directly concerned but also for the question of whether contributory negligence existed in the first place.[13] As Lord Wright observed, the cases decided before 1945 are therefore 'apt to be unsatisfactory and misleading' as a guide to the modern position.[14] And the other preliminary point is that the criticisms that are sometimes directed at the expression 'contributory negligence' are in our view unfounded. It is objected, for example, that it implies, wrongly, that the claimant must have committed actionable negligence against the defendant.[15] However, this objection rests on the false assumption that the word 'negligence' necessarily connotes 'tortious negligence', that is, conduct that gives rise to liability in the tort of negligence. However, in the phrase 'contributory negligence', negligence is synonymous with 'fault', and bears its ordinary legal meaning of conduct that falls below a standard of reasonable care. And the negligence is of course 'contributory' in the sense that it contributes (along with the wrongful conduct of the defendant) to the claimant's damage.[16] **1.07**

[11] J Steele, 'Law Reform (Contributory Negligence) Act 1945: Collisions of a Different Sort' in TT Arvind and J Steele (eds), *Tort Law and the Legislature: Common Law, Statute and the Dynamics of Legal Change* (Hart Publishing 2012) 165 (the doctrine is 'operated chiefly by lawyers and other negotiators, rather than by courts'). On the significance of contributory negligence in the settlement process, see the summary of the findings of the reports cited in the previous footnote in *Goudkamp and Nolan*, paras 1.09–1.12.

[12] See also *Williams*, ch 14.

[13] For other knock-on consequences, see J Goudkamp, 'Rethinking Contributory Negligence' in SGA Pitel et al (eds), *Tort Law: Challenging Orthodoxy* (Hart Publishing 2013) 338–44.

[14] Lord Wright, 'Contributory Negligence' (1950) 13 MLR 2, 10.

[15] See, eg, A Bartlett, 'Attribution of Contributory Negligence: Agents, Company Directors and Fraudsters' (1998) 114 LQR 460, 460.

[16] The appropriateness of the language is brought out by the following definition in the *Restatement (Second) of the Law of Torts* (1965), § 463: 'Contributory negligence is conduct on the part of the plaintiff which falls below the standard to which he should conform for his own protection, and which is a legally contributing cause co-operating with the negligence of the defendant in bringing about the plaintiff's harm'.

1. The History of the Doctrine

(1) The development of the doctrine

1.08 There is a great deal that could be said about the history of the contributory negligence doctrine, but in a work of this kind only a brief overview is possible.[17] The 1809 decision in *Butterfield v Forrester*[18] is generally regarded as marking the birth of the modern doctrine, but it does not follow that in earlier times the fact that the claimant was partly to blame for the damage for which they were claiming was irrelevant. On the contrary, this would frequently lead to the failure of the claim.[19] However, before the nineteenth century the fault of the claimant did not trigger the application of a distinct doctrine, but instead went to the broader question of causation.[20] According to Ernest Turk, as far back as the fifteenth century, lawyers were 'familiar with the fact that a man was not to be held liable if his acts were not the proximate cause of the injury', and it was a truism 'that if the act which had caused the damage was the act of the plaintiff himself, there could be no cause of action'.[21] This idea of what we now term 'contributory negligence' as constituting the 'proximate cause' of the injury survived the development of a distinct legal doctrine of contributory negligence, and is observable in case law and commentary throughout the nineteenth and early twentieth centuries.[22]

1.09 The familiarity of these ancient notions of proximate cause to the lawyers of the early nineteenth century explains why the contributory negligence doctrine was ushered into the common law world in 1809 not with a bang but with a whimper. The claimant in *Butterfield v Forrester* was riding home from a public house at dusk when he collided with a pole that the defendant had placed across the highway, and suffered injury. The jury returned a verdict for the defendant, having been directed to do so if they considered that the claimant had been riding too fast, and that if he had been riding with ordinary care, he would have seen the obstruction and avoided it. That verdict was upheld by Lord Ellenborough CJ, who treated it as a given that the claimant's negligence barred his claim.

---

[17] For a more detailed treatment, focusing in particular on the early history, see van Dongen and Verdam (n 1). And for an outstanding account of the history of comparative fault in civil law systems, see EGD van Dongen, *Contributory Negligence: A Historical and Comparative Study* (Brill Nijhoff 2014).

[18] (1809) 11 East 60, 103 ER 926.

[19] See van Dongen and Verdam (n 1) 61–64.

[20] See ibid 61 ('the legal concept of contributory . . . negligence as we know it today was unknown in the medieval and early modern periods'); DJ Ibbetson, *A Historical Introduction to the Law of Obligations* (OUP 1999) 177 ('Contributory negligence . . . had impeccable medieval antecedents, but in the nineteenth century it took on a far more precisely delineated character').

[21] EA Turk, 'Comparative Negligence on the March' (1949) 28 Chi-Kent L Rev 189, 195. As Turk goes on to point out, in the early law what mattered was that it was the *act* of the claimant that caused the damage, not their *negligence* (ibid, 196). See also WS Holdsworth, *A History of English Law*, vol 8 (Methuen 1925) 459–62; Ibbetson (n 20) 59–60.

[22] See, eg, *Thomas v Quartermaine* (1887) 18 QBD 685 (CA) 694 (Bowen LJ) ('[c]ontributory negligence in a plaintiff only means that he himself has contributed to the accident in such a sense as to render the defendant's breach of duty no longer its proximate cause'); F Pollock, *The Law of Torts* (Stevens & Sons 1887) 441–43; A MacMurchy, 'Contributory Negligence: Should the Rule in Admiralty and the Civil Law Be Adopted?' (1923) 1 Can Bar Rev 844, 845; Holdsworth (n 21) 461 ('The substance of the defence . . . is not the fact that the plaintiff has been negligent; but that his negligent act is the direct cause of the accident'). On the mid-nineteenth century case law, see M Lobban, 'Tort' in W Cornish et al, *The Oxford History of the Laws of England: Volume XII* (OUP 2010) 932–34.

'One person being in fault', he said, 'will not dispense with another's using ordinary care for himself.'[23]

(2) The last opportunity rule and other ameliorative measures

The conception of the common law defence of contributory negligence that developed after *Butterfield* as a causal concept explains its all-or-nothing nature. If the claimant's negligence was the sole legal cause of the damage, then it followed that the defendant was not legally responsible for it at all. Hence the doctrine operated as a complete defence: it yielded a verdict for the defendant. At the same time, however, the development of contributory negligence as a distinct doctrine after 1809 restricted the room for manoeuvre that the courts had previously enjoyed when claimant fault was buried within broader notions of legal causation. The result was that the courts were in effect driven to conclude that it was (as a matter of principle, at least) irrelevant that the claimant's share of the responsibility for the damage was small relative to the defendant's,[24] a consideration that might well have tipped the balance under the old, more general, rule of proximate cause.[25] **1.10**

The practical consequences of these developments were not lost on the judges and juries who tried the cases. Their response was to develop a range of ameliorative measures, of which the most important was the exception known as the last opportunity (or 'last clear chance') rule.[26] According to this rule, the claimant's contributory negligence was not a defence to the claim if the defendant had had the last opportunity to avoid the occurrence of the damage. Like the doctrine of contributory negligence itself, this exception was grounded in notions of legal causation: in such a case (it was argued) the defendant's omission, rather than the claimant's act, was the proximate cause of the injury.[27] The last opportunity rule dates back to the 1842 decision in *Davies v Mann*,[28] where the defendant's wagon had mowed down and killed a donkey which the claimant had left grazing at the side of a road. The jury having found for the claimant, the defendant moved for a retrial on the ground of misdirection. This was rejected by the Court of Exchequer. Even if it had been negligent of the claimant to leave his donkey unattended, Lord Abinger CB said, 'it would have made no difference, for as the defendant might, by proper care, have avoided injuring the animal, and did not', he alone bore legal responsibility for the damage.[29] **1.11**

The last opportunity doctrine 'developed into a plastic instrument for allocating the loss to either plaintiff or defendant in accordance with the court's view of whose was the **1.12**

---

[23] (1809) 11 East 60, 61; 103 ER 926, 927.

[24] See *Cayzer, Irvine & Co v Carron Co* (1884) 9 App Cas 873 (HL) 881 (Lord Blackburn) ('the rule of law is that if there is blame causing the accident on both sides, however small that blame may be on one side, the loss lies where it falls').

[25] See *Woods and Deere*, 6.

[26] See further on this rule, F James Jr, 'Last Clear Chance: A Transitional Doctrine' (1938) 47 Yale LJ 704; *Williams*, ch 9.

[27] Hence the rule was described as 'a limitation which inheres in the defense of contributory negligence itself (rather than one which avoids the effect of contributory negligence)' and as a 'logical application' of the principle underlying the defence: James (n 26) 707. See also Ibbetson (n 20) 177 ('a straightforward causal test'). For a more sceptical view of the relationship between the rule and the law of legal causation, see *Williams*, 236–55.

[28] (1842) 10 M & W 546, 152 ER 588.

[29] ibid 548, 589.

disproportionately greater share of responsibility'.[30] The plasticity of the rule was exemplified by its extension to cases of 'constructive' last opportunity, where the defendant did not actually have the last opportunity to avoid the damage, but would have had it but for their prior negligence, as where the defendant's train hit the plaintiff's wagon on a level crossing because the train's brakes were defective.[31] The complexity and 'casuistry'[32] to which the last opportunity rule gave rise has been well documented[33] and was partly responsible for the twentieth-century reform of the law. As early as 1922 the rule was lambasted as 'an intellectual tyranny, giving rise to confusion, embarrassment and injustice'.[34] Later writers were no less scathing, describing it as 'intolerably subtle and complex',[35] and 'one of the worst tangles known to the law'.[36] It became virtually impossible to give a direction on the rule that was comprehensible to a jury.

1.13 The last opportunity rule was far from being the only mechanism that the courts developed to mitigate the harshness of the common law defence of contributory negligence. Other examples included the principle that the defence did not apply where the claimant's conduct was the very thing which the defendant was under a duty to prevent;[37] the notion that momentary inadvertence did not amount to contributory negligence, especially if the claimant was an employee engaged in repetitive and mind-numbing work on the defendant's behalf;[38] and perhaps also the 'agony of the moment' principle, according to which the claimant was generally absolved of negligence if they made the wrong choice, or acted less than ideally, when confronted with an emergency created by the defendant.[39] Furthermore, it was notorious that when faced with a case of relatively trivial fault on the part of the claimant, a sympathetic jury was likely to return a verdict for him or her regardless.[40] In such cases, the jury might even achieve apportionment on the sly, by reducing the claimant's rightful damages in proportion to the contribution which the jury considered they had made to their own injury.[41]

(3) Reform

1.14 The complex network of common law principles that developed to deal with contributory fault was generally regarded as highly unsatisfactory. On the one hand, it was thought unjust for claimants to be denied recovery altogether on account of comparatively venial fault. On the other hand, where the 'last opportunity' rule—or some other exception or ameliorative device—applied, it was considered unfair for the defendant to be made to pay for the entirety of the claimant's damage even though the claimant was partly (and maybe

---

30 *Fleming*, 305.
31 *British Columbia Electric Railway Co Ltd v Loach* [1916] 1 AC 719 (PC).
32 *Fleming*, 305.
33 For other twentieth-century glosses on the rule, see van Dongen and Verdam (n 1) 70–71.
34 J O'Connor, 'Contributory Negligence' (1922) 38 LQR 17, 17.
35 P Cane and J Goudkamp, *Atiyah's Accidents, Compensation and the Law* (9th edn, CUP 2018) 46.
36 WL Prosser, 'Comparative Negligence' (1953) 51 Mich L Rev 465, 473.
37 See 3.29.
38 See 3.31–3.32.
39 See 3.33.
40 See van Dongen and Verdam (n 1) 66.
41 See *Joslyn v Berryman* [2003] HCA 34, (2003) 214 CLR 552 [17]; *Fleming*, 305; W Cornish et al, *Law and Society in England: 1750–1950* (2nd edn, Hart Publishing 2019) 468–69.

even principally) responsible for it.[42] Furthermore, the complexity and obscurity of the law made it increasingly difficult to understand or apply. The result was that:[43]

> The contributory negligence doctrine made no one happy in the early twentieth century. Practising lawyers and judges found it uncertain and complicated. Many legal academics damned it as outdated and out of step with modern society. Business felt it failed to protect them from lawsuits by careless plaintiffs. The injured, on the other hand, felt threatened that the law would completely bar recovery for their losses.

The harshness of the common law rule was commented upon as early as 1887, when Lindley LJ remarked in *The Bernina* that he 'did not profess to understand' why the damages should not be apportioned in cases of contributory negligence.[44] It was no coincidence that that observation was made in a case involving a collision at sea, where the admiralty courts had long adhered to a principle of apportionment, which required that the damages be equally divided between the negligent parties.[45] The equal division rule for maritime collisions was replaced by a more sophisticated statutory apportionment regime in 1911, which provided for apportionment based on 'the degree in which each ship was in fault',[46] unless it was impossible to establish different degrees of fault, in which case the rule of equal division still applied. The existence of a fault-based apportionment regime for maritime collisions provided a clear alternative to the all-or-nothing rule governing other instances of contributory fault, and the first statutory reform of contributory negligence in what is now the Commonwealth[47] came three years later, with the passage of legislation in Ontario which replaced the complete defence in claims by employees against employers with apportionment based on the formula used in the 1911 Act ('in proportion to the degree to which each party was at fault').[48] Some years later the Ontario legislature passed a statute of general application replacing the common law defence of contributory negligence with apportionment based on relative fault.[49] The early adoption of apportionment in Ontario has been attributed not only to the example provided by the maritime collisions regime but also to the influence of the 'faute commune' principle recognized in the civil law of Quebec.[50] **1.15**

[42] The point being that ameliorative doctrines such as the last opportunity rule did not produce just results, but simply replaced injustice to the claimant with injustice to the defendant. See Prosser (n 36) 474 ('[t]he whole floundering, haphazard, makeshift device operates in favor of some plaintiffs by inflicting obvious injustice upon some defendants').

[43] RB Brown and N Yhard, 'The Harshness and Injustice of the Common Law Rule Has Frequently Been Commented On: Debating Contributory Negligence in Canada, 1914–1919' (2013) 36 Dalhousie LJ 137, 167.

[44] (1887) 12 PD 58 (CA) 89.

[45] See van Dongen and Verdam (n 1) 71.

[46] Maritime Conventions Act 1911, s 1(1). See now the Merchant Shipping Act 1995, s 187 (discussed in 2.25).

[47] There were apparently earlier examples in the United States in the workmen's compensation/employers' liability context: see EST, 'Again the Last Clear Chance Doctrine' (1920) 29 Yale LJ 896, 899.

[48] Workmen's Compensation Act 1914 (Ont) ss 107–108.

[49] Contributory Negligence Act 1924 (Ont). See further on the Ontario Act, JC Kleefeld, 'Concurrent Fault at 90: A History of Ontario's Negligence Act and Canada's Uniform Contributory Negligence Act' in E Quill and R Friel (eds), *Damages and Compensation Culture: Comparative Perspectives* (Hart Publishing 2016).

[50] Brown and Yhard (n 43) 151.

1.16 In England, change was longer in coming, but it did come in the end. In addition to the examples provided by the Maritime Conventions Act 1911 and the Canadian legislation, other drivers of reform can be identified. One was the proliferation of the motor car in the early decades of the twentieth century, and the concomitant increase in the road accidents which, more than any other area of social life, raised issues of contributory fault.[51] The potential injustice of the all-or-nothing rule in this context was shown by cases such as *M'Lean v Bell*,[52] where the pursuer was a girl who had suffered catastrophic injuries after being hit by a car while crossing a street in Glasgow. Two separate jury findings for the pursuer had been set aside by the Court of Session on the ground that she had been contributorily negligent, and it took an appeal to the House of Lords for the jury's decision to be reinstated on the (somewhat strained) basis that it had been entitled to conclude that her negligence was not a legal cause of the accident. Cases such as this raised the question of why there was an apportionment regime for accidents at sea but not on land, and the problems were compounded by the difficulty of applying the last opportunity rule when two motor vehicles collided at speed.[53] It is unsurprising that the proponents of the reform legislation framed it as an extension of the apportionment rules applicable to collisions at sea to 'collisions of a different sort'.[54] Another important driver of reform was the decline of the civil jury, a process in train since the late nineteenth century, but which accelerated in the aftermath of the First World War. This was important for two reasons. First, because juries had frequently mitigated the harshness of the all-or-nothing rule by simply refusing to make a finding of contributory negligence, as in *M'Lean v Bell*. And, secondly, because it was sometimes thought that apportionment based on relative fault was too complex a task for juries to undertake.[55] (The persistence of jury trial doubtless explains why reform came relatively late to the United States, and why the law of contributory fault there has many distinctive features not observable in other common law systems.)

1.17 The immediate catalyst for reform was a report of the Law Revision Committee, which was published in 1939.[56] The Committee had been asked to consider possible changes to the law of contributory negligence, with particular reference to the apportionment rules governing maritime collisions and the advent of contribution between tortfeasors following the passage of the Law Reform (Married Women and Tortfeasors) Act 1935.

---

[51] The importance of road accidents for the reform of contributory negligence is emphasized by Jenny Steele, who comments that the framers of the reforming legislation 'would appear ... to have been almost entirely focused on road traffic accidents': Steele (n 11) 163. Even today, road accidents account for a larger proportion of the litigated cases on contributory negligence than any other contextual category: see *Goudkamp and Nolan*, para 4.04.

[52] (1932) SC (HL) 21.

[53] See, eg, *Swadling v Cooper* [1931] AC 1 (HL).

[54] See the subtitle of Steele (n 11), an illuminating analysis of the 1945 Act and the circumstances surrounding its enactment.

[55] Concern as to the capacity of juries to effect apportionment is manifest in the contemporary literature: see, eg, 'Again the Last Clear Chance Doctrine' (n 47) 901; CLB Lowndes, 'Contributory Negligence' (1934) Georgetown LJ 674, 683 ('an undertaking which [it is] perilous to entrust to a jury'). It is also telling that the original version of the bill that became the Ontario Act of 1924 had assigned the apportionment of damages to the judge, though the Act itself gave the task to the jury: see JC Kleefeld, 'The Contributory Negligence Act at Seventy' (2015) 78 Sask L Rev 31, 41. In the maritime collision cases, where apportionment based on relative fault had been introduced in 1911, it was undertaken by a judge sitting in the Admiralty Division.

[56] Law Revision Committee, *Eighth Report (Contributory Negligence)* (Cmd 6032, 1939). See further, *Mitchell*, ch 13.

The Committee recommended that the complete defence of contributory negligence be replaced with an apportionment regime modelled on that of the Maritime Conventions Act 1911. After a delay of six years (largely attributable to the exigencies of wartime) the Committee's recommendations were implemented by the passing of the Law Reform (Contributory Negligence) Act 1945, albeit with some significant modifications.[57] The 1945 Act applied to all parts of the United Kingdom except for Northern Ireland, in respect of which reforming legislation was passed three years later.[58] The central provision of the 1945 Act is section 1(1), which reads as follows:

> Where any person suffers damage as a result partly of his own fault and partly of the fault of any other person or persons ... the damages recoverable in respect thereof shall be reduced to such extent as the court thinks just and equitable having regard to the claimant's share in the responsibility for the damage.

In the years immediately following its passage, 'there were significant doubts about the extent to which the Act had done away with the complexities of the old law'.[59] However, it 'gradually became clear that the statute had (or at least would be regarded as having) removed most of the difficulties' in question.[60] In particular, while the impact of the legislation on the last opportunity rule was not immediately apparent,[61] judicial decisions soon established that it had in fact sounded the death knell for that troublesome doctrine.[62] Although criticisms can be made of the 1945 Act,[63] it cannot seriously be doubted that the statutory apportionment regime which it introduced was infinitely more straightforward, more sophisticated and more just than the common law doctrine it replaced.

2. Justifications for the Doctrine

Although the law regarding contributory negligence is of ancient origin,[64] surprisingly little has been said about the doctrine's rationales.[65] To a considerable degree, it seems simply to have been assumed that a claimant's fault should count against him or her. Thus, Sir **1.18**

[57] The 1945 Act is reproduced in appendix 2.

[58] Law Reform (Miscellaneous Provisions) Act (Northern Ireland) 1948. This Act is reproduced in appendix 3.

[59] Cane and Goudkamp (n 35) 46.

[60] ibid.

[61] See *Williams*, ch 10.

[62] A key decision in this regard was *Davies v Swan Motor Co (Swansea) Ltd* [1949] 2 KB 291 (CA), where Denning LJ said (at 321) that since the Act was passed the doctrine of last opportunity was 'no longer a practical test and should disappear from the books'. Three years later the same judge observed that '[i]t can now be safely asserted that the doctrine of last opportunity is obsolete': *Jones v Livox Quarries Ltd* [1952] 2 QB 608 (CA) 615.

[63] See, eg, R Stevens, 'Should Contributory Fault be Analogue or Digital?' in A Dyson et al (eds), *Defences in Tort* (Hart Publishing 2015).

[64] See 1.08–1.09.

[65] The position is otherwise on the other side of the Atlantic: see, eg, FH Bohlen, 'Contributory Negligence' (1908) 21 Harv L Rev 233; F James, 'Contributory Negligence' (1953) Yale LJ 691, 696–703; G Schwartz, 'Contributory and Comparative Negligence: A Reappraisal' (1978) 87 Yale LJ 697; K Simons, 'The Puzzling Doctrine of Contributory Negligence' (1995) 16 Cardozo L Rev 1693. However, this literature is often concerned with specific aspects of the law of contributory negligence indigenous to the United States and is hence of limited utility for UK lawyers and those based elsewhere in the Commonwealth.

Percy Winfield complained that the judgments in the foundational decision in *Butterfield v Forrester*[66] 'are so jejune that the doctrine seems to have been taken for granted'.[67] The position has not changed greatly since Winfield's time and, certainly, the courts have not clearly stated that the law in this area rests on any particular justification. In these circumstances, several possible reasons why the law recognizes the doctrine of contributory negligence are sketched below. Some of the potential justifications do not withstand scrutiny and none is entirely free from difficulty. Of course, it would be surprising if the doctrine, which is recognized throughout the common law world as well as in many civil law jurisdictions,[68] was unjustified, although that possibility cannot be excluded.[69] But the fact remains that the quest for a convincing rationale is incomplete.

(1) Punishment

1.19 Early cases concerning the doctrine of contributory negligence were sometimes explained as exercises in punishment.[70] Consistent with this, in *Wakelin v London & South Western Railway Co* Lord Halsbury LC wrote that where the defendant establishes that damage is the result of 'the joint negligence' of both parties, the claimant will 'fail . . . because "*in pari delicto potior est conditio defendentis*"'.[71] This maxim, which today is typically associated with the illegality defence,[72] has a distinctly penal flavour. Whether or not the law in this area in bygone times could be justified on the basis of a retributive theory, a concern with punishment provides no support for the doctrine of contributory negligence in its modern guise. Claimants who are contributorily negligent might merit no sanction at all. Although we sometimes punish through the criminal law persons who risk their own safety but not that of others (eg persons who fail to wear a seat belt), such prohibitions are usually animated more by concerns about avoiding social costs than a desire to inflict retribution, and we would not normally think that self-endangerment deserves punishment. Further, because the standard of care by which claimants are judged is generally objective,[73] a claimant might have been incapable of exercising the degree of care necessary to avoid a finding of contributory negligence. It is only in rare circumstances that such a claimant will deserve to be censured. Even where, unusually, claimants merit a sanction for failing to take reasonable care of their own interests, the penalty imposed by the reduction in damages threatens to be disproportionate to the gravity of the claimant's conduct concerned. This is because the size of the sanction that is imposed by reducing the claimant's damages ultimately depends on the quantum of the claimant's loss (the greater the loss, the greater the punishment the apportionment mechanism imposes and vice versa). The problem that this causes for a retributive account of the law of contributory negligence is that the punishment dispensed is thus a matter of fortuity.

---

[66] (1809) 11 East 60, 61; 103 ER 926, 927.

[67] PH Winfield, *A Text-book of the Law of Tort* (4th edn, Sweet & Maxwell 1948) 418.

[68] The position in several civil law jurisdictions is addressed in M Martin-Casals and U Magnus (eds), *Unification of Tort Law: Contributory Negligence* (Kluwer Law International 2003).

[69] For argument that the doctrine should be abolished, see Stevens (n 63) 253–54.

[70] See, eg, W Schofield, '*Davies v Mann*: Theory of Contributory Negligence' (1890) 3 Harv L Rev 263, 271.

[71] (1886) 12 App Cas 41 (HL) 45.

[72] See, eg, *Patel v Mirza* [2016] UKSC 42, [2017] AC 467 [96]–[97]. Regarding the connection between the defence of illegality and the law of contributory negligence, see 5.08–5.09.

[73] See 3.06.

(2) Deterrence

Law-and-economics accounts of tort law endeavour to explain the rules regarding contributory negligence on the basis that they achieve optimal deterrence.[74] The idea, in short, is that since claimants may be the most efficient loss avoider, the law provides them with a spur to action by withholding part of their damages where they fail to take efficient precautions regarding their own safety. Familiar objections to deterrence-based explanations of tort law can be levelled at such efficiency-inspired accounts of the doctrine of contributory negligence. Deterrence-based theories of tort law implausibly assume that injurers are readily susceptible to being influenced by the economic incentives that the rules generate. This behavioural assumption is no more realistic when applied to most classes of victim. It 'lacks all reality'[75] to suppose that many claimants, in deciding whether to run certain risks and whether to take particular precautions, will carefully evaluate the way in which the law of contributory negligence might respond to careless conduct on their part in the event that they happen to be tortiously injured. This is at least partly because the details of the relevant law will usually be unknown to them and hence incapable of influencing their decision-making. Further, most claimants already have incentives to take reasonable care of their own interests that are far more potent than those supplied by the law of contributory negligence. These include, most obviously, a concern not to end up seriously injured irrespective of whether compensation is recovered.[76] Given the foregoing, it is unsurprising that even prominent proponents of economic accounts of tort law admit that there is a considerable divergence in this area of the law between rules that would be efficient and the principles that in fact exist. Thus, William Landes and Richard Posner concede that the modern law of contributory negligence is less efficient than the all-or-nothing approach that obtained historically because 'it costs more to administer' and that these 'additional administrative costs generate no social benefit'.[77] **1.20**

(3) Endangering others

In searching for a rationalization of the doctrine of contributory negligence, some writers emphasize that claimants who are contributorily negligent will sometimes also endanger others.[78] For example, claimants who drive too quickly are likely not only to be contributorily negligent but to breach the duty of care that they owe to other road users as well. But this cannot explain why the doctrine of contributory negligence extends to **1.21**

[74] Deterrence-based explanations of the law of contributory negligence significantly pre-date the rise of modern law-and-economics scholarship: see, eg, Schofield (n 70) 270 ('the ultimate justification of the rule is in reasons of policy, viz, the desire to prevent accidents by inducing each member of the community to act up to the standard of due care set by the law'). However, it is convenient to consider deterrence arguments through the prism of the law-and-economics movement.

[75] Prosser (n 36) 468.

[76] For further criticism of law-and-economics accounts of the law of contributory negligence, see G Calabresi, 'Optimal Deterrence and Accidents' (1975) 84 Yale LJ 656, 662–63; Schwartz (n 65) 703–21.

[77] W Landes and R Posner, *The Economic Structure of Tort Law* (Harvard University Press 1987) 27. cf at 82 where the authors retreat from this position somewhat ('if the potential victims and injurers are risk averse . . . if insurance is unavailable and if the cost of apportionment is small, the sharing of the damages may be preferable to having one party bear all the losses').

[78] Gary Schwartz flirted with this argument but ultimately considered it to be unconvincing for reasons that are in the end rather different from those sketched here: Schwartz (n 65) 723–24.

situations where the claimant's carelessness did not endanger anyone else. If this analysis were sound, much conduct that constitutes contributory negligence, such as a failure to wear a seat belt, should fall outside the doctrine's scope. More fundamentally, this line of reasoning cannot account for the fact that the focus of the law of contributory negligence is ultimately not on conduct that consists in a breach of a duty of care owed to a defendant or third party but on self-regarding fault.[79] In other words, even where there is negligence towards others combined with negligence towards oneself, it is the carelessness with respect to the claimant's own interests that in the end matters for the purposes of the doctrine of contributory negligence. As Lord Wright observed, '[t]he plaintiff in contributory negligence may owe a duty to the defendant as well, but primarily the question is simply one of his failing to take ordinary care of himself and his property'.[80] Finally, the doctrine of contributory negligence is hardly needed to ensure that account is taken of claimants' contributory fault that endangers others. If such fault causes damage to another, a claim in the tort of negligence will usually be available in respect of it.

(4) Protecting the defendant's interests

1.22 Another attempt at rationalizing the law involves focusing on the fact that the defendant's interests are engaged and set back if the claimant can recover full damages despite having been contributorily negligent. Thus, Gary Schwartz wrote:[81]

> The plaintiff's original act of contributory negligence may not have been morally improper, since it created a risk only to the plaintiff himself. When that risk eventuates in an injury to the plaintiff, however, and when the plaintiff then seeks to collect in tort for that injury against a negligent defendant, at the time of this lawsuit the harm involved in the plaintiff's original conduct 'reaches' the defendant, another person. The defendant, concededly, has engaged in negligent conduct that has contributed to the plaintiff's accident. Nevertheless, that accident would never have occurred had the plaintiff himself not behaved in a foolish way. In these circumstances, it would be basically unfair for the law to ignore entirely the plaintiff's conduct by imposing full liability on the negligent defendant.

Notice that Schwartz stops short of explaining precisely why the unfairness to which he refers would obtain absent the doctrine of contributory negligence. He simply observes the consequences that would follow if there were no contributory negligence doctrine, which is that the defendant would need to bear the full cost of the claimant's damages. Because Schwartz does not actually go on to identify any reason why the alleged unfairness would exist unless account is taken of the claimant's contributory negligence, his analysis does not rise above the level of assertion.

(5) Parity of treatment

1.23 Having considered several arguments that are especially vulnerable to attack, we now turn to two rationales that seem to be more plausible. The first such argument rests on the idea of parity of treatment. It is often said that tort law (and private law more generally) is a two-sided affair. This claim comes in weaker and stronger forms. For some, it simply

[79] See 3.02.
[80] Wright (n 14) 7.
[81] Schwartz (n 65) 724–25 (footnotes omitted).

means that the interests of both parties are reflected in the law's framework.[82] Others argue that tort law's bilateral structure means that the parties must be treated strictly as equals.[83] Both variations of the claim suggest, however, that the doctrine of contributory negligence is justified on the basis that it results in the parties being treated even-handedly. The basic idea is that the quid pro quo for claimants being entitled to recover compensation in respect of a defendant's deficient conduct is that their own inadequate actions should count against them. For example, Ernest Weinrib writes that the law of contributory negligence 'expresses an idea of transactional equality: the plaintiff cannot demand that the defendant should observe a greater care than the plaintiff with respect to the plaintiff's safety'.[84] Lord Ellenborough CJ seemed to have much the same idea in mind when he said in *Butterfield v Forrester* that 'one person being in fault will not dispense with another taking ordinary care for himself'.[85] One possible response to this argument focuses on the fact that, as a purely practical matter, the law of contributory negligence likely has an unequal impact upon claimants. It can safely be assumed that most defendants who are sued in tort have liability insurance and that very few claimants have first-party insurance in respect of (at least) the risk of personal injury.[86] This means that whereas defendants who incur liability in tort rarely pay damages awards personally, claimants who are found to have been contributorily negligent are generally saddled with uninsured losses. Putting things in monetary terms, a claimant who suffers a loss of £100,000 but whose damages are reduced by 25 per cent for contributory negligence in substance has their net worth reduced by £25,000. Accordingly, it might be said that any notion that the law of contributory negligence involves parity of treatment is an illusion. In reply, defenders of this argument might say that insurance arrangements are beside the point[87] and are not something to which the law should pay any attention. They might also say that, in any event, claimants are entirely at liberty to contract for first-party insurance.

(6) Causation

Another possibility is that the law regarding contributory negligence can be justified by principles of causation. In earlier times, when contributory negligence resulted in judgment for the defendant, it was often considered that this outcome was supportable on the basis that the claimant had caused their own damage.[88] For example, in *Thomas v Quartermaine*, Bowen LJ said that the law of contributory negligence 'rests upon the view that though the defendant has in fact been negligent, yet the plaintiff has by his own carelessness severed the causal connection between the defendant's negligence and the accident which has occurred; and that the defendant's negligence accordingly is not the true proximate cause of the injury'.[89] And in *Caswell v Powell Duffryn Associated* **1.24**

[82] See, eg, P Cane, *The Anatomy of Tort Law* (Hart Publishing 1997).

[83] See, eg, EJ Weinrib, *The Idea of Private Law* (Harvard University Press 1995).

[84] ibid 169 fn 53. To similar effect, see A Beever, *Rediscovering the Law of Negligence* (Hart Publishing 2009) 342.

[85] (1809) 11 East 60, 61; 103 ER 926, 927.

[86] Patrick Atiyah regarded this as axiomatic: see PS Atiyah, *The Damages Lottery* (Hart Publishing 1997) 118.

[87] For discussion, see J Stapleton, 'Tort, Insurance and Ideology' (1995) 58 MLR 820; EJ Weinrib, 'The Insurance Justification and Private Law' (1985) 14 J Leg Stud 681.

[88] See 1.08.

[89] (1887) 18 QBD 685 (CA) 697.

Collieries Ltd Lord Atkin remarked that he found 'it impossible to divorce any theory of contributory negligence from the concept of causation'.[90] However, the force of this causation explanation as regards the position at common law is debatable.[91] It might be said that, if it were sound, there would not, in fact, have been any space at all for any rule regarding contributory negligence. On this view, because a defendant must have caused the damage that is the subject of a claim before the issue of contributory negligence could properly fall for consideration,[92] it was impossible to justify the all-or-nothing rule on the basis that it was concerned with instances in which the claimant's conduct caused their loss. In the era of apportionment, a causal account might be thought to be more compelling. Writing in 1948 and hence a few years after the apportionment legislation was enacted, Sir Percy Winfield claimed that '[t]he theory of causation is the predominant [account of the law of contributory negligence] at the present day and it is submitted that, upon the whole, it is the most satisfactory'.[93] The idea appears to be that in discounting the claimant's damages, the courts are in effect isolating that part of the damage for which the claimant is causally responsible and precluding recovery in respect of it.

3. The Situs of the Doctrine

1.25 Where, specifically, does the doctrine of contributory negligence fit within the structure of (in particular) tort law?[94] It is often described as a 'defence'.[95] However, even prior to the enactment of the apportionment legislation this categorization was contestable. It was debatable whether the rule, when enlivened, prevented the elements of the wrong for which the claimant sued from being satisfied (specifically, the causation element on the theory that contributory negligence operated as an intervening cause of the claimant's damage[96]) or whether it precluded liability from arising even where all of the elements of the claimant's cause of action were present.[97] According to one view, only rules that operate in the latter way are genuinely defences.[98]

1.26 Characterizing the contributory negligence doctrine as a 'defence' is even more contentious in the era of apportionment since, when enlivened, it merely affects the recoverable damages and not the defendant's liability. In the age of apportionment, it is difficult to see how the plea of contributory negligence can qualify as a defence (or even a partial defence[99])

---

[90] [1940] AC 152 (HL) 165.

[91] Overwhelming objections are identified in James (n 65) 697–98 (on which the analysis here draws).

[92] Regarding the location of the doctrine of contributory negligence within the analytical structure of tort law, see 1.25–1.30.

[93] Winfield (n 67) 414.

[94] For further discussion, see Goudkamp (n 13) 336–38.

[95] Among countless examples, see *Reeves v Commissioner of Police of the Metropolis* [2000] 1 AC 360 (HL) 371; *Corr v IBC Vehicles Ltd* [2008] UKHL 13, [2008] 1 AC 884 [19].

[96] See 1.08.

[97] 'The plea of contributory negligence is either an argumentative traverse of the necessary averment that the defendant's negligence was the sole cause of the injury, or a plea in confession and avoidance': *Logan v O'Donnell* [1925] 2 IR 211 (SC) 227 (Kennedy CJ).

[98] For discussion, see J Goudkamp, *Tort Law Defences* (Hart Publishing 2013) 1–5.

[99] Regarding the concept of a partial defence, see J Goudkamp, 'Defences in Tort and Crime' in M Dyson (ed), *Unravelling Tort and Crime* (CUP 2014) 233–37.

without that concept being distorted. If the plea is conceived of as a defence myriad other rules that restrict the damages awarded to a claimant who establishes liability, such as the doctrine of remoteness and the limitations on the assessment of punitive and aggravated damages, would in principle need to be counted as defences too.

It might be replied that the doctrine of contributory negligence is different from these and other restrictions on the damages awarded because, as discussed in more detail later,[100] the defendant bears the burdens of pleading and proof in relation to contributory negligence. Thus, Tony Weir wrote that '[c]ontributory negligence is unquestionably a defence . . . [since] it is for the defendant to plead and prove it'.[101] This response is unsatisfying. The difficulty with it is that the allocation of the incidence of pleading and proof is not determinative of whether a doctrine is generally regarded as a defence since various rules that are so regarded do not need to be pleaded by defendants. An example is the doctrine of illegality, which the court can raise on its own motion.[102] Similarly, certain defences need to be disproved by the claimant, such as limitation defences. Once the defendant has pleaded a time bar, the claimant carries the onus of showing that the claim was issued within time.[103] **1.27**

In these circumstances, it is preferable to categorize the law of contributory negligence as belonging to the field of remedies (or damages) rather than to that of defences. This characterization is consistent with the fact that it features in books on remedies.[104] Similarly, some tort textbooks house their treatment of the doctrine of contributory negligence not in chapters on defences but in those concerned with remedies (or damages).[105] Treating the contributory negligence doctrine as a remedial principle rather than as a defence has practical implications. Four examples can be given, at least some of which might also reinforce the case for categorizing the doctrine as part of the law of remedies. First, because the issue of the appropriate remedial response will not become live unless and until liability is established, the question of contributory negligence does not fall to be addressed until the rules that affect liability have been applied.[106] As the authors of a recent American study on the issue of sequencing in damages observe, it 'is emphatically not the case that comparative fault is a "liability" inquiry and thus should always go first' (in other words, the doctrine should not necessarily be applied before rules relevant to damages).[107] As we shall see, this sequencing point can have a significant impact on the quantum of the **1.28**

[100] See 6.06–6.07, 6.09.

[101] T Weir, *An Introduction to Tort Law* (2nd edn, Clarendon Press 2006) 129. See also Stevens (n 63) 248–52.

[102] *Cross v Kirkby*, The Times, 5 April 2000 (CA); Law Commission, *The Illegality Defence: A Consultative Report* (Law Com CP No 189, 2009) para 7.22.

[103] '[T]he claimant has the burden of disproving a limitation defence where the defendant has pleaded one': Law Commission, *Limitation of Actions* (Law Com No 270, 2001) para 5.29. See also Law Commission, *Limitation of Actions* (Law Com CP No 151, 1998) paras 9.23–9.25; *Lloyds Bank plc v Crosse & Crosse* [2001] EWCA Civ 366, [2001] PNLR 34 [41]; *Fiona Trust & Holding Corp v Privalov* [2010] EWHC 3199 (Comm) [315].

[104] See, eg, *Harder*, chs 9–11 (observing at 129 that '[t]he issue of contributory negligence has thus become a proper part of the law of damages. It features in most textbooks on damages or remedies in general'); *Burrows*, 132–44; *Luntz*, 260–91; *McGregor*, ch 7 (though treating only apportionment—and not the existence of contributory negligence—as falling within the scope of a book on damages).

[105] See, eg, NJ McBride and R Bagshaw, *Tort Law* (6th edn, Pearson 2018) ch 23; *Winfield & Jolowicz*, ch 23.

[106] On temporal sequencing in tort law more generally, see Goudkamp (n 98) 13–14.

[107] EK Cheng et al, 'Sequencing in Damages' (2022) 74 Stanford L Rev 353, 378.

claimant's recovery.[108] The second practical implication is that the fact that judgment has been entered against the defendant on the issue of liability will not ordinarily preclude the defendant from being able to raise contributory negligence in connection with the assessment of damages.[109] The third ramification concerns costs. Where a claimant succeeds in establishing liability, their costs should generally be borne by their opponent. Conversely, success on remedial issues does not generally have this effect. Thus, a defendant who is adjudged liable but who establishes that the claimant was contributorily negligent will generally still need to pay the claimant's costs.[110] The final point relates to pleading. For a defendant to put a defence into issue, it is, strictly speaking, unnecessary that it be specifically pleaded. It is enough to allege the facts that undergird it.[111] A different rule applies to the doctrine of contributory negligence. A defendant who wishes to invoke it must rely upon it in terms in their statement of case.[112]

1.29 Beyond the issue of whether the doctrine of contributory negligence is a defence or remedial rule, a question arises as to whether it should be bracketed together with certain other principles. In *Meadows v Khan*,[113] Lord Hodge and Lord Sales sought to reconceptualize the structure of the tort of negligence.[114] They suggested that it should be broken down into six stages as follows:[115]

> (1) Is the harm (loss, injury, and damage) which is the subject matter of the claim actionable in negligence? (the actionability question)
> (2) What are the risks of harm to the claimant against which the law imposes on the defendant a duty to take care? (the scope of duty question)
> (3) Did the defendant breach his or her duty by his or her act or omission? (the breach question)
> (4) Is the loss for which the claimant seeks damages the consequence of the defendant's act or omission? (the factual causation question)
> (5) Is there a sufficient nexus between a particular element of the harm for which the claimant seeks damages and the subject matter of the defendant's duty of care as analysed at stage 2 above? (the duty nexus question)
> (6) Is a particular element of the harm for which the claimant seeks damages irrecoverable because it is too remote, or because there is a different effective cause (including novus actus interveniens) in relation to it or because the claimant has mitigated his or her loss or has failed to avoid loss which he or she could reasonably have been expected to avoid? (the legal responsibility question)

The foregoing makes it clear that Lord Hodge and Lord Sales considered that the sixth enquiry extends to the doctrine of remoteness[116] and mitigation as well as the rules

---

108 See 4.04, 4.06, 4.12–4.14.

109 See 6.11.

110 See 6.11.

111 Consider CPR 16.5(1), which requires defendants simply to deal with every allegation advanced in the Particulars of Claim.

112 See 6.06.

113 [2021] UKSC 21, [2022] AC 852. See also *Manchester Building Society v Grant Thornton UK LLP* [2021] UKSC 20, [2022] AC 783.

114 For analysis, see D Nolan and J Plunkett, 'Keeping Negligence Simple' (2022) 138 LQR 175.

115 [2021] UKSC 21, [2022] AC 852 [28].

116 See also ibid [56].

regarding legal causation. Later in their reasons, they explained that it also encompasses the principles governing contributory negligence as well as the plea of *volenti non fit injuria*.[117] Lord Hodge and Lord Sales described all these rules as 'legal filters' that 'reflect the court's judgment of the extent of a defendant's liability for his or her wrongdoing'.[118] The merits of this vision for the structure of the tort of negligence are debatable.[119]

The relationship between the law regarding contributory negligence and the other rules that form part of Lord Hodge and Lord Sales's sixth enquiry is addressed in detail later.[120] At this stage we observe simply that the notion that the plea of *volenti non fit injuria* is concerned with the 'extent' of the defendant's legal responsibility perhaps casts doubt on the coherence of the enquiry generally. The plea, when successful, does not limit the extent of the defendant's legal responsibility, or at least does not do so in the same way as the doctrine of contributory negligence. Rather, it extinguishes the defendant's responsibility and, moreover, arguably does so *ab initio* by precluding the defendant from becoming a tortfeasor in the first place. **1.30**

117 ibid [57].
118 ibid.
119 Lower courts appear generally to be sceptical of the new structure and have sometimes either ignored it or otherwise declined to follow it: see, eg, *Cunningham v Rochdale MBC* [2021] EWCA Civ 1719 [23]; *Rushbond plc v JS Design Partnership LLP* [2021] EWCA Civ 1889, [2022] PNLR 9 [74].
120 See 4.12–4.14.

2

THE SCOPE OF THE DOCTRINE

1. Introduction

2.01 Unlike defences such as consent and illegality, contributory negligence is not a doctrine of general application across the law of tort, but is applicable only to certain causes of action, most notably negligence. In this chapter, we consider the causes of action to which it applies. The scope of the doctrine is a difficult and controversial issue. This is partly attributable to the apportionment legislation: indeed, it has been observed that perhaps the main criticism that can be made of the Law Reform (Contributory Negligence) Act 1945 is that 'it failed to make absolutely clear when apportionment might be available'.[1] However, some of the blame must also be laid at the feet of the courts, which have failed to establish a set of clear principles to govern the issue. The result is that the authorities on the scope of contributory negligence consist of a series of apparently ad hoc decisions which lack overall coherence.

2.02 We begin our consideration of the scope of the contributory negligence doctrine with a discussion of the rule that apparently prevents the courts from extending the doctrine to causes of action in respect of which the complete defence of contributory negligence was not available before 1945 (the '1945 cause of action rule'). We then consider the application of the doctrine to the intentional torts (such as battery), before proceeding to look at the position with regard to, respectively, other common law torts, statutory torts, breach of contract, and equitable wrongs.

2. The 1945 Cause of Action Rule

2.03 The scope of the modern doctrine of contributory negligence has been profoundly affected by the wording of the Law Reform (Contributory Negligence) Act 1945, even though that legislation was not primarily concerned with this issue. According to section 1(1) of the Act:

> Where any person suffers damage as a result partly of his own fault and partly of the fault of any other person or persons ... the damages recoverable in respect thereof shall be reduced to such extent as the court thinks just and equitable having regard to the claimant's share in the responsibility for the damage.

[1] *Mitchell*, 326.

Contributory Negligence. Second Edition. James Goudkamp and Donal Nolan, Oxford University Press.
 DOI: 10.1093/oso/9780192867919.003.0002

Section 4 of the Act defines 'fault' to mean 'negligence, breach of statutory duty or other act or omission which gives rise to a liability in tort or would, apart from this Act, give rise to the defence of contributory negligence'. The orthodox reading of that definition (the 'split definition') was summed up by Lord Hoffmann in *Standard Chartered Bank v Pakistan National Shipping Corp (Nos 2 and 4)*:[2]

> In my opinion, the definition of 'fault' is divided into two limbs, one of which is applicable to defendants and the other to plaintiffs. In the case of a defendant, fault means 'negligence, breach of statutory duty or other act or omission' which gives rise to a liability in tort. In the case of a plaintiff, it means 'negligence, breach of statutory duty or other act or omission' which gives rise (at common law) to a defence of contributory negligence.

This reading of the definition of 'fault' has been held to have significant repercussions for the scope of the contributory negligence doctrine. By in effect interpreting the words 'which . . . would, apart from this Act, give rise to the defence of contributory negligence' as meaning 'which could have given rise to the complete defence of contributory negligence at common law', the courts concluded that if contributory negligence was not a defence to a given cause of action when the Act was passed, then the doctrine cannot now apply to that cause of action.[3] In *Standard Chartered*, Lord Hoffmann argued that this was 'in accordance with the purpose of the Act, which was to relieve plaintiffs whose actions would previously have failed and not to reduce the damages which previously would have been awarded against defendants'.[4] Although there is unquestionably some force in this observation, from a policy perspective, the 1945 cause of action rule is unfortunate. It means that the permissibility of apportioning damages for contributory negligence depends on accidents of history rather than the merits of extending the apportionment regime to a given cause of action. By preserving the law relating to the scope of contributory negligence in aspic as of 1945, the courts are prevented from considering afresh the question of its applicability to a particular cause of action, and hence from developing the law in the light of changing conditions and attitudes. Furthermore, it is plausible to suppose that the scope of the common law doctrine was kept narrow precisely because it was a complete defence. Now that a finding of contributory negligence no longer leads to the denial of the claim in its entirety but only to a reduction in the damages commensurate with the extent of the parties' responsibility for the damage, there may be a strong case for extending the doctrine to causes of action where its operation as a complete defence would clearly have been undesirable.[5] Hence, as Joshua Pike points out:[6]

> [The 1945 cause of action rule] is illogical because the reason for the introduction of apportionment is also given as the reason for restricting its use despite the fact that

[2] [2002] UKHL 43, [2003] 1 AC 959 [11]. See also *Reeves v Commissioner of Police of the Metropolis* [2000] 1 AC 360 (HL) 369, 382. In New Zealand, this definition was favoured by Prichard J in *Rowe v Turner Hopkins & Partners* [1980] 2 NZLR 550 (HC).

[3] For applications of this reasoning, see the *Standard Chartered* case itself (deceit) and *Pritchard v Co-operative Group Ltd* [2011] EWCA Civ 329, [2012] QB 320 (battery). See further on these decisions 2.18 and 2.07–2.09 respectively.

[4] *Standard Chartered* [2002] UKHL 43, [2003] 1 AC 959 [12].

[5] See *Todd*, 1158–59.

[6] J Pike, 'Contributory Negligence and Intentional Trespass to the Person: Rethinking *Pritchard* and the Section 4 Definition of Fault' (2015) 4 Oxf Univ Undergrad LJ 3, 9.

apportionment provides the means of rectifying the unjust results the complete defence would have otherwise resulted in.

Ironically, therefore, while the introduction of apportionment could have paved the way for a significant expansion in the scope of the contributory negligence doctrine, the wording of the apportionment legislation has been interpreted as preventing any such extension.[7] But is there any way of avoiding this conclusion?

2.04 One possible way round the 1945 cause of action rule is to adopt a different definition of the word 'fault' in the 1945 Act. Instead of the conventional 'split definition', it is possible to read 'fault' as applied to claimants to mean 'negligence, breach of statutory duty or other act or omission' which *either* 'would, apart from this Act, give rise to the defence of contributory negligence' *or alternatively* 'gives rise to a liability in tort'. However, this does not really solve the problem. For although this interpretation enables the doctrine to extend to torts in which contributory defence was not a defence at common law, its application in those torts is then limited to cases in which the conduct said to amount to contributory negligence is itself tortious, a restriction that seems even more irrational than the 1945 cause of action rule. Furthermore, on this interpretation the cause of action rule still applies where the conduct said to amount to contributory negligence was not tortious. In any case, although there are some apparent examples of judicial support for this rival approach before *Standard Chartered*,[8] that decision is a clear endorsement of the more orthodox interpretation in which the definition of 'fault' is split into two quite separate limbs (one applicable to claimant fault and the other to defendant fault), an interpretation also favoured by commentators such as Glanville Williams,[9] and correctly described as 'a far more natural reading' of the relevant words.[10]

2.05 The other line of attack on the 1945 cause of action rule is to question whether that rule follows from the split definition of fault. Many distinguished commentators, such as Williams,[11] have assumed that it does, but others are not so sure. According to John Fleming, the statutory formula is 'ambiguous on the question of whether it authorises apportionment only in cases where contributory negligence was a defence before the Act or whether there is room for a developing common law which would now allow a reduction of damages in cases where formerly a complete denial seemed too punitive'.[12] And Andrew Burrows has argued that an alternative interpretation of the second limb of the split definition (relating to claimant 'fault') would be that:[13]

---

[7] In evaluating the 1945 cause of action rule, it is instructive to bear in mind the sorry history of a similar rule that once applied in the law governing punitive damages. In *AB v South West Water Services Ltd* [1993] QB 507 (CA), it was held that punitive damages could be awarded only if the cause of action in question was one in respect of which an award of punitive damages had been made by the courts prior to the decision of the House of Lords in *Rookes v Barnard* [1964] AC 1129 (HL). Following a torrent of criticism, this 'cause of action' test was scrapped in *Kuddus v Chief Constable of Leicestershire Constabulary* [2001] UKHL 29, [2002] 2 AC 122.

[8] See *Murphy v Culhane* [1977] QB 94 (CA) 99 (Lord Denning MR); *Forsikringsaktieselskapet Vesta v Butcher* [1989] AC 852 (CA) 862 (O'Connor LJ); *Alliance and Leicester Building Society v Edgestop Ltd* [1994] 2 All ER 38 (QBD) 50 (Mummery J). See also *Dairy Containers Ltd v NZI Bank Ltd* [1995] 2 NZLR 30 (HC) 111–12.

[9] *Williams*, 318.

[10] *Todd*, 1158.

[11] *Williams*, 318.

[12] *Fleming*, 318.

[13] *Burrows*, 138.

> [T]he conduct of the claimant must be of the sort that at common law would have given rise to the total defence of contributory negligence, if the claimant had been suing for a tort to which the defence indisputably applied, for example, the tort of negligence.

Another way of arriving at the same result would be to argue that the words 'would, apart from this Act, give rise to the defence of contributory negligence' should be understood to mean not 'would *in 1945*' give rise to the defence, but rather 'would *now*' give rise to the defence had the Act not been passed, an interpretation that would enable the courts to determine for themselves whether at the time of the court's decision it would have been appropriate to have extended the common law defence to a given cause of action in the absence of the Act.[14] (This interpretation does, however, run into a problem, which is that the courts may be minded to expand the scope of the doctrine precisely because, the Act having in fact *been* passed, its application now results in apportionment and not a complete defence.[15]) Finally, Pike has argued that what he calls the 'dual limb' approach to the definition of fault only retains the common law test for contributory negligence (namely whether the claimant took reasonable care for their own safety) and does not otherwise limit the scope of the apportionment provision to cases where the common law defence would previously have applied.[16] He points out that when it passed the Torts (Interference with Goods) Act 1977, Parliament seems itself to have assumed an interpretation along the lines that he suggests, since section 11(1) of that Act expressly states that contributory negligence is not a defence in cases of intentional trespass to goods, a provision rendered entirely superfluous by the 1945 cause of action rule, since contributory negligence was clearly not a defence to such a claim at common law.[17]

3. The Intentional Torts

Whether the contributory negligence doctrine should apply to intentional torts such as battery is a topic that has troubled courts in many common law jurisdictions. Unfortunately, in English law the 1945 cause of action rule has overshadowed this issue, with the result that the normative question of whether an intentional wrongdoer should ever be able to rely on the contributory negligence of the victim has not always been front and centre of the analysis. In the discussion that follows we first consider the positive law on this question and then explore that normative question. **2.06**

(1) The positive law

The leading English case on the question of whether a defendant who has committed an intentional trespass to the person can rely on the doctrine of contributory negligence is *Pritchard v Co-operative Group Ltd*.[18] The authorities before *Pritchard* were inconclusive, **2.07**

[14] See *Dairy Containers Ltd v NZI Bank Ltd* [1995] 2 NZLR 30 (HC) 111 (Thomas J) ('I am not prepared to construe the words "or would, apart from this Act, give rise to the defence of contributory negligence" ... to mean that the defence must have been available *prior* to the Act ... The Act states, "apart from this Act" not "prior to this Act". I can see no sound reason for reading "apart" to mean "prior" ... In the year 2047 such an approach could well prove to be ludicrous' (emphasis in original).)

[15] See 1.07.

[16] Pike (n 6).

[17] See *Pritchard v Co-operative Group Ltd* [2011] EWCA Civ 329, [2012] QB 320, 337–38.

[18] [2011] EWCA Civ 329, [2012] QB 320.

although in *Murphy v Culhane* Lord Denning had made clear his opinion that provocation or contributory negligence by a claimant in a trespass to the person action could result in a deduction from their damages applying the 1945 Act.[19] Furthermore, at the time that *Pritchard* was decided the leading commentaries on English tort law considered that the doctrine of contributory negligence probably applied to claims for trespass to the person.[20] However, *Pritchard* firmly closed the door on that possibility. The claimant in the case was employed by the defendant company in one of its stores. After the store manager refused the claimant's telephoned request to stay at home on the ground of illness, the claimant went with two other people to the store, where she launched a tirade of abuse at the manager. Following the claimant's refusal to leave the premises after being asked to do so, the manager took hold of her arm to eject her, and a struggle ensued. The claimant later sued the defendant for damages for psychiatric illness which she claimed to have suffered as a result of these events. At first instance, the judge held that the manager had committed the torts of assault and battery (for which the defendant was vicariously liable), and that no deduction from the claimant's damages was possible in respect of the provocative conduct on her part that had triggered their commission. The Court of Appeal agreed.

2.08 The reasoning of Aikens LJ (with whom Smith LJ and Sir Anthony May agreed) in *Pritchard* rested in part on the 1945 cause of action rule, as definitively set down by Lord Hoffmann in the *Standard Chartered* case. It followed from that rule that contributory negligence could be relied on in a claim for assault and battery only if at common law there had been a possible defence of contributory negligence to a claim in those torts. However, the defendant had not managed to find any cases before 1945 in which contributory negligence had operated as a defence to such a claim.[21] Furthermore, Lord Denning's suggestions that a deduction from the claimant's damages was possible for provocative conduct were based on an interpretation of the word 'fault' in the 1945 Act which had been decisively rejected in *Standard Chartered*.[22] It followed that, as a matter of principle, it was not open to a court to rely on the 1945 Act to make a deduction from the claimant's damages for contributory negligence where the claim was brought in assault or battery. Aikens LJ also held that the claimant's conduct had in any case not been sufficiently threatening to amount to contributory negligence on the facts. In a concurring judgment, Smith LJ agreed with Aikens LJ on the basis that the wording of the 1945 Act compelled the conclusion that contributory negligence was not available for battery. However, she reached this conclusion with regret because she thought that apportionment ought to be available to a defendant in such a case 'where the claimant has, by his misconduct, contributed to the happening of the incident, for example, by provocative speech or behaviour'.[23] Had she been free to do

---

[19] *Murphy v Culhane* [1977] QB 94 (CA) 98–99. cf *Lane v Holloway* [1968] 1 QB 379 (CA) 387, where the same judge said that while '[p]rovocation by the plaintiff can properly be used to take away any element of aggravation', it cannot 'reduce the real [ie, compensatory] damages'.

[20] See MA Jones (ed), *Clerk & Lindsell on Torts* (20th edn, Sweet & Maxwell 2010) para 3-54 ('balance of authority' suggests that contributory negligence available); WVH Rogers, *Winfield & Jolowicz on Tort* (18th edn, Sweet & Maxwell 2010) 365 (the courts 'now seem to accept that the Act may be applicable to cases of intentional trespass to the person, given sufficiently serious conduct on the part of the claimant').

[21] For a thorough analysis of the early English authorities on contributory negligence and trespass to the person, see *Horkin v North Melbourne Football Club Social Club* [1983] 1 VR 153 (SC).

[22] See 2.03.

[23] [2011] EWCA Civ 329, [2012] QB 320 [82].

so, Smith LJ would have held that the claimant's damages should be reduced by one-third for contributory negligence.

The decision in *Pritchard* was later followed (albeit 'not without some measure of reluctance') in a Northern Irish case concerning battery[24] and has been held to apply to the tort of false imprisonment.[25] The Supreme Court of Victoria has also held that the plea of contributory negligence is not available in an action for battery.[26] However, in *Hoebergen v Koppens*, the Supreme Court of New Zealand reduced the damages awarded in a battery claim pursuant to the apportionment provision. There had been a history of ill feeling between the parties in that case, which included threats of violence. After the plaintiff called the defendant a 'Dutch bastard' during an argument in a petrol station, the defendant assaulted him. The plaintiff's damages for the assault were reduced by 15 per cent for contributory negligence. Canadian courts have similarly discounted damages for contributory negligence in intentional torts cases.[27] **2.09**

(2) The normative question

When considering whether—setting aside the implications of the wording of the 1945 Act—apportionment for contributory negligence should be extended to claims for trespass to the person, it is important to distinguish between consequences intended by the defendant and the unintended consequences of an intentional wrong. It has often been said to be inappropriate to apply the doctrine of contributory negligence to intended consequences—Fleming James even went so far as to observe that this is a proposition on which 'all agree'.[28] Cavanagh J of the New South Wales Court of Appeal recently summed up the argument for this position:[29] **2.10**

> In my view, there are good policy reasons why contributory negligence should not be a defence to the intended consequences of an intentional tort such as battery ... Allowing a person who intentionally injures another to escape the consequences of his conduct merely because the injured person might have carelessly contributed seems somewhat counterintuitive.

This view that 'intention to injure the plaintiff negatives all excuses' is of long standing.[30] Williams commented that 'it is a result of the ordinary human feeling that the defendant's wrongful intention so outweighs the plaintiff's wrongful negligence as to efface it altogether'.[31]

---

[24] *McAleer v Chief Constable of the PSNI* [2014] NIQB 53.

[25] *R (on the application of Diop) v Secretary of State for the Home Department* [2018] EWHC 3420 (Admin) [74].

[26] *Horkin v North Melbourne Football Club Social Club* [1983] 1 VR 153 (SC). See also *Irlam v Byrnes* [2022] NSWCA 81, 108 NSWLR 285 (though the ratio is limited to the intended consequences of an intentional tort).

[27] See L Klar, 'Contributory Negligence and Apportionment in Canadian Tort Law' in K Barker and R Grantham (eds), *Apportionment in Private Law* (Hart Publishing 2019) 154–55.

[28] F James Jr, 'Contributory Negligence' (1953) 62 Yale LJ 691, 707. See similarly, CLB Lowndes, 'Contributory Negligence' (1934) 22 Georgetown LJ 674, 687 (defence should not apply where 'a defendant has intentionally injured the plaintiff', or 'been recklessly indifferent to the plaintiff's safety').

[29] *Irlam v Byrnes* [2022] NSWCA 81 [237].

[30] *Quinn v Leathem* [1901] AC 495 (HL) 537 (Lord Lindley). cf the criticisms of this statement by J Goudkamp, 'Contributory Negligence and Trespass to the Person' (2011) 127 LQR 519, 520.

[31] *Williams*, 198.

2.11 Clearly the argument for the availability of the plea of contributory negligence is much stronger when it comes to the unintended consequences of an intentional tort. This is especially so now that the doctrine's application leads only to a reduction in damages.[32] It is therefore no surprise to see that there is considerable support for the extension of the doctrine to cases where the consequence for which the claimant is seeking damages was not intended by the defendant.[33] A possible objection to the extension of the contributory negligence rule to unintended consequences is that it may not be at all obvious what consequences were 'intended' by, say, a defendant who punched the claimant in the face. However, this problem can largely be avoided by taking a broad view of intention for this purpose and by extending the concept of intention to encompass recklessness, so that a defendant would be barred from relying on contributory negligence if they either intended the consequence in question, or had been reckless as to the occurrence of that consequence. A more serious problem with a test of unintended consequences is that it may not extend the protection of the contributory negligence doctrine to all meritorious defendants. Suppose, for example, that a surgeon amputates the left leg of a patient instead of the right leg because of a mix up for which the patient is partly to blame.[34] Were the contributory negligence doctrine to be extended to battery, then this would surely be one type of case where it might be thought appropriate to apply it, and yet the surgeon *did* intend the consequence in respect of which the patient will claim, namely the loss of the left leg. Similarly, suppose that the defendant assaulted the claimant because of an unreasonable but honestly held belief that the claimant was about to attack them. Since the complete defence of self-defence is not available in such a case,[35] arguably the court should be able to make a deduction for contributory negligence where the claimant was partly to blame for the formation of the defendant's mistaken belief, even if the test of unintended consequences is not met.

2.12 There are two possible ways of solving the problem posed by the apparent under-inclusiveness of an intended consequences test. One is to abandon that test and instead employ a more general test of intention to inflict harm.[36] The other, proposed by Williams,[37] is to supplement the test by holding that the contributory negligence doctrine is available where the consequences were intended if the defendant thought that they had a right to do as they did. Neither solution is itself free from difficulty, however. For example, as regards the first, what is meant by 'harm' here? And as regards the second, there is clear potential for the expanded test to be exploited by an unmeritorious defendant who might argue, for

[32] See Pike (n 6) 10 (unsurprising that the courts did not apply contributory negligence to intentional torts when this would bar recovery altogether).

[33] See, eg, *Williams*, 199; *Venning v Chin* (1974) 10 SASR 299 (SC) 317; Klar (n 27) 154–55.

[34] See the analogous contribution case of *Parnley v Parnley* [1945] SCR 635 (SCC) (cited by *Williams*, 95), where a dentist removed teeth which a patient had not consented to being removed after the dentist misunderstood the instructions of a doctor.

[35] *Ashley v Chief Constable of Sussex Police* [2008] UKHL 25, [2008] 1 AC 962.

[36] See, eg, *Prosser & Keeton*, 462. See also *Restatement (Second) of the Law of Torts* (1965) § 481 (contributory negligence does not bar recovery 'for a harm caused by conduct of the defendant which is wrongful because it is intended to cause harm to some legally protected interest of the plaintiff or a third person'); *Pritchard v Co-operative Group Ltd* [2011] EWCA Civ 329, [2012] QB 320 [82] (Smith LJ) ('I do not think that [the defendant] intended to harm [the claimant], only to remove her').

[37] *Williams*, 201.

example, that they believed that they had the right to assault the claimant for trespassing on the defendant's property.[38]

Four final points should be made about the possible application of the contributory negligence doctrine to the intentional torts. The first is that if the scope of the doctrine were to be extended in this way, then there would doubtless be cases in which, although it could be said that the claimant was partly to blame for what happened, any such contribution would pale into insignificance when compared with the conduct of the defendant.[39] In such cases it would be open to the courts to make only a very small deduction from the claimant's damages, or perhaps even to decide that it would not be just and equitable to make any deduction at all.[40] It is important to remember in this connection that the extension of the scope of the doctrine would simply enable the courts to 'judge each case on its merits',[41] as opposed to the current rigid rule that no deduction for contributory negligence can ever be made where the claim is brought in trespass to the person. The second point is that the present rule forces a court to choose between an award of full damages or finding some basis on which the claim can be denied altogether. Not only does this present the court with 'a stark and unattractive choice',[42] but it may also produce a reverse injustice, whereby in the absence of the possibility of apportionment for contributory negligence the court prefers to stretch an alternative doctrine beyond its appropriate scope in order to bar the claim completely rather than allowing the claimant to recover in full.[43] The third point is that there is nothing to stop a claimant from suing a defendant who acted intentionally in the tort of negligence, and this has been used as an argument for limiting the scope of torts that require proof of intention.[44] It seems strange that in some cases of intentional conduct (pleaded in negligence) apportionment for contributory negligence is possible, but in others it is not. And the final point (this time in favour of the status quo) is that to the extent that the law recognizes a separate doctrine of provocation capable of leading to a reduction in compensatory damages, this relieves at least some of the pressure to reverse the *Pritchard* decision and extend contributory negligence to the intentional torts.[45] **2.13**

[38] This concern might be ameliorated by modifying the test to cover only cases where the defendant 'believed at the time of the tort in the existence of facts that would constitute a defence if true' (ibid, 94, discussing a similar issue in the context of contribution between tortfeasors). But to the extent that such a test would require a distinction to be drawn between mistakes of fact and mistakes of law it would doubtless give rise to other difficulties.

[39] For an example of such a case, see Goudkamp (n 30) 522.

[40] There is some uncertainty as to whether the courts are entitled to refuse to discount the claimant's damages once a finding of contributory negligence has been made, although the weight of authority suggests that they are: see 4.18.

[41] *Harder*, 132.

[42] *Hicks v Young* [2015] EWHC 1144 (QB) [30] (Edis J).

[43] Smith LJ hints at this possibility in *Pritchard v Co-operative Group Ltd* [2011] EWCA Civ 329, [2012] QB 320 [83].

[44] See, eg, *Wainwright v Home Office* [2003] UKHL 53, [2004] 2 AC 406 (tort of intentional infliction of physical or emotional harm).

[45] See Goudkamp (n 30) 522. On the relationship between contributory negligence and provocation, see 5.22–5.23.

4. Other Common Law Torts

(1) Breach of statutory duty and nuisance

2.14 At common law, the defence of contributory negligence applied to claims for breach of statutory duty,[46] and nowadays these are subject to the apportionment regime set out in the 1945 Act. In many of the cases discussed elsewhere in this volume—especially those involving employers' liability—the claim was brought in this tort, sometimes alongside a negligence action. It is also crystal clear that the contributory negligence doctrine applies to public nuisance—indeed *Butterfield v Forrester*,[47] the decision that is generally taken to mark the inception of contributory negligence as a separate defence,[48] was a public nuisance case involving the obstruction of a highway.[49] The plea of contributory negligence is also available in private nuisance claims,[50] although it is more likely to be relevant in the type of nuisance action where it must be established that the defendant was at fault, a category of cases closely analogous to negligence.[51] By contrast, in the more typical case where the nuisance takes the form of an ongoing interference caused by intentional conduct (such as noise from the operation of a factory) there is unlikely to be conduct of the claimant comparable to the contributory fault that can be found in, say, an accident case.

(2) *Rylands v Fletcher* and strict liability

2.15 Since the strict liability rule in *Rylands v Fletcher* concerns one-off escapes that cause physical damage to the claimant's land, there is likely to be more scope for the operation of the contributory negligence doctrine in that cause of action than in the related tort of private nuisance. However, there is very little authority on the question,[52] and the position is complicated by the complete defence of default of the claimant, which applies where the claimant was wholly to blame for the damage that they suffered.[53] Three approaches are possible. The first is to say that the complete defence is available in cases where the claimant was (in law) wholly responsible for the escape that caused the damage, and the plea of contributory negligence where they were only partly responsible.[54] The second is to say that default of the claimant and contributory negligence were essentially the same defence at common law, albeit with different names, and that the continued existence of

---

[46] *Caswell v Powell Duffryn Associated Collieries Ltd* [1940] AC 152 (HL). See also *Davies v Adelaide Chemical and Fertilizer Co Ltd* (1946) 74 CLR 541 (HCA).

[47] (1809) 11 East 60, 103 ER 926.

[48] See 1.08.

[49] See also *Farrell v John Mowlem & Co* [1954] 1 Lloyd's Rep 437 (QBD) (where the plea of contributory negligence failed on the facts); *Trevett v Lee* [1955] 1 WLR 113 (CA) 122.

[50] See generally WA Seavey, 'Nuisance: Contributory Negligence and Other Mysteries' (1952) 65 Harv L Rev 984; James (n 28) 715–21.

[51] See *Williams*, 204. On this type of nuisance case, which generally involves an occupier who has not themselves created the nuisance, see *Winfield & Jolowicz*, paras 15-043 et seq.

[52] In two Australian cases it has been suggested that the contributory negligence doctrine does not apply: see *Burnie Port Authority v General Jones Pty Ltd* (1994) 179 CLR 520 (HCA) 590; *Martin's Camera Corner Pty Ltd v Hotel Mayfair Ltd* [1976] 2 NSWLR 15 (SC) 27. However, contributory negligence is a partial defence to a claim under the analogous American doctrine of strict liability for harm caused by ultra-hazardous activities: *Restatement (Third) of Torts: Liability for Physical and Emotional Harm* (2010), § 25.

[53] On the relationship between contributory negligence and this defence, see 5.12–5.15.

[54] See *Fleming*, 386–87.

the complete defence today would therefore be at odds with the 1945 Act.[55] Applying this reasoning, all instances of claimant fault in the *Rylands* context ought now to be treated as contributory negligence and met with apportionment. Finally, it could be argued that the complete defence of default of the claimant should continue to apply where its very strict conditions are met, but that in lesser cases of claimant fault, no deduction should be made for contributory negligence. The rationale of this approach would be that the complete defence was intended to exhaust the effect on a *Rylands* action of claimant fault. This argument could be supplemented by one based on the 1945 cause of action rule, to the effect that, since contributory negligence was not a defence to claims under the rule before 1945, it ought not to trigger apportionment today (although this argument fails if default of the claimant and contributory negligence are in fact synonymous).

Of these three options, the first is probably to be preferred, on the ground that default of the claimant is functionally equivalent to the novus actus interveniens doctrine that is still capable of barring recovery in other torts,[56] and that there is no particular reason why in lesser instances of claimant fault a reduction in damages should not be made (especially bearing in mind that the rule is one of strict liability, so that the defendant may be entirely free from blame).[57] It is also noteworthy that this approach was taken in two statutory strict liability provisions, one concerning escapes of gas and the other escapes of water, both of which recognize a complete defence akin to default of the claimant but are also subject to the provisions of the 1945 Act.[58] Were this approach to be adopted in *Rylands* cases as well, then where, for example, the claimant themselves caused the escape in full knowledge of the risk posed by the defendant's accumulation, the claim would be defeated by the default of the claimant defence, whereas if the claimant merely acted unreasonably in failing to protect their property from the consequences of an escape for which they were not responsible their damages would be reduced for contributory fault. **2.16**

There are occasional rumblings of concern about the application of contributory negligence to strict liability torts, but these concerns are baseless, and it is noteworthy that Parliament frequently makes express provision for the contributory negligence rule to apply to statutory torts of strict liability.[59] Lord Macmillan's claim that it was 'technically inaccurate' to speak of a guest's contributory negligence in a strict liability claim against an innkeeper[60] seems to have been based on the mistaken assumption that 'contributory **2.17**

---

[55] See *Williams*, 210.

[56] See 5.02–5.07. Default of the claimant is arguably best understood as a doctrine founded on causal reasoning: see 5.14.

[57] In support of this latter point, it could also be argued that since contributory negligence applies to private nuisance, and since the courts have held that the *Rylands* rule is a species of nuisance (*Transco plc v Stockport MBC* [2003] UKHL 61, [2004] 2 AC 1), then contributory negligence ought also to apply in *Rylands* cases.

[58] Gas Act 1965, s 14; Water Industry Act 1991, s 209. See further on these provisions, 2.23.

[59] See 2.23. The application of contributory negligence to strict product liability was endorsed by the Law Commission in *Liability for Defective Products* (Law Com No 82, 1977) paras 107–10, and by the Pearson Commission: *Royal Commission on Civil Liability and Compensation for Personal Injury* (Cmnd 7054, 1978) paras 1256–57. Provision for contributory negligence in cases of strict product liability was also made in the 1985 EC Directive on Liability for Defective Products (85/374/EEC) Art 8(2), and in the *Restatement (Third) of Torts: Products Liability* (1997), § 17. The Law Commission also recommended that contributory negligence apply to statutory strict liability for damage done by dangerous animals: *Civil Liability for Animals* (Law Com No 13, 1967) para 21.

[60] *Shacklock v Ethorpe Ltd* [1939] 3 All ER 372 (HL) 374.

negligence' means negligence concurrent with negligence of the defendant, when in fact it means negligence that contributes to the suffering of the damage.[61] Indeed, as Williams pointed out, the common law defence applied to the strict liability of both innkeepers and common carriers.[62] Similarly, although it is sometimes said to be inappropriate to apply apportionment in cases of strict liability on the ground that it is impossible to compare the fault of the claimant with the strict liability of the defendant,[63] there is no force in this objection,[64] and in fact the courts have apportioned responsibility countless times in cases of breach of a strict statutory duty.[65] Two further arguments can be made against the idea that the contributory negligence doctrine ought not to apply to torts of strict liability. One is that this would produce the strange result that a defendant held liable regardless of fault would be in a worse position than a defendant held liable because at fault. And the other is that there is a danger that a court unhappy with this outcome might be tempted to avoid it by expanding complete defences in the strict liability context, thereby depriving claimants of the benefits of apportionment. This is not to deny that there may be good reasons why contributory negligence should not be applied to particular instances of strict liability—it is merely to reject the misguided notion that the doctrine is somehow inherently out of place where the liability is strict.

(3) Deceit and negligent misrepresentation

2.18 There are some parallels between the issue of the application of contributory negligence to deceit and its application to the intentional torts, though there are also some important differences, most obviously that whereas it is possible for an innocent person to commit battery or false imprisonment, one cannot by definition be inadvertently deceitful. The deceit issue came before the House of Lords in *Standard Chartered Bank v Pakistan National Shipping Corp (Nos 2 and 4)*.[66] A fraudulent misrepresentation had been made by the managing director of the fourth defendant company, which was the beneficiary under a letter of credit confirmed by the claimant bank. His argument that he was not liable because he had made the representation on behalf of the fourth defendant was rejected, which left the question of whether the claimant's damages should be reduced on account of its contributory negligence. Applying the 1945 cause of action rule, the House of Lords held that as the complete common law defence of contributory negligence had not applied to deceit, nor did the apportionment provisions of the 1945 Act. With respect, this is unconvincing. As Lord Rodger pointed out, to have recognized the common law defence in deceit cases would have had the effect of absolving the fraudulent defendant of all liability.[67] But of course the position under the 1945 Act is quite different, and with the advent of apportionment the question of the application of contributory negligence to deceit should therefore have been considered *de novo*, rather than being determined by

[61] *Williams*, 207–208.

[62] ibid 208–209.

[63] See, eg, Klar (n 27) 156, who also cites the claim by a Canadian judge that it is 'doctrinally counter-intuitive' to do this.

[64] See 4.37.

[65] On the apportionment exercise in cases of strict liability, see 4.38.

[66] [2002] UKHL 43, [2003] 1 AC 959. See also the earlier decision to the same effect in *Alliance & Leicester Building Society v Edgestop* [1993] 1 WLR 1462 (QBD).

[67] [2002] UKHL 43, [2003] 1 AC 959 [42].

the position at common law. Having said that, the House also considered that as a matter of legal policy a fraudulent defendant ought not to be allowed to rely on contributory negligence. According to Lord Hoffmann:[68]

> It would not seem just that a fraudulent defendant's liability should be reduced on the grounds that, for whatever reason, the victim should not have made the payment which the defendant successfully induced him to make.

This is clearly a forceful argument, and the narrow scope of the tort of deceit means that the question of contributory negligence is perhaps more clear-cut in this context than in the case of the intentional torts—as Tony Weir put it, 'the con-man can hardly complain that it was stupid of his dupe to be taken in'.[69] Nevertheless, it is worth remembering that an entirely innocent employer or principal can be held liable for the deceit of their employee or agent on the basis of vicarious liability, and in a case of this kind it may be questioned whether it is fair that the contributory fault of the claimant should be entirely irrelevant. This is particularly so where the conduct of the claimant that contributed to their loss was itself deceitful, as was the case in one of the appeals heard by the House of Lords in *Standard Chartered.* Indeed, Sir Anthony Evans had been so concerned by this scenario when that appeal had come before the Court of Appeal that he dissented on the issue of contributory negligence, holding that a discount should be made for the contributory negligence of the deceitful claimant.[70]

Where the defendant's misrepresentation is *negligent* rather than fraudulent, there is no **2.19** objection in principle to the reduction of damages for contributory fault, and there are many examples of such reductions being made.[71] It has sometimes been argued that the claimant's unreasonable reliance on a negligent misrepresentation cannot amount to contributory negligence,[72] but it is not entirely clear why that is. It may be that this is an example of a rule appropriate to an all-or-nothing doctrine (in this instance rescission of a contract for misrepresentation) being applied unthinkingly in the apportionment context. Or it may be that the objection is that, if the claimant's reliance was unreasonable, then by definition no relevant duty of care was owed by the defendant (in which case the appropriate outcome is no liability, not reduced damages).[73] If so, the objection is weak. Simply asserting that no duty of care is owed begs the question of whether denial of liability or apportionment is the appropriate response to this scenario. And any such objection also rests on the rather strange idea that the reasonableness of the reliance on a statement determines whether a duty of care existed at the earlier time when the statement was made.[74] There are in any case many negligent misrepresentation claims in which the

[68] ibid [16].

[69] T Weir, *An Introduction to Tort Law* (2nd edn, OUP 2006) 124. Though cf J Murphy, 'Misleading Appearances in the Tort of Deceit' (2016) 75 CLJ 301, 328–29 (querying why a reckless defendant held liable for deceit should be barred from relying on a reckless or even deliberate lack of self-regard on the part of a claimant).

[70] *Standard Chartered Bank v Pakistan National Shipping Corp (No 4)* [2001] QB 167 (CA).

[71] See *Goudkamp and Nolan*, ch 8.

[72] *Gran Gelato Ltd v Richcliffe (Group) Ltd* [1992] Ch 560 (CA) 574. See also *JEB Fasteners Ltd v Marks, Bloom & Co* [1981] 3 All ER 289 (QBD) 297.

[73] See Klar (n 27) 153, who cites some Canadian cases in support of this reasoning.

[74] cf D Nolan, 'Assumption of Responsibility: Four Questions' (2019) 72 CLP 123, 155.

contributory negligence of a claimant does not take the form of unreasonable reliance on the representation, as where a bank makes an imprudent loan partly because a surveyor negligently over-valued the property on which the loan was secured, and partly because the bank failed properly to assess the creditworthiness of the mortgagor. In such cases there is no doubt that apportionment is both available and appropriate.[75]

(4) Other causes of action

2.20 The common law authorities were unclear as to whether the contributory negligence doctrine extended to conversion, though the weight of authority was against.[76] Parliament provided clarity in section 11(1) of the Torts (Interference with Goods) Act 1977, which states that the doctrine does not apply in proceedings founded on conversion or intentional trespass to goods.[77] Shortly after the enactment of that provision an exception was made for certain cases involving conversion of cheques.[78] The contributory negligence doctrine is also inapplicable to the torts of inducing breach of contract[79] and conspiracy.[80] It seems never to have been argued in a claim for defamation,[81] and it can be assumed that the courts would not entertain it in actions where liability requires proof of bad faith on the defendant's part, such as malicious prosecution and misfeasance in a public office.

2.21 Finally, it is unclear whether the contributory negligence doctrine extends to the action on the case for injury to a reversionary interest, which is an action that persons with certain types of interests in property can invoke in respect of damage to the property concerned where they cannot sue in conversion or trespass because they were out of possession and did not have a right immediately to possess the property when it was damaged. Andrew Tettenborn suggests that such actions are subject to the law of contributory negligence,[82] although it seems that there is no directly relevant authority in this regard, and it might be argued by analogy with the position in conversion[83] that the plea of contributory negligence should not be available in such cases.

---

[75] This is a common scenario in the case law: see, eg, *Paratus AMC Ltd v Countrywide Surveyors Ltd* [2011] EWHC 3307 (Ch), [2012] PNLR 12; *Webb Resolutions Ltd v ESurv Ltd* [2012] EWHC 3653 (TCC), [2013] PNLR 15. See further *Goudkamp and Nolan*, paras 8.24–8.27.

[76] The outlier was *Lumsden & Co v London Trustee Savings Bank* [1971] 1 Lloyd's Rep 114 (QBD), applying the defence. *Lumsden* was criticized as inconsistent with the earlier cases by JR Spencer, 'Widening Scope of Defence of Contributory Negligence' [1972A] CLJ 27, who however accepted that an innocent converter should be able to rely on the doctrine. Williams also considered that contributory negligence should be available in at least some cases of conversion (*Williams*, 210–12). In New Zealand, contributory negligence does apply to conversion: see, eg, *Helson v McKenzies (Cuba Street) Ltd* [1950] NZLR 878 (CA), where the owner of a handbag was held partly to blame for the defendant's having given it by mistake to a third party.

[77] There is some nuance to the wording of this provision, and its operation can lead to surprising results. See further, *Clerk & Lindsell*, para 16-130.

[78] Banking Act 1979, s 47: 'In any circumstances in which proof of absence of negligence on the part of a banker would be a defence in proceedings by reason of section 4 of the Cheques Act 1957, a defence of contributory negligence shall also be available to the banker notwithstanding the provisions of section 11(1) of the Torts (Interference with Goods) Act 1977.'

[79] *Corporacion Nacional del Cobre de Chile v Sogemin Metals Ltd* [1997] 1 WLR 1396 (Ch D) 1405.

[80] ibid; *Dellabarca v Northern Storemen and Packers Union* [1989] 2 NZLR 734 (HC) 757.

[81] Though cf *Williams*, 210.

[82] A Tettenborn, 'Damages in Conversion—The Exception or the Anomaly?' (1993) 52 CLJ 128, 144; A Tettenborn, 'Reversionary Damage to Chattels' (1994) 53 CLJ 326, 340–41.

[83] See 2.20.

5. Statutory Torts

The question of whether the contributory negligence doctrine applies to a statutory tort is often answered by the legislation itself making clear that it does, usually by stating that the liability created by the statute falls within the meaning of 'fault' in section 4 of the 1945 Act.[84] The additional clarity provided by this approach is welcome, as is the fact that it sidesteps the 1945 cause of action rule. **2.22**

Statutory torts to which the contributory negligence doctrine applies by virtue of an express provision to that effect tend to concern strict liability. A possible explanation for this is that the legislation in question works by imposing a primary liability rather than a duty (breach of which gives rise to a secondary liability to pay damages).[85] The draftsman may therefore have been concerned that since the conduct of the defendant that gives rise to the liability is not necessarily a breach of duty it might not otherwise fall within the definition of 'fault' in section 4 of the 1945 Act.[86] Examples of such provisions can be found in, for example, legislation imposing strict liability in respect of damage caused by the discharge or escape of oil from ships at sea,[87] a defective product,[88] the escape of gas from a gas storage facility,[89] unauthorized waste deposits,[90] and the escape of water from a pipe vested in a water undertaker.[91] Similarly, section 10 of the Animals Act 1971 provides for the application of the contributory negligence doctrine to the strict liabilities established by sections 2–4 of that Act, which encompass damage caused by dangerous animals, injuries to livestock by dogs and damage and expenses caused by trespassing cattle. By contrast, where the legislation in question imposes a duty, there tends not to be an express stipulation that the liability amounts to 'fault' for the purposes of the 1945 Act, but there is no difficulty in reaching that conclusion in any case, so that the courts simply assume that the apportionment regime applies. This is true, for example, in the case of the duty of care owed by an occupier to a visitor by virtue of the Occupiers' Liability Act 1957 and of the duty of care that an occupier may owe to a trespasser under the Occupiers' Liability Act 1984.[92] It is surely also true of the various duties created by the Defective Premises Act 1972, though there appears to be no authority on the matter. **2.23**

Damages claims for negligent pre-contractual misrepresentations under section 2(1) of the Misrepresentation Act 1967 are subject to the contributory negligence doctrine at least **2.24**

---

[84] See, eg, Consumer Protection Act 1987, s 6(4); Environmental Protection Act 1990, s 73(9).

[85] The legislation therefore imposes a 'liability rule', ie a rule that simply states that in circumstance *x*, *y* has a claim against *z*. On the distinction between liability rules and wrongs, see D Nolan and A Robertson, 'Rights and Private Law' in D Nolan and A Robertson (eds), *Rights and Private Law* (Hart Publishing 2011) 15–18.

[86] Note for instance the very careful wording of the Consumer Protection Act 1987, s 6(4): 'Where any damage is caused partly by a defect in a product and partly by the fault of the person suffering the damage, the [1945 Act] ... shall have effect *as if the defect were the fault of every person liable by virtue of this Part for the damage caused by the defect*' (emphasis added).

[87] Merchant Shipping Act 1995, s 153(8) and 154(4).

[88] Consumer Protection Act 1987, s 6(4). On the operation of contributory negligence in the product liability context, see D Fairgrieve and R Goldberg, *Product Liability* (3rd edn, OUP 2020) paras 17.123–17.134.

[89] Gas Act 1965, s 14(3). It is also a complete defence that the damage was the claimant's own fault. This is best understood as a statutory form of the 'default of the claimant' defence, as to which see 5.12–5.15.

[90] Environmental Protection Act 1990, s 73(9)(b).

[91] Water Industry Act 1991, s 209(4).

[92] See P North, *Occupiers' Liability* (2nd edn, OUP 2014) paras 8.02–8.05 and 11.42 respectively.

where liability also arises concurrently in common law negligence.[93] It could in theory be argued that since the 'fiction of fraud' in section 2(1) has been held to have implications for the assessment of damages,[94] and since contributory negligence does not apply to deceit,[95] it ought also not to apply to claims under that provision. However, this argument has little appeal, and is unlikely to be accepted by the courts. Where a claim is brought under section 2(1) of the 1967 Act but no concurrent claim lies in negligence, it has been suggested that contributory negligence is not available by analogy with the position in breach of contract.[96] However, since liability under section 2(1) is itself a form of liability in tort the analogy seems weak and the better view is that in these cases too contributory negligence should be available.[97]

2.25 There are three statutes that lay down apportionment provisions in respect of contributory negligence that differ somewhat from the otherwise applicable provisions of the 1945 Act, or which are in some other respect distinctive. The most important of these in practice is the Merchant Shipping Act 1995, section 187 of which is the modern equivalent of section 1 of the Maritime Conventions Act 1911, and provides for distinctive rules of apportionment in cases involving collisions between ships.[98] Section 187(1) stipulates that:

> Where by the fault of two or more ships, damage or loss is caused to one or more of those ships, to their cargoes or freight, or to any property on board, the liability to make good the damage or loss shall be in proportion to the degree in which each ship was in fault.

If it is not possible to establish different degrees of fault, responsibility for the damage 'shall be apportioned equally'.[99] Despite the different phrasing, section 187 and the apportionment provision in the 1945 Act generally apply in a similar way.[100] The main exception to this seems to be that the courts in proceedings to which section 187 applies tend to ask in apportioning responsibility how many more times at fault one party is relative to the other,[101] an approach not used under the 1945 Act. A different approach

---

93 *Gran Gelato Ltd v Richcliff (Group) Ltd* [1992] Ch 560 (Ch D).

94 See the controversial decision in *Royscot Trust Ltd v Rogerson* [1991] 2 QB 297 (CA).

95 See 2.18.

96 See *Gran Gelato Ltd v Richcliff (Group) Ltd* [1992] Ch 560 (Ch D) 574. On the position in contract, see 2.26–2.31.

97 See *Burrows*, 137 fn 301.

98 Full discussion of s 187 and the substantial case law that has sprung up around it is beyond the scope of this volume and should be sought in specialist texts. A leading (albeit dated) analysis of the regime is H Brandon, 'Apportionment of Liability in British Courts under the Maritime Conventions Act of 1911' (1977) 51 Tulane L Rev 1025.

99 Merchant Shipping Act 1987, s 187(2).

100 *Davies v Swan Motor Co (Swansea) Ltd v James* [1949] 2 KB 291 (CA) 319; *The Miraflores and The Abadesa* [1966] P 18 (CA) 33; *Nordlake (Owners) v Seaeagle (Owners)* [2015] EWHC 3605 (Admlty), [2016] 1 Lloyd's Rep 656 [145]. It is true that while the 1945 Act speaks of apportionment by reference to the claimant's share of *responsibility* for the damage, the 1995 Act speaks only of the *fault* of the ships, a formula which appears to exclude causal considerations from the analysis. However, in practice it seems that the Admiralty courts have interpreted the word 'fault' broadly (there being no definition of the term in the 1995 Act or its predecessor), such that it is doubtful whether there is in fact a significant difference between the two regimes in terms of how the apportionment exercise is conducted.

101 See, eg, *Samco Europe v MSC Prestige* [2011] EWHC 1580 (Admlty), [2011] 2 Lloyd's Rep 579 [81]. This follows the suggestion of Brandon (n 98) at 1041 that 'it may be found helpful to consider whether the degree of fault of the ship more to blame is one and a half times as great, twice as great, or three, four, five, or even more times as great, as the degree of the fault of the ship less to blame'.

to the issue of contributory fault is also applicable in respect of harm caused by ionizing radiation. Pursuant to section 13 of the Nuclear Installations Act 1965, the amount of compensation due to the claimant is to be reduced 'only if, and to the extent that, the causation of that injury or damage is attributable to [an] act of the [claimant] committed with the intention of causing harm to any person or property or with reckless disregard for the consequences of his act'. This is clearly a much narrower test than is ordinarily used to assess the existence of contributory negligence, and the kind of conduct that would trigger the application of this provision would in other scenarios be likely to amount to a novus actus interveniens relieving a defendant of liability altogether.[102] Finally, a somewhat complex set of provisions governing contributory fault are to be found in the Automated and Electric Vehicles Act 2018,[103] which imposes strict liability on the insurer—or, if there is no insurer, the owner—of an automated vehicle for damage that results from an accident caused by the vehicle when driving itself. According to section 3(1):

> Where ... the accident, or the damage resulting from it, was to any extent caused by the injured party, the amount of the liability is subject to whatever reduction under the Law Reform (Contributory Negligence) Act 1945 would apply to a claim in respect of the accident brought by the injured party against a person other than the insurer or vehicle owner.

This somewhat opaque application of apportionment for contributory negligence[104] is supplemented by a more draconian provision which provides the insurer or owner with a complete defence where the claim is brought by the person in charge of the vehicle at the relevant time and the accident 'was wholly due to the person's negligence in allowing the vehicle to begin driving itself when it was not appropriate to do so'.[105] The wording of this provision is reminiscent of the language used to qualify certain other statutory forms of strict liability,[106] and the defence it creates is analogous to the 'default of the claimant' defence applicable to certain strict liability causes of action at common law.[107]

6. Breach of Contract

The question of the application of the doctrine of contributory negligence to breach of contract is a complex one, and in a book focused primarily on the law of tort, it is not feasible to explore every aspect of that question.[108] The starting point for the analysis of this **2.26**

[102] See 5.02–5.07.

[103] For discussion, see J Goudkamp, 'Automated Vehicle Liability and AI' in E Lim and P Morgan (eds), *The Cambridge Handbook of Private Law and Artificial Intelligence* (CUP 2023).

[104] For analysis of this provision, which is rightly described as 'difficult to follow', see Law Commission and Scottish Law Commission, *Automated Vehicles: A Joint Preliminary Consultation Paper* (Law Com CP 240, Scot Law Com DP 166, 2018) paras 6.31–6.39.

[105] Automated and Electric Vehicles Act 2018, s 3(2).

[106] See Gas Act 1965, s 14; Environmental Protection Act 1990, s 33(7); Water Industry Act 1991, s 209(2).

[107] See 5.12–5.15. Unlike the common law defence, the s 3(2) defence is only applicable to certain claimants, and in certain closely defined circumstances. However, where an accident was wholly due to the fault of the claimant, but the case does not fall within the ambit of s 3(2), the same result could perhaps be arrived at by the court holding that the accident was not 'caused' by the vehicle in the first place.

[108] For more detailed treatments, see NE Palmer and PJ Davies, 'Contributory Negligence and Breach of Contract: English and Australian Attitudes Compared' (1980) 29 ICLQ 415; J Swanton, 'Contributory Negligence as a Defence to Actions for Breach of Contract' (1981) 55 ALJ 278; Law Commission, *Contributory Negligence as a Defence in Contract* (Law Com No 219, 1993); *Harder*, ch 24; *Burrows*, 138–44.

issue is that it seems clear that contributory negligence was not a defence at common law to a claim in contract, as it was for a claim in tort. No mention was made of contributory negligence as a contract defence in works on contract or pleading before 1945, and '[n]o case can be found in the books where contributory negligence, as such, was ever held to be a defence to an action for breach of contract'.[109] This fact alone could be taken as precluding the possibility of apportionment for contributory negligence in contract cases, applying the 1945 cause of action rule discussed earlier,[110] and indeed an argument along these lines was relied on by a majority of the High Court of Australia in *Astley v Austrust Ltd*.[111] However, with regard to cases of concurrent liability in contract and tort, this argument is somewhat disingenuous. Before 1945, concurrent liability was limited to the duties of carriers, employers, bailees for reward, occupiers (towards contractual entrants), and the so-called 'common callings', and it does not seem to have been seriously suggested in those types of case that a claimant could circumvent the application of the complete defence of contributory negligence by suing in contract rather than tort.[112] Besides, we have seen that the 1945 cause of action rule is open to objection on numerous grounds,[113] and even if it did dictate an answer to the question of the application of the contributory negligence doctrine to breach of contract, that answer would be a crude and simplistic one.

2.27 Turning our attention to the relationship between contributory negligence and breach of contract in the era of apportionment, it is conventional to divide up breaches of contract into three categories. The first category is breaches of a strict contractual duty ('category 1 cases'). The second category is breaches of a contractual duty of care which do not also give rise to a claim in the tort of negligence ('category 2 cases'). And the third category is breaches of a contractual duty of care which do give rise to a claim in the tort of negligence ('category 3 cases'). This threefold categorization was first adopted in the leading case of *Forsikringsaktieselskapet Vesta v Butcher*,[114] where the Court of Appeal held that the doctrine of contributory negligence extended to category 3 cases (unless the parties have agreed otherwise), but that it did not extend to category 1 or category 2 cases.[115] This decision has been followed in later case law.[116] On one view, it is consistent with the wording of the Law Reform (Contributory Negligence) Act 1945, which defines

[109] *Astley v Austrust Ltd* [1999] HCA 6, (1999) 197 CLR 1 [76] (Gleeson CJ, McHugh, Gummow and Hayne JJ). See also *Forsikringsaktieselskapet Vesta v Butcher* [1989] AC 852 (CA) 879. There would have been conceptual obstacles to contributory negligence as a defence in contract, most obviously that the doctrine was causation-based (see 1.08), while breach of contract is actionable per se, so that causation is not an element of the cause of action: see *Belous v Willetts* [1970] VR 45 (SC) 46–48; R Stevens, 'Should Contributory Fault be Analogue or Digital?' in A Dyson et al (eds), *Defences in Tort* (Hart Publishing 2015) 260–61.

[110] See 2.03–2.05.

[111] [1999] HCA 6, (1999) 197 CLR 1 [58]–[59], [80].

[112] See *Williams*, 214–15.

[113] See 2.03–2.05.

[114] [1989] AC 852 (CA).

[115] The decision in *Vesta v Butcher* is consistent with an earlier Court of Appeal decision, *Sayers v Harlow Urban District Council* [1958] 1 WLR 623 (CA), where an award of damages for personal injury was discounted for contributory negligence in circumstances where the claim could have been brought in contract or tort.

[116] See, eg, *Barclays Bank plc v Fairclough Building Ltd* [1995] QB 214 (CA) (category 1); *Raflatac Ltd v Eade* [1999] 1 Lloyd's Rep 506 (QBD) (category 2); *UCB Bank plc v Hepherd Winstanley & Pugh (a firm)* [1999] Lloyd's Rep PN 963 (CA) (category 3).

'fault' for defendant purposes[117] as 'negligence, breach of statutory duty or other act or omission which gives rise to a liability in tort', a description that encompasses only those breaches of contract that also give rise to a concurrent liability in tort. (Indeed, it was this definition that persuaded the Court of Appeal in *Vesta* to exclude category 2 cases on the ground that the defendant's conduct does not 'give rise to liability in tort'.) Furthermore, the dividing line drawn in *Vesta* seems to fit with the intentions of the drafters of the apportionment legislation, as there is evidence that they 'wanted to avoid incursion of the statutory division of responsibility into plain contractual cases', but 'were troubled by cases of overlap in contract and tort duties and equally keen to have the reform assist the claimant in these cases'.[118] Conversely, it might be objected that *Vesta* is not in fact an exercise in statutory interpretation at all (the 1945 Act is barely mentioned in the decision) and that the courts have simply imposed a taxonomy on this area of the law, and derived consequences therefrom, that do not necessarily comport with Parliament's intention.[119]

In *Vesta v Butcher*, O'Connor LJ regarded it as axiomatic that the doctrine of contributory negligence applied where there were concurrent and co-extensive contractual and tortious duties of care:[120] **2.28**

> The category (3) question has arisen in very many different types of case and the answer is treated as so obvious that it passes without any comment. It is commonplace that actions are brought by persons who have suffered personal injuries as the result of the negligence of the person sued and that there is a contractual as well as tortious relationship. In such cases apportionment of blame is invariably adopted by the court notwithstanding that the plaintiff could sue in contract as well as in tort.

It does indeed seem that it would be problematic for a claimant to be able to evade a discount for contributory negligence simply by pleading their case in contract. This is particularly true where the claim is a routine personal injury action that just happens to be between contracting parties, as where a passenger is suing a carrier, an employee an employer, or a patient a private healthcare provider.[121] It is unsurprising, therefore, that not a single respondent to the Law Commission's consultation on this topic opposed the application of the doctrine of contributory negligence in category 3 cases.[122] Conversely, a majority of the High Court of Australia held in *Astley v Austrust Ltd* that the doctrine of contributory negligence was inapplicable to claims for breach of contract even where there was a concurrent and co-extensive liability in tort.[123] The majority did so principally

117 As interpreted by the courts, anyway. See 2.03.

118 J Steele, 'Law Reform (Contributory Negligence) Act 1945: Collisions of a Different Sort' in TT Arvind and J Steele (eds), *Tort Law and the Legislature: Common Law, Statute and the Dynamics of Legal Change* (Hart Publishing 2012) 183. For other evidence that the drafters of the legislation envisaged it applying in at least some cases of breach of contract, see *Williams*, 330–31 (pointing out, inter alia, that a provision to the effect that the legislation should not apply to any claim arising under a contract was removed from the Bill that became the Act).

119 See *Astley v Austrust Ltd* [1999] HCA 6, (1999) 197 CLR 1 [69].

120 [1989] AC 852 (CA) 860–61.

121 See *Astley v Austrust Ltd* [1999] HCA 6, (1999) 197 CLR 1 [135]; JLR Davis, 'Contributory Negligence and Breach of Contract: *Astley v Austrust Ltd*' (1999) 7 Torts LJ 117, 126–28.

122 Law Commission (n 108) para 3.42.

123 [1999] HCA 6, (1999) 197 CLR 1. Most commentators have rejected this position. An exception is Stevens (n 109) 262–63.

on the basis that contributory negligence had not apparently been a defence to claims for breach of contract (pointing out that the great works on the law of contract written before 1945 were silent on the subject of contributory negligence).[124] They also emphasized that the apportionment legislation was intended to improve rather than worsen the position of claimants,[125] a point also taken at the highest level in England.[126] It should be recognized, however, that *Astley* has been the subject of stinging criticism by commentators,[127] and met with a uniform response from the Australian state legislatures, all of which rapidly overturned it.[128]

2.29 Whether contributory negligence should also extend to category 2 cases is not a very significant issue in practice, since such cases are rare following the acceptance by the House of Lords of concurrent liability in contract and tort in *Henderson v Merrett Syndicates Ltd (No 1)*.[129] Be that as it may (and setting aside the issue of statutory construction that proved decisive in this regard in *Vesta v Butcher*) it is not altogether clear why a distinction should be made in this regard between breaches of contractual duties of care that give rise to tort liability and those that do not, and in its report on the law in this area the Law Commission recommended that the scope of contributory negligence ought to be extended to category 2 cases.[130] A possible counter-argument is that, while it should be easy for a court to determine whether there is a concurrent obligation of care in contract and tort, where this is not the case it may sometimes be difficult to tell whether a contractual duty is appropriately characterized as a duty of care as opposed to a stricter obligation.[131]

2.30 A more important question is whether the scope of the contributory negligence doctrine should be extended to breach of contract in general, by applying it to category 1 cases. The Law Commission opposed such an extension, arguing that it would create too much uncertainty by introducing arguments about comparative fault into otherwise routine contract cases.[132] This was also the view of the New Zealand Law Commission, which said:[133]

> We think it obvious that, where the terms of the contract are such that the plaintiff is entitled to rely entirely on the defendant's performance, there can be no question of reducing the plaintiff's damages for any failure to monitor the performance of the defendant or anticipate default. The plaintiff should be able to rely on the defendant to perform as specified.

---

[124] [1999] HCA 6, (1999) 197 CLR 1 [76]–[80].

[125] [1999] HCA 6, (1999) 197 CLR 1 [81].

[126] See 2.03.

[127] See, eg, Davis (n 121); G Masel and D Kelly, 'Contributory Negligence and the Provision of Services: A Critique of Astley' (2000) 74 ALJ 306.

[128] See, eg, Law Reform (Miscellaneous Provisions) Amendment Act 2000 (NSW); Wrongs (Amendment) Act 2000 (Vic). It should be appreciated, however, that these statutes were passed at the height of an 'insurance crisis' in Australia and that the legislatures might well have acted in part because of a concern that the decision in *Astley* would place upward pressure on insurance premiums.

[129] [1995] 2 AC 145 (HL). There are, however, occasional examples of category 2 cases that post-date *Henderson*: see, eg, *Raflatac Ltd v Eade* [1999] 1 Lloyd's Rep 506 (QBD); *Haugesund Kommune v Depfa ACS Bank* [2010] EWCA Civ 579, [2012] QB 549.

[130] Law Commission (n 108) para 3.41. See also New Zealand Law Commission, *Apportionment of Civil Liability: A Discussion Paper* (NZLC PP19, 1992) paras 190–91.

[131] See JC Kleefeld, 'The Contributory Negligence Act at Seventy' (2015) 78 Sask LR 31, 94.

[132] Law Commission (n 108) paras 3.39–3.40.

[133] New Zealand Law Commission (n 130) para 193.

However, a majority of the Law Commission's consultees favoured the extension of contributory negligence to all breaches of contract, and this was also the position adopted by the Scottish Law Commission in a recent report, where it recommended that the 1945 Act be amended to include within the definition of 'fault' a breach of contract by either party.[134] It is sometimes argued in support of this view that the unavailability of contributory negligence for breach of a strict contractual duty may drive a court faced with a culpable claimant to employ an all-or-nothing doctrine—such as novus actus interveniens, remoteness or mitigation of damage—in circumstances where a reduction in the claimant's damages would be a fairer response.[135] Furthermore, the strength of the arguments on which the Law Commission relied in coming to the contrary conclusion is open to question.[136] Proponents of the extension of the doctrine have also pointed out that in Ireland the doctrine of contributory negligence applies to all types of breach of contract, and that this does not appear to have given rise to significant problems.[137]

Although a case can be made for the position at which English law has arrived on the question of contributory negligence and breach of contract, including in the light of the wording of the 1945 Act, it does generate some apparent anomalies.[138] As Andrew Burrows points out, the distinction drawn between category 2 and 3 cases 'encourages an odd reversal of roles in that a blameworthy claimant will be better off ... if it can establish that the defendant was merely liable for breach of a contractual duty of care ... and was not also liable for the tort of negligence'.[139] It also means that the claimant who is the victim of two wrongs is worse off than the claimant who is the victim of one. Similarly, as regards the distinction between category 1 and category 3 cases, it seems strange that a defendant who was negligent is better off than one who was not. **2.31**

7. Equitable Wrongs

There is relatively little authority on the possible application of the doctrine of contributory negligence to equitable wrongs in English law. Although Blackburne J rejected the idea of apportionment for contributory fault in *Nationwide Building Society v Balmer Radmore*,[140] in that case the finding of breach of fiduciary duty rested on the deliberate withholding of information by a firm of solicitors from its client, and the judge distinguished New **2.32**

[134] Scottish Law Commission, *Report on Review of Contract Law: Formation, Interpretation, Remedies for Breach, and Penalty Clauses* (SLC No 252, 2018). The possibility of apportionment would be subject to any contrary stipulation in the contract itself.

[135] Law Commission (n 108) para 3.22. For a possible example of this phenomenon, see the unreported case of *Schering Agrochemicals Ltd v Resibel* (CA, 26 November 1992), cited by *Burrows*, 162–63.

[136] See J O'Sullivan, 'Contributory Negligence and Strict Contractual Obligations Revisited' in A Dyson et al (eds), *Defences in Contract* (Hart Publishing 2017).

[137] Civil Liability Act 1961 (Ire) s 34(1). See also the UNIDROIT Principles of International Commercial Contracts, Art 7.4.7.

[138] For further discussion, see J Goudkamp, 'The Contributory Negligence Doctrine: Four Commercial Law Problems' [2017] LMCLQ 213, 223–25.

[139] *Burrows*, 142.

[140] [1999] PNLR 606 (QBD). See also *de Beer v Kanaar & Co (a firm)* [2002] EWHC 688 (Ch) [92] (breach of trust); *Mosley v News Group Newspapers Ltd* [2008] EWHC 1777 (QB), [2008] EMLR 20 [224] (breach of confidence).

Zealand authorities in which apportionments had been made on the ground that they concerned unintentional breaches of fiduciary duty. Furthermore, in a recent Scottish case it was accepted that apportionment might be appropriate where a breach of fiduciary duty was unintentional.[141] The terms of the 1945 Act may have some bearing on the issue. According to section 4 of the Act, as far as defendants are concerned the word 'fault' means 'negligence, breach of statutory duty or other act or omission which gives rise to liability in tort', a formula which would appear not to encompass equitable wrongs. As in the case of breach of contract, however, the statutory wording provides some support for the view that a defendant ought to be entitled to rely on contributory negligence where there is concurrent liability in negligence and in an equitable wrong such as breach of trust or breach of fiduciary duty, since in that case the conduct of the defendant *would* give rise to liability in tort (as well as in the equitable wrong concerned).

2.33 The application of the contributory negligence doctrine to equitable wrongs was embraced by the New Zealand Court of Appeal in *Day v Mead*.[142] On the advice of his solicitor, the plaintiff in the case had bought shares in a company in which (as the plaintiff knew) the solicitor had a financial interest. Having become interested in the company and its operations, the plaintiff later made a further investment. The company went into liquidation and the plaintiff lost his money. The solicitor was found to have breached his fiduciary duty to the plaintiff, but the plaintiff was held to have been partly to blame for the second investment, since by then he ought to have realized that the company was in difficulties. His compensation in respect of the second investment was reduced by half for his contributory fault. *Day v Mead* was followed in a later New Zealand case, *Mouat v Clark Boyce*,[143] where a solicitor who had acted for the elderly plaintiff and her son was held liable for breach of fiduciary duty and negligence for not doing more to protect the plaintiff's interests in a transaction whereby she had mortgaged her home as security for a loan to her son.[144] The plaintiff's compensation was again reduced by 50 per cent for contributory fault, this time in not taking independent advice and in concealing her doubts about the transaction from the defendant.

2.34 The New Zealand decisions have been welcomed by some commentators. According to Joachim Dietrich, it ought to be possible for a court to reduce an award of equitable compensation on account of contributory negligence because of 'the wide range of factual circumstances which may amount to a breach of fiduciary duty, and the wide range of possible consequent losses arising from many different causative factors'.[145] While the circumstances in which apportionment for contributory fault would be appropriate might be 'exceptional', situations would doubtless arise in which a fiduciary honestly breaches their duty 'or merely carelessly disregards the possibility of a conflict of duty and interest' and can point to conduct of the claimant so disregardful of their own interests as to

[141] *Kidd v Paull & Williamsons LLP* [2017] CSOH 16 [69].

[142] [1987] 2 NZLR 443 (CA). See also *Canson Enterprises Ltd v Boughton & Co* [1991] 3 SCR 534 (SCC) 585 (expressing agreement with *Day v Mead* on this point).

[143] [1992] 2 NZLR 559 (CA).

[144] The finding of liability was reversed on appeal to the Privy Council: [1994] 1 AC 428 (PC).

[145] J Dietrich, 'The Decline of Contributory Negligence and Apportionment: Choosing the Black or White of All-or-Nothing Over Many Shades of Grey?' (2003) 11 Torts LJ 51, 56.

warrant a reduction in the compensation awarded.[146] Similarly, Sirko Harder argues that there are 'no cogent reasons for disallowing an apportionment of equitable compensation on the ground of contributory negligence', and a very good reason to allow it, 'namely the fact that equitable liability is often concurrent with liability at common law', where apportionment is often available.[147] It would, he maintains, be 'illogical' if a claimant were able to 'circumvent the apportionment looming at common law by pleading her case in equity'.[148] As against this, it might be said that 'circumvention' in one area of law of rules in another area of law is routinely permitted by the courts, and is indeed an inevitable consequence of the acceptance of concurrent liability. Further, there is strong resistance in some quarters to the idea of applying contributory negligence to equitable wrongdoing. In *Pilmer v Duke Group Ltd (in liq)*, for example, a majority of the High Court of Australia said that '[c]ontributory negligence focuses on the conduct of the plaintiff, fiduciary law upon the conduct of the defendant',[149] while Kirby J observed that 'the attempt to push common law notions of contributory negligence ... into equitable remedies collapses in the face of unsurmountable obstacles'.[150] Similarly, in the *Nationwide Building Society* case, Blackburne J warned that introducing apportionment into the law of fiduciary duty risked 'subverting the fundamental principle of undivided and unremitting loyalty' which was at the core of the fiduciary's obligation, and of further complicating the 'already complex' law in this area.[151]

8. Conclusion

There seems to be very little, if anything, to explain why the contributory negligence doctrine applies to certain causes of action but not to others. The law as described in this chapter appears to be largely the product of historical accident rather than rational development. A good example is the tort of conversion, to which the contributory negligence doctrine does not apply.[152] That tort can be committed both innocently (as where a defendant buys at an auction property which, unbeknownst to them, belongs to someone other than the vendor) and dishonestly (as where a defendant deliberately destroys property they know belongs to the claimant). It is therefore no explanation of the inapplicability of the doctrine here that it applies unless the defendant acted intentionally or in bad faith. An alternative explanation might be that the contributory negligence doctrine does not apply to property torts. Andrew Tettenborn, for example, speaks of 'English lawyers' dislike of apportionment solutions in English property law'[153] and observes that the inapplicability **2.35**

[146] ibid 57. See also *Hodgkinson v Simms* [1994] 3 SCR 377 (SCC) 444 (La Forest J) ('courts should strive to treat similar wrongs similarly, regardless of the particular cause of action or causes of action that may have been pleaded').
[147] *Harder*, 173.
[148] ibid. See also *Martin v Goldfarb* (1998) 163 DLR (4th) 639 (Ont CA) [34] (plaintiffs should not be able to recover higher damages merely by claiming in breach of fiduciary duty as opposed to tort or breach of contract).
[149] [2001] HCA 31, (2001) 207 CLR 165 [86] (McHugh, Gummow, Hayne and Callinan JJ).
[150] ibid [173].
[151] [1999] PNLR 606 (QBD) 677.
[152] See 2.20.
[153] Tettenborn (n 82 [1993]) 138.

of the defence in such cases dovetails with the fact that, in the law of negligence, an owner does not owe third parties a duty of care to safeguard their own property. However, this understanding would not explain the existing law either: many of the causes of action to which the doctrine does not apply have no necessary connection with any property, and it seems that the doctrine does apply in the property tort of private nuisance.[154] And even if the current rules could be explained in this way, it is far from clear that there is a compelling reason for singling out property torts for separate treatment as far as the law of contributory negligence is concerned.

2.36 The fact is that the entire law of contributory negligence gets off to a bad start because the rules regarding the doctrine's applicability lack any obvious justification. It is very unfortunate that the law in this area has not been developed by reference to any sound theory or argument. The question of which causes of action should be subject to the contributory negligence doctrine has never been analysed by the courts in a thoroughgoing way. Moreover, many difficulties have been caused by the wording of the apportionment legislation, which has often proved decisive on questions of the scope of the doctrine, even though there is little to suggest that the drafting of the statute was done with those questions in mind. Ultimately, the extent of the doctrine's application should be resolved primarily by reference to the reason why the law recognizes the doctrine in the first place, but unfortunately that, too, is a matter in respect of which there is little in the way of reasoned analysis in the case law.[155]

154 See 2.14.
155 See 1.18–1.24.

3

THE EXISTENCE OF CONTRIBUTORY NEGLIGENCE

In this chapter we consider the circumstances in which a court will make a finding of contributory negligence. The consequences of such a finding are considered in chapter 4. Here we focus on what contributory negligence means, and whose claims will be affected by it. A finding of contributory negligence requires (i) that the claimant failed to take reasonable care in respect of their own safety or interests (the 'negligence requirement'), and (ii) that this failure was a cause of some or all of the claimant's damage (the 'causation requirement'). After looking at these two requirements in turn, we conclude our analysis of the existence of contributory negligence by considering when the contributory negligence of a third party will be imputed to the claimant (the 'doctrine of identification'). **3.01**

1. The Negligence Requirement

(1) Introduction

Whereas the negligence that grounds liability consists in a failure to take reasonable care for the safety or interests of others, contributory negligence involves a failure by the claimant to take care of their own safety or interests.[1] Hence while a defendant's negligence creates 'an undue risk of harm to others', contributory negligence creates 'an undue risk of harm to the person who sustains it'.[2] Of course, it is true that conduct constituting contributory negligence will often also ground liability,[3] but at the same time it is perfectly possible to endanger oneself without risking the safety of another person.[4] Since contributory negligence is self-regarding fault, there is no need to establish that the claimant owed the defendant (or anyone else) a duty of care,[5] nor that the claimant's fault was actionable **3.02**

---

[1] 'Contributory negligence is a man's carelessness in looking after *his own* safety': *Froom v Butcher* [1976] QB 286 (CA) 291 (Lord Denning MR) (emphasis added).

[2] *Restatement (Second) of the Law of Torts* (1965) § 463, cmt b.

[3] See, eg, *Carrier v Bonham* [2001] QCA 234, [2002] 1 Qd R 474 (bus driver awarded damages for psychiatric injury he suffered after the defendant stepped in front of his bus in a suicide attempt).

[4] Among countless examples, see *Jones v Livox Quarries Ltd* [1952] 2 QB 608 (CA); *Froom v Butcher* [1976] QB 286 (CA); and *Reeves v Commissioner of Police of the Metropolis* [2000] 1 AC 360 (HL).

[5] See *Davies v Swan Motor Co (Swansea) Ltd* [1949] 2 KB 291 (CA) 324 (Denning LJ): 'When a man steps into the road he owes a duty to himself to take care for his own safety, but he does not owe any duty to a motorist who is going at an excessive speed to avoid being run down.' See also *Jones v Livox Quarries Ltd* [1952] 2 QB 608 (CA) 615.

Contributory Negligence. Second Edition. James Goudkamp and Donal Nolan, Oxford University Press.
 DOI: 10.1093/oso/9780192867919.003.0003

at the instance of the defendant or a third party. Note also that not all blameworthy conduct on the claimant's part will amount to contributory negligence, but only conduct that exposes the claimant to unreasonable risks of harm.[6] In *Westwood v Post Office*,[7] an employee of the defendant entered a lift motor room despite a notice forbidding entry. He fell through a trap door in the floor and was killed. In an action by the employee's widow, it was held by a majority of the House of Lords that no deduction should be made from the damages for contributory negligence, since he had had no reason to suppose that the room was dangerous. For the purposes of the Law Reform (Contributory Negligence) Act 1945, 'fault' meant unreasonable disregard for one's own safety, and not other forms of blameworthy behaviour, such as disobedience.

3.03 As in the case of the negligence that grounds liability, there must be some *conduct* on the part of the claimant that falls below the standard of reasonable care for a finding of contributory negligence to be made.[8] Hence, a person who while unconscious through drink is put by others in a car which is then driven by a clearly intoxicated driver is not guilty of contributory negligence 'because they have done no voluntary act'.[9] Similarly, a claimant who sleepwalks into the road and is run over by a speeding motorist is not guilty of contributory negligence since there was no voluntary act on their part that fell below the standard of reasonable care. It is important to emphasize, however, that this requirement of conduct encompasses both acts and omissions, and that the latter are particularly likely to feature in the contributory negligence context, where—in the absence of a duty of care requirement—the complications attendant on omissions *liability* in negligence do not arise. It is also important to remember that (as with defendant negligence) the fact that contributory negligence is negligent *conduct* makes the claimant's 'subjective mental or emotional state' at the time of the relevant act or omission generally irrelevant.[10]

3.04 It is often suggested that the questions of defendant fault and claimant fault are mirror images of each other. Indeed, some Australian state legislatures have even passed legislative provisions to this effect. According to section 5R(1) of the New South Wales Civil Liability Act 2002, for example:

> The principles that are applicable in determining whether a person has been negligent also apply in determining whether the person who suffered harm has been contributorily negligent in failing to take precautions against the risk of that harm.

In particular, it is commonly believed that the standard of care applied to claimants is the same as the standard of care applied to defendants.[11] However the mirror image principle

[6] See I Fagelson, 'The Last Bastion of Fault: Contributory Negligence in Actions for Employers' Liability' (1979) 42 MLR 646, 654.

[7] [1974] AC 1 (HL).

[8] On this issue in the case of defendants, see J Goudkamp, *Defences in Tort* (Hart Publishing 2013) 49–50.

[9] *Campbell v Advantage Insurance Co Ltd* [2021] EWCA Civ 1698 [53] (Underhill LJ). Of course, it could be argued in such a case that getting unconscious through drink is itself a form of contributory negligence, but that is a separate issue.

[10] *Allen v Chadwick* [2015] HCA 47, (2015) 256 CLR 148 [52] (French CJ, Kiefel, Bell, Keane and Gordon JJ).

[11] See, eg, *Casson v Spotmix Ltd (in liq)* [2017] EWCA Civ 1994 [6] (Sir Terence Etherton MR) ('uncontroversial' that the standard of care applied to claimants 'is the same as that applied when considering negligence from the perspective of breach of duty'); *Restatement (Third) of Torts: Apportionment of Liability* (2000) § 3 ('Plaintiff's negligence is defined by the applicable standard for a defendant's negligence').

may oversimplify the true position. For example, we shall see that the standard of care applied to claimants is more subjective than the standard of care applied to defendants in that the courts are more inclined to take account of the claimant's personal characteristics.[12] Furthermore, when it comes to the application of the standard of care, there is reason to suppose that the courts take a more lenient approach when faced with allegations of claimant fault than they do when faced with allegations of defendant fault.[13] As Glanville Williams noted:[14]

> In theory the same standard should be required of a plaintiff ... [as of a defendant], but one cannot help feeling in reading the cases that the actual standard required has often been lower ... In a word, the reasonable defendant is not allowed lapses, but the reasonable plaintiff is.

A moment of inadvertence by an employee while performing a repetitive task may well be judged not to constitute contributory negligence,[15] for example, but there is little doubt that if it resulted in injury to a third party then it would constitute negligence for the purposes of a claim by that third party against the employee (or their employer).[16] The historical roots of this leniency towards claimants undoubtedly lie in the draconian effect of the common law defence of contributory negligence. But although Williams thought that this tendency might not survive the advent of apportionment,[17] there is abundant evidence that a stricter approach is still taken to defendant negligence than to claimant negligence today. The explanation for the survival of this tendency may be the courts' awareness that defendants are generally insured and so do not themselves bear the cost of liability, whereas deductions from damages for contributory negligence almost always leave claimants with uninsured losses.[18]

In defence of the mirror image principle, the reporters for the *Restatement (Third) of* **3.05**
Torts: Apportionment of Responsibility argue that the task of comparing 'the responsibility of various actors, including the plaintiff, whose conduct combines to cause an injury ... is difficult if different rules apply to the same actor in different parts of a lawsuit', as the same person might be both a plaintiff and a defendant in the same lawsuit.[19] It is true that where counterclaims are involved, the simplicity of the mirror image principle is appealing. However, this consideration carries more weight in the United States, where trial by jury is the norm in tort cases, than it does in jurisdictions in which the trier of fact is a judge. An English trial judge should have no difficulty in applying different standards to claimants and defendants, even where there are counterclaims. Furthermore, there may be good reasons for doing this, which justify the additional complexity involved.

---

[12] See 3.08–3.19.

[13] See also *Fleming*, 320 ('the *actual* standard of care for plaintiffs is without much doubt often appreciably lower than that for defendants'); *Todd*, 1159 ('In practice ... the plaintiff's standard tends to be less exacting').

[14] *Williams*, 353.

[15] See 3.31–3.32.

[16] J Dietrich and I Field, 'The "Reasonable Tort Victim": Contributory Negligence, Standard of Care and the "Equivalence Theory"' (2017) 41 Melb UL Rev 602, 639–40. See also *Munkman*, para 6.7.

[17] *Williams*, 354.

[18] *Fleming*, 309.

[19] *Restatement (Third) of Torts: Apportionment of Liability* (2000) § 3, cmt a.

(2) The standard of care

3.06 Like a defendant in a negligence case, a claimant 'is not required to attain a standard of perfection'.[20] Rather, the standard that a claimant is expected to achieve is one of reasonable care, which standard must take account of 'the realities of ordinary everyday life'.[21] The use of a reasonable care test shows that the default position is that where contributory negligence is alleged the standard is objective.[22] The starting point for the analysis is whether in all the circumstances of the case the conduct of the claimant fell below the standard of the reasonable person. Consequently, and as Lord Denning MR explained in *Froom v Butcher*:[23]

> In determining [the issue of contributory negligence], the law eliminates the personal equation. It takes no notice of the views of the particular individual or of others like him. It requires everyone to exercise all such precautions as a man of ordinary prudence would observe.

Hence, in *Froom* itself, it was irrelevant that the claimant believed, wrongly, that using a seat belt increased the probability of suffering serious injury.[24] Similarly, where the alleged contributory negligence is taking a lift with an intoxicated driver, the question is not whether the claimant knew (or was aware of signs indicating) that the driver was intoxicated, but what a reasonable person in their position would have known.[25] Furthermore, it would make no difference in such a case that the claimant did not realize that the driver was intoxicated because the claimant was in the same condition. This is because the law does not treat 'the fact that the claimant is drunk as a characteristic that can be taken into account in deciding whether he or she took reasonable care'.[26]

3.07 It is, however, important to distinguish between the standard of care itself and the circumstances which are taken into account when applying it. In *Allen v Chadwick*,[27] the plaintiff was a passenger in a car being driven by a drunken driver, who suffered serious injuries after the car crashed into a tree. One issue that arose was whether it had been contributorily negligent of the plaintiff to re-enter the car after she had left the vehicle (which she had been driving) to go to the toilet, during which time the intoxicated defendant had taken the wheel without her consent. The High Court of Australia took

[20] *Crew v Ash* [2008] EWHC 3068 (QB) [28] (Lloyd Jones J).

[21] *Howe v Houlton* [2009] EWHC 3344 (QB) [123] (Swift J).

[22] See *Rose v South East London and Kent Bus Co Ltd* [2004] EWHC 1106 (QB) [4]; *Badger v Ministry of Defence* [2005] EWHC 2941 (QB), [2006] 3 All ER 173 [7]. See also *McHale v Watson* (1966) 115 CLR 199 (HCA) 214–15; and *Joslyn v Berryman* [2003] HCA 34, (2003) 214 CLR 552 [34], both rejecting the suggestion in an earlier Australian case that the standard of care applicable to plaintiffs was what they were 'in fact capable of' (*Cotton v Commission for Road Transport and Tramways* (1942) 43 SR(NSW) 66 (Full Ct) 69 (Jordan CJ)).

[23] [1976] QB 286 (CA) 294.

[24] See also *Astley v Austrust Ltd* [1999] HCA 6, (1999) 197 CLR 1 [35].

[25] See *Joslyn v Berryman* [2003] HCA 34, (2003) 214 CLR 552 [36]–[38].

[26] *Campbell v Advantage Insurance Co Ltd* [2021] EWCA Civ 1698 [50] (Underhill LJ). See also ibid [36] et seq; *Joslyn v Berryman* [2003] HCA 34, (2003) 214 CLR 552 [38]; *Charlesworth*, para 4–53 ('The excuse of intoxication, whether by drink or drugs, must be disregarded when considering contributory negligence'); and the cases collected in appendix 1, Part 2 of this volume ('2. Intoxicated Pedestrian Injured by Motorist'). The position might of course be otherwise were the intoxication involuntary.

[27] [2015] HCA 47, (2015) 256 CLR 148.

account not only of the fact that the plaintiff would otherwise have been left alone on a dark country road late at night in an unfamiliar location, but also of the fact that she was pregnant at the time. In doing so, the High Court did not modify the standard of care to that of a pregnant woman—they simply asked whether her decision to get back into the car fell below the standard of a reasonable person in the circumstances in which she found herself, which included that she was pregnant.[28] As Joachim Dietrich and Iain Field point out:[29]

> [P]ersonal characteristics may legitimately be framed as part of the 'circumstances', provided that the reasonable person in the position of the person would take the existence of the characteristic into account in making a decision. So framed, the characteristic in question does not modify the standard of care to that of a reasonable person exhibiting those personal characteristics, but rather forms part of the factual matrix within which that person operates.

However, as they also say, it is highly doubtful whether a characteristic that affects a person's '*capacity to reason*, or to respond to or appreciate a risk ... could ever be described as a "circumstance"', since to take account of such a characteristic would involve a departure from the objective standard of the reasonable person, and such a departure 'must clearly be justified as a matter of law (when setting the standard of care)'.[30]

Although it is indisputable that the law starts from the assumption that an objective standard of care applies to claimants, there is disagreement as to whether the only departures which are permitted from that standard are those also made in the case of defendants.[31] In *Joslyn v Berryman*,[32] McHugh J argued that this was in fact the position. Apart from the case of children (where the standard of care is also modified for defendant negligence), his Honour said that 'the plaintiff is held to the standard of care expected of an ordinary reasonable person engaging in the conduct that caused the plaintiff's injury or damage'.[33] It followed that, for example, the 'physical and mental deficits' of a plaintiff were not to be taken into account. But many commentators take issue with this claim, and argue that the courts do and should take a more subjective approach when it comes to contributory negligence. For example, in an article devoted to this question Dietrich and Field reject the view 'that the reasonable person standard should always be applied equivalently (or uniformly) to defendants and plaintiffs' and argue that in some situations it is appropriate for 'the personal characteristics of plaintiffs' to be taken into account.[34] The case for making such an adjustment is particularly strong where the claimant is a vulnerable person whom the defendant is legally obliged to protect, as in Ken Simons' example of a nurse charged with caring for a dementia patient.[35] Were the nurse to be accused of breaching their protective duty to the patient it seems unlikely that the latter's damages would be reduced for contributory negligence on the ground that their conduct fell below the standard of **3.08**

[28] See the discussion of this case in Dietrich and Field (n 16) 616–18.

[29] ibid 618.

[30] ibid (emphasis in original).

[31] See further, K Simons, 'Victim Fault and Victim Strict Responsibility in Anglo-American Tort Law' (2015) 8 J Tort Law 29; Dietrich and Field (n 16).

[32] *Joslyn v Berryman* [2003] HCA 34, (2003) 214 CLR 552.

[33] ibid [35].

[34] Dietrich and Field (n 16) 606.

[35] Simons (n 31) 39.

a reasonable person without dementia.[36] Although the argument for a more subjective approach is especially powerful where there is a protective duty of this sort, it is not limited to cases of this kind. Suppose, for example, that the defendant is to blame for a defect in the brakes of a car, which results in the car careering out of control while descending a hill, mounting the pavement and hitting a pedestrian. In theory, the defendant could argue that it was contributorily negligent of the pedestrian not to have got out of the way of the car once they saw it coming towards them. However, in assessing whether that was the case, it would be very surprising if the court could not take into account that the pedestrian was an elderly person whose infirmity made it impossible for them to do so.

3.09 When assessing whether it is appropriate to take a more subjective approach to claimant negligence than to defendant negligence it is helpful to consider the possible rationales of the objective standard of care as applied to defendants and whether these have equal force in the contributory negligence context. One such rationale is the practical argument that the use of a subjective standard would hugely complicate negligence litigation, because the court would have to determine what the defendant's personal capabilities were before they could set the appropriate standard.[37] This argument also applies to claimant negligence, where it serves as an important counterweight to the drive towards a more subjective approach.[38] However, the same is not true of another rationale, which is Richard Wright's argument that the rights which the law of negligence protects would be too weak and contingent if they were dependent on what the defendant was personally capable of, and that only a right that relates to an objective standard of reasonable care gives adequate protection to our security interests by clearly indicating what we are entitled to expect from others in our interactions with them.[39] Since the self-regarding fault that amounts to contributory negligence does not threaten the rights of others, this argument carries no weight in the context of claimant negligence. Finally, the example of the elderly pedestrian suggests that a counter-argument which can generally be deployed in response to the contention that the application of an objective standard to defendants is unfair is not available to proponents of the objective approach for contributory negligence. An obvious riposte to, say, a defendant motorist who objects to the use of the objective standard of the reasonable driver on the ground that they are unable to reach that standard is that if they are unwilling to accept the consequences of the application of that standard then they should not drive in the first place, but should instead take alternative transport, not least because their driving threatens the security of other road users. That argument is not available against the elderly pedestrian, who can hardly be expected to become a recluse, and whose infirmity probably threatens no-one's security but their own.

[36] See also Dietrich and Field (n 16) 624.

[37] See *Nettleship v Weston* [1971] 2 QB 691 (CA) 707 (Megaw LJ) ('The certainty of a general standard is preferable to the vagaries of a fluctuating standard').

[38] A point emphasized by R Parsons, 'Negligence, Contributory Negligence and the Man Who Does Not Ride the Bus to Clapham' (1957) 1 Melb UL Rev 163, 179–82.

[39] R Wright, 'The Standards of Care in Negligence Law' in DG Owen (ed), *Philosophical Foundations of Tort Law* (OUP 1995) 258–59.

(a) Age

The most prominent exception to the objective test for contributory negligence is childhood, an exception also recognized in the case of defendant negligence.[40] Where the claimant is a child, their conduct will be judged against the benchmark of the reasonable child of the same age.[41] This principle is traceable to the nineteenth-century case of *Lynch v Nurdin*,[42] where a boy of seven who had climbed onto the defendant's unattended horse and cart and was thrown off when the horse moved on was absolved of contributory negligence. According to Lord Denman, 'ordinary care must mean that degree of care which may reasonably be expected from a person in the plaintiff's situation'.[43] The reasonable child is neither 'a paragon of prudence' nor 'a scatter-brained child' but the 'ordinary child'.[44] In English law the standard is fixed for child claimants (and defendants) by reference to age alone. By contrast, some other common law systems also take account of the individual child's intelligence and experience,[45] a more subjective approach that makes allowance 'for the varied rate of development in children's intelligence and learning'.[46] **3.10**

There is no fixed age below which a child will not be found to have been contributorily negligent, but where the claimant is so young that they cannot be expected to take any care for their own safety, no such finding will be made.[47] Hence Channell B's observation in *Gardner v Grace* that '[t]he doctrine of contributory negligence does not apply to an infant of tender age'.[48] A finding of contributory negligence was made against a child aged seven in a recent English case,[49] but in *Boardman v Ministry of Defence*,[50] the judge considered that no blame could attach to a six-year-old boy who had run into the road regardless of the reason why he entered the carriageway. There are admittedly older Scottish decisions in which findings of contributory negligence were made against children aged as young as four,[51] but it seems probable that these would be decided differently today. In practice, it seems that the cut-off age is probably seven. The closer the claimant is to adulthood, the less allowance will be made, and sometimes it seems that in the case of adolescents **3.11**

---

[40] *Mullin v Richards* [1998] 1 WLR 1304 (CA).

[41] *Gough v Thorne* [1966] 1 WLR 1387 (CA).

[42] (1841) 1 QB 29, 113 ER 1041.

[43] ibid 36, 1043.

[44] *Gough v Thorne* [1966] 1 WLR 1387 (CA) 1391 (Salmon LJ).

[45] See *Restatement (Second) of the Law of Torts* (1965) § 464(2) ('a reasonable person of like age, intelligence, and experience'); *Wade v Canadian National Railways* [1978] 1 SCR 1064 (SCC) 1074–76. The High Court of Australia divided on this point in *McHale v Watson* (1966) 115 CLR 199 (HCA), with Kitto J preferring the English formula (at 214), and Owen J the North American (at 229). Owen J's approach has been followed in the subsequent Australian case law: see, eg, *Goldsmith v Bisset (No 3)* [2015] NSWSC 634, (2015) 71 MVR 53 ('developmental delay' of nine-year-old plaintiff taken into account when considering contributory negligence).

[46] *Fleming*, 321.

[47] See *Beasley v Marshall* (1977) 17 SASR 456 (SC) 459 (Bright J) ('there must surely be some age below which nothing is to be expected').

[48] (1858) 1 F & F 359, 359; 175 ER 763, 763.

[49] *N (a child) v Newham LBC* [2007] CLY 2931 (Central London CC) (the claimant punched a pane of glass while at school).

[50] QBD, 12 November 2012 [24].

[51] *Cass v Edinburgh & District Tramways Co Ltd* 1909 SC 1068 (IH) (four); *McKinnell v White* 1971 SLT (notes) 61 (OH) (five); *Banner's Tutor v Kennedy's Trustees* 1978 SLT (notes) 85 (OH) (five); *Harvey v Cairns* 1989 SLT 107 (OH) (six).

no allowance is made at all.[52] The overall position as regards children and contributory negligence was summed up by Lord Denning MR in *Gough v Thorne* as follows:[53]

> A very young child cannot be guilty of contributory negligence. An older child may be. But it depends on the circumstances. A judge should only find a child guilty of contributory negligence if he or she is of such an age as to be expected to take precautions for his or her own safety: and then he or she is only to be found guilty if blame should be attached to him or her.

Finally, where the defendant's negligence created a dangerous situation that acted as an 'allurement' to children, the court may be disinclined to find contributory negligence.[54]

3.12 Even though the existence of the childhood exception to the objective standard in theory operates in favour of child claimants, empirical evidence suggests that such claimants are nevertheless more likely to be found guilty of contributory negligence than adults. According to a study of first instance claims, the plea of contributory negligence succeeded in 59 per cent of the claims where the claimant was known to be an adult, and in 69 per cent of claims where the claimant was known to be a child.[55] Of course, this result may be explicable in large part on the ground that younger claimants (and especially adolescents) tend to act more irresponsibly. However, the figure is nonetheless striking and gives rise to some doubt as to the accuracy of the common perception that the courts treat child claimants leniently with regard to contributory negligence.[56]

3.13 In contrast with the position that prevails in relation to childhood, the courts do not seem disposed to make any allowances for the claimant's reduced ability to look after themselves on account of their advanced age.[57] *Daly v Liverpool Corpn*[58] is sometimes thought to have held the contrary, but the issue there was whether the defendant should have taken into account the fact that some pedestrians are elderly and infirm, not whether the sixty-nine-year-old claimant had himself been contributorily negligent. There are, however, examples in the American case law of the plaintiff's old age being taken into account,[59] and for the reasons given earlier,[60] it is hard to see why it should not be in at least some circumstances, for example when deciding whether the claimant was negligent in not moving out of the path of a speeding vehicle.

---

[52] See, eg, *Phethean-Hubble v Coles* [2012] EWCA Civ 349, [2012] RTR 31 (trial judge should not have taken the age of a sixteen-year-old cyclist into account when fixing the discount for contributory negligence). In the US, the adult standard is frequently applied to a child engaged in an adult activity such as driving: see *Prosser & Keeton*, 181–82.

[53] *Gough v Thorne* [1966] 1 WLR 1387 (CA) 1390.

[54] *Yachuk v Oliver Blais Co Ltd* [1949] AC 386 (PC); *Galbraith's Curator ad Litem v Stewart (No 2)* 1998 SLT 1305 (OH).

[55] *Goudkamp and Nolan*, para 4.25. For fuller discussion of this and other results relating to age in the study, see ibid, paras 4.34–4.38.

[56] See, eg, C Sappideen and P Vines (eds), *Fleming's The Law of Torts* (10th edn, Thomson Reuters Professional (Australia) Ltd 2011) 330 ('The courts have been singularly lenient to children ... in terms of finding them guilty of contributory negligence').

[57] Consider, eg, *Maughan v Boylan* [2006] NIQB 38; *Moreh v O'Neill* [2008] NIQB 28.

[58] [1939] 2 All ER 142 (Assizes).

[59] See *Woods and Deere*, 218–19.

[60] See 3.09.

(b) Physical disability

Exceptions to the objective test for contributory negligence other than age have been recognized on a more ad hoc and sporadic basis and generally without any attempt to explain their recognition. There is, for example, a dearth of authority on whether a claimant's physical disability should be taken into account. However, the better view is that it should.[61] We have seen that many of the rationales put forward for the objective standard for defendant negligence are inapplicable to claimant negligence, and that the only rationale that retains its full force in this context is the practical difficulty of evaluating what could reasonably be expected of the particular claimant. But in the case of a tangible physical disability such as blindness or immobility, this difficulty largely falls away, with the result that not taking account of such a disability when assessing a claimant's conduct would seem to be manifestly unjust, if not absurd. This view is supported by early case law from Ireland and Scotland. In two Irish cases from either side of the turn of the last century, it was held that there was no contributory negligence where a deaf pedestrian failed to get out of the way of a vehicle which he had not heard approaching.[62] Similarly, a Scottish court held in 1920 that a visually impaired pursuer who had fallen into a hole in the pavement caused by the removal of a hydrant cover was not guilty of contributory negligence.[63] According to Lord Salvensen, when it came to contributory negligence, 'you are entitled to take into account the defective eyesight or other infirmity of a person who meets with an accident'.[64] There are also numerous American cases in which allowances have been made for disabled plaintiffs,[65] such as *Weinstein v Wheeler*,[66] where the plaintiff was a blind person who was hit by the defendant's car while crossing the street. According to the Supreme Court of Oregon, it was 'not the policy of the law to discriminate against those who suffer from physical infirmity':[67] **3.14**

> The blind and the halt may use the streets without being guilty of negligence if, in so doing, they exercise that degree of care which an ordinarily prudent person similarly afflicted would exercise under the same circumstances.

A harsher approach is, however, evident in some Australian cases. In *Joslyn v Berryman*, McHugh J remarked that if a pedestrian or driver entered a railway crossing in the face of an oncoming train it would make no difference that they had defective hearing or sight.[68] And

[61] See also *Clerk & Lindsell*, para 3–84; WVH Rogers, 'Contributory Negligence under English Law' in U Magnus and M Martin-Casals (eds), *Unification of Tort Law: Contributory Negligence* (Kluwer Law International 2004) 64 ('[i]t is clear that if a blind person falls into an unfenced excavation on the street he cannot be met by the argument that the danger would have been obvious to a sighted person').

[62] *Smith v Browne* (1891) 28 LR Ir 1 (QBD); *Gaffney v Dublin United Tramways* [1916] 2 IR 472 (CA).

[63] *M'Kibbin v Glasgow Corpn* 1920 SC 590 (IH). For examples of similar cases where an argument of contributory fault either failed or was not made, see *Sleeper v Sandown* 52 NH 244 (NH Sup Ct of Judicature 1872); *Haley v London Electricity Board* [1965] AC 778 (HL).

[64] *M'Kibbin v Glasgow Corpn* 1920 SC 590 (IH) 597.

[65] Writing in the 1950s, Fleming James observed that the vast majority of cases in which American courts have taken physical disability into account concerned disabled plaintiffs: F James Jr, 'The Qualities of the Reasonable Man in Negligence Cases' (1951) 16 Missouri L Rev 1, 21.

[66] 271 P 733 (Or 1928). After a retrial, the case came back to the Supreme Court of Oregon, which reversed a judgment for the defendant: 295 P 196 (Or 1931).

[67] 271 P 733 (Or 1928) 734 (Belt J). On the early American cases, see GB Weisiger, 'Negligence of the Physically Infirm' (1946) 24 NC L Rev 187.

[68] [2003] HCA 34, (2003) 214 CLR 552 [39].

a majority of the Western Australia Court of Appeal adhered to the objective standard in *Town of Port Hedland v Hodder (No 2)*.[69] The plaintiff had cerebral palsy, and suffered from multiple physical and intellectual disabilities, including deafness and visual impairment. He sustained serious injuries after diving into the shallow end of the defendant's swimming pool from a diving block negligently placed there by the defendant. At first instance his claim had succeeded, but with a 10 per cent deduction for contributory negligence. By a majority, the Court of Appeal held that the plaintiff had not been contributorily negligent, but two of the three judges assessed the plaintiff's conduct against an objective standard, with McLure P holding that his conduct had not fallen short of that standard and Murphy JA (dissenting) holding that it had. By contrast, Martin CJ applied a subjective approach, arguing that in such a case:[70]

> The harshness, injustice and unfairness [of using an objective standard] is manifest. It assumes a miracle of biblical proportions and requires the court to assess the question of contributory negligence in some parallel universe in which the blind can see, the deaf can hear, the lame can walk or even run, and the cognitively impaired are somehow restored to full functionality.

These arguments seem difficult to refute, although in fairness to the other judges the civil liability legislation in Western Australia (as in many Australian states) includes an unfortunate provision stating that the principles that determine whether a defendant has been negligent also apply to plaintiffs,[71] which was a significant obstacle to the adoption of a subjective approach on the facts.

3.15 It goes without saying that, regardless of whether the standard of care is modified for physical disability, the fact that the claimant is disabled may be a relevant circumstance when determining whether they took reasonable care for their own safety. Hence, for example, it might be negligent of a disabled pedestrian to cross a road other than at a controlled crossing, even though it would not necessarily be negligent for an able-bodied pedestrian to do so. Similarly, it might be negligent of a blind person to venture out without a white cane or a guide dog.

(c) Mental disability

3.16 When it comes to questions of mental illness and intellectual development, the practical argument for an objective standard retains some force, and so one might expect a greater reluctance to adopt a subjective approach, even where claimants are concerned.[72] Hence Williams's claim (with reference to the American authorities) that 'so far as mental powers are concerned a person of full age is judged by an objective standard', whereas 'in respect of physical situation the individual circumstances are taken into account'.[73] Nevertheless, there are recent English cases in which the courts have taken account of a claimant's impaired mental faculties. In *Spearman v Royal United Bath Hospitals NHS Foundation*

---

[69] [2012] WASCA 212, 43 WAR 383.

[70] ibid [156].

[71] Civil Liability Act 2002 (WA) s 5K(1).

[72] The position regarding defendants is that no allowance will be made, no matter how profound the mental illness: *Dunnage v Randall* [2015] EWCA Civ 673, [2016] QB 639.

[73] *Williams*, 357.

Trust,[74] for example, Spencer J refused to make a finding of contributory negligence where a brain damaged person who had suffered a hypoglycaemic attack suffered injury after either falling from or jumping off a hospital roof. The judge said:[75]

> Just as a young child is not guilty of contributory negligence in running out into a road where the child is so young as not to appreciate the danger of so doing, so too where a person's state of mind is such that, whether temporarily or permanently, they do not appreciate that they are putting themselves in danger and it cannot be said that they should have so appreciated. Otherwise, that would be to penalise a person for being ill or of unsound mind, and the law does not do that.

Similarly, in *Young v Kent County Council*,[76] Morison J bore in mind the learning disability of a child claimant when apportioning responsibility for injuries he suffered after falling through a skylight after climbing onto a school roof. There are also American cases where a subjective standard has been being applied to plaintiffs with mental illness,[77] although the US *Restatements* have taken a relatively harsh line on the issue.[78] Ellen Bublick highlights practical concerns as a possible explanation for the reluctance to extend the protections afforded to child plaintiffs to those with mental incapacities. She writes:[79]

> Not only do infant plaintiffs lack the capacity to meet the standard of care, but they also do so in a way that is easy to judge categorically ... Accordingly, it is not surprising that, in comparative-fault claims against other arguably dependent persons, courts seem to rely upon demonstratable indicia of incapacity for self-care such as institutionalization.

The case for taking mental disability into account is stronger when the defendant is **3.17** charged with taking care of the claimant in the light of that disability,[80] and hence it is not surprising that the American courts have refused to make findings of contributory fault against dementia patients suing a negligent carer.[81] The same is true where the disability is itself the defendant's fault, as in *Corr v IBC Vehicles Ltd*.[82] The claimant's husband had sustained terrible injuries in a workplace accident for which the defendant had admitted responsibility. As a result, he suffered severe depression, and six years after the accident he committed suicide by jumping from the top of a multi-storey car park. When the case reached the House of Lords, it was agreed that the defendant was liable for the consequences of the suicide, but the question of whether the suicide itself amounted to contributory negligence proved controversial. By a majority, the House declined to reduce the claimant's

[74] [2017] EWHC 3027 (QB), [2018] Med L Rev 244.
[75] ibid [74].
[76] [2005] EWHC 1342 (QB).
[77] See the US cases discussed in *Woods and Deere*, 219–21; and *Russell v Rail Infrastructure Corporation* [2007] NSWSC 402 [96].
[78] The *Restatement (Second) of the Law of Torts* (1965), § 464 left open the question of whether plaintiff insanity was taken into account, while making it clear (in comment g) that '[m]ental deficiency which falls short of insanity' was not. And in a misguided quest for symmetry with the position regarding defendants, the *Restatement (Third) of Torts: Apportionment of Liability* (2000) holds that even a plaintiff's insanity is to be disregarded: see § 3, cmt a.
[79] EM Bublick, 'Comparative Fault to the Limits' (2003) 56 Vand L Rev 977, 1003. For a similar focus on practical considerations (and the need for a 'ready reckoner' of incapacity), see Parsons (n 38) 179–82.
[80] See 3.17.
[81] See Bublick (n 79) 1002.
[82] [2008] UKHL 13, [2008] AC 884.

damages, but this was in part because the point had not been fully argued, nor findings made on it below. Lord Walker did not in any case consider it appropriate to characterize the deceased's conduct as negligent when his judgment was impaired by severe depression, while Lord Scott would have reduced the damages for contributory fault, although he accepted that the degree of the deceased's blameworthiness was relatively low. Lord Mance and Lord Neuberger also refused to rule out the possibility that a finding of contributory negligence might be appropriate in this kind of case. According to Lord Neuberger, the mere fact that the deceased's mental state was impaired to some extent by a condition for which the defendant was responsible could not without more rule out such a finding.

(d) Experience

3.18 Finally, there are cases where the courts have considered the claimant's experience when deciding questions of contributory negligence. This tendency is especially pronounced in the employers' liability context, where the employee's level of experience or skill is frequently taken into account. In *Egan v Central Manchester and Manchester Children's University Hospitals NHS Trust*,[83] the claimant, an 'experienced and highly trained nurse', was using a mobile hoist to move a disabled patient into a bath when the hoist came to a sudden stop, causing the claimant to suffer a back injury. The Court of Appeal held that the claimant's employer had breached its statutory obligation to take all appropriate steps to reduce the risk of injury arising from a handling operation to the lowest level that was reasonably practicable, but that the claimant had also been careless, and shared equal responsibility for her injury with her employer. Similarly, in *Mullaney v Chief Constable of the West Midlands*,[84] where the claimant was a probationary police constable who sustained a serious head injury whilst attempting to arrest a suspect without assistance, it was held that in the light of the claimant's inexperience his decision to enter a public lavatory to carry out reconnaissance on his own had not amounted to contributory negligence. Numerous other examples could be given.[85]

3.19 A similar phenomenon is observable in the professional negligence context. For example, in finding that there was no contributory negligence on the part of a company which was suing a law firm, the judge bore in mind the fact that the person who ran the company had 'little or no experience' of property development and limited understanding of the 'intricacies' of agreements of the kind at issue in the case.[86] By contrast, in a rare instance in which a law firm defendant successfully pleaded contributory negligence,[87] the claimant was a government department which the judge held ought not to have relied completely on its legal advisers to remind it to make a vital payment that would have enabled it to exercise a break clause in a lease.

[83] [2008] EWCA Civ 1424, [2009] ICR 585.

[84] [2001] EWCA Civ 700, [2001] Po LR 150.

[85] See, eg, *Byers v Head Wrightson & Co Ltd* [1961] 2 All ER 538 (QBD) 543; *Ball v Richard Thomas & Baldwin Ltd* [1968] 1 All ER 389 (CA) 395, 398; and the cases cited in *Munkman*, para 6.62.

[86] *Akasuc Enterprise Ltd v Farmar & Shirreff (a firm)* [2003] EWHC 1275 (Ch) [21], [80] (Peter Smith J).

[87] *Secretary of State for the Environment, Transport and Regions v Unicorn Consultancy Services Ltd* [2000] NPC 108 (Ch D).

(3) The application of the standard

As with defendant negligence, the question of whether the claimant has fallen below the standard of conduct set by the law is a highly fact-sensitive one, and decisions on the application of the standard of care are not binding in future cases. It is nevertheless possible to identify some general principles that underlie the approach of the courts to this issue. Furthermore, it will be helpful to consider some particular contexts in which the question of contributory fault has frequently arisen, and to seek to identify the considerations that have proven to be significant in the context in question, as well as any general patterns that can be observed in the relevant case law. **3.20**

It is important to remember when looking at previous decisions on the application of the standard of reasonable care to claimants that before 1945 contributory negligence was a complete defence. As a result the courts may have been reluctant to find that the claimant was negligent unless the evidence of fault was very clear.[88] Now that the consequences of a finding of contributory negligence are less draconian, the courts are likely to be more willing to make such a finding, since relatively minor fault can be dealt with by imposing a small discount at the apportionment stage. **3.21**

(a) General observations

There are clear parallels between the question of whether the defendant's conduct fell below the standard of reasonable care for the purposes of liability and the question of whether the claimant's conduct fell below that standard for the purposes of contributory negligence. For example, the principle that whether a defendant failed to take reasonable care is assessed by reference to the circumstances pertaining at the time of the alleged negligence[89] applies equally when it comes to contributory negligence, with the result that the court must adopt the perspective of a person standing in the shoes of the claimant at that time, and not rely on hindsight.[90] In addition, for a finding of contributory negligence to be made the risk of harm must have been reasonably foreseeable to someone in the claimant's position—as Denning LJ said in *Jones v Livox Quarries Ltd*, '[j]ust as actionable negligence requires the foreseeability of harm to others, so contributory negligence requires the foreseeability of harm to oneself'.[91] Examples of claimant conduct held not to amount to contributory negligence on the ground that the risk of harm was not reasonably foreseeable include not noticing obstructions on the ground that there was no reason to expect would be present;[92] slipping on a floor that the claimant had no reason to think would be wet;[93] not asking a driver whether he was so impaired by alcohol consumption that he should not drive;[94] and not catering for the possibility that another driver would allow his vehicle to drift onto the claimant's side of the road,[95] that a car door would be opened unexpectedly,[96] or that a lorry in a stream of traffic would pass too close to an open car door.[97] **3.22**

---

[88] See 1.13.
[89] *Roe v Ministry of Health* [1954] 2 QB 66 (CA).
[90] See, eg, *Smith v Finch* [2009] EWHC 53 (QB) [43].
[91] [1952] 2 QB 608 (CA) 615.
[92] *Nimmo v Secretary of State for Scotland* 2000 Rep LR 14 (OH).
[93] *McLeish v Lothian NHS Board* [2017] CSOH 71, 2017 Rep LR 90 [8].
[94] *Booth v White* [2003] EWCA Civ 1708.
[95] *Gray v Gibson* [2014] EWCA Civ 355.
[96] *Burridge v Air Work Ltd* [2004] EWCA Civ 459.
[97] *Howe v Houlton* [2009] EWHC 3344 (QB).

3.23 As with defendant negligence, where the risk of harm is reasonably foreseeable, the courts in contributory negligence cases attach weight to three matters in particular when considering whether a claimant was negligent in not taking a precaution that would have reduced or eliminated that risk. Those matters are (1) the probability that the risk would materialize; (2) the likely gravity of the harm if the risk did materialize; and (3) the cost or burden of the precaution in question (a matter which may require the court to consider the social utility of the activity in which the claimant was engaged). Numerous instances can be identified of the courts attaching significance to one or other of these considerations. As regards the cost of precautions, for example, it was held to be reasonable for a worker not to wear a safety belt while working on an electricity pylon because it might itself cause a fall,[98] for a police officer to use his patrol car to block the path of an escaping criminal,[99] and for an occupier to continue using the kitchen of her house after reporting the presence of a crack in the ceiling to the landlord.[100] Conversely, a police officer's decision to pursue a criminal suspect at speeds of up to 180 kilometres per hour on a single carriageway road at night was contributorily negligent since the possible public benefit of capturing the suspect was outweighed by the risks that the officer's conduct posed to himself and others.[101]

3.24 In determining whether the claimant took reasonable care for their own safety or interests, it may be relevant to ask whether other persons situated in the same position as the claimant behaved in a like manner. If the claimant acted in much the same way as similarly situated persons, that will tend to suggest that what the claimant did was not unreasonable. In *Casson v Spotmix Ltd (in liq)*, the claimant employee suffered injury to his hand while cleaning a machine. Sir Terence Etherton MR said:[102]

> [T]he fact that every other employee charged with the task of cleaning the machine did exactly what the claimant did is strongly supportive of the conclusion that the extent to which the claimant's conduct could be criticised fell considerably short of that which could properly be categorised as amounting to contributory negligence.

Webb Resolutions Ltd v E.Surv Ltd[103] involved a claim by a lender against surveyors. In considering whether the lender was guilty of contributory negligence, Coulson J said that it was relevant to 'see what was happening elsewhere in the lending market because, if the claimant was doing what its competitors were doing, negligence was unlikely, unless it could be shown that it was irrational or illogical'.[104] However, as with defendant negligence,[105] the fact that the conduct of the claimant was in accordance with common practice is not

[98] *Gibson v British Insulated Callendars Construction Co Ltd* 1973 SLT 2 (HL).

[99] *Hambley v Shepley* (1967) 63 DLR (2d) 94 (Ont CA).

[100] *Greene v Chelsea Borough Council* [1954] 2 QB 127 (CA).

[101] *Hirst v Nominal Defendant* [2005] QCA 65, [2005] 2 Qd R 133.

[102] [2017] EWCA Civ 1994 [15]. For other cases where an employee has been held not to have been negligent in following an established practice, see *Moffat v Atlas Hydraulic Loaders Ltd* 1992 SLT 1123 (OH) (cleaning unguarded machine in motion); *McNeill v Roche Products Ltd (No 2)* 1988 SCLR 629 (OH) (cutting off petrol supply to machine manually).

[103] [2012] EWHC 3653 (TCC), [2013] PNLR 15.

[104] ibid [71]. See also *Paratus AMC Ltd v Countrywide Surveyors Ltd* [2011] EWHC 3307 (Ch), [2012] PNLR 12 [79]–[80]; *Barclays Bank plc v Christie Owen & Davies Ltd* [2016] EWHC 2351 (Ch), [2017] PNLR 8 [232] (Richard Spearman QC) ('if a practice was accepted by a significant section of the banking market at the relevant time, it should not be held to fail to meet the standard of a reasonably competent bank unless plainly illogical').

[105] See *Winfield & Jolowicz*, para 6-026.

conclusive. For example, an employee may still be found to have been negligent even if all their co-workers acted in the same way.[106]

Similarly, whether the claimant complied with the criminal law, or with some other regulatory requirement governing their activity, is highly pertinent when considering the issue of fault, but not necessarily determinative.[107] Examples of criminal conduct that are very likely to amount to fault for the purposes of contributory negligence include speeding,[108] and failing to wear a seat belt while travelling in a vehicle,[109] but in exceptional circumstances such conduct may not be negligent. It might, for example, be reasonable of a claimant to drive in excess of the speed limit in an emergency situation, while in one case it was held not to be negligent to accept a ride in the back of a van which was not fitted with seat belts because it had been designed to carry goods rather than people.[110] Nor does it follow from the fact it is illegal for a cyclist to ride on the pavement that doing so amounts to a failure to take reasonable care for their own safety.[111] Where the claimant has an exemption from, say, wearing a seat belt, then the court will of course take that into account, although there is no reason why it should in itself preclude a finding of fault for civil purposes.[112] **3.25**

Finally, as the application of the standard of care is a question of fact rather than of law, it is contrary to principle for a court to lay down a fixed rule as to what does, or does not, amount to contributory negligence, regardless of the circumstances of the individual case.[113] At times, the courts have sometimes sailed rather close to the wind in this respect, for example in cases where the defendant claimed that it was negligent of the claimant to exercise their right of way as a road user when they were struck by the defendant's vehicle. In *Keam v Chiomey bnf Mercer*,[114] the plaintiff was a child who had cycled from a footpath onto a pedestrian crossing without stopping and was then struck by the defendant's truck. The New South Wales Court of Appeal treated the plaintiff's right of way as determinative and rejected the defendant's argument that it was contributory negligence not to have paused before proceeding onto the crossing to ascertain whether the truck, which the plaintiff saw approaching, would stop. In a similar English case, *Tremayne v Hill*,[115] the **3.26**

---

106 See *Clifford v Charles H Challen & Son* [1951] 1 KB 495 (CA) 499.

107 See, eg, *Lewis v Denye* [1940] AC 921 (HL) 929 (employee's breach of workplace safety regulations does not automatically give an employer a defence to a claim for their own breach of statutory duty, though it may be evidence of contributory negligence). The English position can be contrasted with the principle of contributory negligence per se recognized in some other jurisdictions, according to which a claimant's violation of a regulatory statute automatically amounts to contributory fault, at least where the injury falls within the risks which it was the purpose of the statute to obviate. See, eg, *Tedla v Ellman* 19 NE 2d 987 (NY 1939).

108 See, eg, *Buchan v Whiting* [2008] EWHC 2951 (QB); *Train v Secretary of State for Defence* [2014] EWHC 1928 (QB); *Buswell v Symes* [2015] EWHC 1379 (QB).

109 See, eg, *Froom v Butcher* [1976] QB 286 (CA).

110 *Cross v Smith* 1999 WL 982463 (CA).

111 *Kotula v EDF Energy Networks (Epn) plc* [2010] EWHC 1968 (QB) [44].

112 See *Jones v Morgan* [1994] CLY 3344 (QBD) (relevance of exemption for taxi drivers in seat belt case); *Pace v Cully* 1992 SLT 1073 (OH).

113 The leading case on this principle with regard to defendant negligence is *Qualcast (Wolverhampton) Ltd v Haynes* [1959] AC 743 (HL).

114 [2002] NSWCA 280.

115 [1987] RTR 131 (CA). See also *Joseph Eva Ltd v Reeves* [1938] 2 KB 393 (CA); *Bailey v Geddes* [1938] 1 KB 156 (CA).

claimant was hit when crossing a road by a car which had run a red light. The claimant had not looked in the direction from which the car came before stepping onto the road because he knew that traffic travelling from that direction was faced with a red light. The Court of Appeal agreed with the trial judge that the defendant having run a red light told conclusively against a finding of contributory negligence. However, despite these apparently definitive statements, the position is not in reality quite so clear-cut. On the contrary, there are situations in which a road user who had priority according to the rules of the road was nevertheless found guilty of contributory negligence. Examples include cases where a motorist had entered an intersection with the lights in their favour only to collide with an emergency vehicle which had gone through a red light.[116]

(b) Anticipating the carelessness of others

3.27 The taking of reasonable care may require the claimant to anticipate that others will be careless and to take appropriate precautions against that risk, 'especially where experience has shown such negligence to be likely or where resulting damage can be minimised'.[117] As Denning LJ said:[118]

> A person is guilty of contributory negligence if he ought reasonably to have foreseen that, if he did not act as a reasonable, prudent man, he might be hurt himself; and in his reckonings he must take into account the possibility of others being careless.

A good illustration of this principle is the proposition that it may be contributory negligence for a passenger to accept a lift from the driver of a vehicle 'whom he knows has consumed alcohol in such quantity as is likely to impair to a dangerous degree that driver's capacity to drive properly and safely'.[119] Exceptional cases aside, as where the only apparent alternative to accepting a lift for a young pregnant woman was having to walk an unknown distance on a dark and unfamiliar country road in the early hours of the morning,[120] in this scenario a deduction for contributory negligence is very likely to be made. *McDermott v Pettit*[121] is another example of the same principle. In that case, Parker J, in holding the claimant pedestrian guilty of contributory negligence, remarked that the claimant should have anticipated the possibility that some motorists would be intoxicated at 2.30 am.[122] Similarly, cyclists have been held to be negligent for undertaking a lorry turning left at a traffic light,[123] and for failing to notice and take preventive action when a motorist

[116] *Griffin v Mersey Regional Ambulance* [1998] PIQR P34 (CA); *Purdue v Devon Fire and Rescue Service* [2002] EWCA Civ 1538.

[117] *Charlesworth*, para 4–60.

[118] *Jones v Livox Quarries Ltd* [1952] 2 QB 608 (CA) 615. See also *Grant v Sun Shipping Co Ltd* [1948] AC 549 (HL) 567 (Lord du Parcq) ('a prudent man will guard against the possible negligence of others, when experience shows such negligence to be common').

[119] *Owens v Brimmell* [1977] 1 QB 859 (QBD) 866 (Watkins J). See generally, CR Symmons, 'Contributory Negligence Defences for the Drunken Driver' (1977) 40 MLR 350; K Hogg, 'Guest Passengers: A Drunk Driver's Defences' (1994) 2 Torts LJ 37.

[120] See *Allen v Chadwick* [2015] HCA 47, (2015) 256 CLR 148. See also *Restatement (Second) of the Law of Torts* (1965) § 466, cmt d (not contributory negligence to accept a lift from a driver known to be incompetent if no other way to get one's seriously injured child to hospital).

[121] [2011] EWHC 3074 (QB).

[122] ibid [31].

[123] *McGeer v McIntosh* [2017] EWCA Civ 79.

negligently turned across their path.[124] And in a claim by a government department against a law firm, the judge held that the department was guilty of contributory negligence because it should have had its own system for ensuring that it made a vital payment, and not relied completely on its legal advisers to remind it of the need to do so.[125] The overall principle in play here was described by Williams as being that where 'the danger is sufficiently substantial to induce the reasonable man to take precautions against it, a plaintiff who neglects these precautions will be held guilty of contributory negligence'.[126] It has sometimes been said that this principle does not extend to claims for breach of statutory duty, especially in the area of health and safety at work, since a claimant is entitled to expect that a defendant will comply with their statutory obligations.[127] With respect, however, this is an example of the kind of generalization that is to be deprecated when it comes to the application of the standard of care.[128] The better view is that there may be circumstances in which it would be negligent of a claimant not to take precautions against a possible breach of statutory duty, for example, if the claimant knew that non-compliance with that duty was common.[129]

Having said that, there may of course be cases where the claimant was justified in assuming that others would take reasonable care and hence in not taking precautions to guard against the risk of their negligence. For example, in *Gray v Gibson*,[130] it was held that a reasonable motorist in the claimant's position would not have foreseen the risk that the driver of a lorry would move onto the claimant's side of the road when rounding a bend. Similarly, where a pedestrian was injured by a bus that intruded onto the pavement, the judge rejected the plea of contributory negligence, remarking that '[t]he pursuer, wholly on the pavement, is entitled not to be struck by a vehicle',[131] while a worker who entered an unlighted part of a ship was entitled to assume compliance with the statutory duty to cover the hatchways.[132] An important context in which a claimant will generally be entitled to assume that another will take reasonable care of the claimant's interests is that of professional negligence. That setting is considered later.[133] **3.28**

(c) *Defendant's duty to prevent conduct of claimant alleged to be negligent*

A connected issue is whether a finding of contributory negligence can be made where the defendant was under a duty to anticipate and guard against the very conduct of the **3.29**

[124] *Rickson v Bhaker* [2017] EWHC 264 (QB).

[125] *Secretary of State for the Environment, Transport and the Regions v Unicorn Consultancy Services Ltd* [2000] NPC 108 (Ch D). For similar reasoning in a Canadian case, see *Doiron v Caisse Populaire* (1985) 17 DLR (4th) 660 (NBCA), where it was held that a financial institution was guilty of contributory negligence for failing to check that the loan documents provided by the defendant solicitor complied with its instructions.

[126] *Williams*, 384.

[127] See, eg, *Grant v Sun Shipping Co Ltd* [1948] AC 549 (HL) 567; *Westwood v Post Office* [1974] AC 1 (HL) 16–17; *Cooper v Carillion* [2003] EWCA Civ 1811 [13].

[128] See 3.26.

[129] See *London Passenger Transport Board v Upson* [1949] AC 155 (HL) 176 (unreasonable to ignore negligence when it is common).

[130] [2014] EWCA Civ 355 [20] (Longmore LJ).

[131] *Whyte v Bluebird Buses Ltd* [2015] CSOH 56 [28] (Lord McEwan). See also *Osei-Antwi v South East London & Kent Bus Co Ltd* [2010] EWCA Civ 132 [17].

[132] *Grant v Sun Shipping Co Ltd* [1948] AC 549 (HL). For other examples, see *Williams*, 384.

[133] See 3.35–3.38.

claimant that the defendant alleges amounted to contributory negligence. This question has been most prominent in claims for breach of statutory duty, especially against employers. In *Hutchinson v London & North Eastern Railway Co*, Goddard LJ said:[134]

> It is only too common to find in cases where the plaintiff alleges that a defendant employer has been guilty of breach of a statutory duty, that a plea of contributory negligence has been set up. In such a case I always directed myself to be exceedingly chary of finding contributory negligence where the contributory negligence alleged was the very thing which the statutory duty of the employer was designed to prevent.

It is important to note that these remarks were made when contributory negligence was a complete defence. At that time, to have treated as contributory negligence conduct of the claimant which the defendant was under a statutory duty to prevent would have made it virtually impossible for a claim for the breach of that duty to succeed, which would in turn have threatened to undermine the objectives of the relevant legislation. However, with the advent of apportionment this concern lost most of its force, since defendants would still be held to account for their breach of statutory duty, albeit subject to a deduction for contributory negligence.[135] Hence the concern not to allow the operation of contributory negligence to undermine the legislative purpose of safety legislation has not gone away, but the tendency in the post-1945 case law has been to bring this concern to bear at the apportionment stage, where appeal courts have deprecated very high discounts in such cases, as opposed to holding that no finding of contributory negligence should have been made at all.[136] It is possible, however, to find counter-examples where the old reasoning on the issue has been employed so as completely to absolve a claimant from blame.[137]

3.30 The principle set out by Goddard LJ in *Hutchinson* has not gained much traction outside of the breach of statutory duty context. In *Calvert v William Hill Credit Ltd*,[138] the claimant was a pathological gambler who sued the defendant bookmakers for not preventing him from gambling with them after they had undertaken to do so. Although it was held that no liability arose in the first place for want of causation, had liability been imposed the Court of Appeal would have reduced the damages by 30 per cent for contributory negligence on the ground that the claimant had failed to deal with his addiction despite 'periods of clarity' in which he could have done so. Similarly, in *Reeves v Commissioner of Police of the Metropolis*,[139] the House of Lords held that the suicide of a man in police custody amounted to contributory negligence for the purposes of a claim by his dependants against the police, even though the police conceded that they had owed the deceased a duty to

[134] [1942] 1 KB 481 (CA) 488.

[135] See *Reeves v Commissioner of Police of the Metropolis* [2000] 1 AC 360 (HL) 370–72; Fagelson (n 6) 652–53.

[136] See, eg, *Mullard v Ben Line Steamers* [1970] 1 WLR 1414 (CA) 1418 (deduction reduced from one-half to one-third); *McGuinness v Key Markets Ltd* (1972) 13 KIR 249 (CA).

[137] See, eg, *Stocker v Norprint* (1970) 10 KIR 10 (CA); *Toole v Bolton Metropolitan Borough Council* [2002] EWCA Civ 588 (though in this case it seems that the precaution that it was argued the claimant employee should have taken would have made no difference). See also *Staveley Iron & Chemical Co Ltd v Jones* [1956] AC 627 (HL) 648 (Lord Tucker) ('in Factory Act cases the purpose of imposing the absolute obligation is to protect the workmen against those very acts of inattention which are sometimes relied upon as constituting contributory negligence so that too strict a standard would defeat the object of the statute'); *Ashbridge v Christian Salvensen plc* [2006] CSOH 79, 2006 SLT 697 [25].

[138] [2008] EWCA Civ 1427, [2009] Ch 330.

[139] [2000] 1 AC 360 (HL). See 3.44.

take care to prevent him from killing himself. Nor have the English courts adopted the position sometimes taken elsewhere that the wrongdoing of a company does not amount to contributory negligence for the purposes of a claim by the company against an auditor which failed to uncover it.[140] *A fortiori*, the mere fact that, say, the defendant was engaged to protect the claimant's property from theft does not absolve the claimant of contributory negligence if they leave their property lying about and so make it easier for a thief to take it.[141] As a majority of the High Court of Australia pointed out in *Astley v Austrust Ltd*, it is better for issues such as this one and the one discussed in the previous section to be resolved on a case-by-case basis, rather than by hard-and-fast rules:[142]

> What is reasonable care depends on the circumstances of the case. In many cases, it may be proper for a plaintiff to rely on a defendant to perform its duty. But there is no absolute rule. The duties and responsibilities of the defendant are a variable factor in determining whether contributory negligence exists and, if so, to what degree ... Contributory negligence focuses on the conduct of the plaintiff. The duty owed by the defendant, though relevant, is one of only many factors that must be weighed in determining whether the plaintiff has so conducted itself that it failed to take reasonable care for the safety of its person or property.

(d) Momentary lapses by employees

Another principle that developed in the pre-apportionment era is that where the claimant made an error while engaging in a repetitive activity on behalf of the defendant, that error will not be judged in isolation for the purposes of determining whether it constitutes contributory negligence. Rather, account will be taken of the repetitive nature of the work that the claimant was required to do and of the fatigue and tedium that it was likely to induce, with the result that, provided the claimant generally acted carefully, the court will be unlikely to make a finding of contributory negligence.[143] This idea stands in marked contrast to the position elsewhere in the law of negligence and contributory negligence, where the focus of the court's attention is on the specific conduct of the actor (whether defendant or claimant) that led to the damage, and where the fact that they usually acted competently is generally irrelevant.[144] For example, it is no answer to a negligence claim for a driver who made an error to say that they usually drove well, nor for a surgeon who made a mistake to point to a previous track record of successful operations. **3.31**

The principle that allowances should be made for claimants who are engaged in a repetitive activity on behalf of the defendant applies, classically, in the context of manual labour.[145] In *Flower v Ebbw Vale Steel Iron & Coal Ltd*, Lord Wright quoted with approval the trial judge's remark that 'it is not for every risky thing which a workman in a factory may do in his familiarity with the machinery that a plaintiff ought to be held guilty of contributory negligence'.[146] And a few years later, in *Caswell v Powell Duffryn Associated Collieries Ltd*, **3.32**

---

[140] See *Barings v Coopers and Lybrand (No 7)* [2003] EWHC 1319 (Ch), [2003] Lloyd's Rep IR 566 [698]–[720]; *Singularis Holdings Ltd v Daiwa Capital Markets Europe Ltd* [2018] EWCA Civ 84, [2018] 1 WLR [94]. cf *Livent Inc v Deloitte LLP* [2016] ONCA 11 [103].

[141] *Astley v Austrust Ltd* [1999] HCA 6, (1999) 197 CLR 1 [29].

[142] ibid [30] (Gleeson CJ, McHugh, Gummow and Hayne JJ).

[143] *Caswell v Powell Duffryn Associated Collieries Ltd* [1940] AC 152 (HL) 187.

[144] Although consider the Social Action, Responsibility and Heroism Act 2015, s 3.

[145] For a thorough discussion of the authorities, see *Munkman*, paras 6.50 et seq.

[146] [1936] AC 206 (HL) 214.

Lord Wright referred to 'an error of judgment or heedlessness or inadvertence in regard to [the worker's] own safety not amounting to contributory negligence',[147] while Lord Atkin remarked that a 'different degree of care may well be expected' from a worker in a factory or mine from those 'not exposed continually to the noise, strain, and manifold risks' of such a workplace.[148] Again, however, it should be borne in mind that these authorities predate the 1945 Act. At that time, a finding of contributory negligence absolved the employer of liability altogether, and thereby threatened to undermine the policy on which was founded the protective duty the employer had breached.[149] Furthermore, at a more general level, the principle under discussion can be understood as a manifestation of the 'relaxed standard of care applied to injured workmen', which originated 'as a device for mitigating the Common Law rule that contributory negligence was a complete defence'.[150] It is therefore unsurprising that there has been a greater willingness on the part of the courts to find employees guilty of contributory negligence in the post-1945 case law, even if the discounts imposed in such cases tend to be relatively low.[151] Nevertheless, there are still some recent examples of courts holding that a momentary lapse on the part of an employee does not amount to contributory negligence, especially where the employer had breached a statutory duty designed to protect against precisely such an eventuality.[152] Momentary inattention has been contrasted in this respect with a deliberate decision by an employee to risk their own safety.[153]

(e) Emergencies

3.33 The claimant will usually be absolved of negligence if they made the wrong choice, or acted less than ideally, when confronted with an emergency created by the defendant. According to Blake J in *Rickson v Bhakar*, 'a person placed in a situation of responding to a danger created by another cannot be considered guilty of negligence merely because one of two available options turns out to be less effective'.[154] This 'agony of the moment' principle is particularly associated with two nineteenth-century cases, *Jones v Boyce*,[155] where the claimant jumped from an out-of-control stagecoach, and *The Bywell Castle*,[156] which concerned a collision at sea. In the latter case, Cotton LJ said that 'a man in charge of a vessel is not to be held guilty of negligence … if in a sudden emergency caused by the default or negligence of another vessel, he does something which he might under

147 [1940] AC 152 (HL) 174.

148 ibid 166.

149 For a clear articulation of this thinking, see ibid 179–80.

150 Fagelson (n 6) 650.

151 For detailed analysis, based on an empirical study of the twenty-first century case law, see *Goudkamp and Nolan*, ch 7.

152 See, eg, *McGowan v W & JR Watson Ltd* [2006] CSIH 62, 2007 SC 272; *Kennedy v Chivas Brothers Ltd* [2013] CSIH 57, 2013 SLT 981.

153 *Kennedy v Chivas Brothers Ltd* [2013] CSIH 57, 2013 SLT 981 [38]. For an example of a case of the latter kind, see *Sowmez v Kebaberry Wholesale Ltd* [2008] EWHC 3366 (QB) (deliberate decision to override a safety device).

154 [2017] EWHC 264 (QB) [31]. See also *Crew v Ash* [2008] EWHC 3068 (QB) [23]; *Dickson v Kinsman* [2013] CSOH 111 [47]–[48]; *Nadarajah v Sotnick* [2013] EWHC 3389 (QB) [47].

155 (1816) 1 Stark 493, 171 ER 540.

156 (1879) 4 PD 219 (CA).

the circumstances as known to him reasonably think proper', even if with the benefit of hindsight it can be seen that 'the course which he adopted was not in fact the best'.[157] At the same time, however, claimants will sometimes be expected to act quickly when faced with a need for instant action. For example, it was contributory negligence of a driver to steer into the path of an oncoming vehicle despite being startled by its sudden presence on her side of the road,[158] and for the user of a lift not to remove his hand from in between the closing doors when it became apparent that they would not be automatically retracted.[159] Needless to say, a claimant cannot invoke the 'agony of the moment' principle when they were themselves partly to blame for the emergency situation in which they found themselves.[160] It has sometimes been suggested that the principle in question was another device designed to soften the harshness of the common law all-or-nothing rule, so that the need for it has now gone.[161] There are, however, examples of the principle being applied in the apportionment era, as in a recent case where a novice golfer was absolved of contributory negligence for not responding effectively to a cry of 'fore', when he had less than five seconds to do so and did not know from whence the warning came.[162]

(f) Rescuers

It has long been the clear policy of the law to encourage rescue.[163] Thus, the courts have been reluctant to hold rescuers who make matters worse liable in negligence,[164] and have been similarly slow, where the rescuer is injured, to hold that the rescuer was *volens* to the risk of injury.[165] Likewise, the courts are hesitant to conclude that it was contributorily negligent of an injured rescuer to intervene. As Lord Steyn said in *White v Chief Constable of South Yorkshire*:[166] **3.34**

> The law has long recognised the moral imperative of encouraging citizens to rescue persons in peril. Those who altruistically expose themselves to danger in an emergency to save others are favoured by the law ... A plea of contributory negligence will usually receive short shrift.

In *Tolley v Carr*,[167] it was held not to have been contributorily negligent of the claimant to try to move a car from the fast lane of a motorway, where it posed a threat to other vehicles. Hickinbottom J said that '[t]he law recognises that a rescuer may, in effecting or attempting to effect a reduction of risk to others, imperil his own life and limb: and the greater the risk to others that he is trying to avert, the greater the imperilment to his safety the law will accept as reasonable'.[168] Furthermore, where the claimant has sacrificed their own safety to try to save others, it is clear that the courts will not engage in a fine balancing

[157] ibid 228 (Cotton LJ).

[158] *Bennett v Southwell* [2013] EWHC 2382 (QB).

[159] *Malcolm v Commissioner of Police of the Metropolis* 1999 WL 477408 (QBD).

[160] See, eg, *Hickman v London Central Bus Co Ltd* [2013] EWHC 1703 (QB) [64]–[66].

[161] See, eg, *Williams*, 361; *Fleming*, 319–20.

[162] *Phee v Gordon* [2013] CSIH 18, 2013 SC 379.

[163] A dated, but still the best, analysis of how tort law applies in rescue situations is AM Linden, 'Rescuers and Good Samaritans' (1972) 10 Alta L Rev 89.

[164] See, eg, *Watt v Hertfordshire CC* [1954] 1 WLR 835 (CA).

[165] *Haynes v Harwood* [1935] 1 KB 146 (CA); *Baker v TE Hopkins & Son Ltd* [1959] 1 WLR 966 (CA).

[166] [1999] 2 AC 455 (HL) 498.

[167] [2010] EWHC 2191 (QB), [2011] RTR 7.

[168] ibid [22].

act of risk and benefit, but will give them the benefit of the doubt.[169] Nevertheless, rescuers have occasionally been found contributorily negligent. In *Sparrow v Andre*,[170] the claimant was injured when he attempted to stop a car containing his young children from rolling down a slope towards an electrical switch room and propane gas cylinders. The claimant had accidentally left the car with the ignition switched on and in 'neutral' instead of 'park' mode. The court held that contributory negligence was established, apparently partly on the basis of the claimant's conduct in trying to arrest the movement of the vehicle.[171] Finally, it should be noted that the common law's traditional indulgence towards rescuers has now been reinforced by statute. According to section 4 of the Social Action, Responsibility and Heroism Act 2015, when considering a claim that a person was negligent, a court 'must have regard to whether the alleged negligence ... occurred when the person was acting heroically by intervening in an emergency to assist an individual in danger'. Although mainly directed at defendant negligence, there is no reason why this provision should not be relied upon in cases of alleged contributory negligence as well.[172]

(g) Professional negligence cases

3.35 The courts seem to treat professional negligence cases differently from other types of case as far as contributory negligence is concerned.[173] According to an empirical study of the operation of the contributory negligence doctrine at first instance, the average success rate of the plea of contributory negligence was much lower in professional negligence claims (28 per cent) than in all the claims sampled (58 per cent).[174] There are obvious reasons why a professional will often face 'grave difficulty'[175] and will 'only rarely ... be able to set up allegations of contributory negligence against their clients'.[176] These reasons include the fact that the professional will usually have greater expertise than the client in the relevant field, that the relationship between professional and client is often markedly asymmetrical in terms of power, and that it will often be reasonable for the client to follow professional advice and to rely on the professional to do properly the job that they had been engaged to do. It is therefore unsurprising that, for example, it has been said that it would be rare for a client alleging the negligence of a lawyer in the conduct of litigation to be found guilty of contributory fault.[177]

3.36 It appears to be particularly difficult to establish that a client was contributorily negligent for failing to detect an error committed by a professional defendant or for not remembering

---

[169] See *Restatement (Second) of the Law of Torts* (1965) § 471, cmt a.

[170] [2016] EWHC 739 (QB).

[171] For other examples of rescuers being found guilty of contributory negligence, see *Harrison v British Railways Board* [1981] 3 All ER 679 (QBD); *Jeffrey v Commodore Cabaret* (1995) 128 DLR (4th) 535 (BCSC).

[172] For discussion of section 4, see J Goudkamp, 'Restating the Common Law? The Social Action, Responsibility and Heroism Act 2015' (2017) 37 LS 577, 594–95.

[173] See generally, DW Marks, 'Professional Negligence: Contribution and Contributory Negligence' (1988–1989) 15 U Queensland LJ 209; AM Dugdale and KM Stanton, *Professional Negligence* (3rd edn, Butterworths 1998) 523–32; J Murdoch, 'Client Negligence: A Lost Cause?' (2004) 20 PN 97; *Goudkamp and Nolan*, ch 8.

[174] *Goudkamp and Nolan*, paras 4.07–4.08.

[175] Marks (n 173) 226–27.

[176] *Secretary of State for the Environment, Transport and the Regions v Unicorn Consultancy Services Ltd* [2000] NPC 108 (Ch D) [128] (Rimer J).

[177] *Feakins v Burstow* [2005] EWHC 1931 (QB), [2006] PNLR 6 [109].

to do something which it was the defendant's responsibility to remind the claimant to do. In *Credit Lyonnais SA v Russell Jones & Walker (a firm)*,[178] for example, the defendant law firm had been negligent in not drawing to its client's attention the fact that time was of the essence in relation to a particular payment that needed to be made to exercise a break clause in a lease. The defendant's argument that the claimant (a major bank) had also been guilty of contributory negligence in not making the payment on time was rejected. Similarly, in *Akasuc Enterprise Ltd v Farmar & Shirreff (a firm)*,[179] where the defendant's negligence involved failing to insert a mechanism into a conditional purchase agreement to protect an overage fee, the judge rejected the argument that the corporate client in question had been negligent in not noticing the omission. Finally, in a case where insurance underwriters had settled a claim in reliance on defective advice provided by their solicitors, short shrift was given to the defendant's allegation that the claimants had been guilty of contributory negligence in not realizing that the advice given to them was flawed. Simon J remarked that:[180]

> The defendant was specifically instructed to consider the issue of coverage and it is difficult to see why the client, who has paid the solicitor to do the work, should check that the solicitor has done the task for which he has been employed ... To put the matter more proverbially: if you hire a dog you do not expect to have to bark.

Conversely, in professional malpractice cases, the courts are more willing to make a finding of contributory negligence where there was carelessness on the claimant's part which was independent of the defendant's fault, such as occurs where an institutional lender suffers losses as a result of having lent money due to both a negligent valuation and improper lending practices. Failures to comply with the standard of the reasonable lender have included not taking account of discrepancies between a borrower's statements as to his debts and those revealed by credit checks;[181] failing to make enquiries regarding a borrower's income and ability to service the loan;[182] failing to take account of a borrower's misuse of an earlier loan;[183] and lending sums of money for a project that the lender knew exceeded the project's cost.[184] Furthermore, in cases of this kind, a sophisticated lender may be held to have been at fault simply for not second-guessing the valuation provided by the defendant, though in such a scenario a lower discount can be expected.[185] The courts may also be more willing to find that a client has been negligent where they failed **3.37**

[178] [2002] EWHC 1310 (Ch), [2003] PNLR 2; cf *Secretary of State for the Environment, Transport and the Regions v Unicorn Consultancy Services Ltd* (2000) NPC 108 (Ch D).

[179] [2003] EWHC 1275 (Ch).

[180] *Newline Corporate Name Ltd v Morgan Cole (a firm)* [2007] EWHC 1628 (Comm), [2008] PNLR 2 [69]. For the same argument in respect of other types of professional adviser, see *Chrysalis Scotland Ltd v Clydesdale Bank Insurance Brokers Ltd* [2008] CSOH 144 [58] (financial adviser); *Manorgate Ltd v First Scottish Property Services Ltd* [2013] CSOH 108 [58] (property search company).

[181] See, eg, *Paratus AMC Ltd v Countrywide Surveyors Ltd* [2011] EWHC 3307 (Ch), [2012] PNLR 12; *Webb Resolutions Ltd v E.Surv Ltd* [2012] EWHC 3653 (TCC), [2013] PNLR 15.

[182] See, eg, *Paratus AMC Ltd v Countrywide Surveyors Ltd* [2011] EWHC 3307 (Ch), [2012] PNLR 12.

[183] See, eg, *Barclays Bank plc v Christie Owen & Davies Ltd* [2016] EWHC 2351 (Ch), [2017] PNLR 8.

[184] See, eg, *Lloyds Bank plc v McBains Cooper Consulting Ltd* [2018] EWCA Civ 452.

[185] See, eg, *Speshal Investments Ltd v Corby Kane Howard Partnership Ltd* [2003] EWHC 390 (Ch) (20 per cent discount for failing to subject to critical analysis the disparity between the purchase price of the properties against which the loan was secured and the valuations provided by the defendants).

to furnish the professional with all the information that the latter needs to provide an appropriate service to the former.[186]

3.38 It seems to be particularly unusual for a claimant in a medical malpractice case to be found guilty of contributory negligence.[187] Indeed, the only reported case in which an English court has made such a finding appears to be *Pidgeon v Doncaster HA*,[188] where the judge held that although the negligent evaluation of a cervical smear by the defendants was partly responsible for the claimant's cancerous condition, the bulk of the blame lay with the claimant, who had failed to have further smear tests, despite being repeatedly urged to do so in strong terms by several doctors. The facts of *Pidgeon* were however described as 'extreme' in *Re P (decd) v Pedar*,[189] where the deceased was held not to have been negligent in failing to chase up hospital appointment letters that the defendant GP had sent to the wrong address, with the result that her breast cancer was incurable by the time it was diagnosed.[190] The dearth of contributory negligence case law in the healthcare context is generally attributed to the paternalistic model of the doctor/patient relationship, which 'places responsibility for the patient's health and medical treatment squarely on the shoulders of the doctor without reference to any responsibility the patient may have for his or her own health'.[191] The decline of that model in recent times[192] might therefore be expected to lead to increasing reliance on contributory negligence arguments by health professionals, a phenomenon which has already been observed by commentators in Australia[193] and Canada.[194] In any case, regardless of the model of the doctor–patient relationship which the law favours, it is hard to see why a deduction for contributory negligence should not be made where, for example, a patient fails to disclose highly relevant information, attend a follow-up appointment, or comply with medical advice.

(h) Psychiatric injury cases

3.39 Findings of contributory negligence also appear to be rare in actions for psychiatric injury, especially in the typical accident scenario, where the mental harm results from involvement in, or observation of, a traumatic event.[195] If the claimant sues for psychiatric injury

---

[186] See *Tai v Hatzistavrou* [1999] NSWCA 306 [56] (cited by Dietrich and Field (n 16) 622 fn 68).

[187] *Goudkamp and Nolan*, paras 8.31–8.36. On contributory negligence in this context, see RB Harper, 'The Application of Contributory Negligence Principles to the Doctor/Patient Relationship' (2001) 9 Torts LJ 1; YSH Ventresca et al, 'With Patient Rights Come Patient Responsibilities: Contributory Negligence in Medical Negligence Actions' (2007) 33 Advoc Q 207; J Herring and C Foster, 'Blaming the Patient: Contributory Negligence in Medical Malpractice Litigation' (2009) 25 PN 76.

[188] [2002] Lloyd's Rep Med 130 (Sheffield CC). See also *PPX v Aulakh* [2019] EWHC 717 (QB), where Whipple J would have made a 25 per cent deduction for contributory fault in a medical negligence case had she found the defendant liable.

[189] [2011] EWHC 1266 (QB) [61] (HHJ Mitchell).

[190] See also *Spencer v Hillingdon Hospital NHS Trust* [2015] EWHC 1058 (QB) (not negligent of claimant to fail to report calf pain despite being told to mention 'any problems' experienced post-surgery).

[191] Harper (n 187) 3. See also Herring and Foster (n 187) 83 (under the paternalistic model, '[t]he patient's role is essentially a passive one').

[192] As exemplified by the decision in *Montgomery v Lanarkshire Health Board* [2015] UKSC 11, [2015] AC 1430: see especially at [81].

[193] Harper (n 187) 17. For a survey of the Australian case law, see *Luntz*, para 1.13.25.

[194] EI Picard and GB Robertson, *Legal Liability of Doctors and Hospitals in Canada* (4th edn, Carswell 2007) 369.

[195] On psychiatric injury and contributory negligence, see P Handford, *Tort Liability for Mental Harm* (3rd edn, Thomson Reuters (Professional) Australia 2017) paras 16.30 et seq.

triggered by the defendant's having negligently endangered the bodily integrity of the claimant, the endangerment and hence the trauma could in theory be partly the claimant's fault. However, there do not appear to be any reported cases where a 'primary victim' of this kind has had their damages reduced for contributory negligence. Similarly, a so-called 'involuntary participant' who was actively involved in the events leading up to an accident might in principle be partly to blame for the accident having happened, although thus far the persons who have brought claims on this basis have generally been entirely innocent.[196] As for the 'secondary victim' who suffers psychiatric injury as a result of the death, injury, or imperilment of a third party, the possibility of contributory negligence here is lesser still, as most such cases involve bystanders who play no causal role in the traumatic event. In theory a court might find that a secondary victim should have protected their mental health by, say, leaving an accident scene—or indeed not going there in the first place—but where (as is generally the case) a loved one is involved such a finding is obviously unlikely.[197]

Defendants in work stress claims sometimes argue that the employee was negligent in not taking steps to protect their mental health, but the courts are generally unsympathetic to such attempts to shift the blame. In *Rowntree v Commissioner of Police for the Metropolis*,[198] for example, Nelson J rejected the contention that an overworked police officer had been partly at fault for her psychiatric injury for not complaining, seeking support, and distancing herself from an especially difficult case. Though it was true that these failures were in part causative of her injury, they were not the claimant's fault, but rather 'in part due to the Defendant's own negligence in failing to supervise her properly, failing to give adequate support and failing to spot the warning signs'.[199] Similarly, in a case brought by a Post Office workshop manager, the Court of Appeal upheld the Recorder's finding that he had not been contributorily negligent in burdening himself unnecessarily and not voicing concerns to his supervisors. He was 'both conscientious and vulnerable and could scarcely be blamed for doing his best to undertake the task which he understood to be expected of him, when he had made complaints in the past which had not been heeded'.[200] It should also be borne in mind that even if it is found that the claimant in a work stress case was at fault, the defendant may face an uphill struggle on causation, since in such cases the employer has often failed to respond adequately to complaints when they have been made or to provide support when it has been requested. Similar difficulties in establishing fault and causation for the purposes of contributory negligence are likely to face defendants in analogous scenarios, for example claims against schools for psychiatric illness induced by bullying.[201] **3.40**

196 Though note two cases from other jurisdictions (cited in Handford (n 195) para 16.50) where deductions were made from the damages awarded for psychiatric injury to plaintiffs partly responsible for the traumatic event: see *Kwok v British Columbia Ferry Corporation* (1987) 20 BCLR (2d) 318 (SC); and *Regan v Harper* [1971] Qd R 191 (SC).

197 Note that the contributory negligence of the third party whose death, injury, or imperilment triggers the secondary victim's trauma is not imputed to the secondary victim, whose action against the tortfeasor is an entirely independent one: see 3.63.

198 QBD, 26 October 2001.

199 ibid [109].

200 *Young v Post Office* [2002] EWCA Civ 661, [2002] IRLR 660 [26] (May LJ).

201 See, eg, *Oyston v St Patrick's College* [2011] NSWSC 269 (failure to complain about bullying not contributory negligence).

(i) Addiction and contributory negligence

3.41 We have already seen that the damages awarded to a compulsive gambler who sued a bookmaker for not blocking him from placing bets with it might have been reduced for contributory negligence had liability been established.[202] More generally, the fact that the conduct said to amount to contributory negligence is the result of an addiction will not prevent a finding of contributory negligence being made. In *Badger v Ministry of Defence*,[203] the claimant's husband had died of lung cancer in 2002, at the age of sixty-three. His cancer was attributable in part to his having been exposed to asbestos while working for the defendant, and in part to his having smoked throughout his adult life. The defendant admitted liability but pleaded contributory negligence on the ground that the deceased should have given up smoking once the health dangers of cigarettes became notorious. Stanley Burnton J agreed, holding that a reasonably prudent person in the deceased's position would have stopped smoking in the mid-1970s, and that this would have significantly reduced the risk of his contracting lung cancer. The appropriate deduction from the claimant's damages for this contributory negligence was 20 per cent. Similar conclusions were reached in a later case also concerning smoking and asbestos,[204] and in a case concerning alcoholism.[205] The same approach would presumably also be taken where an addiction to drugs contributed to the damage.[206]

(4) 'No duty' cases

3.42 In the *Restatement (Third) of Torts: Liability for Physical and Emotional Harm*, it is said that: 'An actor ordinarily has a duty to exercise reasonable care when the actor's conduct creates a risk of physical harm.'[207] The reporters stipulate that this statement applies both to the duty of care for the purposes of the tort of negligence and to the doctrine of contributory negligence (or 'comparative responsibility'). They also argue that 'duty' is sometimes 'cancelled' for reasons of public policy:[208]

> Just as special problems of policy may support a no-duty determination for a defendant, similar concerns may support a no-duty determination for plaintiff negligence. By relieving the plaintiff of an obligation to act reasonably for self-protection, these rules eliminate the defense of comparative responsibility that otherwise would diminish the plaintiff's recovery.

Similarly, Ellen Bublick has argued that the American courts should recognize citizen 'no-duty' rules in the context of civil rape cases in order to acknowledge the independent interests of citizens in not being required to shape their conduct around the reality of pervasive rape and fear of rape in modern society.[209] The language of 'no duty' is problematic

---

[202] *Calvert v William Hill Credit Ltd* [2008] EWCA Civ 1427, [2009] Ch 330. See 3.30.

[203] [2005] EWHC 2941 (QB), [2006] 3 All ER 173.

[204] *Blackmore v Department for Communities and Local Government* [2017] EWCA Civ 1136, [2018] QB 471.

[205] *Hughes v Turning Point Scotland* [2019] CSOH 42, 2019 SLT 651 (the discussion of contributory negligence was obiter as the defendant was held not to have been negligent).

[206] Though it will depend on the directness of the link between addiction and damage: see *St George v Home Office* [2008] EWCA Civ 1068, [2009] 1 WLR 1670 (discussed in 3.51–3.53).

[207] *Restatement (Third) of Torts: Liability for Physical and Emotional Harm* (2010) § 7(a).

[208] [1999] 2 AC 455 (HL) 498.

[209] EM Bublick, 'Citizen No-Duty Rules: Rape Victims and Comparative Fault' (1999) 99 Colum L Rev 1413.

in the contributory negligence context, since people cannot owe legal duties to themselves. Nevertheless, shorn of that language, the argument that certain types of conduct are incapable of amounting to contributory negligence, since otherwise wrongdoers would be able to place unacceptable constraints on the freedom of action of potential claimants, is clearly a powerful one.[210] Suppose, for example, that a woman who is raped in the immediate vicinity of a nightclub brings a claim against the operators of the club alleging that they should have done more to protect female patrons from such an attack. In a case of this kind, it would clearly be completely unacceptable for a court to hold that the victim was partly to blame for what happened because, say, she was wearing revealing clothing or had gone to the club on her own. Similarly, in an old American case, the argument that it had been negligent of a landowner to store flax close to a railway track because of the risk of it being set alight by sparks from locomotives was quite rightly rejected.[211] It was his land and he was free to store his goods where he wished. One way of explaining these results is by saying that as a matter of public policy the law will not entertain an allegation of contributory negligence in these circumstances.[212] However, another way of arriving at the same conclusion would be to say that it can never be 'unreasonable' for a woman or a landowner to exercise their freedoms in this regard, with the result that—as a matter of fact, rather than legal policy—such behaviour will never amount to negligence.

William Prosser expressed the idea that seems to underlie decisions of this kind by saying **3.43**
that 'the plaintiff may not be required to surrender a valuable right or privilege because the defendant's conduct threatens him with a risk'.[213] However, he also cautioned that there were 'situations where insistence upon a right ... may clearly involve a risk out of all proportion to its value'[214] and that in such a case a finding of negligence might be made. Suppose, for example, that the defendant has created a danger in the road outside the claimant's house such that the claimant faces a significant risk of death or serious injury if they seek to exercise their public right to use the highway. If the claimant sought to exercise that right anyway, and suffered injury as a result of the danger, then that would doubtless be considered contributory fault.

(5) Intentional self-harm

It might be thought that the notion that intentionally inflicted harm can constitute **3.44**
contributory negligence makes no sense on the basis that the idea of 'intentional negligence' is contradictory. However, this view involves a misunderstanding of the concept of negligence. Negligence, including contributory negligence, is a type of conduct, namely behaviour that falls below the standard of a reasonable person in the circumstances. It is not a state of mind. Accordingly, there is no reason why intentional conduct cannot amount to contributory negligence in an appropriate case. A conclusion to the contrary

[210] These concerns would be especially acute were the scope of contributory negligence to be extended to intentional wrongs such as battery: see the discussion in the *Restatement (Third) of Torts: Apportionment of Liability* (2000) § 3, cmt d.

[211] *Leroy Fibre Co v Chicago, Milwaukee & St Paul Railway Co* 232 US 340 (S Ct 1914).

[212] See J Goudkamp, 'Rethinking Contributory Negligence' in SGA Pitel et al (eds), *Tort Law: Challenging Orthodoxy* (Hart Publishing 2013) 314–23.

[213] *Prosser*, 400.

[214] ibid 401.

would in any event involve the peculiar outcome whereby a person who inadvertently but carelessly caused themselves harm would be liable to have their damages reduced for contributory negligence, whereas a person who engaged in acts of deliberate self-harm would not. After a period of some confusion, the courts confirmed that a claimant's intentional self-harm can constitute contributory negligence in *Reeves v Commissioner of Police of the Metropolis*.[215] The deceased had committed suicide while in police custody. A claim by his dependants and on behalf of the deceased's estate succeeded on the basis that the police had been negligent in not taking precautions to prevent the deceased killing himself, but the damages were reduced by 50 per cent for contributory negligence. It is, however, likely to be rare for the courts to be faced with the question of whether deliberate self-harm amounts to contributory negligence, since in such cases the claimant's conduct will usually be regarded as a novus actus interveniens, and hence the sole legal cause of the damage.[216] *Reeves* was an unusual case in this regard since the police conceded that they had owed the deceased a duty to take care to prevent him from committing suicide, a concession which the House of Lords considered incompatible with the claim that his doing so amounted to a novus actus.

2. The Causation Requirement

3.45 Contributory negligence comprises two elements—fault and causation—and both must be present for the doctrine to apply. It follows that the doctrine will not be engaged by negligence on the part of the claimant which is not a cause of the damage that is the subject of their claim. As Lord Atkin said in *Caswell v Powell Duffryn Associated Collieries Ltd*, 'if the plaintiff were negligent, but his negligence was not a cause operating to produce the damage, there would be no defence'.[217] His Lordship added:[218]

> I find it impossible to divorce any theory of contributory negligence from the concept of causation … and whether you ask whose negligence was responsible for the injury, or from whose negligence did the injury result, or adopt any other phrase you please, you must in the ultimate analysis be asking who 'caused' the injury.

As with liability for negligence,[219] the causation requirement with regard to contributory negligence has both factual and legal aspects. First and foremost, the defendant needs to establish that the negligent conduct of the claimant was historically connected to the damage in respect of which they are bringing the action. We refer to this as the 'factual causation' question. However, even where this factual link has been established, the court may find that the connection between the negligence and the damage is not sufficiently strong for a finding of contributory negligence to be made. We refer to this as the 'legal causation' question.

[215] [2000] 1 AC 360 (HL). See also *Corr v IBC Vehicles Ltd* [2008] UKHL 13, [2008] 1 AC 884 (discussed in 3.17).

[216] The relationship between the contributory negligence doctrine and the law relating to intervening causes is considered in 5.02–5.07.

[217] [1940] AC 152 (HL) 165.

[218] Ibid.

[219] See *Winfield & Jolowicz*, ch 7.

(1) Factual causation

If the damage would have happened even if the claimant had taken reasonable care for their own safety or interests a finding of contributory negligence will not be made. For example, in *Beasley v Alexander*, the contributory negligence doctrine was inapplicable because the claimant motorcyclist, who had been careless in riding too quickly, would still have been injured by the defendant's negligence if he had been travelling at the 'top safe speed'.[220] Similarly, in *Toole v Bolton Metropolitan Borough Council*,[221] an employee's failure to wear protective gloves when cleaning a lavatory did not constitute contributory negligence as it would probably not have prevented the needle-stick injury which he suffered when he tried to pick up a discarded syringe. **3.46**

The burden of proving causation for the purposes of contributory negligence falls on the defendant. In *Owens v Brimmell*,[222] the claimant went on a pub crawl with the defendant in the latter's car. In the early hours of the morning the defendant was driving the claimant home when he lost control of the car, which crashed into a lamp-post. The claimant, who was not wearing a seat belt, sustained very serious injuries, including brain damage. It was not clear whether the brain damage occurred because the claimant sustained a blow to the head (which would probably not have occurred if he had been wearing a seat belt) or whether it was the result of a whiplash injury (which would probably have happened anyway). Watkins J held that the claimant's damages should be reduced by 20 per cent for travelling in a car with a drunken driver, but that no further reduction should be made in respect of his failure to wear a seat belt, since it had not been shown that this would have lessened the severity of his injuries. The judge said that where contributory negligence was alleged, 'the burden of proving on the balance of probabilities that a plaintiff has contributed to the cause of the damage suffered lies upon he who alleged it, namely, the defendant'.[223] **3.47**

The extent to which a defendant alleging contributory negligence can rely on rules that have developed to make it easier for a *claimant* to establish that a *defendant's* negligence was causative is unclear. On the one hand, it is sometimes said or assumed that the rules determining causation for liability purposes are the same as those determining causation for the purposes of contributory negligence.[224] This approach has the appeal of simplicity, and any other might give rise to difficulties in a case where the same exception could potentially benefit both parties. At the same time, however, it should be borne in mind that the rationale for an exception to the need for a claimant to establish causation on the balance of probabilities will not necessarily have the same force in the context of alleged contributory negligence. It is in any case clear that in scenarios falling within the most prominent such exception—the so-called *Fairchild* principle[225]—the courts give both sides the benefit of the exception. So, for example, if the claimant contracts lung cancer and it **3.48**

---

220 [2012] EWHC 2197 (QB) [18] (Sir Raymond Jack). See also *Davis v Schrogin* [2006] EWCA Civ 974 [3], [11] (driving more slowly would have made no difference).

221 [2002] EWCA Civ 588.

222 [1977] 1 QB 859 (QBD).

223 [1976] QB 286 (CA) 292 (emphasis in original).

224 See, eg, *Restatement (Second) of the Law of Torts* (1965) § 465(2).

225 After the decision of the House of Lords in *Fairchild v Glenhaven Funeral Services Ltd* [2002] UKHL 22, [2003] 1 AC 32. See further, *Winfield & Jolowicz*, paras 7-034 et seq.

is unclear whether this was caused by (1) asbestos exposure for which the defendant was responsible, (2) the claimant's smoking, or (3) a combination of the two, then to establish *liability* the claimant need show only that the asbestos exposure materially increased the risk of cancer, and conversely to establish *contributory negligence* the defendant need show only that the smoking did.[226] Finally, it should be noted that in a *Fairchild* case where liability is limited by reference to the proportion of the risk of disease for which the defendant was responsible, any contribution which the claimant's negligence made to that risk will not be treated as contributory negligence, since it will already have served to reduce the extent of the defendant's prima facie liability.[227]

3.49 The contributory negligence that *was* found in *Owens v Brimmell*, namely the decision to travel in the defendant's car knowing of his intoxication, was not a cause of the accident, but it was a cause of the claimant's involvement in it.[228] Since the causation requirement is concerned with the link between the claimant's fault and the claimant's *damage*, that was sufficient. The broader point here is that the defendant need not show that the claimant's negligence was a cause of the event that led to the claimant being injured, but only that, had the claimant not been negligent, their injuries would have been avoided or less severe.[229] The classic statement of this principle is found in another seat belt case, *Froom v Butcher*, where Lord Denning MR said:[230]

> The question is not what was the cause of the accident. It is rather what was the cause of the damage. In most accidents on the road the bad driving, which causes the accident, also causes the ensuing damage. But in seat belt cases the cause of the accident is one thing. The cause of the damage is another. The *accident* is caused by the bad driving. The *damage* is caused in part by the bad driving of the defendant, and in part by the failure of the plaintiff to wear a seat belt. If the plaintiff was to blame in not wearing a seat belt, the damage is in part the result of his own fault. He must bear some share in the responsibility for the damage.

Of course, as *Owens v Brimmell* shows, in such a scenario the defendant may be unable to establish a link between the claimant's injuries and the use of a seat belt or other protective mechanism, in which case no finding of contributory negligence will be made.[231]

---

[226] The both-ways application of the exception seems simply to be assumed by the courts. See, eg, *Badger v Ministry of Defence* [2005] EWHC 2941 (QB), [2006] 3 All ER 173 (smoking after dangers became readily apparent and which significantly increased risk of lung cancer constituted contributory negligence).

[227] See *Barker v Corus UK Ltd* [2006] UKHL 20, [2006] 2 AC 572. The proportionate liability rule set down in *Barker* was subsequently reversed for mesothelioma cases by the Compensation Act 2006, s 3. It follows that in such cases any contribution which the negligence of the claimant made to the risk of damage *is* dealt with as contributory negligence.

[228] This is a common scenario. For other examples, see *Davies v Swan Motor Co (Swansea) Ltd* [1949] 2 KB 291 (CA) (refuse collector hitching a lift on side of dustbin lorry); *Jones v Livox Quarries Ltd* [1952] 2 QB 608 (CA) (worker travelling on back of excavator).

[229] In the light of the wording of s 1(1) of the Law Reform (Contributory Negligence) Act 1945, this seems rather obvious, but apparently it was once controversial: see JR Spencer, 'Widening Scope of Defence of Contributory Negligence' [1972A] CLJ 27.

[230] [1976] QB 286 (CA) 292 (emphasis in original).

[231] See also *Lertora v Finzi* [1973] RTR 161 (QBD) (seat belt); *Stanton v Collinson* [2009] EWHC 342 (QB) (seat belt); *Smith v Finch* [2009] EWHC 53 (QB) (cycle helmet). Whether in cases involving seat belts and the like the court should take account of any additional damage that might have occurred if the claimant *had* used the protective mechanism in question is a difficult issue on which the limited case law is inconsistent: compare

It is frequently true in cases involving seat belts and the like that the claimant's negligence was a cause of some but not all of their injuries. Similarly, it may be that the negligent driving of the claimant was responsible for only some of the damage done to their car in a road accident, or that in a professional negligence case the fault of the claimant was a concurrent cause of only some of the losses that they suffered as a result of the defendant's wrongdoing. Needless to say, in such cases the court will endeavour to separate out the damage or loss attributable to the fault of both parties and the damage attributable to the fault of the defendant alone, so as to apply the deduction for contributory negligence only to the damages for the former.[232] **3.50**

(2) Legal causation

It is not enough to engage the contributory negligence doctrine that the claimant's failure to take reasonable care merely formed part of the background facts. The doctrine will be enlivened only if the connection between the fault of the claimant and the damage sustained is sufficiently strong for the former to count as a legal cause of the latter. In *St George v Home Office*,[233] the claimant, who had a long history of alcohol and drug addiction, was sentenced to a term of imprisonment. Although the prison authorities were aware that he was a drug addict and alcoholic who had previously had withdrawal seizures, he was negligently allocated to an ordinary unit and a top bunk. When he fell from his bunk during a withdrawal seizure, and knocked his head on the floor, this triggered a status epilepticus, which itself caused severe brain damage. The trial judge imposed liability for the negligence of the prison authorities but reduced the claimant's damages by 15 per cent on the ground that he was partly to blame for the damage for having become an addict in the first place. The Court of Appeal allowed the claimant's cross appeal. According to Dyson LJ, the claimant's addictions were not 'a potent cause of the injury',[234] since his fault in becoming an addict 'was too remote in time, place and circumstance and was not sufficiently connected with the negligence of the prison staff'.[235] **3.51**

Dyson LJ argued in *St George v Home Office* that there was a close analogy between the facts of that case and a scenario where a doctor provides negligent medical treatment to a patient whose medical condition is one for which the patient is to blame, such as lung cancer caused by smoking, or liver cirrhosis caused by excessive alcohol consumption.[236] In such a case the claimant's faulty conduct is merely part of the history, and does not amount to contributory negligence. More generally, 'in a case involving negligent rendition of a service ... a factfinder does not consider any plaintiff's conduct that created the condition **3.52**

Mackay v Borthwick 1982 SLT 265 (OH) with *Patience v Andrews* [1983] RTR 447 (QBD). As a matter of principle it is hard to see why the court should not do so, though the evidential difficulties may be severe.

[232] See *O'Connell v Jackson* [1972] 1 QB 270 (CA) 277. However, it may not always be possible for the court to separate out the damage or loss in this way, in which case a more rough and ready approach will be required at the apportionment stage: see 4.05.

[233] [2008] EWCA Civ 1068, [2009] 1 WLR 1670.

[234] ibid [51].

[235] ibid [56]. See also *Calvert v William Hill Credit Ltd* [2008] EWCA Civ 1427, [2009] Ch 330 [70], where it was suggested that if liability had been imposed on the defendant bookmaker for not honouring its undertaking to prevent the claimant from gambling with them, then the claimant's having become a compulsive gambler prior to that undertaking would not have amounted to contributory negligence.

[236] [2008] EWCA Civ 1068, [2009] 1 WLR 1670 [58].

the service was employed to remedy'.[237] This is because the conduct of the claimant that created the condition is not regarded as a legal cause of the injury which results from the service provider's negligence.

3.53 The decision in *St George* suggests that the courts take a more broad-brush approach to the legal causation issue in cases of contributory negligence than they do when it comes to establishing liability. Suppose that when the claimant had fallen from his bunk he had landed on another prisoner, injuring him. Had the other prisoner then sued the claimant, it seems unlikely that the court would have held simply that his becoming an addict lacked 'causal potency'. Instead the court would probably have focused on whether the other prisoner's injury was a foreseeable consequence of the claimant's addiction, or on whether the prison authorities' decision to allocate the claimant to a top bunk was a *novus actus interveniens*. It is not entirely clear why in the context of contributory negligence the courts seem to adopt a less rigorous approach to questions of legal causation.

3.54 The causation requirement in contributory negligence cases also encompasses a distinct principle that the damage sustained must have been within the scope of the risk or risks created by the claimant's lack of reasonable care. As the *Restatement (Second) of the Law of Torts* puts it:[238]

> The fact that the plaintiff has failed to exercise reasonable care for his own safety does not [constitute contributory negligence] unless his harm results from one of the hazards which make his conduct negligent.

In a leading American case, *Smithwick v Hall & Upson Co*,[239] the plaintiff was standing on a platform repairing the defendant's wall when the section above him collapsed, causing him injury. Although he had been told not to use the platform in question because it lacked a guard rail, his negligence in this regard was not a proximate cause of his injury since the accident that took place was in no way linked to the absence of a guard rail. It would have been different if he had fallen from the platform and suffered injury. Consistently with the authorities on the equivalent 'scope of risk' principle applicable to defendant negligence,[240] the courts generally take a broad approach to the characterization of the risks generated by the claimant's fault.[241] As John Fleming wrote, it would be 'a mistake to assess the scope of the apparent risk engendered by the plaintiff's conduct with overdue refinement', especially in the apportionment era.[242] In *Jones v Livox Quarries Ltd*,[243] the claimant was crushed while riding on the back of an excavator when another vehicle struck it from behind. The Court of Appeal held that his riding on the vehicle in defiance of an express prohibition constituted contributory negligence. The risks at which the prohibition was most obviously

---

[237] *Restatement (Third) of Torts: Apportionment of Liability* (2000) § 7, cmt m.

[238] *Restatement (Second) of the Law of Torts* (1965) § 468.

[239] 21 A 924 (Conn 1890).

[240] See *Winfield & Jolowicz*, paras 7-064–7-065.

[241] Hence 'the precise way that the damage or injury' occurred need not have been foreseeable: *Badger v Ministry of Defence* [2005] EWHC 2941 (QB), [2006] 3 All ER 173 [12] (Burnton J). See, eg, *Hanly v Berlin* [1975] Qd R 52 (SC) (plaintiff contributorily negligent for driving with his elbow sticking out of his car window, even if he could not have foreseen the precise manner in which his arm suffered injury).

[242] *Fleming*, 314. American courts faced with the complete defence sometimes engaged in extreme hair-splitting to let negligent claimants off the hook. For some amusing examples, see *Prosser & Keeton*, 457–58.

[243] [1952] 2 QB 608 (CA).

aimed were of a worker falling off a machine or getting trapped in a moving part, 'but those were not the only risks' to which the claimant had subjected himself.[244] In addition, '[h]e had put himself in the dangerous position which ... exposed him to the particular danger which came upon him'.[245] It would have been different, said Denning LJ, if he had been shot by a negligent hunter in an adjoining field.[246]

3. The Doctrine of Identification

(1) Introduction

One person may be identified with another for various purposes in the law of obligations. In the context of contributory negligence, the 'doctrine of identification' may mean that one person suffers a reduction in their damages on account of the contributory negligence of a third party.[247] The historical basis of this doctrine seems to lie in the maxim *qui facit per alium facit* per se ('he who acts through another acts himself'). In *The Bernina*,[248] a collision occurred between two ships because of the negligent navigation of both vessels. When the representatives of a crew member and a passenger who drowned brought a claim against the owners of the other ship, the House of Lords held that the deceased were not identified with those navigating the vessel on which they were travelling. According to Lord Herschell, it had not been argued that 'there was contributory negligence on the part of any third person standing in such a legal relation towards the deceased men *as to cause the acts of that third person ... to be regarded as their acts*'.[249] **3.55**

The doctrine of identification seems not to have been in the forefront of the minds of the drafters of the apportionment legislation, which refers only to a person who 'suffers damage as the result partly of *his own* fault',[250] but the 1945 Act was clearly not intended to affect the doctrine's operation and the courts have held that the words 'his own fault' encompass the fault of a person with whom the claimant is identified applying the doctrine.[251] Where the doctrine of identification applies, the defendant need not of course rely on it if for some reason they prefer to pay full damages to the claimant and then seek contribution from the third party.[252] **3.56**

---

[244] ibid 614 (Singleton LJ).

[245] ibid.

[246] ibid 616.

[247] The literature is extensive. See in particular, C Gregory, 'Vicarious Responsibility and Contributory Negligence' (1932) 41 Yale LJ 831; WP Keeton, 'Imputed Contributory Negligence' (1936) 13 Tex L Rev 161; A Bartlett, 'Attribution of Contributory Negligence: Agents, Company Directors and Fraudsters' (1998) 114 LQR 460.

[248] (1888) 13 App Cas 1 (HL).

[249] ibid 5 (emphasis added). See also at 7–8.

[250] Law Reform (Contributory Negligence) Act 1945, s 1(1) (emphasis added).

[251] *William A Jay & Sons v JS Veevers Ltd* [1946] 1 All ER 646 (QBD). See also *Williams*, 434–36. As Williams points out, applying the '*qui facit*' maxim the act of the employee is legally the act of the employer, in which case the statutory wording would be adequate as it stands. Apportionment legislation elsewhere puts the point beyond doubt: see, eg, Wrongs Act 1954 (Tas) s 4(7) ('A reference in this section to the wrongful act of a person shall be construed as including a reference to a wrongful act for which that person is vicariously liable').

[252] *Todd*, 1162.

3.57 The Law Reform (Miscellaneous Provisions) Act 1934 simply transfers the deceased's cause of action to their personal representatives, with the result that the estate's claim will be reduced in proportion to any contributory fault of the deceased.[253] This is not, however, an application of the doctrine of identification because in law the estate and the deceased are one and the same, so no attribution of a third party's contributory fault is involved. Where, in a case brought under the survival statute, a beneficiary under the estate was partly to blame for the death of the deceased this will not affect the estate's action,[254] although the defendant may be able to recover contribution from the beneficiary.[255] The position is the same where the personal representative who brings the claim on behalf of the estate was partly to blame for the deceased's death.[256]

(2) Where the doctrine of identification applies

(a) Employers and employees

3.58 The principle that underlies the doctrine of identification in the modern law is the 'both ways' test. According to this test, the claimant 'is identified with another if, but only if, that other's negligence would be imputed to him, were he a defendant'.[257] The most obvious application of the both ways test is the vicarious responsibility of an employer for the contributory negligence of an employee in the course of employment, which operates as a sort of mirror image of the employer's vicarious liability.[258] Suppose, for example, that C suffers property damage through the combined fault of both D and X. If X is C's employee, and was acting in the course of employment at the time, then in C's claim against D, X's negligence will be imputed to C for the purposes of the contributory negligence analysis.[259] Rightly or wrongly, the courts appear to have accepted the idea of vicarious responsibility for contributory negligence as the logical corollary of vicarious liability. And although it has been described as the result of a 'misguided sense of symmetry',[260] Andrew Bartlett argues that:[261]

> [The symmetry of the both ways test] has a strong appeal, both because of the inherent attractiveness of a symmetrical solution and because the symmetry enables the court to solve questions of attribution of contributory negligence by having recourse to an existing developed body of law on vicarious liability.

---

253 See, eg, *Davies v Swan Motor Co (Swansea) Ltd* [1949] 2 KB 291 (CA).

254 This follows from the wording of s 1(1) of the Law Reform (Contributory Negligence) Act 1945, since the estate's claim is for damage suffered by the deceased, not the beneficiary. See also *Restatement (Second) of the Law of Torts* (1965) § 493.

255 See *Williams*, 438 et seq.

256 This again follows from the wording of the 1945 Act, as the claim is not for damage suffered by the personal representative. See also *Williams*, 461–63; *Restatement (Second) of the Law of Torts* (1965) § 492.

257 *Fleming*, 323.

258 The law on this point is explored in some detail in PS Atiyah, *Vicarious Liability in the Law of Torts* (Butterworths 1967) 409–14.

259 See, eg, *Chaplin v Hawes* (1823) 3 Car & P 554, 172 ER 543; *William A Jay & Sons v JS Veevers Ltd* [1946] 1 All ER 646 (QBD).

260 *Fleming*, 323 (the doctrine 'has little to commend it'). The principle is however defended in the employment context by Atiyah (n 258) 410. For an exploration of possible justifications for the doctrine of identification, see M MacIntyre, 'The Rationale of Imputed Negligence' (1944) 5 U Toronto LJ 368.

261 Bartlett (n 247) 469.

To some extent whether one thinks that vicarious responsibility should track vicarious liability depends on one's view as to the rationale of the latter doctrine.[262] For example, if one subscribes to the 'master's tort' theory of vicarious liability, which imputes the act (rather than the tort) of the employee to the employer, then the 'both ways' test makes perfect sense. Furthermore, that test also squares with a deterrence rationale for vicarious liability, by adding to the incentives on employers to exercise care in selecting, training and monitoring those they employ. Conversely, other possible rationales for vicarious liability, such as 'deep pockets', or 'enterprise risk', offer no obvious support for a mirror image principle of vicarious responsibility.[263] Having said that, the absence of such a principle might raise eyebrows in a case like *William A Jay & Sons v JS Veevers Ltd*,[264] where a collision between two lorries was the result of the negligence of both drivers, each an employee of the relevant lorry's owner. Had the doctrine of identification not been applied on those facts then each owner would have recovered full damages from the owner of the other lorry, with no allowance being made for the fact that, say, one of the drivers was 80 per cent responsible for the accident and the other only 20 per cent per cent responsible. Would that have been a sensible or fair result? **3.59**

(b) *Companies and principals*

For the purposes of contributory negligence, the fault of a company director will generally be imputed to a company,[265] as will the fault of a person (whether or not an employee) to whom a director delegates their responsibility.[266] The position as regards principals and agents is fuzzier,[267] though it is clear that the 'both ways' test applies in a case where a car owner would be vicariously liable for the negligence of a person driving the car for the owner's purposes within the rule in *Launchbury v Morgans*.[268] **3.60**

(c) *Fraud and intentional misconduct*

It is unclear to what extent a claimant will be identified with a third party who is an agent, employee, or director of the claimant where the third party has acted fraudulently or otherwise engaged in intentional misconduct. Fuller treatment of this difficult issue should be sought in more detailed excurses elsewhere.[269] However, the better view is that in this context the courts should apply the 'both ways' test. An argument in favour of this **3.61**

---

[262] For a discussion of possible rationales of vicarious liability, see *Winfield & Jolowicz*, para 21-006.

[263] See *Fleming*, 323 (arguing that vicarious liability is based primarily 'on the economic policy of assuring effective redress for tortious harm', and that there 'is no corresponding reason for protecting a culpable tortfeasor to the prejudice of his victim').

[264] [1946] 1 All ER 646 (QBD).

[265] See *Daniels v Anderson* (1995) 37 NSWLR 438 (CA) 568–70.

[266] *Barings plc (in liq) v Coopers & Lybrand (a firm)* [2003] EWHC 1319 (Ch), [2003] PNLR 34 [903]. See also Bartlett (n 247) 471–72, criticizing the narrower ruling in *British Racing Drivers' Club Ltd v Hextall Erskine & Co* [1996] 3 All ER 667 (QBD), which would have limited this to cases where the directors constituted the 'directing mind and will' of the company in the transaction in question.

[267] See Bartlett (n 247) 470–71.

[268] [1973] AC 127 (HL). See *Berrill v Road Haulage Executive* [1952] 2 Lloyd's Rep 490 (QBD); *Lampert v Eastern National Omnibus Co Ltd* [1954] 1 WLR 1047 (QBD) (contributory negligence of husband driver attributed to wife owner).

[269] See the helpful discussion in Bartlett (n 247) 472–78.

position is that, as between two innocent parties, it is fairer for the party who employed or otherwise cloaked the fraudster with authority to bear the loss than the one who did not.

(d) Cargo owners and ships

3.62 Finally, for the purposes of the separate apportionment regime for collisions at sea set down by section 187 of the Merchant Shipping Act 1995,[270] the owners of cargo damaged in the collision are (in effect) identified with the ship on which the cargo was being carried.[271] By contrast, a crew member or passenger who suffers personal injury in the collision is not identified with the ship on which they were travelling.[272]

(2) Where the doctrine of identification does not apply

3.63 In earlier times, the negligence of a driver of a vehicle or other conveyance was imputed to their passengers in certain circumstances.[273] This rule was widely ridiculed and was rejected long ago.[274] Spouses are not identified with each other in this sense,[275] and nor is a child identified with the person in the care of whom the child is placed.[276] Accordingly, if a child suffers injury due to the combined fault of a carer and a third party, the carer's negligence does not affect the child's claim against the third party, though it may ground a claim for contribution by the third party against the carer.[277] The trend of modern authority is to the effect that the negligence of a bailee is not imputed to the bailor, even in claims for damage to the chattel bailed.[278] Finally, an action by a 'secondary victim' for psychiatric injury caused by the death, injury or imperilment of another (the 'immediate victim') is not affected by the immediate victim's negligence, since the secondary victim is owed an independent duty of care and their claim is in no manner derivative of any action which may be available to the immediate victim.[279] In this context, it is unlikely that the defendant will obtain contribution from the immediate victim or their estate because of the rule that an immediate victim owes no duty of care to the secondary victim.[280]

---

[270] See 2.25.

[271] This follows from the wording of the Merchant Shipping Act 1995, s 187.

[272] ibid s 188.

[273] *Thorogood v Bryan* (1849) 8 CB 115, 137 ER 452 ('an unfortunate English decision': *Prosser*, 417). See W Cornish et al, *Law and Society in England: 1750–1950* (2nd edn, Hart Publishing 2019) 473–74.

[274] *The Bernina* (1888) 13 App Cas 1 (HL).

[275] *Mallett v Dunn* [1949] 2 KB 180 (KBD); *Drinkwater v Kimber* [1952] 2 QB 281 (CA).

[276] *Oliver v Birmingham and Midland Motor Omnibus Co Ltd* [1933] 1 KB 35 (KBD), overruling *Waite v North Eastern Railway Co* (1858) El Bl & El 719, 120 ER 679 (Exch Ch) ('a still more unfortunate English case' which set down 'a barbarous rule': *Prosser*, 419–20).

[277] As in *Jones v Wilkins* [2001] RTR 19 (CA); *Williams v Williams* [2013] EWCA Civ 455, [2013] PIQR P17.

[278] *Wellwood v Alexander King Ltd* [1921] 2 IR 290 (CA); *Fletcher v Thomas* [1931] 3 DLR 142 (Ont SC); *France v Parkinson* [1954] 1 WLR 581 (CA); *Restatement (Second) of the Law of Torts* (1965) § 489. See, further, *Prosser*, 424–25; JG Fleming, 'Tort Liability for Damage to Hire-Purchase Goods' (1959) 32 ALJ 267, 273–74.

[279] Law Commission, *Liability for Psychiatric Illness* (Law Com No 249, 1998) paras 2.22–2.24, 5.39. This is shown by the fact that the immediate victim may be unhurt and so have no claim of their own: see, eg, *Dooley v Cammell Laird & Co Ltd* [1951] 1 Lloyd's Rep 271 (Assizes). The position is otherwise in some Australian states, where the contributory negligence of the immediate victim is imputed to the secondary victim by virtue of legislative provisions: see, eg, Civil Liability Act 2002 (NSW) s 30(3). For a detailed discussion, see Handford (n 195) paras 16.70–16.180.

[280] *Greatorex v Greatorex* [2000] 1 WLR 1970 (QBD).

(3) Equivalent statutory provisions

(a) *Fatal Accidents Act 1976*

Certain statutory provisions have a similar effect to the doctrine of identification. The most important of these is section 5 of the Fatal Accidents Act 1976, according to which any damages for loss of dependency or bereavement recoverable under that Act shall be reduced in proportion to any contributory negligence of the deceased. The position prior to 1945 had been that the contributory negligence of the deceased barred claims under the fatal accidents legislation altogether.[281] However, the position was changed by s 1(4) of the Law Reform (Contributory Negligence) Act 1945, which had the same effect as section 5 of the 1976 Act, and was replaced by it. Since the dependant's claim under the 1976 Act is derivative of the wrong done to the deceased, it seems logical to (in effect) attribute the contributory negligence of the latter to the former, although some wrongful death legislation in other jurisdictions does not do this.[282] Another possibility is to allow the dependant to recover in full but to give the defendant a right of contribution against the estate of the deceased. Where the beneficiaries of the estate and the dependants are one and the same, this solution simply replicates the effect of section 5, but it will put the dependants in a better position where they are not the beneficiaries or where the estate is insolvent. This approach does however give rise to some complexity. **3.64**

Where a dependant under the 1976 Act is partly to blame for the death of the deceased the damages which they recover from the defendant will be reduced in proportion to the dependant's responsibility.[283] The fault of one dependant is not however attributed to the others, so that their claims are unaffected,[284] although in such a case the defendant may be able to recover contribution from the negligent dependant. Where both the deceased and a dependant are to blame for the former's death, the relevant deductions must be combined. This would presumably be done by first applying the deduction for the deceased's negligence (as this affects the dependency claim as a whole) and then applying the deduction for the dependant's negligence to their prima facie share of the reduced award. **3.65**

If the damages of a dependant are reduced for the contributory fault of the deceased, then arguably the same approach should be applied where an intended beneficiary under a will suffers loss because of the combined negligence of the solicitor charged with drawing it up and the testator who instructed the solicitor to do so. Strictly speaking, the beneficiary's action against the solicitor as recognized in *White v Jones*[285] is (unlike the dependency claim) for the breach of an independent duty of care. However, there is a derivative aspect to the claim, since the content of the solicitor's obligation is determined by the terms of their contract with the testator, and any exclusion or limitation of liability in that **3.66**

281 *Senior v Ward* (1859) 1 El & El 385, 120 ER 954; *Vincent v Southern Railway* [1927] AC 430 (HL).

282 See Wrongs Act 1958 (Vic) s 26(4); Civil Law (Wrongs) Act 2002 (ACT) s 27(1) (subject to exceptions). New South Wales used to have the same rule (Law Reform (Miscellaneous Provisions) Act 1965 (NSW) s 13), but this was largely abrogated by the Civil Liability Act 2002 (NSW) s 5T.

283 *Mulholland v McCrea* [1961] NI 135 (CA). This seems to follow from the wording of the 1945 Act, as the dependant is bringing the claim in respect of 'damage' (namely, the loss of dependency and/or bereavement) for which they are partly to blame.

284 *Dodds v Dodds* [1978] QB 543 (QBD) (fact that widow to blame for death of husband did not affect dependency claim of son).

285 [1995] 2 AC 207 (HL). See *Winfield & Jolowicz*, para 5-064.

contract will affect the action by the beneficiary.[286] In the analogous case of *Gorham v British Telecommunications plc*,[287] Sir Murray Stuart-Smith held that for this reason the damages recoverable by the third-party beneficiary should be reduced by reference to any contributory negligence on the part of the testator (or equivalent). Pill and Schiemann LJJ preferred to leave the point open, although they saw attractions in Sir Murray's view.

(b) Congenital Disabilities (Civil Liability) Act 1976

3.67 Pursuant to section 1(7) of the Congenital Disabilities (Civil Liability) Act 1976, where a child is born disabled as a result of a pre-natal event which was caused by the defendant's wrongful conduct vis-à-vis one of the child's parents, the damages the child can recover from the defendant under the Act are reduced proportionate to any responsibility which the parent in question bears for the child's disability. Where, as is usually the case, that parent is the child's mother, the child generally cannot sue their mother to recover the shortfall, as the mother herself is exempted from liability under the Act.[288] However, under section 2 of the Act a pregnant woman driving a motor vehicle is to be regarded as owing a duty of care to her unborn child, so that if the child's disability were caused by a road accident for which its mother and a third party were both to blame, the child could recoup any shortfall in the damages obtainable from the third party as a result of section 1(7) from its mother's insurer.

[286] ibid.
[287] [2000] 1 WLR 2129 (CA).
[288] Section 1(1).

4

APPORTIONMENT OF RESPONSIBILITY

We have seen that the Law Reform (Contributory Negligence) Act 1945 replaced the complete defence of contributory negligence with an apportionment regime, whereby a court which has made a finding of contributory negligence reduces the claimant's damages in proportion to their responsibility for the damage.[1] In this chapter we consider the process of apportionment that follows once the existence of contributory negligence has been established. The discussion begins by looking at how the courts fix the sum of damages to which the claimant would be entitled but for the fact of their contributory negligence, before moving on to some general observations on the apportionment exercise, which are followed by consideration of the criteria of apportionment, aggravating and mitigating factors, guideline discounts, the discounts employed, and apportionment in cases involving multiple defendants and absent tortfeasors. **4.01**

Before we turn to the first of those questions, it will be helpful to remind ourselves of the key tenets of the statutory apportionment regime. According to section 1(1) of the 1945 Act: **4.02**

> Where any person suffers damage as a result partly of his own fault and partly of the fault of any other person or persons ... the damages recoverable in respect thereof shall be reduced to such extent as the court thinks just and equitable having regard to the claimant's share in the responsibility for the damage.

As interpreted by the courts,[2] section 4 of the 1945 Act defines 'fault' for *defendants* as meaning 'negligence, breach of statutory duty or other act or omission which gives rise to a liability in tort', and for *claimants* as meaning 'negligence, breach of statutory duty or other act or omission' which would give rise to the defence of contributory negligence at common law. Finally, 'damage' is defined in section 4 as including 'loss of life and personal injury', although it is clear that it also encompasses property damage and pure economic loss.

[1] See 1.17. There is a surprising lack of authority as to whether it is possible to contract out of the apportionment regime and back into the all-or-nothing rule. However, section 1(1) of the 1945 Act is said to operate without prejudice 'to any defence arising under a contract', which might be taken to mean that this can indeed be done.

[2] See 2.03.

Contributory Negligence. Second Edition. James Goudkamp and Donal Nolan, Oxford University Press
 DOI: 10.1093/oso/9780192867919.003.0004

1. The Damages to be Reduced

(1) Introduction

4.03 Applying section 1(1) of the 1945 Act, it is the 'damages recoverable' in respect of the damage for which the claimant was partly to blame that are to be reduced for the claimant's contributory negligence. Section 1(2) requires a court making a deduction for contributory negligence to state the quantum of these recoverable damages. In most cases, it is clear which damages should be the subject of the discount. However, there are some issues that may arise in this regard, and these are considered in the discussion that follows.

4.04 Before we turn to those issues, however, a preliminary point should be made regarding the relationship between the assessment of damages and contributory negligence, as it concerns a sequencing issue that is also relevant to the discussion in the remainder of this section. Sometimes, the fact that the claimant is entitled to a substantial award of damages will have a bearing on how the claimant will be assumed to act in the future, which in turn can affect the quantum of damages that need to be awarded to afford the claimant full compensation. In such a case, should the value of the claimant's claim be assessed for these purposes before or after discounting for contributory negligence? This issue arose in *Sowden v Lodge*,[3] where the claimant was held 50 per cent responsible for her personal injuries on account of her contributory negligence. The defendant argued that, because of the large discount that would be made to her damages as a result, she would be unlikely to be able to afford private medical care for the rest of her life. It followed that it would be more appropriate for the claimant to be cared for in a cheaper, public facility and that hence a lower damages award should be made. This argument was rejected on the basis that the claim had to be valued first and any discount for contributory negligence applied only once the damages to which the claimant would have been entitled but for the contributory negligence had been determined. As Pill LJ explained:[4]

> Damages are to be reduced [under section 1 of the Law Reform (Contributory Negligence) Act 1945] having regard only to the 'claimant's share in the responsibility for the damage'. That assumes an assessment of the sum recoverable prior to any reduction for contributory negligence ... The reduction takes account of share of responsibility for the damage but not how the damages are likely to be spent.

(2) Causally relevant damages

4.05 We saw in chapter 3 that contributory negligence requires a causal link to be established between the fault of the claimant and the damage in respect of which they are suing, and that where that link can be shown for only *some* of that damage, then the discount for contributory negligence will be limited to the damages for that harm.[5] Hence if, for example, the claimant's contributory negligence consisted of not wearing a crash helmet while riding a motorbike, but the defendant was entirely to blame for the road accident in which the claimant was injured, then only the damages for injuries which a helmet

[3] [2004] EWCA Civ 1370, [2005] 1 WLR 2129.
[4] ibid [79].
[5] See 3.50.

would have prevented are reduced on account of the contributory fault.[6] This however assumes that a clear dividing line can be drawn between the damage that was caused by the claimant's contributory negligence and the damage that was not. Where this is not the case, the court will have no option but to apply the discount to the whole of the damages, and to take account of the limited causal role of the claimant's negligence when apportioning responsibility.[7] A similar issue can arise where more than one defendant is involved. In such a case, the court will need to identify for each defendant in turn (1) which part of the damage that defendant caused; (2) whether the claimant's negligence was also a cause of all or part of that damage; and (3) the appropriate apportionment of responsibility for any damage of which the contributory negligence was causative.[8]

(3) Mitigation and avoidable losses

Applying the so-called 'avoidable consequences rule', the defendant is not liable for damage or loss that the claimant could have avoided by taking reasonable care.[9] This is because the law treats such loss as having been caused by the claimant alone. Since no damages are recoverable in respect of such losses, it follows that they are not included in the sum of prima facie damages which is then discounted for contributory negligence. Put in terms of sequencing, the mitigation rule is applied first, and apportionment for contributory negligence second.[10] **4.06**

(4) Collateral benefits

Where the quantum of the claimant's damages falls to be reduced on account of their receipt of a collateral benefit arising out of the tort, then this reduction should be made prior to any discount for contributory negligence being made. This follows from the wording of section 1(1) of the 1945 Act.[11] (The position is of course different if the rule regarding the collateral benefit is a legislative one, and the legislation provides otherwise.) Where no deduction is made from the damages for the collateral benefit, but the source of that benefit is to be reimbursed out of the claimant's damages,[12] any discount applied to **4.07**

---

6 *O'Connell v Jackson* [1972] 1 QB 270 (CA) 277–78.

7 This was in fact the position in *O'Connell* itself.

8 See *Restatement (Third) of Torts: Apportionment of Liability* (2000) § 7, cmt e. For apportionment in cases involving multiple defendants responsible for the same damage, see 4.73–4.75.

9 On the relationship between this rule and the doctrine of contributory negligence, see 5.17–5.21.

10 See EK Cheng et al, 'Sequencing in Damages' (2022) 74 Stanford L Rev 353, 362–63.

11 Although it has also been claimed that reversing this sequence would 'unfairly penalise' the claimant (*Luntz*, para 1.13.12), in the case of collateral benefits the sequencing issue is a complex one. As Cheng et al (n 10) 368–75 point out, the collateral benefit is essentially a windfall and in cases of contributory negligence the sequencing analysis determines how that windfall is distributed between the parties. The way in which it should be distributed is not entirely obvious and the American authorities do not speak with one voice. Having said that, applying the discount for contributory negligence before deducting the collateral benefit has the effect of giving the defendant the entirety of the windfall. And, as Cheng et al observe, although in some situations there may be a good reason to do this, it is generally fairer to divide the windfall between the two parties, which is the effect of the rule set out in the text. (They also point out, however, that the *way* in which that rule divides the windfall rewards the more culpable party, a perverse result to which they propose a somewhat complex solution. It is questionable whether the English courts have the freedom to develop such a solution in the light of the wording of the 1945 Act.)

12 See *Hunt v Severs* [1994] 2 AC 350 (HL).

the damages for contributory negligence should be taken into account when determining the amount of the reimbursement.[13] Unfortunately, provision to similar effect has not been made in the statutory regime for recoupment of social security payments made to the claimant in the first five years after the tort, with the result that the full amount of such payments is deducted from the award of damages for lost earnings before any discount is made for contributory negligence, and then recouped by the state from the defendant.[14] As Tony Weir points out, this means that a contributorily negligent claimant who has been in receipt of social security 'may be left with little or nothing (apart from his (reduced) damages for pain and suffering and loss of amenity)'.[15]

(5) Limitations of liability

4.08 Contractual clauses or notices that limit the defendant's liability are given effect according to their proper interpretation unless they are rendered unenforceable by statute.[16] An issue that arises in connection with such provisions is whether they fall to be applied before or after the contributory negligence doctrine. Suppose that D contracts with C that, if C has a claim against D, D's damages will be capped at £1m. And suppose that C has a claim against D in respect of a loss of £1.5m, but that C is guilty of contributory negligence, which is held to merit a 50 per cent reduction being made to his damages. In such a case, is C entitled to damages of £500,000 or £750,000? The better view is that any such clause falls to be applied before any discount for contributory negligence is made, unless the clause provides otherwise. In our example, therefore, C should be entitled to £500,000. This is because the discount is to be applied to the 'damages recoverable' in respect of the relevant damage, and the limitation clause operates to limit the damages that are recoverable in the first place.

4.09 Unfortunately, what little authority there is on this issue takes a contrary view, the logic of which is unclear. In an *ex tempore* judgment in *Natixis SA v Marex Financial Ltd*[17] Bryan J held that the discount for contributory negligence was to be applied to what he called the 'basic loss' (ie the actual loss suffered by the claimant), and then any limitation of liability provision should be applied to the discounted figure. With respect, the learned judge appears to have been led into error in this regard by a misreading of the 1945 Act, coupled with confusion engendered by the difficult decision of a majority of the House of Lords in *Platform Home Loans Ltd v Oyston Shipways Ltd*.[18] As regards the statutory wording, Bryan J focused only on the opening words of section 1(1), and the reference to 'damage' there (which he took to mean the 'basic loss'), apparently overlooking the fact that the discount is not to be applied to the 'damage' but to the 'damages recoverable thereof', which would of course be limited by the limitation clause.[19] A similar mistake appears

---

[13] The same rule applies in Australia in cases where a plaintiff is under a statutory obligation to reimburse a collateral source: see *Luntz*, para 1.13.12.

[14] Social Security (Recovery of Benefits) Act 1997. See further, 6.20.

[15] T Weir, *An Introduction to Tort Law* (2nd edn, OUP 2006) 128. Nor is there an offset for contributory negligence for the *defendant*, with the result that even if the damages after the discount are less than the social security payments made, the defendant must reimburse the state for the full amount of those payments.

[16] Unfair Contract Terms Act 1977, Pt 1; Consumer Rights Act 2015, Pt 2.

[17] [2019] EWHC 3163 (Comm).

[18] [2000] 2 AC 190 (HL). See 4.13–4.14.

[19] Bryan J was fortified in this interpretation by the fact that s 1(1)(b) of the Act provides that where any contract or enactment providing for limitation of liability is applicable to the claim, the amount of damages

to have been made by counsel in another case, cited by Bryan J, where it was conceded that the limitation cap should be applied to the award after discounting for contributory negligence rather than before.[20]

(6) Jurisdictional limits and legislative caps on damages

In *Kelly v Stockport Corp*,[21] a claim was brought in a court the jurisdiction of which was limited to £200, with the claimant claiming that maximum figure. The trial judge found that the claim was worth £300 but that the claimant was guilty of contributory negligence sufficient to warrant reducing the damages by one-third. On appeal, it was unanimously held that the claimant could recover only £133 (being two-thirds of £200) rather than £200 (being two-thirds of £300). Since the jurisdictional limit of the court meant that the claimant could not recover more than £200, those were the 'damages recoverable' under the 1945 Act. Glanville Williams objected to this approach on the ground that a claimant who, perhaps for reasons of procedural convenience, sues in a court of limited jurisdiction and thereby waives the right to claim for any sum in excess of the court's jurisdiction should at least be entitled to recover 'all that the court is entitled to award him under the Contributory Negligence Act'.[22] He suggested that legislation should be introduced to provide that jurisdictional limits of inferior courts should apply not to the claimant's total damages but to the sum actually recoverable. It appears that this outcome has been achieved through judicial decisions in Canada,[23] though it is doubtful whether this solution is open to the UK courts in the light of the wording of the apportionment legislation. **4.10**

When it comes to legislative caps on damages, such as the limits on claims for non-pecuniary losses which apply in many American and Australian states, the answer to the question of whether to apply the cap or the discount for contributory negligence first should in principle be governed by the proper construction of the legislative provision in question.[24] Suppose, for example, that a damages cap of £100m is imposed on negligence claims against auditors so that auditors can obtain adequate insurance cover.[25] Here the law **4.11**

recovered by the claimant by virtue of s 1(1) shall not exceed the maximum applicable amount. However, this provision has nothing to do with the sequencing point. The intention behind it was merely to make it clear that apportionment was not supposed to override any contractual limitation altogether. On the background to this provision and its companion provision (s 1(1)(a)), see J Steele, 'Law Reform (Contributory Negligence) Act 1945: Collisions of a Different Sort' in TT Arvind and J Steele (eds), *Tort Law and the Legislature: Common Law, Statute and the Dynamics of Legal Change* (Hart Publishing 2012) 182–83, who says that the goal of the drafters in including these contractual provisos 'was to ensure that apportionment . . . disturbed neither the law of contract, nor the bargains of the contracting parties'.

[20] See *Newcastle International Airport Ltd v Eversheds LLP* [2012] EWHC 2648 (Ch) [135]–[137]. The point was not in fact in issue as no finding of contributory negligence was made.

[21] [1949] 1 All ER 893 (CA).

[22] *Williams*, 396.

[23] See JC Kleefeld, 'The Contributory Negligence Act at Seventy' (2015) 78 Sask LR 31, 54 fn 113 and cases cited therein.

[24] See Cheng et al (n 10) 367. For an example of a legislative rule analogous to a damages cap which is clearly worded in this respect, see Consumer Protection Act 1987, s 5(4) ('No damages shall be awarded . . . *if the amount which would fall to be so awarded* . . . does not exceed £275' (emphasis added)). In the case of this provision, it is obvious from the wording that the lower limit is to be applied after any discount for contributory negligence is made.

[25] For an example of a (global) damages limit based on insurability concerns, see the optional cap of 70 million ECU in Article 16(1) of Council Directive 85/874/EEC on liability for defective products.

is concerned with the quantum of the final award, which should not exceed the maximum sum recoverable under an insurance policy entered into in the light of the cap. It follows that in this case the better view is that any discount for contributory negligence should be made *before* the cap is applied. (It is questionable, however, whether this approach would be consistent with the reference in the apportionment legislation to the discount being made to the 'damages recoverable', since these are capped at £100m.) By contrast, a statutory limit on claims for non-pecuniary losses can best be understood as the legislature putting a maximum value on such losses, in which case the cap is directed not at the quantum of the final award but at the assessment of prima facie damages that occurs prior to apportionment for contributory negligence. In this case, therefore, the better view is that the discount for contributory negligence should be made *after* the cap is applied.

(7) The *SAAMCO* principle

4.12 The so-called '*SAAMCO* principle'[26] dictates that a defendant is liable only for loss or damage that it was their duty to prevent. Suppose, for example, that a lender suffers loss because the value of the property against which a loan is secured is insufficient to discharge the liability of a defaulting borrower, which is the result of the property having been negligently overvalued. Applying the *SAAMCO* principle, the lender can recover from the valuer the whole of the loss flowing from his entry into the loan transaction, *except for loss that he would still have suffered had the valuation been accurate*. Another way of putting this is to say that the damages awarded to the lender cannot exceed the difference between the inaccurate valuation given by the valuer and the amount of an accurate valuation. Let us imagine, for example, that C makes a loan of £900,000 to X on the security of a property valued by D at £1m when an accurate valuation would have been £800,000. When, on X's default, the property is sold, it realizes only £500,000 because of a general fall in the market. C's total loss from entering into the loan is £400,000 but D's liability is only £200,000 because the balance of £200,000 is the loss which C would have suffered even if the valuation had been accurate (or, put differently, because C's losses are capped at the difference between the inaccurate valuation and an accurate one, which is £200,000).

4.13 In *Platform Home Loans Ltd v Oyston Shipways Ltd*[27] the issue arose as to the relationship between the *SAAMCO* principle and the doctrine of contributory negligence. Suppose now that in our example C was guilty of contributory negligence in the order of 25 per cent because C should have realized that X would be unable to service the loan. The actual loss suffered by C is £400,000. However, the recoverable loss (applying *SAAMCO*) is £200,000. If the discount for contributory negligence is applied to the total loss (reducing it to £300,000), and the *SAAMCO* cap is applied *subsequently*, then C recovers £200,000. By contrast, if the discount is applied to the recoverable loss of £200,000, then C recovers only £150,000. Since the discount is to be applied to the 'damages recoverable' under section 1(1), it seems rather obvious that the latter is the correct approach. However, in the *Platform Home Loans* case a majority of the House of Lords (Lord Cooke dissenting) held that the discount for contributory negligence should be applied to the *total* loss and not to

[26] After the decision in *South Australia Asset Management Corp v York Montague Ltd* [1997] AC 191 (HL).
[27] [2000] 2 AC 190 (HL).

the *recoverable* loss. According to Lord Hobhouse, for example, 'the traditional percentage reduction' should be applied to the lender's 'basic loss [ie total loss] before making any further deduction on account' of the *SAAMCO* principle.[28] It is not surprising that this decision has been widely criticized.[29]

The reasoning of Lord Hobhouse and Lord Millett for the majority in *Platform Home Loans* is not always easy to follow. However, it seems to rest on the assumption that there is something unusual about the *SAAMCO* principle, such that it places an artificial limit on the liability of defendants in cases in which it applies,[30] which it would not be 'just and equitable' to compound by applying the discount for contributory negligence to the damages recoverable in the light of the principle. This assumption is however hard to square with two recent Supreme Court decisions in which it has been emphasized that the *SAAMCO* analysis is entirely orthodox, and that the '*SAAMCO* cap' is merely a working through of the implications of that orthodoxy.[31] In our view *SAAMCO* is indeed orthodox, and best understood as a straightforward application of ordinary remoteness principles.[32] On that alternative understanding the *Platform Home Loans* decision seems (with respect) to be clearly incorrect, since it is not in doubt that in other cases where the claimant has suffered losses that are too remote, any discount for contributory negligence is made only to the damages in respect of the non-remote losses.[33] Three further points can be made. One is that it is questionable whether it was appropriate of the majority in *Platform Home Loans* to seek to justify their decision by reference to the words 'just and equitable' in section 1(1) of the 1945 Act, since the courts have generally eschewed any notion that those words confer on them an open-ended discretion as to how they should proceed when apportioning damages.[34] The second point is that Lord Hobhouse placed weight on the fact that the claimant in one of the appeals heard by the House of Lords in the *SAAMCO* case itself had been contributorily negligent, and Lord Hoffmann had applied 'the percentage reduction ... to the lender's basic loss ... not to the cap'.[35] With respect, it is difficult to understand why Lord Hobhouse considered that this lent weight to his view on the sequencing issue, since in the appeal in question the 'basic loss' was *less than* the '*SAAMCO* cap', so it was obviously the basic loss figure which was discounted for contributory negligence (the discount was hardly going to be applied to a figure greater than any conceivable measure of the loss suffered by the claimant) and the sequencing **4.14**

[28] ibid 212.

[29] See, eg, the notes on the case by J Stapleton (1999) 115 LQR 527; D McLauchlan [1999] LMCLQ 355; and D Howarth (2000) 8 Tort L Rev 85.

[30] See also *Clerk & Lindsell*, para 3-103 (referring to the 'artificial *SAAMCO* cap' in an apparent defence of the *Platform Home Loans* decision).

[31] See *Hughes-Holland v BPE Solicitors* [2017] UKSC 21, [2018] AC 599; *Manchester Building Society v Grant Thornton UK LLP* [2021] UKSC 20, [2022] AC 783.

[32] See D Nolan and J Plunkett, 'Keeping Negligence Simple' (2022) 138 LQR 175. Admittedly, in the two cases referred to in the previous footnote a majority of the Supreme Court chose to classify the *SAAMCO* principle as one going to the scope of the duty owed, rather than remoteness. However, for present purposes what matters is that the Justices considered *SAAMCO* to be an application of general negligence principles, and not which particular principle they considered it to be an application of.

[33] See R Stevens, 'Should Contributory Fault be Analogue or Digital?' in A Dyson et al (eds), *Defences in Tort* (Hart Publishing 2015) 261; *Todd*, 1163.

[34] See 4.23, 4.29–4.36, 4.60–4.66.

[35] *Platform Home Loans Ltd v Oyston Shipways Ltd* [2000] 2 AC 190 (HL) 208.

question was therefore irrelevant. And finally, it should be noted that the approach taken in *Platform Home Loans* produces the somewhat bizarre result that, in the example used in the previous paragraph, the lender C, despite being held 25 per cent to blame for their losses, recovers precisely the same amount as if they had not been at fault at all.

(8) Aggravated and punitive damages

4.15 While the basic principle that compensatory damages are to be reduced for contributory negligence is not in doubt, the position is less clear in relation to other types of damages. There is, for example, no authority as to whether aggravated damages are amenable to reduction for contributory negligence. Cases which raise this issue are likely to be rare, but given that aggravated damages are compensatory in nature,[36] there is no reason in principle why they should not be reduced by reference to the claimant's contributory fault.

4.16 There is also little English authority on the relationship between the doctrine of contributory negligence and awards of punitive damages. This is no doubt attributable to the fact that the torts for which such awards are most frequently made[37] (such as battery, false imprisonment and deceit) are not causes of action to which the doctrine of contributory negligence applies.[38] It may also be linked to the fact that punitive damages will generally not be awarded where the claimant was partly to blame for what happened.[39] Although commentators have argued that the apportionment legislation is 'capable of encompassing exemplary damages',[40] the better view is that awards of punitive damages should *not* be amenable to reduction for contributory negligence. After all, under section 1(1) of the 1945 Act discounts for contributory negligence are to be applied to the *damages recoverable in respect of the damage*, which would seem to imply damages intended to compensate the claimant for loss suffered, rather than damages intended to punish the defendant. Furthermore, because punitive damages are awarded to punish the defendant, the quantum of the award is set with that goal in mind. And once the court has decided on a sum deemed appropriate for that purpose, it makes little sense to reduce that sum to reflect the claimant's partial responsibility for the damage. It is therefore unsurprising that in an Australian case in which punitive damages were awarded the judge simply assumed that they did not fall to be reduced for the plaintiff's contributory negligence,[41] and that in the United States there is 'nearly uniform case law' to the same effect.[42]

---

[36] Aggravated damages 'are primarily to be awarded to compensate the plaintiff for injury to his proper pride and dignity and the consequences of his being humiliated': *Thompson v Commissioner of Police of the Metropolis* [1998] QB 498 (CA) 512 (Lord Woolf MR).

[37] See J Goudkamp and E Katsampouka, 'An Empirical Study of Punitive Damages' (2018) 38 OJLS 90.

[38] See chapter 2.

[39] *Thompson v Commissioner of Police of the Metropolis* [1998] QB 498 (CA) 518.

[40] M Tilbury and H Luntz, 'Punitive Damages in Australian Law' (1995) 17 Loy LA Int'l & Comp LJ 769, 790. See also Law Commission, *Aggravated, Exemplary and Restitutionary Damages* (Law Com No 247, 1997) 81 fn 475 (arguable that the 1945 Act applies to awards of punitive damages).

[41] *Ali v Hartley Poynton Ltd* [2002] VSC 113, [2002] Aust Torts Reports 81–665.

[42] *Restatement (Third) of Torts: Apportionment of Liability* (2000) § 7, cmt l. See also *Woods and Deere*, 165–66.

2. The Apportionment Exercise Generally

(1) Introduction

Once the sum of recoverable damages has been calculated, section 1(1) of the 1945 Act instructs the court to reduce those damages to such extent as the court thinks just and equitable having regard to the claimant's share in the responsibility for the damage. The procedure pursuant to which the court arrives at the appropriate discount has been determined by judicial convention. According to that convention, the court first assesses the claimant's share of responsibility for the damage as a percentage. The court then reduces the claimant's damages by the percentage of responsibility that it has assigned to him or her. This approach assumes that the claimant's share of responsibility for the damage is the sole consideration that the judge should take into account when assessing what discount from the claimant's damages would be 'just and equitable'. As Patrick Atiyah pointed out,[43] this approach does not necessarily follow from the legislative wording. After all, the fact that a judge must 'have regard to' the claimant's share of responsibility does not preclude the possibility that the judge might have regard to other considerations as well. Nevertheless, it is clear that in general the courts have given these words a more restrictive interpretation, and besides it is not entirely obvious which other considerations it would be appropriate for them to take into account.[44] **4.17**

(2) Is making no discount at all permissible?

Some uncertainty exists as to whether the courts are entitled to refuse to discount the damages once a finding of contributory negligence has been made.[45] On the one hand, the language of the 1945 Act seems to be imperative in this regard ('the damages shall be reduced'). On the other hand, the statute requires the court to reduce the damages 'to such extent as the court thinks just and equitable', and it can be argued that a court might legitimately conclude that any contributory negligence is *de minimis* such that it is not just and equitable to make any reduction at all. There are conflicting judicial statements on the issue. In *Boothman v British Northrop Ltd*, Stephenson LJ held that the wording of the Act did not permit a court not to reduce the claimant's damages once a finding of contributory negligence had been made,[46] a sentiment with which Stanley Burnton J concurred in *Badger v Ministry of Defence*.[47] However, the weight of authority is the other way. There are many examples of judges assuming that, were they to make a finding of contributory negligence, it would then be open to them to make no reduction in the claimant's damages.[48] Most of **4.18**

---

43 PS Atiyah, 'Causation, Contributory Negligence and Volenti Non Fit Injuria' (1965) 43 Can Bar Rev 609, 614–15.

44 ibid.

45 Compare *Williams*, 392–93 and *Harder*, 142 (courts entitled to do this) with *Munkman*, para 6.15 (courts not entitled to do this).

46 (1972) 13 KIR 112 (CA) 121–22.

47 [2005] EWHC 2941 (QB), [2006] 3 All ER 173 [15].

48 See, eg, *Hawkins v Ian Ross (Castings) Ltd* [1970] 1 All ER 180 (QBD) 188; *Stocker v Norprint Ltd* (1970) 10 KIR 10 (CA) 14; *Vacwell Engineering Co Ltd v BDH Chemicals Ltd* [1971] 1 QB 88 (QBD) 110; *Cullip v Horsham DC* 1981 WL 687310 (CA); *Sahib Foods Ltd v Paskin KyriaKides Sands (a firm)* [2003] EWCA Civ 1832, [2004] PNLR 22 [69]; *Corr v IBC Vehicles Ltd* [2008] UKHL 13, [2008] AC 884 [22], [44]; *St George v Home Office* [2008] EWCA Civ 1068, [2009] 1 WLR 1670 [60]–[63]; *Haughton v Patel* [2017] EWHC 2316 (QB) [98].

the relevant remarks are dicta, but in *Pankhurst v White*[49] no discount was made despite a finding of contributory negligence. The claimant was a cyclist who suffered injury after a collision with a car driven by the defendant, who was unlicensed and uninsured. Wilkie J found the defendant liable but also held that the claimant had been guilty of contributory negligence for cycling too fast. However, he refused to reduce the damages, on the ground that the claimant's share in the responsibility for his damage was negligible.

(3) Is a 100 per cent discount permissible?

4.19 A not dissimilar issue arises at the other end of the apportionment scale, which is whether it is permissible for a judge to reduce the claimant's damages to nil by making a 100 per cent discount for contributory negligence. This possibility seems clearly to be inconsistent with the apportionment legislation, since it amounts to a finding that the claimant was entirely responsible for their damage, and yet no question of apportionment arises under section 1(1) of the 1945 Act unless the damage was the result partly of the fault of the claimant and partly of the fault of the defendant. It follows that where the court considers that the claimant was entirely responsible for the damage the only course open to it is to find that the defendant is not liable at all. Despite this, for a time the courts insisted on their power to impose a discount of 100 per cent.[50] However, it has now been confirmed by the Court of Appeal in *Anderson v Newham College of Further Education* that such a discount is impermissible. According to Sedley LJ, if the evidence shows that the entire fault lies with the claimant then there is no liability on the defendant. And if there is liability, then 'contributory negligence can reduce its monetary quantification, but it cannot legally or logically nullify it'.[51]

4.20 It has been argued that the courts should be allowed to impose a discount of 100 per cent for contributory negligence because 'there may be cases in which the plaintiff's relative responsibility for the injuries suffered is so great that it seems fair to deny the plaintiff any damages at all'.[52] But while the premise of this argument can readily be accepted, the conclusion drawn from it cannot. It may indeed sometimes be fair to deny the claimant any damages because their responsibility for the damage is so much greater than any responsibility of the defendant. However, this can be done (and sometimes is done) by finding that the defendant's fault was not a legal cause of the damage.[53] It is

[49] [2006] EWHC 2093 (Admin).

[50] *ICI Ltd v Shatwell* [1965] AC 656 (HL) 672; *McMullen v National Coal Board* [1982] ICR 148 (QBD) 154–55; *Jayes v IMI (Kynoch) Ltd* [1985] ICR 155 (CA) 159; *Reeves v Commissioner of Police of the Metropolis* [1999] QB 169 (CA) 195; *McEwan v Lothian Buses plc* [2006] CSOH 56, 2006 SCLR 592 [32]–[35]. In Australia, state legislation often authorizes a court to make a finding of 100 per cent contributory negligence: see, eg, Civil Liability Act 2002 (NSW) s 5S.

[51] [2002] EWCA Civ 505, [2003] ICR 212 [19]. See similarly, *Pitts v Hunt* [1991] 1 QB 24 (CA) 50; *Wynbergen v Hoyts Corp Pty Ltd* (1997) 72 ALJR 65 (HCA); *Buyukardicli v Hammerson UK Properties plc* [2002] EWCA Civ 683 [7]; *Brumder v Motornet Service and Repairs Ltd* [2013] EWCA Civ 195, [2013] 1 WLR 2783 [4].

[52] Commonwealth of Australia, *Review of the Law of Negligence: Final Report* (2002) para 8.24. *Harder* (143–44) also favours the permissibility of 100 per cent discounts and argues that they are consistent with the wording of the 1945 Act.

[53] See 5.02–5.07.

therefore unnecessary, as well as incoherent, to make a finding of 100 per cent contributory negligence.

(4) A comparative exercise

The apportionment process requires the court to compare the claimant's share of responsibility with that of the defendant. It is therefore impermissible to look at the fault of one of the parties in isolation. As Hale LJ explained in *Eagle v Chambers*, the apportionment provision 'is premised on both parties being at fault' and, as such:[54] **4.21**

> It is ... impossible to consider the claimant's 'share' [of responsibility] without also considering that of the defendant. Moreover, the court has to do what is 'just and equitable' which includes being fair to the claimant as well as to the defendant. Realistically, therefore the court has to compare the one with the other.

Because the apportionment exercise involves comparing the responsibility of both parties, the same act of contributory negligence may attract quite different discounts in different cases depending on the defendant's degree of responsibility. Moreover, in theory, a claimant who is guilty of a minor fault may be met with a higher discount than a claimant who is guilty of more serious negligence if in the former case the defendant's conduct is less culpable and/or causally potent.

(5) A discretionary exercise

The apportionment exercise is also a discretionary one.[55] As Lord Wright said in a maritime collision case:[56] **4.22**

> [Apportionment of responsibility is a] question, not of principle or of positive findings of fact or law, but of proportion, of balance and relative emphasis, and of weighing different considerations. It involves an individual choice or discretion, as to which there may well be differences of opinion by different minds.

The reasons why apportionment should be discretionary were set out by the 'Ipp Panel' in its report for the governments of Australia on possible changes to the tort system in that country:[57]

> [C]ontributory negligence come[s] in an infinite variety of forms. From one case to another, the respective culpability of the plaintiff and defendant, and their relative causal contributions to the death or injury may differ widely. ... The Panel considers that any fettering of judicial discretion to apportion damages for contributory negligence is undesirable.

The discretionary nature of apportionment explains its description as 'a matter of individual judicial impression',[58] and as an 'art and not a science'.[59] It also explains why, as Lord Reed

---

[54] [2003] EWCA Civ 1107, [2004] RTR 9 [14].

[55] See generally, J Goudkamp, 'Apportionment for Contributory Negligence: A Fixed or Discretionary Approach?' (2015) 35 LS 621.

[56] *British Fame (Owners) v Macgregor (Owners)* [1943] AC 197 (HL) 201.

[57] Commonwealth of Australia, *Review of the Law of Negligence: Final Report* (2002) para 8.16.

[58] *Hughes-Jukes v Etti* [2006] EWHC 2493 (QB), [2007] RTR 2 [31] (Holland J).

[59] *Powell v Hansen* 2001 WL 753470 (QBD) [131] (Mr Recorder Thorn QC). See also *Woods v Police Service of Northern Ireland* [2009] NIQB 35 [38] (McCloskey J) ('the court is not required to engage in a scientific exercise').

said in *Jackson v Murray*, '[i]t is not possible for a court to arrive at an apportionment which is demonstrably correct'.[60] The *Jackson v Murray* case itself shows how judges can arrive at very different discounts on the same facts.[61] At first instance the damages awarded to a child who had run in front of an oncoming vehicle were reduced by 90 per cent.[62] On appeal, the Inner House of the Court of Session lowered the discount to 70 per cent.[63] And on a second appeal a bare majority of the Supreme Court lowered it further to 50 per cent, although two of the five Justices dissented, as they would not have interfered with the decision of the Inner House.[64]

4.23 Although the discretionary nature of the apportionment exercise clearly gives trial judges a great deal of freedom when fixing the discount for contributory negligence, section 1(1) of the 1945 Act does place some limits on that freedom by stipulating that the discretion must be exercised having regard to 'the claimant's share in the responsibility for the damage'. Since the courts have generally interpreted this instruction to mean that the claimant's share of responsibility is the sole basis on which they should arrive at the appropriate discount,[65] it follows that certain facts are necessarily excluded from consideration. For example, in the light of this instruction it would be wrong for the court to attach weight to the fact that the claimant risked the defendant's safety or the safety of third parties, since that does not relate to the claimant's share in the responsibility *for the damage*, by which is meant the damage suffered by the claimant.

(6) Relevance of other cases

4.24 The discretionary nature of the apportionment exercise, coupled with the fact that it involves a comparison of the parties' respective shares of responsibility, means that the discount imposed in any single case is not, in principle, immediately relevant to the discount that should be imposed in another case. Accordingly, judges sometimes remark that being referred to other apportionment decisions is of 'limited assistance'[66] or 'not ... particularly helpful'[67] because they are all 'fact-specific'.[68] It has been said, for example, that 'it will seldom be appropriate to choose a figure for contributory negligence as between two vehicles in a road traffic accident solely by reference to an assessment in another case, even if that case bears points of similarity with the case under consideration'.[69] Nevertheless, it is

[60] *Jackson v Murray* [2015] UKSC 5, [2015] 2 All ER 805 [27]. See also at [46].

[61] See also *Watt v Bretag* (1982) 41 ALR 597 (HCA), where the discounts different judges would have imposed were 15 per cent (two judges); 33.3 per cent (one judge); 40 per cent (three judges); and 50 per cent (two judges). Wide variations were also observed when study participants were given the same set of facts and asked to apportion responsibility between two culpable parties: see AM Votruba, 'Dividing Responsibility: The Role of the Psychology of Attribution' (2020) 69 DePaul L Rev 721, 744.

[62] *Jackson v Murray* [2012] CSOH 100, 2012 SCLR 605.

[63] [2012] CSIH 100, 2013 SCLR 429.

[64] [2015] UKSC 5, [2015] 2 All ER 805.

[65] See 4.17.

[66] *Lightfoot v Go-Ahead Group plc* [2011] EWHC 89 (QB), [2011] RTR 27 [51] (McCombe J). See also *Jackson v Murray* [2015] UKSC 5, [2015] 2 All ER 805 [50] (Lord Hodge) ('little assistance').

[67] *Sahakian v McDonnell* [2007] EWHC 3242 (QB), [2008] RTR 19 [17] (HHJ Foster QC).

[68] *Tavares v Hudson-Rotin* [2012] EWHC 3171 (QB) [49] (Globe J).

[69] *Wagner v Grant* [2016] CSIH 34, 2016 SLT 699 [40] (Lord Menzies).

not uncommon for judges to refer extensively to discounts imposed in other cases,[70] often to reinforce a conclusion to which the judge was already attracted. Christopher Clarke J summarized the approach that the courts take as follows:[71]

> Every case depends on its own facts and limited guidance is to be found in the apportionment determined in other cases with different facts. At the same time, some guidance may be drawn from the approach which the court has taken in cases with features similar to [the proceedings at hand].

(7) Different discounts in respect of different time periods

Where the conduct constituting contributory negligence is of long duration, different apportionments of responsibility may be made in respect of different periods of time. For example, in *Barings plc (in liq) v Coopers & Lybrand (a firm)*,[72] Evans-Lombe J fixed the claimant's responsibility at 50 per cent, 60 per cent, and 80 per cent in relation to three temporal windows spread over around eighteen months. **4.25**

(8) Third-party cases

Where the claimant's damages are to be reduced because of the contributory negligence of a third party (such as an employee) with whom the claimant is identified for this purpose,[73] it is the third party's share in the responsibility for the damage that is taken into account, and not the claimant's.[74] Similarly, where the liability of the defendant is vicarious, then for the purpose of weighing the relative culpability of the parties, it is the primary tortfeasor's conduct which is relevant.[75] Having said that, in a case of the latter kind it is possible that the defendant was also guilty of personal fault, and where that fault was tortious—so that, for example, an employer is liable for the same damage both personally and vicariously—then the defendant's personal fault should be taken into account when apportioning responsibility.[76] By contrast, where there is some faulty conduct on the part of a vicariously liable defendant which does not amount to a wrong against the claimant, the better view is that the court should not take it into account when apportioning responsibility, since it does not amount to 'fault' for the purposes of the 1945 Act.[77] **4.26**

(9) Counterclaims

Where, for example, two vehicles collide and both drivers are at fault, a claim and a counterclaim may well be brought. Since the word 'claim' in section 1(1) of the 1945 Act obviously encompasses counterclaims, a finding of contributory negligence will inevitably be made against both parties. Where this is the case, the apportionment in the initial **4.27**

[70] See, eg, *Lunt v Khelifa* [2001] All ER (D) 428 (QBD); *McCreery v Letson* [2015] CSOH 153 [78]; *Buck v Ainslie* [2017] CSOH 73 [99]–[103].

[71] *Toropdar v D* [2009] EWHC 2997 (TCC) [16] (Christopher Clarke J).

[72] [2003] EWHC 1319 (Ch) [1069].

[73] See 3.53–3.67.

[74] See *Restatement (Third) of Torts: Apportionment of Liability* (2000) § 7, cmt j.

[75] See PS Atiyah, *Vicarious Liability in the Law of Torts* (Butterworths 1967) 408.

[76] ibid 408–409.

[77] On the meaning of 'fault' in the Act, see 2.03.

claim will almost certainly be the mirror image of the apportionment in the counterclaim. Thus, if the claimant is held to be 75 per cent responsible for the damage for the purposes of the claim against the defendant, then the defendant will very likely be held to be 25 per cent responsible for the damage in the counterclaim. According to Hale LJ, while in cases of this kind 'one might not wish to rule out the possibility that there might be an exceptional case in which different apportionments were possible, no one has yet thought of an example where this would be so'.[78] In one case involving a claim and counterclaim, *Black v McCabe*,[79] the jury reduced the claimant's damages by 31 per cent,[80] and then reduced the defendant's damages on the counterclaim by 25 per cent. The verdict was set aside on the ground that the shares of responsibility assigned to the two parties must add up to 100 per cent.

4.28 The same issue is raised by cases where two employees are injured in an accident which is the fault of both (and of no-one else). Is it open to a court in a case of this kind to impose discounts on the two employees that do not add up to 100 per cent? In *ICI Ltd v Shatwell*, the House of Lords did not have to deal with this question because liability was denied altogether on the ground that the employees were *volenti*. However, Lord Pearce was clearly troubled by the point, observing:[81]

> Apportionment of loss through contributory negligence ... is of no avail in solving this problem. For if one man is held, owing to his greater fault, entitled only to twenty per cent of his loss, then as a general rule, the other must be entitled to eighty per cent of his loss; and the total result would still offend against common sense.

It is not entirely clear why Lord Pearce thought that this result would 'offend against common sense'. One possibility is that his view of the situation was coloured by the fact that the actual defendant in both claims was the employer, which was entirely free from fault. We have just seen, however, that in principle the fact that the defendant's liability is vicarious is irrelevant to the apportionment exercise, where what matters is the share of responsibility of the employee or employees for whose torts the employer is liable.[82] Another possibility is a feeling that—as Atiyah puts it—in such a case 'each party was primarily responsible for his own injury, and that although the other may have contributed something, this was only a small, perhaps negligible factor'.[83] However, even if Atiyah is right that 'one feels that a person may be more responsible in relation to his own injuries than he is in relation to the injuries of the other party',[84] the law (as he concedes) has clearly set its face against this idea. As the law stands, therefore, the assumption that on the facts of a case like *Shatwell* the shares of responsibility of the two employees will add up to 100 per cent seems sound.

[78] *Eagle v Chambers* [2003] EWCA Civ 1107, [2004] RTR 9 [15].
[79] [1964] NI 1 (CA).
[80] The explanation for this rather bizarre deduction is that the jury decided to reduce the damages *to* a round figure (£1000) rather than *by* a round figure (such as 30 per cent).
[81] [1965] AC 656 (HL) 684.
[82] See 4.26.
[83] Atiyah (n 43) 615.
[84] ibid.

3. The Criteria of Apportionment

(1) The twin criteria

In the earliest apportionment regime in English law, for collisions at sea, apportionment was based solely on the 'fault' of the vessels involved.[85] By contrast, the Law Reform (Contributory Negligence) Act 1945 Act uses the word 'responsibility', and this was understood by the courts as an invitation to take into account causation as well as culpability. Hence in a case decided shortly after the passage of the Act, Denning LJ remarked that apportionment of responsibility involved 'a consideration not only of the causative potency of a particular factor, but also of its blameworthiness'.[86] And in *Stapley v Gypsum Mines Ltd*, Lord Reid said:[87] **4.29**

> A court must deal broadly with the problem of apportionment and in considering what is just and equitable must have regard to the blameworthiness of each party, but 'the claimant's share in the responsibility for the damage' cannot, I think, be assessed without considering the relative importance of his acts in causing the damage apart from his blameworthiness.

These twin criteria of relative culpability and relative causal potency (or variations thereon) are also employed in most other common law jurisdictions when apportioning responsibility for contributory negligence,[88] as well as being used by the English courts when apportioning responsibility between wrongdoers in contribution proceedings.[89]

The twin criteria are flexible tools, and, as Lord Walker observed in *Corr v IBC Vehicles Ltd*, they 'are not precise or mutually exclusive tests'.[90] It follows that it can sometimes be difficult to draw a clear distinction between the two;[91] indeed, in *Starks v Chief Constable of Hertfordshire*[92] Underhill LJ said that on the facts no such distinction could be made. And it also follows that a given consideration may relate to both criteria and that 'the overall assessment of responsibility should not be affected' by the heading under which a particular consideration is taken into account.[93] An example of a consideration that may be difficult to pigeon-hole in this regard is the fact that the defendant was under a duty to prevent the very act that amounted to contributory negligence.[94] **4.30**

---

[85] Maritime Conventions Act 1911, s 1 (see now Merchant Shipping Act 1995, s 187(1)).

[86] *Davies v Swan Motor Co* [1949] 2 KB 291 (CA) 326.

[87] [1953] AC 663 (HL) 682.

[88] See, eg, *Podrebersek v Australian Iron and Steel Pty Ltd* (1985) 59 ALJR 492 (HCA) 494. In the United States, whether causal factors should play a role at the apportionment stage is controversial, but the view that both fault and causal contribution are relevant is adopted by the *Restatement (Third) of Torts: Apportionment of Liability* (2000) § 8, and by 'most of the cases' (*Woods and Deere*, 119). By contrast, in Canada apportionment is based solely on relative culpability, largely because of the wording of the apportionment statutes: see J Goudkamp and L Klar, 'Apportionment of Damages for Contributory Negligence: The Causal Potency Principle' (2016) 53 Alta L Rev 1, 10–11. However, the Law Reform Commission of Manitoba recommended that the legislation there be amended so as to base apportionment on both blameworthiness and causation: *Contributory Fault: The Tortfeasors and Contributory Negligence Act* (Report No 128, 2013) 11–12.

[89] *Brian Warwicker Partnership plc v HOK International Ltd* [2005] EWCA Civ 962, 103 Con LR 112 [37].

[90] [2008] UKHL 13, [2008] 1 AC 884.

[91] See *Rehill v Rider Holdings Ltd* [2012] EWCA Civ 628, [2013] RTR 5 [30].

[92] [2013] EWCA Civ 782 [17].

[93] *Jackson v Murray* [2015] UKSC 5, [2015] 2 All ER 805 [40] (Lord Reed).

[94] For cases where this factor was taken into account at the apportionment stage, see, eg, *Mullard v Ben Line Steamers* [1970] 1 WLR 1414 (CA); *McGuinness v Key Markets Ltd* (1972) 13 KIR 249 (CA).

4.31 One facet of the flexibility inherent in the use of the twin criteria is that they need not be accorded equal weight in the apportionment exercise. In *Blackmore v Department for Communities and Local Government*,[95] the deceased had died of lung cancer through the combined effect of smoking (which amounted to contributory negligence) and asbestos exposure (which was the fault of the defendant employer). Although the trial judge had found that the relative contribution of the smoking to the risk was two or three times that of the asbestos exposure, his decision to impose a discount of 30 per cent for contributory negligence was upheld by the Court of Appeal. On the facts the much greater blameworthiness of the defendant in consistently violating its statutory duties outweighed the greater causal contribution of the deceased's conduct.

(2) Relative culpability

4.32 The criterion of relative blameworthiness is concerned, not with moral culpability, but with the extent to which the conduct of each party fell below the standard of reasonable care in the circumstances.[96] Although English tort law has traditionally been wary of attaching significance to degrees of negligence when it comes to defendants,[97] doing so is routine in the case of apportionment for contributory negligence. Three further points can be made about this criterion. First, only fault that was causative of the damage should be taken into account when assessing relative culpability.[98] Secondly, although it has sometimes been suggested that the fact that the defendant endangered others while the claimant endangered only themselves is relevant to the assessment of relative blameworthiness,[99] since contributory negligence is by definition self-regarding fault,[100] this seems likely to cause confusion, and the claim cannot be supported as far as English law is concerned. Finally, since the standard of care is modified to take account of the young age of the claimant,[101] it follows that account should also be taken of this when determining their relative blameworthiness.[102] There is however some inconsistency on this question in road accident cases involving claimants who were almost of age. Where a pedestrian aged seventeen was hit by a police car after he stepped into the road without looking, the judge said that it was 'particularly important to bear in mind the youth and relative inexperience' of the claimant.[103] Conversely, in *Phethean-Hubble v Coles*, the Court of Appeal held that the trial judge had been wrong to impose a discount of one-third rather than one-half for a cyclist's contributory negligence on the ground that he was aged sixteen at the time of

---

[95] [2017] EWCA Civ 1136, [2018] QB 471. As to whether a finding of contributory negligence should even be made in a case like this, see 3.48.

[96] *Pennington v Norris* (1956) 96 CLR 10 (HCA) 16 (Dixon CJ, Webb, Fullagar, and Kitto JJ).

[97] See D Nolan, 'Varying the Standard of Care in Negligence' (2013) 72 CLJ 651.

[98] *Natixis SA v Marex Financial Ltd* [2019] EWHC 2549 (Comm) [450].

[99] This idea has gained some traction in Australia: see, eg, *Pennington v Norris* (1956) 96 CLR 10 (HCA) 16; and *Luntz*, para 1.13.9 (and cases there cited).

[100] See 3.02.

[101] As regards contributory negligence, see 3.10–3.13.

[102] See *Fleming*, 322. The majority view is, however, otherwise in the United States, perhaps because there causal considerations play a more dominant role in the apportionment analysis: see *Woods and Deere*, 216–17.

[103] *Scutts v Keyse* 2000 WL 33201536 (QBD). See also *Eagle v Chambers* [2003] EWCA Civ 1107, [2004] RTR 9 [18].

the accident.[104] There was no reason to treat the claimant as anything other than an adult in respect of his cycling.

(3) Relative causal potency

The law regarding the causal potency criterion is underdeveloped,[105] and the meaning of the concept has never been explained by the courts. On one account the concept is little more than a screen behind which judges can impose the discount which they think justice requires. Proponents of this view often support it with the claim that there are no such things as degrees of causation. However, while this is undoubtedly true of causation as a purely factual concept (where either X caused Y or not), the doctrine of legal causation (or 'intervening cause') does appears to rest on the idea that some causes are more 'potent' than others.[106] This line of analysis depends, however, on the causal potency criterion being understood as concerned with legal rather than factual causation. In any case, commentators have tried to give some substance to the notion of causal potency in the contributory negligence context by characterizing it as the tendency of conduct of the type in question to produce damage.[107] According to John Fleming:[108] **4.33**

> What [causal potency] must mean is that weight be given to the comparative gravity of the risk. In situations, for instance, where even slight negligence is fraught with exceptional peril to others, the main blame must fall on him who created that danger or brought to the accident the dangerous subject matter ....

Fleming's analysis is consistent with case law suggesting that the conduct of the party who created a danger will generally be regarded as more causally potent than another party's failure to avert that danger once created.[109] And it is also consistent with the fact that in road accident cases motorists are usually treated as playing a more causally potent role in bringing about damage than pedestrians or cyclists on account of the significant destructive potential of motor vehicles.[110] It is important to note that considerations such as these are capable of outweighing relative culpability, with the result that even if A is more negligent than B, B may still bear greater responsibility for the damage if they have 'brought to the accident its dangerous subject matter or control ... the instrument or the more potent instrument for causing damage'.[111] In *The Marimar*,[112] for example, the causal potency of steering an improper course was held to be greater than the causal potency of sailing too

---

[104] [2012] EWCA Civ 349, [2012] RTR 31.

[105] See generally, Goudkamp and Klar (n 88).

[106] Once the law has accepted the departure from 'the philosophical theory of causation' inherent in the concept of legally relevant (as opposed to purely historical) causes, 'it would seem unreasonable to deny the possibility of further differentiation ... between the "effectiveness" of particular causes': NP Gravells, 'Three Heads of Contributory Negligence' (1977) 93 LQR 581, 596.

[107] See HLA Hart and T Honoré, *Causation in the Law* (2nd edn, OUP 1985) 233.

[108] *Fleming*, 308.

[109] *Samco Europe v MSC Prestige* [2011] EWHC 1580 (Admlty), [2011] 2 Lloyd's Rep 579 [84]; *Nettleton v Rondeau* [2014] NSWSC 903 [81]; *Sabir v Osei-Kwabena* [2015] EWCA Civ 1213 [16].

[110] *Sinclair v Joyner* [2015] EWHC 1800 (QB) [73]; *Sabir v Osei-Kwabena* [2015] EWCA Civ 1213 [16]; cf *Belka v Prosperini* [2011] EWCA Civ 623 (causal potency of driver's and pedestrian's conduct equal where latter ran across road in front of former's car).

[111] JA Redmond, 'Fault and Apportionment Acts' (1957) 31 ALJ 520, 526.

[112] [1968] 2 Lloyd's Rep 165 (PD).

fast and not attending to the ship's radar, even if on the facts it was less blameworthy. This was because while the former conduct put the two ships on a collision course, the latter conduct meant only that the resultant collision was not averted or its seriousness lessened.

4.34 The notion of causal potency also appears to encompass intuitive judgments about relative responsibility. In *Stapley v Gypsum Mines Ltd*,[113] for example, the House of Lords clearly considered that the decision of a miner (Stapley) to go back to working under a dangerous roof which then collapsed and killed him was more causally potent than the failure of his co-worker (Dale) to try to prevent him from doing so. According to Lord Reid, Stapley's contribution to the accident was much more 'direct' than Dale's:[114]

> It may be that in this case Dale was not much less to blame than Stapley, but Stapley's conduct in entering the stope contributed more immediately to the accident than anything that Dale did or failed to do.

Similarly, in an Australian case it was held that the causative potency of driving a motor vehicle while drunk was greater than that of handing over the keys to the driver, since the law rightly attached primary responsibility in such a case to the person who 'gets behind the driver's wheel in a car and sets it in motion', as opposed to the person who (by handing over the keys) permits, but does not compel, this to happen.[115]

4.35 One final point worth making about the use of causal potency as a criterion for apportionment is that it might make it easier to arrive at appropriate discounts in cases of strict liability.[116] However, it is important not to fall into the trap of thinking that where the defendant's liability is strict, there is necessarily no room to enquire as to their relative blameworthiness, since a party who is strictly liable may in fact have been at fault.

(4) Additional criteria?

4.36 It is unclear whether the twin criteria of relative blameworthiness and relative causal potency are the only factors that the courts take into account when determining the appropriate apportionment of responsibility. In *Reeves v Commissioner of Police of the Metropolis*, the deceased, who was of sound mind, committed suicide while in police custody. The police were in breach of the duty of care that they owed him to safeguard him from self-harm. Lord Hoffmann said: 'The apportionment must recognise that a purpose of the duty accepted by the commissioner in this case is to demonstrate publicly that the police do have a responsibility for taking reasonable care to prevent prisoners from committing suicide.'[117] Lord Hoffmann did not say, however, whether this factor was relevant in its own right, or because it went to one or both of the criteria of relative blameworthiness and causal potency.

---

[113] [1953] AC 663 (HL).

[114] ibid 682.

[115] *Williams v Government Insurance Office (NSW)* (1995) 21 MVR 148 (NSWCA) 154 (Kirby J).

[116] See 4.37–4.38. For criticism of the South African legislation requiring apportionment on the basis of fault alone, see R Zimmermann, *The Law of Obligations* (OUP 1996) 1048–49.

[117] [2000] 1 AC 360 (HL) 372.

(5) Cases of strict liability

The apportionment exercise is sometimes thought to be rendered more complex or even confounded altogether where the defendant's liability is strict. The concern seems to be that it is impossible to assess the parties' respective shares of responsibility where the defendant is strictly liable. However, these concerns are overstated. For one thing, although strict liability is liability irrespective of fault, a defendant who is subject to strict liability will often in fact have been at fault. Where this is the case, it is entirely proper for the court to factor it into the apportionment analysis.[118] Furthermore, apportionment is concerned with relative responsibility, and a party can be responsible (in the sense of that word that matters for these purposes) without being at fault. As Lord Hoffmann observed in the *Reeves* case, '[a] person may be responsible although he has not been careless at all, as in the case of a breach of an absolute statutory duty'.[119] Indeed, as we have just seen, the case law on contributory negligence itself demonstrates that responsibility is not exclusively a matter of fault, since the apportionment exercise involves a consideration not only of the parties' relative culpability but also of the relative causative potency of their conduct. **4.37**

In a case where the defendant was not in fact at fault, it is inevitable that the culpability criterion will play a lesser role in the apportionment analysis, and that the significance of the relative causal potency of the parties' conduct will be much heightened.[120] This latter consideration might involve the court attaching importance, for example, to the level of danger posed by the defendant's activity in a claim under the rule in *Rylands v Fletcher*, or to the nature and extent of the risk posed by the defendant's animal in a claim under section 2 of the Animals Act 1971.[121] **4.38**

4. Aggravating and Mitigating Factors

There are certain circumstances that tend either to increase or decrease the discount that is made for contributory negligence. Although these factors are inevitably related to the criteria discussed in the previous section (in that they increase or decrease the relative culpability or causal potency of the conduct of one of the parties) it is helpful to separate them out for the purposes of discussion. We begin by considering factors that tend to increase the discount before turning to factors that tend to decrease it. It is important to emphasize that although these factors tend to have respectively an inflationary or deflationary effect, whether they have this effect in a particular case will depend on all the circumstances. **4.39**

[118] See, eg, *Quintas v National Smelting Co* [1961] 1 WLR 401 (CA), where in a case involving a breach of a strict statutory duty, the trial judge found that the defendant had not been at fault and imposed a discount of 75 per cent, while the Court of Appeal did find fault and accordingly reduced the discount to 50 per cent.

[119] [2000] 1 AC 360 (HL) 371.

[120] See D Fairgrieve and R Goldberg, *Product Liability* (3rd edn, OUP 2020) para 17.132 (discussing American decisions on strict product liability). See also *North*, para 2.164 (the twin criteria 'have to be considered by the court in a flexible manner in cases of strict liability').

[121] For a helpful discussion, see *Restatement (Third) of Torts: Liability for Physical and Emotional Harm* (2010) § 25, cmt d.

(1) Aggravating factors

(a) The claimant was experienced in the activity in question

4.40 The discount will tend to be increased where the claimant had significant relevant experience. For example, in *Ringe v Eden Springs (UK) Ltd*,[122] the court emphasized when imposing a discount of 80 per cent that the claimant was an experienced motorcyclist who was familiar with the road, and with the type of traffic that usually travelled on it. In *Causby v Seagoe Technologies Ltd*, the claimant suffered injuries at work. When determining the claimant's share of responsibility for an injury which he suffered while unloading pallets in an unsafe manner, McCloskey J attached significance to his 'experience in the activity in question'.[123]

(b) The claimant was aware of the risk of injury

4.41 Where the claimant was subjectively aware of the danger that led to their being injured this will tend to lead to a higher discount. For example, in *Russell v West Sussex CC*,[124] the judge attached weight to the fact that the claimant driver knew that the road was slippery on account of the presence of frost but did not reduce her speed as a result. Similarly, the fact that the claimant was given but did not heed a warning regarding the risk that materialized will also tend to weigh in favour of a higher discount.[125]

(c) The claimant was driving or riding too quickly

4.42 A paradigmatic aggravating factor in road accident cases is driving or riding too quickly in all the circumstances. It is routine for judges to take travelling at too high a speed into account in fixing the discount, and significant weight will often be attached to it.[126] This factor tends to inflate the discount even when the claimant was travelling below or around the speed limit but nonetheless faster than was safe in the circumstances.[127]

(d) The claimant crossed a road diagonally

4.43 Judges regularly place weight on the fact that the claimant was crossing a road diagonally.[128] Crossing a road in this way is presumably treated as an aggravating factor because the claimant is exposed to the risk of being struck by oncoming traffic for longer than they would have been had they taken a perpendicular path.

---

[122] [2012] EWHC 14 (QB).

[123] [2009] NIQB 24. See also *Hicks v British Transport Commission* [1958] 1 WLR 493 (CA) (experienced shunter); *Akel v Havering LBC* 1999 WL 982477 (CA) (experienced gym user); *Stephen v Peter* 2005 Rep LR 53 (CSOH) [38] (experienced lorry driver); *Sandison v Coope* 2016 Rep LR 70 (Tayside, Central and Fife Sheriff Court) (experienced cyclist).

[124] [2009] EWHC 1063 (QB).

[125] See, eg, *Eagle v Chambers* [2003] EWCA Civ 1107, [2004] RTR 9 [18].

[126] See, eg, *Buchan v Whiting* [2009] EWHC 2951 (QB) [42]–[44]; *Train v Secretary of State for Defence* [2014] EWHC 1928 (QB); *Buswell v The Motor Insurers Bureau* [2015] EWHC 1379 (QB) [54].

[127] See, eg, *Jones v Lawton* [2013] EWHC 4108 (QB) [44].

[128] See, eg, *Kane v New Forest Council* 2001 WL 1903436 (QBD); *Markowski v Elson* [2001] CLY 4477 (Weymouth CC); *Lightfoot v Go-Ahead Group plc* [2011] EWHC 89 (QB), [2011] RTR 27 [40]; *Smith v Bluebird Buses Ltd* [2014] CSOH 75, 2014 Rep LR 91 [27].

(e) The claimant was wearing dark clothing at night

Judges routinely attach significance in road accident cases to the fact that a claimant pedestrian was wearing dark clothing at night, and hence was more difficult for motorists to observe.[129] It appears that this consideration goes only to causal potency rather than to relative blameworthiness, although it may be that it also reduces the defendant's culpability.[130] Conversely, the fact that the claimant was wearing light-coloured clothing at night may operate in their favour.[131] **4.44**

(f) The claimant failed to use a nearby pedestrian crossing

Judges often emphasize the fact that a claimant pedestrian struck by a vehicle failed to use a nearby pedestrian crossing.[132] **4.45**

(g) Intoxication

Judges regularly place significant weight on the fact that the claimant was intoxicated at the time of the accident,[133] albeit only where this contributed to the damage, as what matters for the purposes of the contributory negligence doctrine is causally relevant fault.[134] Conversely, judges have sometimes remarked that the fact of intoxication by itself is unimportant for the purposes of the apportionment exercise because intoxication 'merely ... serves to explain why [the claimant] failed to take proper care for his own safety'.[135] Similarly, Lord Boyd said in *Smith v Bluebird Buses Ltd* that '[t]he critical issue is not whether [the pursuer] was under the influence of alcohol but what his actions were'.[136] **4.46**

(h) Proceeding without priority or against a red light

In *Rehill v Rider Holdings Ltd*, Richards LJ referred to the fact that the claimant had crossed a road at 'a controlled pedestrian crossing with the red man showing against pedestrians',[137] and said that this 'was a strong reason in itself why the claimant should not have attempted to cross'.[138] His Lordship concluded that the claimant's conduct was 'seriously blameworthy' and the discount of one-third that had been imposed at first instance was increased to one-half. In *Malasi v Ahmed*, the claimant cyclist ran a red light and was struck by a taxi. The judge said that 'the balance of fault' lay 'very heavily' with the claimant because 'had [he] **4.47**

[129] See, eg, *Scutt v Keyse* 2000 WL 33201536 (QBD); *Lunt v Khelifa* [2001] All ER (D) 428 (QBD); *Carpenter v Lunnon* [2004] EWHC 3079 (QB) [62]–[63]; *Callier v Deacon* [2009] EWHC 245 (QB) [26]; *Bruma v Hassan* [2017] EWHC 3209 (QB) [73].

[130] *Carpenter v Lunnon* [2004] EWHC 3079 (QB) [63].

[131] Consider *Eagle v Chambers* [2003] EWCA Civ 1107, [2004] RTR 9 [17].

[132] *McDermott v Pettit* [2011] EWHC 3074 (QB) [31], [40]; *Smith v Bluebird Buses Ltd* [2014] CSOH 75, 2014 Rep LR 91 [26], [29]; *Adams v Gibson* [2016] EWHC 3209 (QB) [46]; *Bruma v Hassan* [2017] EWHC 3209 (QB) [73].

[133] See, eg, *Barrett v Ministry of Defence* [1995] 1 WLR 1217 (CA); *McCaughey v Mullan* [2014] NIQB 132 [16].

[134] *Lightfoot v Go-Ahead Group plc* [2011] EWHC 89 (QB), [2011] RTR 27 [38]. On the necessity for the fault to be causally relevant for it to count in the apportionment exercise, see 4.05.

[135] *McNab v Bluebird Buses Ltd* [2007] CSOH 36 [11] (Lord Brodie). See also *Lightfoot v Go-Ahead Group plc* [2011] EWHC 89 (QB), [2011] RTR 27 [39]; *Adams v Gibson* [2016] EWHC 3209 (QB) [48].

[136] [2014] CSOH 75, 2014 Rep LR 91 [26].

[137] [2012] EWCA Civ 628, [2013] RTR 5.

[138] ibid [31].

not chosen to disregard a red traffic signal, he would not have exposed himself to the risks of those circumstances which have eventuated'.[139]

(i) Failing to keep a proper lookout

4.48 A classic aggravating factor is failing to keep a proper lookout for danger. This consideration is of particular significance in road accident cases where brief moments of inattention can have catastrophic consequences.[140] Judges regularly remark, in particular, that pedestrians are expected to look in both directions before entering the carriageway.[141] Even a claimant who uses a designated crossing area may still be expected to keep a lookout for oncoming traffic. For example, in a case from the 1970s, *Clifford v Drymond*,[142] the claimant, who was using a zebra crossing, failed to keep an approaching vehicle under observation. Her damages were reduced by 20 per cent, although it has been suggested that the case might be decided differently today.[143] It has also been said that claimants who walk on the road should face oncoming traffic.[144]

(j) Becoming distracted or otherwise paying insufficient attention

4.49 The fact that the claimant allowed themselves to become distracted will tend to increase the discount. For example, in fixing the appropriate discount, judges have taken account of the fact that the claimant's attention was on a mobile telephone,[145] a heart-rate monitor,[146] and the rear wheel of the bicycle in front.[147]

(k) Disobeying orders

4.50 As the authors of *Munkman* observe, in the context of an employers' liability claim, '[a] decision to breach or ignore instructions, warnings or orders will often result in a significant finding of contributory negligence'.[148] In *Stapley v Gypsum Mines Ltd*,[149] for example, a discount of 80 per cent was imposed where the deceased miner had disobeyed an order to make a roof safe before returning to work beneath it. Similarly, a discount of 50 per cent was made where a stevedore had been injured after failing to heed a foreman's instruction as to the manner in which bags should be unloaded from the hold of a ship.[150]

(l) Disregarding an obvious danger

4.51 The fact that the claimant disregarded an obvious danger is another aggravating factor.[151] Examples of such conduct on the part of employees include placing piece-work too close

139 [2011] EWHC 4083 (QB) [28].

140 See, eg, *Jones v Lawton* [2013] EWHC 4108 (QB) [44]; *McAllister v Campbell* [2014] NIQB 24 [21]; *Wagner v Grant* [2015] CSOH 51 [17].

141 See, eg, *Honnor v Lewis* [2005] EWHC 747 (QB) [52], [63]; *Ehrari v Curry* [2006] EWHC 1319 (QB) [11]; *Adams v Gibson* [2016] EWHC 3209 (QB) [46].

142 [1976] RTR 134 (CA).

143 *Sabir v Osei-Kwabena* [2015] EWCA Civ 1213 [17].

144 *Carpenter v Lunnon* [2004] EWHC 3079 (QB) [62]; *McNab v Bluebird Buses Ltd* [2007] CSOH 36 [11].

145 *Joseph v Braid* 2003 Rep LR 133 (OH) [60].

146 *McAllister v Campbell* [2014] NIQB 24 [9], [21].

147 *Daly v Heeps* 2018 GWD 2–45 (Lothian and Borders Sheriff Court) [36].

148 *Munkman*, para 6.73.

149 [1953] AC 663 (HL).

150 *Williams v Port of Liverpool Stevedoring Co Ltd* [1956] 2 All ER 69 (Assizes).

151 Regarding the significance of this in the employers' liability context, see *Munkman*, para 6.74.

to a moving machine part,[152] leaning over a machine to catch a pigeon,[153] and lying about knowing how to use a circular saw.[154] A pedestrian who deliberately courted danger by running across a road in front of an oncoming vehicle had his damages reduced by two-thirds for contributory negligence.[155]

(m) Engaging in criminal conduct

Just as participating in criminal conduct will often amount to contributory negligence,[156] so too will it tend to be highly pertinent to the apportionment exercise. As Edis J explained in *Hicks v Young*, '[t]hat is because criminal or reckless conduct is morally more blameworthy than conduct which is merely careless'.[157] *McCracken v Smith*[158] is a good illustration of a case in which criminal conduct by the claimant was highly relevant to the apportionment of responsibility. In that case, a pillion passenger on a trail bike was injured in an accident for which the defendant minibus driver was partly responsible. The parties agreed that a 15 per cent discount was warranted on account of the claimant's failure to wear a helmet. However, other acts of contributory negligence, which included the fact that the claimant had allowed himself to be carried as a pillion passenger when he knew that this was not permitted, and also that the bike's driver was unlicensed and uninsured, led the Court of Appeal to impose a total discount of 65 per cent.[159] In another case involving criminal conduct, *Groves v Studley*,[160] the claimant threatened the defendant driver and jumped onto the bonnet of his car, whereupon the defendant accelerated and swerved, causing the claimant to fall from the vehicle and suffer injury. The claimant's damages were reduced by 40 per cent. **4.52**

(2) Mitigating factors

(a) Vulnerability

The vulnerability of the claimant is often cited as a powerful mitigating consideration. For example, in *Powell v Hansen*,[161] Mr Recorder Thorn QC placed weight on the fact that, as a motorcyclist, the claimant belonged to a class of persons especially prone to suffer serious injury.[162] And in *Jones v Lawton*, Burnett J said that the vulnerability of the claimant motorcyclist 'tilt[ed] the balance decisively in [his] favour' as regards causal potency.[163] Similarly, it is widely acknowledged that the fact that pedestrians are particularly vulnerable to being injured by vehicles means that the apportionment exercise is skewed in their favour. For example, in *McCreery v Letson*, Lord Bannatyne said that 'it is clear from the **4.53**

---

152 *Johnson v J Stone & Co (Charlton) Ltd* [1961] 1 All ER 869 (QBD).
153 *Uddin v Associated Portland Cement Manufacturers Ltd* [1965] 2 All ER 213 (CA).
154 *Kerry v Carter* [1969] 1 WLR 1372 (CA).
155 *Belka v Prosperini* [2011] EWCA Civ 623.
156 See 3.25.
157 [2015] EWHC 1144 (QB) [35].
158 [2015] EWCA Civ 380, [2015] PIQR P19.
159 ibid [83].
160 [2014] EWHC 1522 (QB).
161 2001 WL 753470 (QBD) [128].
162 See also the remarks in *McAllister v Campbell* [2014] NIQB 24 [21] and *McGeer v McIntosh* [2017] EWCA Civ 79 [28] (both referring to cyclists).
163 [2013] EWHC 4108 (QB) [44].

case law that in a road traffic case one factor which should be had regard to is the potential destructive disparity between the pedestrian and the person driving the vehicle'.[164] In *Jackson v Murray*, Lord Reed identified this consideration as a factor to be taken 'into account when assessing blameworthiness', although he added that 'the overall assessment of responsibility should not be affected by the heading under which' it was taken into consideration.[165] In *Eagle v Chambers*, Hale LJ said that '[i]t is rare indeed for a pedestrian to be found more responsible than a driver unless the pedestrian has suddenly moved into the path of an oncoming vehicle',[166] and in *Lunt v Khelifa* Latham LJ observed that the law 'has consistently imposed on the drivers of cars a high burden to reflect the fact that a car is potentially a dangerous weapon'.[167]

(b) Socially beneficial conduct

4.54 The courts sometimes emphasize that allowances should be made for the fact that the claimant was engaged in some socially worthwhile activity when injured, or doing something that was required by their employment. For example, in *Gilfillan v Barbour*, Lord Reed took into account the fact that the claimant, although he was driving 'much too fast in the circumstances', was fulfilling his duties as a police officer at the time.[168]

(c) The claimant had priority

4.55 In road accident cases, the fact that the claimant had priority (for example, because they were on the more major road) will tend to lead to a lower discount where the defendant failed to give way and an accident then occurred.[169] The position will be otherwise where it was the defendant who had priority, which the claimant failed to respect.[170]

(d) The defendant's negligence created the danger

4.56 Where the claimant did not create the risky situation, but merely reacted to an emergency that was brought about by the defendant's negligence, the courts will often assign the bulk of the responsibility for the damage to the defendant. Thus, if the defendant negligently pulled in front of the claimant's vehicle and the claimant's reaction was inadequate, the defendant will typically be held to have been primarily responsible.[171] In *The Miraflores and The Abadesa*, Lord Pearce said:[172]

> It is axiomatic that a person who embarks on a deliberate act of negligence should, in general, bear a greater degree of fault than one who fails to cope adequately with the resulting crisis which is thus thrust upon him. This generality is subject, of course, to the

---

[164] [2015] CSOH 153 [76].

[165] [2015] UKSC 5, [2015] 2 All ER 805 [40].

[166] [2003] EWCA Civ 1107, [2004] RTR 9 [16]. See also *Smith v Bluebird Buses Ltd* [2014] CSOH 75, 2014 Rep LR 91 [28]. This approach is not limited to cars but has been extended to motorcycles: *Greenwood v Cummings* (QBD, 9 April 2008).

[167] [2002] EWCA Civ 801 [20].

[168] 2003 SLT 1127 (OH) [40].

[169] See, eg, *Nicolson v Willis* [2006] EWHC 2402 (QB) [49].

[170] *Joseph v Braid* 2003 Rep LR 133 (OH) [61]; *Flavio v Jeffrey* [2008] EWHC 2331 (QB) [13]; *Armsden v Kent Police* [2009] EWCA Civ 631, [2009] RTR 31 [24]. See also 4.47.

[171] See *Jones v Lawton* [2013] EWHC 4108 (QB) [44] (33.3 per cent). See also *Nicolson v Willis* [2006] EWHC 2402 (QB) [51] (33.3 per cent); *Rickson v Bhakar* [2017] EWHC 264 (QB) [32] (20 per cent).

[172] [1967] 1 AC 826 (HL) 847–48.

> particular facts. And it may be that the initial act was so slight or easily avoidable and the subsequent failure to take avoiding action so gross that the blame for the accident falls more largely or even (if the interval and opportunity for avoidance are sufficiently great) wholly upon the person who failed to avoid the consequences of another's negligence. … But the driver who deliberately goes round a corner on the wrong side should, as a rule, find himself more harshly judged than the negligent driver who fails to react promptly enough to the unexpected problem thereby created. For all humans can refrain from deliberately breaking well-known safety rules; but 'tis not in mortals to command the perfect reaction to a crisis, and many fall short at times of that degree which reasonable care demands.

(e) The claimant was walking rather than running

In pedestrian cases, the courts generally look sympathetically on claimants who were walking rather than running across a road.[173] The justification for this approach is doubtless that slower-moving pedestrians usually afford drivers a greater opportunity to take evasive measures. Conversely, claimants injured after suddenly darting out into the carriageway tend to have their damages discounted by larger amounts.[174] If, however, the claimant was already part of the way across the carriageway and broke into a run to avoid being struck by an oncoming vehicle, the court may regard that as a mitigating factor.[175] **4.57**

(f) Pedestrian activity in the area was likely

Extra care is required of defendant motorists when passing through an area where nearby facilities (such as schools, shops, pubs, bus stops and underground stations) suggest that pedestrian activity is likely.[176] Thus, the mere fact that the area was 'built up' or 'shop-lined' tends to work in the claimant's favour when it comes to apportionment,[177] as does the presence of parked cars[178] or a stationary minibus that has its hazard lights activated.[179] **4.58**

(g) The defendant put the claimant under pressure or condoned the claimant's conduct

Where the claimant engaged in the conduct that amounted to contributory negligence at the defendant's urging, that will tend to diminish the discount, especially if the defendant was in a position of responsibility relative to the claimant.[180] The same is true where the defendant condoned the negligent conduct of the claimant.[181] **4.59**

---

[173] See, eg, *Sedge v Prime* [2011] EWHC 820 (QB) [37]; *Bruma v Hassan* [2017] EWHC 3209 (QB) [72].

[174] See, eg, *Belka v Prosperini* [2011] EWCA Civ 623 (66.6 per cent); *Paramasivan v Wicks* [2013] EWCA Civ 262 (75 per cent).

[175] *Hickman v London Central Bus Co Ltd* [2013] EWHC 1703 (QB) [66], [69]; cf *Hughes-Jukes v Etti* [2006] EWHC 2493 (QB), [2007] RTR 2 [30].

[176] See, eg, *Eagle v Chambers* [2003] EWCA Civ 1107, [2004] RTR 9 [17]; *Bruma v Hassan* [2017] EWHC 3209 (QB) [72].

[177] See, eg, *Bruma v Hassan* [2017] EWHC 3209 (QB) [72]; *Sabir v Osei-Kwabena* [2015] EWCA Civ 1213 [13], [16].

[178] See, eg, *Brownlow v Knight* [2003] NIQB 71 [18].

[179] *Jackson v Murray* [2015] UKSC 5, [2015] 2 All ER 805.

[180] See, eg, *Ministry of Defence v Radclyffe* [2009] EWCA Civ 635.

[181] See *Bennett v Brinks Ltd* [1999] CLY 1378 (Leeds CC); *Palmer v Perrins Hill Partnership* [2019] 4 WLUK 542 (QBD) (both involving failures by employees of the defendants to wear seat belts).

5. Guideline Discounts

4.60 In *Froom v Butcher*,[182] Lord Denning MR famously promulgated guideline discounts in seat belt cases.[183] He argued that guidelines would save the cost and time required to enquire into the individual circumstances of each and every such case. According to his Lordship:[184]

> Sometimes the evidence will show that the failure [to wear a seat belt] made no difference. The damage would have been the same, even if a seat belt had been worn. In such cases the damages should not be reduced at all. At other times the evidence will show that the failure made all the difference. The damage would have been prevented altogether if a seat belt had been worn. In such cases I would suggest that the damages should be reduced by 25 per cent. But often enough the evidence will only show that the failure made a considerable difference. Some injuries to the head, for instance, would have been a good deal less severe if a seat belt had been worn, but there would still have been some injury to the head. In such cases I would suggest that the damages attributable to the failure to wear a seat belt should be reduced by 15 per cent.

4.61 A degree of flexibility is observable in the use of these guidelines by the courts. In *Froom* itself, for example, where the evidence was that some of the claimant's injuries would have been completely avoided had the claimant used a seat belt, while other injuries would have been incurred regardless, the damages were reduced by 20 per cent. And a 20 per cent discount was also imposed in *Hazlett v Robinson*, where the judge found that had a seat belt been used, the damage would have been 'very [much] less severe'.[185] However, the courts rarely depart from the guidelines altogether. In *Capps v Miller*, Croom-Johnson LJ said that it was important that the courts followed the guidelines 'for the sake of the swift conduct, and it may be settlement, of litigation'.[186] While it could not be said that they should never be departed from, 'ordinarily they should be adhered to'.[187] The defendant carries the onus of showing that the guidelines should not be applied,[188] which onus will be discharged only where the case is 'rare or exceptional'.[189] A case that apparently fits that description is *Bennett v Brinks Ltd*,[190] where the damages were reduced by only 10 per cent because the defendant employer had condoned the failure by the claimant employee to wear a seat belt.[191]

---

[182] [1976] QB 286 (CA).

[183] See, generally, Goudkamp (n 55). *Froom* concerned a passenger in a car. In *Welsh v Messenger* [2006] CLY 2875 (Newcastle upon Tyne CC) it was held that a coach passenger's failure to wear a seat belt did not amount to contributory negligence at all, in the light of the fact that it was not then compulsory to use a seat belt on a coach and that there had been no government campaign to encourage such use. As it is now mandatory to use a seat belt on a coach where fitted, one would expect a different outcome today, though it is not clear whether the *Froom* guidelines would be followed in such a case.

[184] [1976] QB 286 (CA) 296.

[185] [2014] NIQB 17 [53] (Gillen J).

[186] [1989] 1 WLR 839 (CA) 850.

[187] ibid.

[188] *Stanton v Collinson* [2009] EWHC 342 (QB) [140] (Cox J).

[189] *Gawler v Raettig* [2007] EWHC 373 (QB) [26] (Gray J).

[190] [1999] CLY 1378 (Leeds CC).

[191] See also *Palmer v Perrins Hill Partnership* [2019] 4 WLUK 542 (QBD).

When *Froom* was decided, it was compulsory for cars to be fitted with seat belts but not mandatory to wear them. After their use became mandatory, it was thought that the *Froom* guidelines might need to be revisited, and *Froom* has thus been challenged on several occasions. However, those challenges have been forcefully rejected,[192] and it appears that the courts have little appetite for reconsidering *Froom*. On the contrary, the *Froom* guidelines have been extended to contribution proceedings where a parent negligently failed properly to secure their infant child inside a car.[193] The guidelines have also been extended beyond the seat-belt context to failures by motorcyclists[194] and bicyclists[195] to wear crash helmets,[196] although it is less clear whether they are closely adhered to in those settings, partly because there have been relatively few recent cases of this kind. **4.62**

How should responsibility be apportioned where there is another act of contributory negligence, coupled with one to which a guideline discount applies? One possibility would be for the court to consider what discount would be appropriate for the additional act of contributory negligence on its own, and then to add that to the guideline discount to arrive at the total. However, although there are apparent examples of this approach being employed,[197] it has generally been rejected. In *Clark v Farley*,[198] Yip J said that 'the correct approach is to look at relative blameworthiness and causative potency as a whole, rather than assessing elements of contributory negligence separately and adding the percentages together'. The result was a discount of 40 per cent for travelling as a pillion passenger on an off-road motorcycle in dangerous circumstances while not wearing a helmet, it having been agreed that on its own the failure to wear a helmet would have merited a discount of 12.5 per cent. Similarly, in *Gleeson v Court*,[199] HHJ Foster QC considered that while on the facts a discount of 25 per cent would have been appropriate for travelling in the boot of a car, and a discount of 20 per cent for accepting a lift from a drunk driver, the composite discount for both acts of contributory negligence taken together should be 30 per cent. Aggregating the two figures to produce a discount of 45 per cent would have failed to reflect the relative blameworthiness of the two parties.[200] **4.63**

---

[192] *Gawler v Raettig* [2007] EWHC 373 (QB) [39]–[46]; *Stanton v Collinson* [2010] EWCA Civ 81, [2010] RTR 26 [26].

[193] *Jones v Wilkins* [2001] RTR 19 (CA); *Williams v Williams* [2013] EWCA Civ 455, [2013] PIQR P17.

[194] 'I see no reason to distinguish between seat belt cases and crash helmet cases and I would apply the dictum of Lord Denning to crash helmets': *Capps v Miller* [1989] 1 WLR 839 (CA) 847 (Croom-Johnson LJ).

[195] 'In my judgment the observations of Lord Denning MR ... should apply to the wearing of helmets by cyclists': *Smith v Finch* [2009] EWHC 53 (QB) [44] (Griffith Williams J); cf *Sinclair v Joyner* [2015] EWHC 1800 (QB) [71], where Cox J doubted whether failing to wear a helmet while riding a bicycle amounted to contributory negligence, although it is not entirely clear whether she was speaking generally or only in the context of that particular case.

[196] For discussion, see J Fulbrook, 'Cycle Helmets and Contributory Negligence' [2004] JPIL 171.

[197] See, eg, *McCracken v Smith* [2015] EWCA Civ 380, [2015] PIQR P19 (agreed discount of 15 per cent for failing to wear a helmet while travelling on a motorcycle added to 50 per cent discount for agreeing to go on a joyride).

[198] [2018] EWHC 1007 (QB), [2018] PIQR P15.

[199] [2007] EWHC 2397 (QB), [2008] RTR 10.

[200] See also *Gregory v Kelly* [1978] RTR 426 (QBD) (40 per cent discount for failing to wear a seat belt while travelling in a car which the claimant knew had defective brakes); and two Scottish decisions in which discounts of 33.3 per cent were made for not wearing a seat belt as well as travelling in a car with a drunken driver: *Sloan v Triplett* 1985 SLT 294 (OH); *Hill v Chivers* 1987 SLT 323 (OH).

4.64 Guideline discounts are suitable for cases involving seat belts and crash helmets because 'the negligent conduct is readily identifiable, repetitive and generally uniform'.[201] The same is not true of other recurrent forms of contributory negligence, which are not concerned with the failure to use a safety mechanism of this kind. In other types of case the courts have therefore generally not tried to formulate guidelines. It is true that in *Best v Smyth,* Tugendhat J said that since *Owens v Brimmell*[202] 'the figure of 20% is commonly regarded as the appropriate reduction for a claimant who has got into a vehicle when he must have known that the driver had had too much to drink'.[203] However, in cases of this kind the circumstances vary widely, and in some the claimant is clearly much more culpable than in others, for example, because the claimant encouraged the defendant to drink knowing that they would later be driving.[204] It is therefore unsurprising that judges have denied that *Owens* sets the figure of 20 per cent in stone,[205] and that in practice the discounts in such cases frequently depart from that figure.[206]

4.65 In some jurisdictions, the discount for particular types of contributory negligence is fixed by statute. For example, in some Australian states, legislation provides that the plaintiff's damages must be reduced by 25 per cent for failing to wear a seat belt.[207] And in South Australia, if the claimant is guilty of contributory negligence in having relied on an intoxicated defendant, a discount of 25 per cent must be imposed, which increases to 50 per cent where the defendant was intoxicated to a sufficient degree.[208] None of these statutory fixed reduction rules give the court the power not to apply the prescribed discount.

4.66 There is clearly a conflict between the use of guideline discounts of the kind set down in *Froom* and the usual discretionary approach to apportionment based on the twin criteria of relative culpability and relative causal potency. Suppose, for example, that a passenger is injured in a car accident due to the negligence of the driver, and that the passenger would have escaped unharmed had a seat belt been worn. Following *Froom*, the passenger's damages will almost certainly be reduced by 25 per cent. Now consider the same scenario with the following modifications made to it: first, that the driver was intoxicated (in circumstances where the claimant did not know and could not reasonably have known this); and second, that the driver is an adult whereas the passenger is a teenager. The driver surely bears a significantly greater proportion of responsibility for the claimant's damage in the modified scenario than in the original scenario, with the result that, if the usual approach to apportionment were employed, the discount would undoubtedly be lower in the modified scenario than in the original scenario. Yet, by virtue of *Froom*, the damages will be reduced by 25 per cent in both cases. At least three arguments can be made in favour of this departure from the general discretionary approach.[209] One is that guideline discounts

201 *Fleming*, 316.

202 [1977] QB 859 (QBD).

203 [2010] EWHC 1541 (QB) [12].

204 See, eg, *Duncan v Bell* [1967] Qd R 425 (SC).

205 *Stinton v Stinton* [1993] PIQR P135 (QBD) 140; *Currie v Clamp's Executor* 2002 SLT 196 (OH) [22].

206 For a list of recent cases of this kind, where the discounts range from 15 per cent to 33.3 per cent, see A1.82.

207 Motor Accidents (Compensation) Act (NT) s 11(1); Civil Liability Act 1936 (SA) s 49(3); cf Motor Accidents (Liabilities and Compensation) Act 1973 (Tas) s 22(4) (15 per cent). The Northern Territory and South Australian Acts extend to failure to wear a safety helmet.

208 Civil Liability Act 1936 (SA) s 47(3), (6).

209 See Goudkamp (n 55) 638–40.

make the outcome of litigation more certain, which in turn facilitates settlement.[210] Another is that guideline discounts help to keep the cost of litigation proportionate to the value of the underlying claims (many of which may be for modest amounts) by leaving less room for evidence to be called and submissions made regarding apportionment.[211] And finally, guideline discounts promote consistency, and thereby reduce the risk that similar cases will be treated differently (even if, as in the example just given, they also sometimes mean that very different cases are treated the same). None of these three values—certainty, proportionality and consistency—is itself capable of making a particular rule a good one. Merely because a rule is, for example, certain in its application does not make it just. But all three of these values might nevertheless be thought to be important to any legal system that aspires to be fair. Each of the arguments that have been sketched thus offers some support for the adoption of guideline discounts.

6. Discounts Imposed

(1) Discounts in general

According to an empirical study of first instance decisions in the United Kingdom between 2000 and 2016, the average discount by which damages were reduced for contributory negligence across all types of claim was 40 per cent.[212] The average discount by contextual category was found to be as follows: road accident (43 per cent); employers' liability (32 per cent); occupiers' liability (47 per cent); professional negligence (52 per cent); public liability (35 per cent); sports injury (38 per cent); and 'other' (37 per cent).[213] **4.67**

Consistently with the fact that the apportionment exercise is discretionary and that it does not admit of a demonstrably correct answer,[214] the courts take a broad-brush approach to apportionment[215] and tend to reduce the claimant's damages either by the fractions used most frequently in everyday life (such as one-half, one-quarter, and one-third) or by percentages that are multiples of 10 (10 per cent, 20 per cent, etc).[216] Judges strive not to become 'bogged down by fine-shadings of percentages'.[217] **4.68**

---

[210] See *Jones v Wilkins* [2001] RTR 19 (CA) [18]; *Stanton v Collinson* [2010] EWCA Civ 81, [2010] RTR 284 [26].

[211] See *Froom v Butcher* [1976] QB 286 (CA) 296 (Lord Denning MR) (arguing that the apportionment exercise 'should not be prolonged by an expensive inquiry into the degree of blameworthiness on either side').

[212] *Goudkamp and Nolan*, para 4.12.

[213] ibid paras 4.14–4.18.

[214] See 4.22–4.23.

[215] See *Stapley v Gypsum Mines Ltd* [1953] AC 663 (HL) 682; *Badger v Ministry of Defence* [2005] EWHC 2941 (QB), [2006] 3 All ER 173 [16] (Stanley Burnton J) (apportionment decisions should be 'dealt with in a broad, jury-like and commonsense way').

[216] See *Goudkamp and Nolan*, para 4.20 (by far the most frequently observed discount in first instance cases was 50 per cent, followed by 25 per cent, 20 per cent, and 33.3 per cent). The same broad-brush approach is observable in the case law on apportionment in maritime collision cases, where the most common divisions of responsibility have been one-quarter/three-quarters; half/half; and one-third/two-thirds: see H Brandon, 'Apportionment of Liability in British Courts under the Maritime Conventions Act of 1911' (1977) 51 Tul L Rev 1025, 1041. As to why divisions of responsibility tend to be broad-brush assessments, see Votruba (n 61).

[217] *Powell v Hasen* 2001 WL 753470 (QBD) [131] (Mr Recorder Thorn QC). By contrast, *juries* sometimes proceed differently. In a New Zealand case, *Joll v Watson* [1953] NZLR 788 (SC), a jury reduced the plaintiff's damages by 52 per cent. And in a recent Scottish case, a jury reduced the pursuer's damages by 96.5

4.69 As the average discount of 40 per cent suggests, there are many more discounts below 50 per cent than above 50 per cent. In some types of case, it is extremely unlikely that a discount as high as 50 per cent would be made. One example is where the claimant's negligence consisted solely of accepting a lift from an intoxicated driver.[218] It is also unlikely that the damages awarded to an employee suing an employer for breach of statutory duty will be discounted by more than 50 per cent, and indeed it has been claimed that there is a 'rule of thumb' to this effect.[219] Clearly, however, any such rule must be subject to possible exceptions as it would otherwise operate as an unwarranted fetter on the discretion which the judge has under the statutory apportionment regime.

(2) **Very low and very high discounts**

4.70 Discounts that fall at the extremes of the spectrum cast doubt on whether the contributory negligence doctrine is properly applicable in the first place. A discount of, say, 5 per cent suggests that the claimant was not really guilty of contributory negligence in the first place. Similarly, a discount of 95 per cent suggests that the claimant was, in reality, wholly responsible for the damage, so that the defendant ought not to have been held liable at all. The practice of the courts is broadly consistent with these propositions. Thus, discounts of less than 10 per cent are unusual.[220] In *Cooper v Carillion plc*, Keane LJ said that '[t]he issue in this case, given the low figure of 10 per cent attributed by the judge in respect of the claimant's contributory negligence, is whether the judge was right to find that there was contributory negligence at all on the part of the claimant'.[221] Discounts approaching 100 per cent are also rare. In *Hodkinson v Henry Wallwork & Co Ltd*,[222] the damages of an employee who took an 'amazing risk' while attempting to fix a machine were reduced by 90 per cent. And in *Barings plc (in liq) v Coopers & Lybrand (a firm)*,[223] the judge would have discounted the damages by 95 per cent in respect of conduct committed over a given period of time had he found that the primary negligence remained operative during that period. In the empirical study adverted to earlier, the lowest discount imposed was 10 per cent, and the highest was 90 per cent.[224]

per cent: see https://www.scotcourts.gov.uk/about-the-scottish-court-service/scs-news/2017/05/09/first-civil-jury-trial-for-all-scotland-sheriff-personal-injury-court (accessed 31 December 2017).

[218] See *Williams v Government Insurance Office (NSW)* (1995) 21 MVR 148 (NSWCA) 157 (apparently no example in New South Wales of a discount higher than 40 per cent being imposed in such a case).

[219] See *Munkman*, para 6.19.

[220] But see *Pasternack v Poulton* [1973] 1 WLR 476 (QBD) (5 per cent); *Snushall v Fulsang* (2006) 258 DLR (4th) 425 (Ont CA) (5 per cent); *Nominal Defendant v Rooskov* [2012] NSWCA 43, (2012) 60 MVR 350 (5 per cent). See also the discussion (see 4.18) regarding whether the courts have a discretion not to reduce the claimant's damages at all where contributory negligence has been established.

[221] [2003] EWCA Civ 1811 [11]. Consider also Sedley LJ's remark in *Butcher v Cornwall CC* [2002] EWCA Civ 1640 [13] that '10% is so nearly a token figure that one's first reaction is that it betokens an absence of significant fault on the claimant's part'.

[222] *Hodkinson v Henry Wallwork & Co Ltd* [1955] 3 All ER 236 (CA).

[223] [2003] EWHC 1319 (Ch) [1068] (Evans-Lombe J).

[224] *Goudkamp and Nolan*, para 4.20.

(3) Professional negligence cases

Empirical research suggests that pleas of contributory negligence succeed relatively rarely in professional negligence cases,[225] but that when they do the discount tends to be high. In the study in question, the average discount in professional negligence claims at first instance was considerably higher (52 per cent) than the average discount across all first instance claims (40 per cent). One possible explanation for this inverse relationship between the success rate of the plea of contributory negligence and the average discount is that claimants need to do something particularly unreasonable for a finding of contributory negligence to be made in the professional negligence setting. If this is correct, then judges may conclude that claimants who have been found guilty of contributory negligence in this type of case deserve to have their damages discounted by a sizeable amount. Another possible explanation for the relatively high discounts in professional negligence cases is that in other types of case, such as road accident claims, considerations of causative potency play a greater role in the apportionment decision,[226] whereas in professional negligence claims the focus is often exclusively on the relative fault of the parties, which more often leads to the conclusion that an equal division of responsibility is appropriate. **4.71**

High discounts for contributory negligence are more likely in the professional negligence setting where the claimant's fault is independent of that of the defendant (in that it does not lie in not checking or verifying the professional's work), or where the thing that the claimant ought to have done, or which the claimant failed properly to do, did not require technical competence. A good example of a case in which the claimant's fault was independent of that of the defendant is *Sahib Foods Ltd v Paskin KyriaKides Sands (a firm)*,[227] where liability was imposed on the defendant architects for the inadequate fireproofing of a food preparation room in the claimant's factory, but the damages were reduced by two-thirds because the claimant's employees had both caused the fire that did the damage, and contributed to its spreading by misinforming the defendants about the nature of the cooking process involved. Similarly, in *Logical Computer Supplies Ltd v Euro Car Parks Ltd*,[228] the compensation awarded to a company for damage to its computer files caused by employees of an IT firm hired to supply an email system was reduced by 50 per cent on account of the company's failure to apply 'business common sense and risk management'[229] by properly backing up its data. **4.72**

7. Multiple Defendants

Difficult issues arise at the apportionment stage when two or more defendants are liable for the same damage, and the claimant is also contributorily negligent. In such a case, should the claimant's damages be reduced by reference to their share of responsibility as against the defendants collectively, or as against a given defendant individually? Suppose, for example, that C is 25 per cent responsible for the damage, D1 25 per cent responsible, and D2 50 **4.73**

[225] See 3.35.
[226] See 4.33.
[227] [2003] EWCA Civ 1832, [2004] PNLR 22.
[228] 2001 WL 825094 (QBD).
[229] ibid [14] (Richard Fernyhough QC).

per cent responsible. If C sues both D1 and D2, should the damages for which D1 is liable be reduced by one-quarter or by one-half? Since s 1(1) of the 1945 Act refers to a situation in which a person suffers damage 'as the result partly of his own fault and partly of the fault of any other person *or persons*', and states that in such a case the damages are to be reduced 'having regard to *the claimant's share of responsibility* for the damage', the former approach seems to be the right one, and that was indeed confirmed by the House of Lords in *Fitzgerald v Lane*.[230]

4.74 The claimant in *Fitzgerald v Lane* had been struck by two cars in succession while crossing a road at a pedestrian crossing when the lights were against him. The trial judge found that all three parties had been negligent and that they were 'equally to blame'. According to Lord Ackner, for the purposes of apportionment, the claimant's conduct had to be compared 'with the totality of the tortious conduct of the defendants'.[231] The responsibility of the defendants *inter se* was not a matter that concerned the claimant but was relevant only to subsequent contribution proceedings between them. Somewhat confusingly, however, the House refused to interfere with the apportionment of the Court of Appeal, which had replaced the discount of one-third imposed by the trial judge (consistently with his allocation of the blame) with a discount of one-half. However, the explanation for this seems to have been that the House of Lords considered the trial judge's allocation of the blame to be clearly erroneous, and that the claimant was as much to blame for the damage as the two defendants taken together. The same basic approach was in any case adopted by the New South Wales Court of Appeal in *Barisic v Devenport*[232] in a more carefully reasoned and transparent analysis where close attention was paid to the wording of the relevant apportionment legislation (which was similar to that of the 1945 Act). As well as being consistent with the legislation, the solution adopted in *Fitzgerald v Lane* has the advantage of simplicity, since the damages are reduced by the same percentage for each defendant.

4.75 When coupled with the rule of joint and several liability, the decision in *Fitzgerald v Lane* means that where C, D1, and D2 are all responsible for the same damage, C can recover full damages from, say, D1, minus a deduction based on C's share of responsibility for the damage. If this results in D1 paying more than their 'fair share', D1 can seek contribution from D2. However, if D2 is insolvent, or his share is otherwise uncollectable, the joint and several liability rule leaves D1 to bear the entirety of the burden that correlates to D2's share of responsibility. In other cases of joint and several liability, that is considered to be a fair outcome because D1 wrongfully caused the damage and C was entirely innocent. But where C was contributorily negligent some of the responsibility for the damage lies with C. There is therefore often thought to be a strong argument for distributing D2's uncollectable share between C and D1 in proportion to their shares of responsibility *inter se*.[233] However, while some common law jurisdictions have developed systems for

[230] [1989] AC 328 (HL). This accorded with the view taken by Denning LJ in *Davies v Swan Motor Co* [1949] 2 KB 291 (CA) 325.

[231] [1989] AC 328 (HL) 367.

[232] [1978] 2 NSWLR 111 (CA).

[233] See, eg, JG Fleming, 'Foreword: Comparative Negligence at Last—By Judicial Choice' (1976) 64 Calif L Rev 239, 251–52.

distributing the burden of an insolvent defendant's share of responsibility in this way,[234] English law has not done so. Another possible solution is to replace liability *in solidum* with proportionate liability in this type of case, which is the approach taken in the maritime collision context.[235] But since the effect of this is to shift the entirety of the burden of the uncollectable share from the solvent defendant(s) to the claimant it simply perpetuates any injustice inherent in the current approach and so cannot be supported.

8. Absent Tortfeasors

Finally, where more than one tortfeasor caused the same damage, an issue arises as to whether it is right for the court to consider the extent of the responsibility of a wrongdoer who is not a party to the proceedings.[236] For example, if C suffers damage due to the wrongs of both D1 and D2, as well as C's own carelessness, and C sues only D1, then when determining C's share of responsibility for the damage should the court consider the fault of D2 as well as the fault of the parties to the action? The fact that section 1(1) of the 1945 Act refers to one or more 'persons' who are partly at fault for the damage (as opposed to 'parties') might be taken to mean that the court *should* do so, although the little authority there is on the point is inconsistent.[237] It is in any case clear that any conclusion to which the court comes regarding D2's share of responsibility will not be binding on D2, while the lack of case law suggests that the issue may not be a significant one in practice, perhaps because claimants generally proceed against all possible defendants in a single claim, or because the defendant(s) sued will join any others in third-party proceedings.[238] **4.76**

[234] See, eg, US Uniform Comparative Fault Act, s 2(d) (discussed in *Woods and Deere*, 507–508); Civil Liability Act 1961 (Ire) s 38. This solution was endorsed by *Williams*, 403–405.

[235] *The Miraflores and The Abadesa* [1967] 1 AC 826 (HL). This is said to follow from the wording of the relevant legislation, which states that, where loss is caused by the fault of two or more vessels, 'the liability to make good the damage or loss shall be in proportion to the degree in which *each ship* was in fault' (Merchant Shipping Act 1995, s 187(1) (emphasis added)).

[236] See Fleming (n 233) 256–59.

[237] Compare *Barisic v Devenport* [1978] 2 NSWLR 111 (CA) 122–23 and *Nordlake (Owners) v Seaeagle (Owners)* [2015] EWHC 3605 (Admlty), [2016] 1 Lloyd's Rep 656 [146] (permitting such account to be taken) with *Vail v Formato* (1989) 10 MVR 12 (SAFC) (forbidding it).

[238] See Fleming (n 233) 256–57.

5

RELATED DOCTRINES

5.01 The fact that the claimant failed to take reasonable care for their own safety or interests may be relevant to doctrines other than the contributory negligence doctrine. These doctrines and their relationship with the law of contributory negligence are discussed in this chapter, along with doctrines (such as contribution between wrongdoers) that are related to the doctrine of contributory negligence in other ways. The related rules considered in this chapter are: (i) legal causation ('novus actus interveniens'); (ii) illegality; (iii) *volenti non fit injuria*; (iv) default of the claimant; (v) contribution between wrongdoers; (vi) the avoidable consequences rule; (vii) provocation; (viii) limitation of actions; and (ix) the principle in *Ginty v Belmont Building Supplies Ltd*,[1] which excludes claims in breach of statutory duty where the breach was brought about solely by the wrongful conduct of the claimant. In the case of illegality and *volenti*, the doctrine in question is often relied upon in addition to contributory negligence.[2] By contrast, in the case of legal causation and mitigation a court may need to choose between the application of these doctrines and the doctrine of contributory negligence, and the dividing line between them is not always clear. In the case of the other five doctrines considered here the nature of the relationship between the doctrine in question and the doctrine of contributory negligence varies. Finally, it is worth noting that the relationship between contributory negligence and other legal principles or rules is also the subject of some of the discussion in other chapters of this work.[3]

1. Legal Causation (Novus Actus Interveniens)

5.02 Where the claimant's contributory negligence plays a sufficiently significant role in bringing about their damage it may constitute an intervening cause of that damage (or 'novus actus interveniens'). When that is the case, the effect will usually be that the claim fails in its entirety for lack of legal causation, and there will be no scope for the doctrine of contributory negligence to operate. Sometimes, however, the intervening cause analysis will render only a particular item of damage or loss irrecoverable, as opposed to defeating the claim altogether.[4] Such an outcome is conceptually distinct from the type of partial recovery that the law of contributory negligence yields, since recovery in respect of the full

---

[1] [1959] 1 All ER 414 (QBD).

[2] See, eg, *Berry v Hayden* [2008] NIQB 134.

[3] See, eg, 4.12–4.14 (contributory negligence and the *SAAMCO* principle); 4.08–4.09 (contributory negligence and exclusion and limitation clauses); 4.04 (contributory negligence and the compensatory principle).

[4] See, eg, *McKew v Holland & Hannen & Cubitts (Scotland)* [1969] 3 All ER 1621 (HL).

Contributory Negligence. Second Edition. James Goudkamp and Donal Nolan, Oxford University Press.
 DOI: 10.1093/oso/9780192867919.003.0005

amount of the specific damage or loss concerned will be denied. It should be remembered that the distinction between an intervening cause and mere contributory negligence only really became significant with the enactment of the apportionment legislation, as previously contributory negligence also operated as a complete bar on recovery.

The law that determines when the claimant's conduct will amount to an intervening cause as opposed to mere contributory negligence is 'imprecise'.[5] However, in principle, an intervening cause analysis applies only where the claimant's conduct is such that 'it obliterates the wrongdoing of the defendant'.[6] For this to be the case, it has been said that the claimant's conduct must be 'reckless or worse than reckless',[7] although on other occasions it has been held that recklessness is not required.[8] The leading case is *McKew v Holland & Hannen & Cubitts (Scotland)*.[9] The defender negligently injured the pursuer, who later fell down a staircase which he should not have tried to descend without assistance in view of his injuries. The pursuer sustained further injury in the fall. It was held that the defender was not liable for the additional injuries because the pursuer's decision to descend the stairs unaided was a novus actus that broke the chain of causation between the defender's negligence and those injuries. Lord Reid said:[10] **5.03**

> [I]f the injured man acts unreasonably he cannot hold the defender liable for injury caused by his own unreasonable conduct. His unreasonable conduct is *novus actus interveniens*. The chain of causation has been broken and what follows must be regarded as caused by his own conduct and not by the defender's fault or the disability caused by it.

Where the defendant was under a duty to prevent the conduct of the claimant in question that conduct will not generally amount to an intervening cause, although it may still constitute contributory negligence.[11] In *Bhatt v Fontain Motors Ltd*, the claimant employee fell from a ladder in the defendant employer's car showroom. The defendant had breached a statutory duty that required work at height to be avoided altogether if it was reasonably practicable to carry out the work otherwise than at height. Richards LJ said:[12] **5.04**

> [The claimant's] failure to follow the prescribed procedure when doing work he should not have been required to do at all, and when using equipment that he should not have been required to use if the work was to be done, does not mean that the accident was caused by him alone. It goes only to contributory negligence.

The position is otherwise where there is wilful misconduct on the claimant's part,[13] save where the defendant is under a duty of care to prevent deliberate self-harm, in which

---

[5] *Hicks v Young* [2015] EWHC 1144 (QB) [44] (Edis J).

[6] *Stephen v Peter* 2005 Rep LR 53 (CSOH) [36] (Lord Menzies).

[7] *Clift v Hawes* 1999 WL 1457275 (CA) (Sedley LJ).

[8] 'In my judgment there does not have to be recklessness and nothing less than recklessness ...': *Lambert v Lewis* [1982] AC 225 (CA) 252 (Roskill LJ) (reversed on other grounds on appeal).

[9] [1969] 3 All ER 1621 (HL). For a similar Canadian decision, see *Priestley v Gilbert* (1972) 28 DLR (3rd) 553 (Ont HC).

[10] [1969] 3 All ER 1621 (HL) 1623.

[11] On the possibility of contributory negligence in this type of case, see 3.29–3.30.

[12] [2010] EWCA Civ 863, [2010] PIQR P17 [34]. See also *Neil v East Ayrshire Council* 2005 Rep LR 18 (OH) [27]–[29] (Lord Brodie).

[13] See *Charlesworth*, para 13-93 ('a deliberate act of folly'); and K Stanton et al, *Statutory Torts* (Sweet & Maxwell 2003) para 9.021, along with the cases they cite.

case such conduct will not amount to a novus actus, though it may again constitute contributory negligence.[14]

5.05 The connection between the novus actus doctrine and contributory negligence is strong, since both doctrines rest on the fundamental premise that the claimant is responsible (at least to some extent) for their own damage. For present purposes, the key difference between them is that a finding of intervening cause expresses the conclusion that the claimant is *wholly* responsible for the damage, while a finding of contributory negligence expresses the conclusion that the claimant is *partly* responsible for it. This is, however, a difference 'of degree rather than kind',[15] and the distinction between these two scenarios can be a fine one. It is instructive in this regard to contrast the outcome in *McKew* with that in the more recent case of *Spencer v Wincanton Holdings Ltd*.[16] The claimant in *Spencer* had injured his knee in a work accident for which the defendant was responsible. Three years later, this injury led to the amputation of his right leg. A few months after the amputation, the claimant was filling his car with petrol when he fell and suffered a further injury. The Court of Appeal held that the claimant's failure to use his prosthesis or walking sticks at the time of the second accident was not a novus actus, although his damages were reduced by one-third for contributory negligence. Aikens LJ emphasized that the line between conduct that amounted to contributory negligence and conduct that amounted to a novus actus was not 'capable of precise definition'.[17] Each case would depend on its facts and the court would have to make a value judgment. To the extent that *McKew* had suggested that any unreasonable conduct of the claimant in a case of this kind would constitute an intervening cause, the court held that that was not so.[18] Instead, it depended on *how* unreasonable the conduct was, although the suggestion that only reckless or deliberate conduct would have this effect was rejected.

5.06 It is sometimes argued that with the possibility of apportionment of responsibility following a finding of contributory negligence, there is now no reason for the courts to employ intervening cause analysis to deny the claimant's action altogether.[19] However, this seems not to have been the view that was taken in the immediate aftermath of the apportionment legislation,[20] and even today the courts continue to use the intervening cause technique in a small category of cases where the conduct of the claimant is regarded as so grossly negligent or reckless as altogether to eclipse the contribution of the defendant.[21] A recent example is

[14] *Reeves v Commissioner of Police of the Metropolis* [2000] 1 AC 360 (HL). On the application of contributory negligence to intentional self-harm, see 3.44.

[15] D Payne, 'Reduction of Damages for Contributory Negligence' (1955) 18 MLR 344, 350.

[16] [2009] EWCA Civ 1404, [2010] PIQR P8. See also *The Calliope* [1970] P 172 (PD).

[17] [2009] EWCA Civ 1404, [2010] PIQR P8 [45].

[18] This must surely be correct, since if *any* unreasonable conduct of the claimant amounted to a novus actus there would be no scope for the operation of contributory negligence in this type of case, and yet there are many examples of its being employed by the courts.

[19] See, eg, ID Field, 'Contributory Negligence and the Rule of Avoidable Losses' (2018) 38 OJLS 475, 487 ('it seems contrary to the terms and spirit of the apportionment legislation to treat subsequent claimant negligence as an intervening act, provided its occurrence is foreseeable').

[20] See, eg, *Davies v Swan Motor Co (Swansea) Ltd* [1949] 2 KB 291 (CA) 323 (Denning LJ).

[21] The same is true in many US jurisdictions that employ a 'pure comparative fault' approach analogous to the apportionment regime in the 1945 Act: see *Woods and Deere*, 100–102; PT Hayden, '*Butterfield* Rides Again: Plaintiff's Negligence as Superseding or Sole Proximate Cause' (2000) 33 Loy LA L Rev 887. And the same pattern is observable in cases involving third parties, where the courts sometimes decide that the intervening act of a third party broke the chain of causation between the defendant's negligence and the

Clay v TUI UK Ltd,[22] where the claimant and members of his family had become trapped on the balcony of a hotel room in Tenerife when the door leading to the balcony locked after being closed from the outside. After waiting for about thirty minutes, the claimant tried to cross to an adjacent balcony, but a ledge on which he stood collapsed, and he fell some distance to the ground, fracturing his skull. A majority of the Court of Appeal refused to overturn the finding of the trial judge that a defect in the door's lock was not a legal cause of the claimant's injuries because his attempting a life-threatening manoeuvre to escape a predicament that was no more than an inconvenience was a novus actus. Moylan LJ dissented, holding that the claimant's conduct had not been sufficiently unreasonable to eclipse the causative effect of the defective lock, and that it amounted only to contributory negligence, for which a discount of 45 per cent was appropriate. Like the contrast between the outcomes in *McKew* and *Spencer*, the disagreement in *Clay* demonstrates the difficulty of drawing a clear line between intervening causes and mere contributory negligence. It also illustrates the extent to which decisions in this area are matters of individual judgment, based on close analysis of the facts of the particular case.

It seems right that the courts should still be entitled to deny a claim altogether on the ground that the claimant's conduct was a novus actus. If an act of a third party can have the effect of negating the defendant's responsibility, then it is hard to see why the same should not be true of an act of the claimant. Furthermore, since the wording of the 1945 Act is inconsistent with a 100 per cent reduction in the damages for contributory negligence,[23] the continuing availability of this solution provides the courts with a safety valve for use in cases where the claimant's conduct is so outrageous or reckless that it seems unfair that the defendant should be required to pay any damages at all.[24] It is also hard to see any real force in the argument that such a solution is incompatible with the apportionment regime introduced by the 1945 Act, the driver of which was the injustice of the all-or-nothing nature of the common law defence of contributory negligence, rather than the operation of the novus actus principle. Having said all that, it is important to emphasize that the use of intervening cause analysis to deny recovery is relatively rare, and that generally the more appropriate response to intervening claimant conduct will be an apportionment of responsibility following a finding of contributory negligence. Hence courts should 'strive to invoke [legal causation analysis] only in situations where the plaintiff's fault, or causal contribution, is truly extraordinary, overwhelming, or gross compared to that of the defendant'.[25] **5.07**

claimant's damage, rather than holding both the third party and the defendant jointly and severally liable, and then apportioning responsibility via the rules on contribution between tortfeasors: see, eg, *Knightley v Johns* [1982] 1 WLR 349 (CA).

22 [2018] EWCA Civ 1177, [2018] 4 All ER 672. For discussion of a similar American case, see Hayden (n 21) 937–38.

23 See 4.20.

24 For example, Hayden (n 21) describes proximate cause (ie legal causation) analysis (at 945) as a 'doctrinal safety valve that is necessary for systems of [pure comparative fault] to remain acceptable and thus viable' in the American context.

25 Hayden (n 21) 945.

2. Illegality

5.08 The relationship between the illegality and contributory negligence doctrines is complex, not least because the law governing the former has undergone significant development lately,[26] and the full implications of those developments have not yet been worked out.[27] It is however clear that conduct that amounts to contributory negligence may constitute a criminal offence or other serious 'turpitude' and hence also trigger the illegality doctrine (*ex turpi causa non oritur actio*).[28] And it is also clear that, where that is the case, the claimant's action will fail entirely on account of the illegality, unless the illegality affects only a specific head of damages.[29] It must be emphasized, however, that the mere fact that the claimant was engaged in illegal conduct at the time of the alleged tort will not necessarily amount to contributory negligence, since many such forms of behaviour do not expose the perpetrator to unreasonable risk of injury, and even where they do they may not be causative of the damage. Hence, for example, if the claimant was involved in a head-on collision caused entirely by the driver of the other vehicle, then the fact that he was carrying illegal drugs in his car would not amount to contributory fault. Conversely, contributorily negligent conduct will often be perfectly lawful,[30] or constitute a trivial offence insufficiently serious to enliven the illegality doctrine.[31] For example, failing to wear a seat belt or driving a little in excess of the speed limit is generally a breach of the criminal law, but in the tort context such behaviour is dealt with exclusively by reference to the doctrine of contributory negligence.[32] Indeed, even in the case of relatively serious criminal conduct, the illegality defence may for some reason be held not to apply, but a deduction made for contributory negligence instead.[33]

5.09 When considering the relationship between illegality and contributory negligence, it is important to note the argument that the possibility of apportionment via contributory negligence ought to limit the operation of the illegality defence. In *Hall v Hebert*,[34] the

[26] See especially *Patel v Mirza* [2016] UKSC 42, [2017] AC 467; *Henderson v Dorset Healthcare University NHS Foundation Trust* [2020] UKSC 43, [2021] AC 563; *Energizer Supermarket Ltd v Holiday Snacks Ltd* [2022] UKPC 16.

[27] For a conspectus of the law, see J Goudkamp, 'The Law of Illegality After *Patel v Mirza*: Identifying the Issues' in A Bogg and S Green (eds), *Illegality After Patel v Mirza* (Hart Publishing 2018).

[28] See, eg, *Pitts v Hunt* [1991] 1 QB 24 (CA); *Vellino v Chief Constable of Greater Manchester* [2001] EWCA Civ 1249, [2002] 1 WLR 218.

[29] See, eg, *Burns v Edman* [1970] 2 QB 541 (QBD); *Gray v Thames Trains Ltd* [2009] UKHL 33, [2009] AC 1339.

[30] See, eg, *Badger v Ministry of Defence* [2005] EWHC 2941 (QB), [2006] 3 All ER 173; *Anderson v Lyotier* [2008] EWHC 2790 (QB).

[31] See *Vellino v Chief Constable of Greater Manchester* [2001] EWCA Civ 1249, [2002] 1 WLR 218 [70], where Sir Murray Stuart-Smith said that criminal conduct had to be 'sufficiently serious' for the illegality doctrine to apply, although generally speaking crimes punishable with imprisonment 'could be expected to qualify'. See also *Les Laboratoires Servier v Apotex Inc* [2014] UKSC 55, [2015] AC 430.

[32] See 3.25. The position in this regard used to be less clear, though before 1945 little turned on the distinction between illegality and contributory negligence, as both were complete defences. See further, *Williams*, 333–35.

[33] See, eg, *Revill v Newbery* [1996] QB 567 (CA) (attempted burglary); *McCracken v Smith* [2015] EWCA Civ 380, [2015] PIQR P19 (claim against third party by pillion passenger on stolen trails bike being driven dangerously).

[34] [1993] 2 SCR 159 (SCC). See also *British Columbia v Zastowny* [2008] SCC 4, [2008] 1 SCR 27.

Supreme Court of Canada severely curtailed the scope of the illegality defence, essentially confining it to situations where, were the claimant able to recover damages, tort law would stultify the operation of the criminal law. In a concurring opinion, Cory J argued that the enactment of apportionment legislation in Canadian jurisdictions weighed strongly in favour of this limiting of the illegality doctrine. According to his Honour, there was 'a great deal to be said for the position that apportionment legislation goes far towards removing *ex turpi causa* as a defence'.[35] A similar view was expressed by Sedley LJ in his dissenting judgment in *Vellino v Chief Constable of Greater Manchester*.[36] The claimant in that case had thrown himself out of a second-floor window to avoid being arrested by the police. At first instance, Elias J held that attempting to escape from custody was a sufficiently serious offence to bring into play the illegality doctrine, and that the claim therefore failed on this ground. But he went on to hold that, if he was wrong on that point, then the claimant's damages should in any case be reduced by two-thirds for contributory negligence. On appeal, the majority of the Court of Appeal agreed that the illegality doctrine defeated the claim in its entirety. However, Sedley LJ disagreed, holding that the claimant should have judgment for one-third of his damages in accordance with the trial judge's contingent holding on contributory negligence. This was, he considered, a fairer solution than the application of the *ex turpi causa* principle. Since the passage of the Law Reform (Contributory Negligence) Act 1945, he said, 'the power to apportion liability between claimant and defendant in tort actions of all kinds has afforded a far more appropriate tool for doing justice than the blunt instrument of turpitude'.[37] The view of Cory J and Sedley LJ was however implicitly rejected by Lord Walker in *Stone & Rolls Ltd v Moore Stephens*.[38] His Lordship accepted that illegality was a 'blunt instrument', but was 'far from convinced' that if the defence were not available 'contributory negligence would provide a more sensitive or effective tool'.[39] And in *Miller v Miller*, the High Court of Australia also rejected the argument that the greater flexibility of the apportionment legislation warranted reconsideration of the scope of the illegality defence.[40] It is also worth noting in this regard that the route suggested by Cory J and Sedley LJ might be complicated by the fact that illegality is a defence to all torts, but contributory negligence applies only to some,[41] and by the fact that (as was pointed out above) not all illegal conduct of the claimant at the time of the tort constitutes contributory negligence. Turning finally to the positive law on this issue, it is clear that the English courts have not adopted Sedley LJ's approach, and that they continue to use the illegality doctrine to deny recovery altogether, even though on the facts apportionment for contributory negligence was also a possibility.[42]

---

35 [1993] 2 SCR 159 (SCC) 207.

36 [2001] EWCA Civ 1249, [2002] 1 WLR 218.

37 Ibid [55].

38 [2009] UKHL 39, [2009] AC 1391.

39 Ibid [185].

40 *Miller v Miller* [2011] HCA 9, (2011) 242 CLR 446 [97]. cf *Jackson v Harrison* (1978) 138 CLR 438 (HCA) 465 (Murphy J).

41 See chapter 2.

42 See, eg, *McCracken v Smith* [2015] EWCA Civ 380, [2015] PIQR P19 (claim by pillion passenger on stolen trails bike against driver of bike barred for illegality).

3. *Volenti Non Fit Injuria*

5.10 Like illegality, the defence of *volenti non fit injuria* (often referred to as 'voluntary assumption of risk') is a general defence applicable across the law of tort, although outside of negligence it usually goes by the name of consent. In negligence cases, the defence applies where the claimant consented to the lack of reasonable care that created the risk of injury that materialized.[43] There is a considerable degree of overlap between *volenti* and contributory negligence, and the two defences often fall for consideration on the same facts.[44] Indeed, it is likely to be rare for a claimant who is *volens* not also to be considered to have been contributorily negligent.[45] (Note that the reverse is not true—there are many acts of contributory negligence that in no way evince consent to the defendant's breach.) However, despite the overlap between the two doctrines, there are also significant differences between them.[46] Although it is unnecessary to enumerate all the respects in which they are distinctive,[47] one example can be given. While the *volenti* doctrine requires that the claimant be subjectively aware of the risk generated by the defendant's conduct,[48] no such requirement exists in the law of contributory negligence, where (at least prima facie) a more objective approach prevails.[49] Hence in a case where the claimant took a lift in a car driven by an intoxicated driver, *volenti* would not be available if the claimant did not know that the driver was drunk but should reasonably have realized this, whereas contributory negligence would.[50]

5.11 Prior to the enactment of the apportionment legislation, there was little reason rigorously to distinguish between *volenti* and contributory negligence, since both were complete bars to liability. Nowadays, however, the distinction is highly pertinent since *volenti* remains a complete defence while contributory negligence goes only to quantum. As with illegality,[51] it can be argued that the remit of the complete defence should be limited in the light of the possibility of apportionment for contributory negligence, and this argument has

---

43 *Wooldridge v Sumner* [1963] 2 QB 43 (CA) 69 (Diplock LJ).

44 See, eg, *Morris v Murray* [1991] 2 QB 6 (CA); *Reeves v Commissioner of Police of the Metropolis* [2000] 1 AC 360 (HL); *Corr v IBC Vehicles Ltd* [2008] UKHL 13, [2008] 1 AC 884.

45 Though the claim that 'contributory negligence will be available as a defence in any case in which voluntary assumption of risk is available' (Commonwealth of Australia, *Review of the Law of Negligence: Final Report* (2002) para 4.20) may be exaggerated. For a possible counter-example, see *Murray v Harringay Arena Ltd* [1951] 2 KB 529 (CA) (though query whether this was not really a 'no breach' case).

46 See *Fleming*, 327: 'Obviously [the defence of *volenti non fit injuria*] bears much resemblance to contributory negligence. Most often, indeed, the two defences overlap ... But, like intersecting circles, some cases support one defence without the other; thus to assume the risk may in some circumstances be perfectly reasonable or (per contra) the risk, though unreasonable, may not be fully appreciated and assumed.'

47 For an attempt to do so, see FH Bohlen, 'Contributory Negligence' (1908) 21 Harv L Rev 233, 243–51.

48 *Bartlett v English Cricket Board Association of Cricket Officials* 2015 WL 5037730 (Wolverhampton CC) [55] (HHJ Lopez) ('*Volenti* has no application as the Claimant has not perceived there is a risk'); *Lear v Hickstead Ltd* [2016] EWHC 528 (QB), [2016] 4 WLR 73 [101] (Picken J) ('[the claimant] was unaware of the risk of the ramp falling on him. He cannot, therefore, be regarded as having voluntarily accepted the risk that what happened to him would happen').

49 See 3.06.

50 See K Hogg, 'Guest Passengers: A Drunk Driver's Defences' (1994) 2 Torts LJ 37, 58.

51 See 5.09.

gained considerable traction in the *volenti* context.[52] This may be partly because the scope of the *volenti* defence is so unclear in the first place, and partly because its rationale is not so easily differentiated from the rationale of contributory negligence as is the rationale of illegality.[53] There was in any case a widespread perception in the post-war years that the advent of apportionment had contributed to the decline of *volenti*. Hence Lord Pearce said in 1964 that since contributory negligence had ceased to be a total defence and it had 'become possible to produce a fair result by apportionment, the reluctance to find the total defence of *volenti non fit injuria* has become more marked',[54] and seven years later Lord Denning MR remarked that '[n]ow that contributory negligence is not a complete defence ... the defence of [*volenti*] has been closely considered and, in consequence, it has been severely limited'.[55] These observations were echoed by McHugh J in a later Australian case involving a claim by an injured passenger against an intoxicated driver:[56]

> It is difficult to escape the conclusion that the introduction of apportionment legislation has influenced the courts in characterising the conduct of the passenger as contributory negligence, rather than as a voluntary assumption of risk ... Apportionment legislation enables the court to apportion responsibility for the plaintiff's damages according to the respective responsibility of the plaintiff and the defendant for that damage. Since the introduction of apportionment legislation, contributory negligence has been the preferred characterisation of the conduct of the plaintiff who accepts a lift from a driver known to be intoxicated.

Today, very few negligence claims fail on the ground of *volenti*, and many of the cases in which the language of 'voluntary assumption of risk' is employed seem to be using that terminology to express the conclusion that there was either no breach of duty or no causal link between any such breach and the claimant's damage.[57] Nevertheless, the view of a Canadian judge that there is no place for a complete defence of *volenti* in the era of apportionment[58] has not been accepted by the English courts, and in a narrow band of cases where the claimant has willingly accepted conduct of the defendant involving a high risk of injury, the *volenti* doctrine will still operate to defeat their claim in its entirety.[59] English law has therefore arrived at the solution advocated by John Fleming in the 1970s for Californian law, of letting the defence of *volenti* survive 'as an embodiment of the

[52] Indeed, in some US jurisdictions, the legislation introducing apportionment for contributory negligence either abolished the *volenti* defence or merged it into the new 'comparative negligence' regime: see *Woods and Deere*, 13.

[53] According to an early American commentator, 'It is often said that ... the two principles [ie *volenti* and contributory negligence] are identical: and throughout the cases there is the greatest confusion between them' (C Warren, 'Volenti Non Fit Injuria in Actions of Negligence' (1895) 8 Harv L Rev 457, 459).

[54] *ICI Ltd v Shatwell* [1965] AC 656 (HL) 686. See also at 672 (Lord Reid); *Stapley v Gypsum Mines Ltd* [1953] AC 663 (HL) 677 (Lord Porter); *McMath v Rimmer Bros (Liverpool) Ltd* [1962] 1 WLR 1.

[55] *Nettleship v Weston* [1971] 2 QB 691 (CA) 701.

[56] *Joslyn v Berryman* [2003] HCA 34, (2003) 214 CLR 552 [27] (footnote omitted).

[57] For discussion, see J Goudkamp, *Tort Law Defences* (Hart Publishing 2013) 55–58.

[58] *Crocker v Sundance Northwest Resorts Ltd* [1988] 1 SCR 1186 (SCC) 1202 (Wilson J).

[59] The leading modern examples are *Imperial Chemical Industries Ltd v Shatwell* [1965] AC 656 (HL) and *Morris v Murray* [1991] 2 QB 6 (CA).

still vital individual freedom to forgo one's right to sue for negligence', but redefining its conditions 'so that it would only be applicable on stringent proof of genuine consent'.[60]

4. Default of the Claimant

5.12 'Default of the claimant' is recognized as a defence to certain strict liability causes of action, most notably the rule in *Rylands v Fletcher*. The gist of the defence is that the claimant was wholly to blame for the damage that they suffered. The leading case in the *Rylands* context is *Dunn v Birmingham Canal Co*,[61] where the claimant worked mines beneath a canal without supporting the surface, even though he knew that this created a risk that water would escape from the canal into his mines. The mine workings were indeed flooded, and the claimant sought damages from the owners of the canal under *Rylands v Fletcher*. According to Cockburn CJ:[62]

> I cannot think that, where an injury results to a man, not from the danger alone to which the act of another has exposed him, but from his own wilful and intentional exposure to such danger, as its proximate and immediate cause, he, who has thus brought the injury on himself, can maintain an action in respect of it.

Where the injury was brought about by an act of the claimant done with knowledge 'that the injury would be the probable consequence of the act',[63] Cockburn CJ continued, it would defeat his claim. And since on the facts the claimant had seen (and even courted) the danger, his action was dismissed.

5.13 The same defence of default of the claimant was recognized at common law in actions for cattle trespass[64] and for damage inflicted by a dangerous animal. Hence a claimant who had entered a stable of zebras without permission, and then patted one of them, resulting in a kick that forced him into the stall of another zebra, which bit him on the hand, failed in his action against their keeper because he was considered to have brought his injuries upon himself.[65] In the animals context, the common law defence has been superseded by section 5(1) of the Animals Act 1971, which states that a person is not liable under sections 2–4 of that Act—encompassing not only damage caused by dangerous animals and cattle trespass, but also injuries to livestock caused by dogs—'for any damage which is due wholly to the fault of the person suffering it'.[66] 'Fault' in this provision has the same meaning as in the Law Reform (Contributory Negligence) Act 1945.[67] Another statutory provision that

---

[60] JG Fleming, 'Foreword: Comparative Negligence at Last—By Judicial Choice' (1976) 64 Calif L Rev 239, 266.

[61] (1872) LR 7 QB 244 (QBD).

[62] ibid 260. See also *Rylands v Fletcher* (1866) LR 1 Exch 265 (Exch Ch) 279–80 (Blackburn J).

[63] (1872) LR 7 QB 244 (QBD) 260, 261.

[64] See, eg, *Crow v Wood* [1971] 1 QB 77 (CA).

[65] *Marlor v Ball* (1900) 16 TLR 239 (CA). The defence was not however available where a dog wandering unattended in the street bit a man who patted it on the head (*Gordon v Mackenzie* 1913 SC 109 (IH)), nor where a lion mauled a child who relieved herself next to its cage (*Pearson v Coleman Bros* [1948] 2 KB 359 (CA)).

[66] For a full discussion of s 5(1) and its common law antecedents, see P North, *Civil Liability for Animals* (OUP 2012) paras 2.154 et seq.

[67] Animals Act 1971, s 11.

imposes strict liability subject to a complete defence of default of the claimant is section 209 of the Water Industry Act 1991, which concerns escapes of water.[68]

The relationship between the common law 'default of the claimant' defence and contributory negligence is unclear. According to Glanville Williams, the former was synonymous with the common law defence of contributory negligence,[69] in which case it would in effect have been abolished by the Law Reform (Contributory Negligence) Act 1945, with the result that where it would previously have applied to defeat liability the position would now be governed by the apportionment regime established by the Act. However, an alternative view is that default of the claimant was a distinct doctrine, going to (legal) causation. This interpretation is consistent with the requirement that the claimant must have been wholly to blame for the damage, as well as the language of legal causation employed by Cockburn CJ in *Dunn* ('proximate and immediate cause'). It is also consistent with the view that the three principal defences to a claim under *Rylands v Fletcher*—act of God, act of a stranger, and default of the claimant—are causation-based, with the event that gives rise to them being treated as the proximate cause of the claimant's injury.[70] If that interpretation is accepted, then it would seem to follow that the complete defence of default of the claimant survived the 1945 Act and would today operate to defeat a claim where the requirements set down for its application are met. (Clearly the position is *a fortiori* when it comes to s 5(1) of the Animals Act, which was passed into law decades after the 1945 Act was enacted.) **5.14**

That still leaves the question of whether the partial defence of contributory negligence would be available to a defendant in a *Rylands* claim who was unable to establish the more onerous requirements of the complete defence, which question is considered elsewhere in this work.[71] One final point to note is that, even if the defendant succeeds in establishing a complete defence to a *Rylands* claim, there is still the possibility of liability in negligence, where (subject to a possible legal causation argument) any contributory fault of the claimant would serve only to reduce the damages.[72] It is however hard to imagine circumstances in which negligence liability would arise where the defence of default of the claimant was made out. **5.15**

---

[68] See Water Industry Act 1991, s 209(2) (defence where 'the escape was due wholly to the fault of the person who sustained the loss or damage or of any servant, agent or contractor of his'). Where the damage is only partially the fault of the claimant, there is apportionment for contributory negligence: s 209(4). See also the strict liability for escape of gas from a storage facility, which is again subject to a de facto default of the claimant defence which operates alongside contributory negligence: Gas Act 1965, s 14(3).

[69] *Williams*, 210.

[70] See *Transco v Stockport MBC* [2003] UKHL 61, [2004] 2 AC 1 [59] (Lord Hobhouse): '[The defences to a claim in *Rylands v Fletcher*] were the same as those used elsewhere in the common law in relation to strict liabilities and related to the causal connection between the relevant damage and the conduct of the defendant'. Compare the rival view that defences such as default of the claimant have been developed in order to link the rule in *Rylands* 'more closely to the pervasive concept of fault liability' (*Fleming*, 385), a view endorsed by a majority of the High Court of Australia in *Burnie Port Authority v General Jones Pty Ltd* (1994) 179 CLR 520 (HCA) 545.

[71] See 2.15–2.17. As regards liability for animals, the defence of contributory negligence is clearly available to a defendant unable to establish the more onerous requirements of s 5(1) of the Animals Act: see 2.23.

[72] See L Klar, 'Contributory Negligence and Apportionment in Canadian Tort Law' in K Barker and R Grantham (eds), *Apportionment in Private Law* (Hart Publishing 2019) 157.

5. Contribution Between Wrongdoers

5.16 The law of contributory negligence and the rules relating to contribution between wrongdoers are intimately related. Both deal with situations in which more than one person is regarded as responsible for the same damage, and both respond to these situations by seeking to apportion the responsibility for that damage between the two (or more) parties regarded as responsible for it.[73] The difference between them is that while the law of contributory negligence deals with the apportionment of responsibility between the wrongdoer and the victim of the wrong, the law of contribution deals with the apportionment of responsibility between wrongdoers *inter se*. The law of contribution is outside the scope of this work, and detailed discussion of it should be sought elsewhere.[74] Nevertheless, because both contributory negligence and contribution between wrongdoers are concerned with the apportionment of responsibility between persons who have caused the same damage, there are many parallels between them, as a result of which it can be illuminating when considering contributory negligence to look at the equivalent aspect of the law of contribution. Hence, for example, the court is required to determine a wrongdoer's contribution based on what is 'just and equitable having regard to the extent of that person's responsibility for the damage in question'.[75] As we have seen,[76] a similar test is used when determining the discount for contributory negligence, and the courts take into account the same considerations in the two contexts, namely the relative culpability of the parties and the relative causal potency of their actions.[77] Similarly, in both contexts the decision as to apportionment is regarded as highly discretionary, as a result of which appellate intervention is discouraged.[78] Furthermore, the guideline discounts set down in respect of failure to wear a seat belt[79] have also been applied in contribution cases.[80] Finally, the two doctrines can be engaged on the same set of facts, where the claimant suffers injury as a result of the fault of more than one wrongdoer and of the claimant themselves. In such cases, it has been held that the questions of contributory negligence and contribution must be kept separate, with the court first determining the extent of the claimant's responsibility

---

73 See Civil Liability (Contribution) Act 1978, s 2.

74 See C Mitchell, *The Law of Contribution and Reimbursement* (OUP 2003); *Winfield & Jolowicz*, paras 22-007 et seq.

75 Civil Liability (Contribution) Act 1978, s 2(1).

76 See 4.02.

77 For contributory negligence, see 4.29–4.35; and for contribution, see *Downs v Chappell* [1997] 1 WLR 426 (CA); *Madden v Quirke* [1989] 1 WLR 702 (QBD). Unlike in contributory negligence cases, the courts in contribution cases have sometimes taken into account conduct that was not causative of the relevant damage, such as an attempt by a wrongdoer to conceal their involvement: see, eg, *Re-Source America International Ltd v Platt Site Services Ltd* [2004] EWCA Civ 665, 95 Con LR 1. It can however be questioned whether this is consistent with the wording of s 2(1) of the 1978 Act.

78 On appellate intervention with apportionment for contributory negligence, see 6.25–6.27; and for the equivalent principles in contribution cases, see, eg, *Kerry v Carter* [1969] 1 WLR 1372 (CA) 1376.

79 See 4.60–4.66.

80 See *Jones v Wilkins* [2001] RTR 19 (CA); *Williams v Williams* [2013] EWCA Civ 455, [2013] PIQR P17. Both cases concerned the failure of a parent safely to secure a child in a vehicle, and in both the court followed *Froom v Butcher* [1976] QB 286 (CA) in apportioning to the parent 25 per cent of the responsibility for the injuries the child suffered in a subsequent accident.

as against the defendants collectively, and then proceeding to determine the responsibility of the defendants inter se.[81]

6. The Avoidable Consequences Rule

One of the three central rules concerning mitigation of damage is that the defendant is not liable for loss that the claimant could have avoided by taking reasonable care.[82] For example, if a claimant unreasonably fails to undergo treatment for an injury caused by the defendant, the claimant will be unable to recover compensation in respect of losses that would have been avoided had the treatment been given.[83] This rule is generally known as the 'avoidable consequences' (or 'avoidable losses') rule. There are both similarities and differences between the contributory negligence doctrine and the avoidable consequences rule. One obvious similarity is that both are governed by objective tests, in that they are concerned with the reasonableness of what the claimant did. Conversely, two important distinctions between the two doctrines should be highlighted. One is that the avoidable consequences rule applies to all civil wrongs, whereas contributory negligence extends only to some. Hence, for example, no apportionment for contributory negligence is possible in a claim for battery,[84] but if a victim of a tortious physical assault 'heedlessly fails to care for his wounds so that gangrene sets in and he loses a limb, he cannot recover for that aggravation of his original injury' applying the avoidable consequences rule.[85] And the other important distinction is that contributory negligence results only in the claimant's recovery of damages being scaled back, with a deduction being made following an apportionment of responsibility as between the parties. By contrast, where a claimant has failed to mitigate their loss applying the avoidable consequences rule no damages are recoverable in respect of that loss at all. **5.17**

The chief difficulty when it comes to the relationship between the rules regarding contributory negligence and the avoidable consequences principle is in identifying the dividing line between the two.[86] This question is of paramount importance in the light of the second of the differences between the doctrines identified in the previous paragraph, namely that the mitigation rule bars recovery of the relevant losses completely, while contributory negligence leads only to a reduction in the damages awarded. The orthodox view as to the nature of the distinction is that contributory negligence is concerned with pre-tort fault whereas mitigation of damage relates to post-tort fault.[87] **5.18**

[81] See *Fitzgerald v Lane* [1989] AC 328 (HL); *Nationwide Building Society v Dunlop Haywards (DHL) Ltd* [2009] EWHC 254 (Comm), [2010] 1 WLR 258. For more extended discussion of the operation of the contributory negligence doctrine in cases concerning multiple defendants, see 4.73–4.75.

[82] On mitigation, see generally *Burrows*, 127–32. The other two principal rules of mitigation concern reasonable action (as opposed to unreasonable inaction) and so are far removed from the contributory negligence doctrine.

[83] See, eg, *McAuley v London Transport Executive* [1957] 2 Lloyd's Rep 500 (CA).

[84] See 2.06–2.09.

[85] F James Jr, 'Contributory Negligence' (1953) 62 Yale LJ 691, 708.

[86] For a thorough recent discussion of this issue, see ID Field, 'Contributory Negligence and the Rule of Avoidable Losses' (2018) 38 OJLS 475. See also *Williams*, ch 11.

[87] See, eg, *McGregor*, para 6-018 ('Distinguishing between the application of contributory negligence and that of mitigation is comparatively easy. In this context, contributory negligence comes in only before the

According to William Prosser (writing of contributory negligence as a complete defence):[88]

> The statement commonly made as to the distinction between the two [rules] is that contributory negligence is negligence of the plaintiff before any damage, or any invasion of rights, has occurred, which bars all recovery. The rule of avoidable consequences comes into play after a legal wrong has occurred, but while some damages may still be averted, and bars recovery only for such damages. Thus, if the plaintiff is injured in an automobile collision, his contributorily negligent driving before the collision will prevent any recovery at all, but his failure to obtain proper medical care for his broken leg will bar only his damages for the subsequent aggravated condition of the leg.

Drawing the distinction in this way generally makes it straightforward to apply, other than in the unlikely scenario of negligent conduct of the claimant which begins before the time at which the cause of action crystallizes and which continues until after that time.[89] The orthodox approach to the distinction between contributory negligence and mitigation is also consistent with the fact that in English law the avoidable consequences rule never applies to pre-tort conduct, so that, for example, in a road accident case any additional damage caused by the claimant's failure to wear a seat belt will be dealt with by the apportionment regime rather than the rules on mitigation.[90] A third point in favour of this way of making the distinction is that it fits with the fact that contributory negligence used to be a complete defence to liability. As Robert Stevens points out:[91]

> Prior to 1945 it was quite clear that contributory negligence only applied to the claimant's fault before the commission of a wrong. The defence operated as a complete bar ... It never operated so as to, say, generally rule out a head of loss where the defendant was negligent in subsequently failing to take steps to avoid it. This area was, and is, governed by the law of mitigation.

Stevens goes on to say that there is nothing in the 1945 Act that necessitates that the same approach be taken today. However, it could be argued that since the courts have held that only conduct of the claimant that would have given rise to the complete defence of contributory negligence before 1945 can amount to 'fault' capable of triggering the

commission of the wrong, mitigation necessarily after its commission'); *Luntz*, para 1.12.11 ('The demarcation line between the two doctrines is thus one of the dates at which the plaintiff's conduct occurred'). See also *Restatement (Second) of the Law of Torts* (1965) § 918(1) (avoidable consequences rule applies to harm that could have been avoided 'by the use of reasonable effort or expenditure *after the commission of the tort*' (emphasis added)); *Richardson v Schultz* (1980) 25 SASR 1 (SC) 17–20.

88 *Prosser*, 398.

89 It may also be difficult in a pure economic loss case to identify precisely when the tort occurs. In the negligent misrepresentation case of *Webb Resolutions Ltd v ESurv Ltd* [2012] EWHC 3653 (TCC), [2013] PNLR 15, it was said (at [144]–[146]) that if the claimant's unreasonable conduct came after they had irrevocably committed themselves to a transaction in reliance on the defendant's advice, then that might be a case of failure to mitigate rather than contributory negligence, presumably on the ground that that was when the cause of action arose.

90 See 4.60–4.66. See also *Williams*, 288 ('[m]itigation of damages does not come in until the first damage has been sustained'); *Richardson v Schultz* (1980) 25 SASR 1 (SC) (Williams J) ('in English and Australian law a plaintiff is not required to take steps to mitigate damages until he has suffered a wrong at the hands of the defendant causing actual or potential damage').

91 R Stevens, 'Should Contributory Fault be Analogue or Digital?' in A Dyson et al (eds), *Defences in Tort* (Hart Publishing 2015) 259.

apportionment regime,[92] post-tort conduct (which would not have given rise to the complete defence) is incapable of having this effect, and must therefore be dealt with by applying the avoidable consequences rule instead.

There are, however, several difficulties with the orthodox way of drawing the distinction between contributory negligence and mitigation. The first is that there are cases in which the courts have simply assumed (without addressing the issue) that the 1945 Act is capable of applying to post-tort conduct, including *Spencer v Wincanton Holdings Ltd*,[93] a decision of the Court of Appeal discussed earlier in this chapter with reference to the relationship between intervening causes and contributory negligence.[94] Another such case is *The Calliope*,[95] where the claimant's vessel was damaged in a collision with the defendant's vessel for which both ships were to blame. In view of the damage sustained by the ship, it was decided to undertake certain manoeuvres to protect her, but one of these was undertaken carelessly, as a result of which she suffered further damage. Brandon J held that the defendant was liable for that further damage, subject to a deduction for contributory negligence. He found it 'difficult to see why, as a matter of principle, it should make any difference that, in relation to a particular part of the damage arising, or alleged to arise, from the casualty, the later negligence of [the claimant] should follow rather than precede the casualty itself'.[96] It might, of course, be replied that these cases were wrongly decided and are not good authority for the point in issue since they did not grapple with it. But they are nevertheless hard to dismiss out of hand. A second difficulty with the orthodox approach is that its strict application produces results that might be considered to be counter-intuitive. Consider, for example, a case in which a fire begins in the claimant's house because of the defendant's negligence. Once the fire is well underway the claimant arrives home, but negligently fails to call the fire brigade as soon as they ought to have, a failure which results in additional damage being done to the house. According to the orthodox approach, the avoidable loss rule would govern this situation since the claimant's negligence occurred after their cause of action arose, which was once the house had suffered damage that was more than negligible.[97] However, unless the claimant's failure amounts to an intervening legal cause,[98] one would expect to see the court apply the 1945 Act here, and apportion responsibility for the additional damage between the parties. The final and perhaps most serious objection to the orthodox approach is that it is not clear *why* whether the claimant acted unreasonably before or after the tort was committed should determine whether responsibility for the relevant harm is apportioned between the parties (contributory negligence) or laid entirely at the claimant's door (mitigation).[99] As Williams 5.19

[92] See 2.03.

[93] [2009] EWCA Civ 1404, [2010] PIQR P8.

[94] See 5.05.

[95] [1970] P 172 (PD).

[96] ibid 182.

[97] See *Homburg Houtimport BV v Agrosin Private Ltd (The Starsin)* [2003] UKHL 12, [2004] 1 AC 715. Field points out that another type of case that poses significant problems for the orthodox distinction is where the claimant's post-tort negligence contributes to a second occurrence of damage which is indivisible from the first: see Field (n 86) 485–87.

[98] As to which, see 5.02–5.07.

[99] See Field (n 86) 478 and sources there cited.

pointed out, drawing the line in this way can result in apparently arbitrary distinctions being drawn.[100]

5.20 A possible solution to these difficulties would be to abolish the avoidable consequences rule in tort cases and extend the remit of the contributory negligence doctrine to all post-tort fault on the part of the claimant, thereby replacing the current all-or-nothing allocation of responsibility for post-tort fault with an approach based on apportionment. This radical step was taken in the *Restatement (Third) of Torts: Apportionment of Liability*,[101] in which it is said that:[102]

> The underlying premise of comparative responsibility is that a plaintiff's negligence should reduce, not bar, the plaintiff's recovery for any damages caused both by that conduct and by the defendant's conduct. A plaintiff's failure to mitigate damages should no longer constitute a bar to recovering those damages. Under comparative responsibility, a plaintiff's negligent failure to mitigate damages is a factor to consider when assigning percentages of responsibility. It does not totally exclude recovery of the damages caused by the plaintiff's failure to mitigate.

However, there are serious problems with this approach, which arise out of the underlying rationale of the avoidable consequences rule. That rule is best understood as an aspect of the fundamental remedial principle that a person who commits a wrong is obliged to put the victim into the position that they would have been in had the wrong not been committed. Part and parcel of that remedial principle is the limitation of recovery to what we might call 'reasonable losses', which is to say losses that flow naturally from the wrong and which are not suffered by the claimant simply because of their unreasonable conduct.[103] As Iain Field points out, 'unreasonable or extravagant conduct on the claimant's part has no real bearing on the measure of the claimant's reasonable losses and thus the sum in damages awarded', and hence it would be unfair to require a defendant to pay for a portion of an avoidable loss.[104] Suppose, for example, that a claimant chooses to repair a damaged car at an unreasonably high price. Would it not be absurd to suggest that some of the additional cost should be payable by the defendant responsible for the damage? A further difficulty with this proposal is that mitigation applies to all torts and contributory negligence does not.[105] This means that were this proposal to be adopted in English law then either contributory negligence would have to be extended to all torts, or a bizarre situation would arise whereby a claimant who sues in, say, deceit or battery would potentially be left worse off than a claimant who brings proceedings in negligence, as the avoidable consequences rule would still apply in the former torts even after its replacement with contributory negligence in the latter.

---

[100] See his discussion of *Anderson (Commander of The Flying Fish) v Hoen* (1865) 3 Moo PC NS 77, 16 ER 29 (PC) (*Williams*, 288–89). Other problems with the orthodox distinction are flagged by Williams at 289 et seq.

[101] *Restatement (Third) of Torts: Apportionment of Responsibility* (2000) § 3, cmt b ('No rule about mitigation of damages or avoidable consequences . . . categorically excludes recovery'). See also *Williams*, 290 et seq; Y Adar, 'Comparative Negligence and Mitigation of Damages: Two Sister Doctrines in Search of Reunion' (2013) 31 Quinnipiac L Rev 783.

[102] *Restatement (Third) of Torts: Apportionment of Responsibility* (2000) § 3, cmt b.

[103] See Field (n 86) 494–97.

[104] ibid 496.

[105] A point emphasized by J Goudkamp, 'Rethinking Contributory Negligence' in SGA Pitel et al (eds), *Tort Law: Challenging Orthodoxy* (Hart Publishing 2013) 332.

An alternative way of drawing the distinction between contributory negligence and the avoidable consequences rule has recently been put forward by Field, who argues that:[106] **5.21**

> [T]he preferable distinction between contributory negligence and the rule of avoidable losses lies simply in whether the claimant's unreasonable conduct (i) contributes to the claimant's damage (contributory negligence) or (ii) explains why certain losses actually suffered by the claimant do not fall within the range of reasonable losses that flow from the damage, and which are not compensable in damages for this reason (the rule of avoidable losses).

Field's solution rests heavily on the distinction between damage (a setback to the claimant's interests capable of giving rise to liability in negligence) and loss (the deleterious knock-on effects of that damage, such as monetary losses flowing from a physical injury).[107] Field's approach appears to avoid the difficulties attendant on both the orthodox pre-tort/post-tort distinction and the alternative solution of contributory negligence supplanting the avoidable consequences rule altogether. Two other merits of his proposal should be highlighted. The first is that it seems to be consistent with the wording of the 1945 Act, which makes apportionment conditional on the fault of the claimant contributing to 'damage', a concept defined as including 'loss of life and personal injury' (section 6(1)) and which is clearly distinct from the 'damages' which are to be reduced once a finding of contributory negligence has been made. Secondly, since Field's concept of 'damage' encompasses post-tort harms capable of giving rise to an independent cause of action (such as the loss of a leg following an earlier injury to that leg), his proposal has the merit of explaining the post-1945 case law, where the application of contributory negligence to post-tort fault has occurred only in cases where that fault led to the occurrence of a separate injury which could itself have grounded a negligence claim.[108] Having said all that, Field's solution may give rise to difficulties of its own. In particular, while the application of an approach based on a distinction between damage and loss should work well in negligence claims for personal injury or property damage, it may prove more problematic in torts which are actionable without proof of damage (or where 'damage' might carry a different meaning than in negligence), and in negligence claims for pure economic loss, where the distinction between damage and loss may be harder, or perhaps even impossible, to draw.[109]

7. Provocation

The law of torts in all the major common law jurisdictions recognizes the doctrine of provocation. When applicable, this doctrine diminishes awards of punitive damages,[110] and there is some support for the proposition that provocation is also capable of reducing compensatory damages.[111] There is clearly a degree of affinity between the doctrine of **5.22**

106 ibid 479.

107 See D Nolan, 'Rights, Damage and Loss' (2017) 37 OJLS 255, 270–74.

108 This was true in both *Spencer v Wincanton Holdings Ltd* and *The Calliope*, the cases discussed in 5.19.

109 See Nolan (n 107) 263.

110 *Fontin v Katapodis* (1962) 108 CLR 177 (HCA); *Lane v Holloway* [1968] 1 QB 379 (CA); *Hoebergen v Koppens* [1974] 2 NZLR 597 (SC).

111 *Murphy v Culhane* [1977] QB 94 (CA) 98; *McAleer v Chief Constable of the PSNI* [2014] NIQB 53 [28]; *Rennie v Morrison* [2014] CSOH 123, 2014 SLT 862 [17]. In Canada, the 'weight of authority' supports this proposition (Klar (n 72) 154 fn 63): see, eg, *Hurley v Moore* (1993) 107 DLR (4th) 664 (Nfld CA).

contributory negligence and the rules regarding provocation, and some scholars take the view that the latter are merely a specific application of the former. For instance, Lewis Klar claims that:[112]

> Contributory negligence can be defined as any unreasonable conduct on the part of a plaintiff which contributes to his injury. Provocation can be viewed as a specific type of contributorily negligent behaviour. [Reliance on both doctrines involves the defendant] arguing that the plaintiff's provocatory conduct was unreasonable and contributed to his own injury.

Likewise, David Cheifetz writes that 'the doctrine of provocation ... seems suspiciously like contributory fault'.[113] He concludes 'that the doctrine of provocation in relation to intentional torts is in fact a restatement of contributory fault'[114] and that 'provocation is flagrant contributory fault—something more than mere carelessness for one's own safety'.[115]

5.23 However, the better view is that, although the two doctrines may overlap, they are distinct. There are at least two arguments in support of this position. The first is that, whereas contributory negligence by definition involves fault on the part of the claimant, it is doubtful whether provocation requires the claimant to have been at fault.[116] And the second argument is that, unlike the doctrine of contributory negligence, the provocation doctrine seems to require close scrutiny of the nature of the defendant's response. For example, and by analogy with the criminal law,[117] it is relevant to enquire whether the defendant lost self-control[118] and to consider the gravity of the provocation to which the defendant was exposed.[119] No parallel enquiries are made in asking whether the claimant is guilty of contributory negligence. In the light of these fundamental differences between the two doctrines, the view that one is a sub-category of the other cannot be supported. Nevertheless, it must be acknowledged that were contributory negligence to be recognized as a defence to an intentional tort[120] there would be a significant potential overlap between the spheres of operation of the two doctrines. On the assumption that provocation may lead to a reduction in compensatory damages, this could be considered to be an argument against extending the contributory negligence doctrine to these torts, since it may be supposed that in this context the most egregious cases of contributory fault will already amount to provocation.[121]

---

[112] L Klar, 'Recent Developments in Canadian Law: Tort Law' (1985) 17 Ottawa L Rev 325, 336–37.

[113] D Cheifetz, *Apportionment of Fault in Tort* (Canada Law Book Ltd 1981) 197.

[114] ibid 197–98.

[115] ibid 199.

[116] For an extreme example from the criminal law, see *R v Doughty* (1986) 83 Cr App R 319 (CA) (provocation consisted in the incessant crying of a seventeen-day-old baby). cf *Rennie v Morrison* [2014] CSOH 123, 2014 SLT 862 [17], where Lord Jones remarked that 'the act of provocation must be a wrongful act, otherwise an entirely innocent act which happens to anger an irrational wrongdoer would operate to exclude or mitigate damages for injury caused by the irrational wrongdoer's unlawful act'.

[117] Coroners and Justice Act 2009, ss 54, 56(1).

[118] In *McAleer v Chief Constable of the PSNI* [2014] NIQB 53 [31], Gillen J held that no deduction from the claimant's damages should be made for provocation because the defendant had displayed no 'loss of control, anger or retaliation'.

[119] *Hurley v Moore* (1993) 107 DLR (4th) 664 (Nfld CA) [73].

[120] As to which see 2.06–2.09.

[121] See J Goudkamp, 'Contributory Negligence and Trespass to the Person' (2011) 127 LQR 519, 522.

8. Limitation of Actions

The doctrine of contributory negligence and the defence of limitation are, at first glance, apparently unrelated doctrines save that both can be relied upon by a defendant in response to a claim brought against them. However, the doctrine of contributory negligence and defence of time bar are linked with each other by virtue of section 1(5) of the 1945 Act, which states: **5.24**

> Where, in any case to which [the apportionment provision] applies, one of the persons at fault avoids liability to any other such person or his personal representative by pleading the Limitation Act 1939, or any other enactment limiting the time within which proceedings may be taken, he shall not be entitled to recover any damages from that other person or representative by virtue of the said subsection.

This clumsily drafted provision[122] appears to be aimed at situations in which C and D, when both at fault within the meaning of section 1(1) of the 1945 Act, sue each other (whether or not in the same set of proceedings) and one of the claims fails because of the expiry of the limitation period. Suppose that D, who has been sued for negligence, pleads a time bar. Suppose also that D counterclaims, which claim C defends by alleging contributory negligence. The effect of section 1(5) seems to be that if D's limitation defence succeeds, the all-or-nothing rule will apply to D's counterclaim, with the result that if D is indeed contributorily negligent, D's claim will fail in its entirety (subject to any points that might conceivably be taken as regards the last opportunity and cognate rules which might be revived together with the all-or-nothing rule[123]).

Section 1(5) appears not to have been considered by the courts,[124] presumably because in most cases in which there are claims and counterclaims the same limitation period will apply to both causes of action with the result that there will be no scope for section 1(5) to operate. Academic commentary regarding it is all but non-existent[125] save for a brief discussion in Williams's book. Although Williams considered that it was 'admirable in its conception'[126] even if imperfectly drafted, it is in fact vulnerable to significant objections. For one thing, it is a trap for the unwary. If D successfully pleads a time bar in defence of C's claim, D's own claim will be defeated by the all-or-nothing rule if D is contributorily negligent. Litigants cannot reasonably be expected to anticipate that succeeding in a defence to an opponent's claim could result in the defeat of their own. More fundamentally, the justification for the provision is unclear. It proceeds on the footing that the party with the benefit of a longer limitation period should not be able to rely on a time bar to defeat their opponent's claim while at the same time recovering partial damages in their own **5.25**

---

122 For various defects in the drafting, see *Williams*, 337–39.

123 Consider ibid 338.

124 Equivalent or otherwise similar provisions are found in several other jurisdictions: see, eg, Contributory Negligence Act 1947 (NZ) s 3(5); Law Reform (Miscellaneous Provisions) Act 1965 (NSW) s 14; Contributory Negligence and Personal Injuries Act (Singapore) s 3(6). None of these equivalents seems to have been the subject of judicial consideration either.

125 Several significant studies on the history of the 1945 Act are silent in relation to it: see, eg, J Steele, 'Law Reform (Contributory Negligence) Act 1945: Collisions of a Different Sort' in TT Arvind and J Steele (eds), *Tort Law and the Legislature: Common Law, Statute and the Dynamics of Legal Change* (Hart Publishing 2012); *Mitchell*, chs 7 and 13.

126 *Williams*, 337.

pursuant to the apportionment provision. According to Williams, it was 'designed to avoid unfairness resulting from the lop-sided working of statutes of limitation',[127] but it is not clear where the unfairness is thought to lie. We would not ordinarily think that a litigant must surrender a defence in a claim against them in order to benefit in connection with a separate claim from a rule that would ordinarily work to their advantage. Note also that a litigant who can defeat an opponent's claim by virtue of a time bar is entitled to capitalize in their own claim on *any* rule except for the apportionment provision. What is special about the apportionment provision relative to the many other rules that might enable a litigant to recover damages where none might otherwise be recoverable? Finally, it should be noted that litigants might be able to bypass the provision. There is nothing to prevent D from suing first and recovering partial damages from C pursuant to the apportionment provision, and then later invoking a time bar to defeat any claim that C issues.

9. The *Ginty* Principle

5.26 In *Ginty v Belmont Building Supplies Ltd*,[128] the claimant had fallen through an asbestos roof and suffered injury. His failure to use the crawling boards provided put both himself and his employer in breach of the same statutory duty. Pearson J dismissed his claim against his employer on the ground that their breach was caused solely by his own wrongful act in working on the roof without using the boards provided.[129] It was subsequently confirmed by the House of Lords in *Boyle v Kodak*[130] that an employer is not liable for a breach of statutory duty if it can prove that its breach was entirely coterminous with a breach by the employee bringing the claim, and that it had done all that it could to ensure the employee's compliance with the duty in question. Although in one case of this kind, the court held that the employee's damages should be discounted by 100 per cent for contributory negligence,[131] we have seen that such a deduction is not permitted applying the wording of the Law Reform (Contributory Negligence) Act 1945.[132] Where the conditions for the application of the *Ginty* principle are met, the correct analysis is rather that the rule operates as a complete defence to liability, so that the issue of contributory negligence does not arise.[133] Conversely, where the conditions for the principle's application are not satisfied—for example because the employer is judged to have been partly to blame for what happened—then liability is imposed subject to a possible deduction for contributory negligence.[134]

---

[127] ibid.

[128] [1959] 1 All ER 414 (QBD).

[129] See further on this principle, *Clerk & Lindsell*, paras 12-89–12-90; *Winfield & Jolowicz*, para 8-020.

[130] [1969] 1 WLR 661 (HL).

[131] *Jayes v IMI (Kynoch) Ltd* [1985] ICR 155 (CA). This was also done at first instance in *Brumder v Motornet Service and Repairs Ltd* [2013] EWCA Civ 195, [2013] 1 WLR 2783.

[132] See 4.19–4.20.

[133] For a recent example, which required the extension of the principle to a breach by the employee of a duty owed to the employer, see *Brumder v Motornet Service and Repairs Ltd* [2013] EWCA Civ 195, [2013] 1 WLR 2783.

[134] See, eg, *Anderson v Newham College of Further Education* [2002] EWCA Civ 505, [2003] ICR 212 (50 per cent deduction).

One of the justifications that Pearson J gave for recognizing the *Ginty* principle was that the common law position had always been that a person was barred from recovery where the damage was caused solely by his own negligence, and that this rule had not been affected by the 1945 Act, which dealt only with cases where the claimant was *partly* to blame for the damage.[135] However, while there is admittedly some force in this contention, it is questionable whether it is wise to elevate it into a general principle of law above and beyond specific applications of the idea in the context of particular doctrines such as legal causation.[136] There is also a mismatch between this justification and the scope of the *Ginty* principle, which applies not merely because the employee was wholly to blame for the damage, but because he was himself in breach of duty, and hence a wrongdoer. For these reasons, it seems preferable to ground the rule on the other two justifications that Pearson J provided for it, namely the principle that a person should not be allowed to benefit from his own wrong, and the need to avoid circuity of action. **5.27**

[135] [1959] 1 All ER 414 (QBD) 424.
[136] See 5.02–5.07.

6

PROCEDURE AND APPEALS

6.01 This chapter is concerned with procedural issues that arise in relation to contributory negligence as well as with appeals regarding the existence of contributory negligence and apportionment. Although appeals concerning contributory negligence do not merely raise procedural points, because issues of procedure are so important in this connection, it is convenient to deal with both topics within a single chapter. By and large, general principles governing procedure and appeals apply to contributory negligence cases. However, there are some respects in which contributory negligence cases present special issues in this connection, as will be seen from the discussion that follows.

1. Procedure

(1) Pre-action protocols

6.02 Where there are grounds for alleging contributory negligence, the defendant would generally be expected to raise them in correspondence sent in response to the claimant's pre-action letter and to supply as much detail as is reasonably practicable. This requirement is mandatory in the case of claims to which the Pre-Action Protocol for Personal Injury Claims below the Small Claims Limit in Road Traffic Accidents applies ('the RTA Small Claims Protocol'),[1] that is to say, claims for less than £5,000 in respect of personal injuries suffered in a road traffic accident and for less than £10,000 overall.

6.03 The RTA Small Claims Protocol also lays down detailed procedural steps that the parties must take in cases that involve a failure to wear a seat belt. Following the exchange of the initial letters, the claimant must inform their medical expert whether contributory negligence is alleged[2] and ask them to comment on the effect, if any, of the failure to wear a seat belt on their injuries.[3] The medical expert must then state in their report whether the claimant's injuries or any part of them would have been reduced or avoided altogether had they worn a seat belt.[4] Thereafter, the insurer must consider that report and, if it supports the insurer's position regarding contributory negligence, state in its obligatory settlement offer the discount that has been applied to it.[5] The insurer must not specify the discount

---

[1] Pre-Action Protocol for Personal Injury Claims below the Small Claims Limit in Road Traffic Accidents, para 6.21(4).

[2] ibid, para 7.9(1)(c).

[3] ibid, para 7.9(1)(d).

[4] ibid, para 7.12.

[5] ibid, para 8.10. See also para 8.12(3).

Contributory Negligence. Second Edition. James Goudkamp and Donal Nolan, Oxford University Press.
 DOI: 10.1093/oso/9780192867919.003.0006

that they consider should be applied for contributory negligence until the claimant has disclosed the report.[6]

Various other pre-action protocols contain provisions relevant to contributory negligence albeit none is as prescriptive as those found in the RTA Small Claims Protocol. For example, where contributory negligence is alleged claims that would otherwise be governed by the Pre-Action Protocol for Low Value Personal Injury Claims in Road Traffic Accidents or the Pre-Action Protocol for Low Value Personal Injury (Employers' Liability and Public Liability) Claims will instead proceed under the Pre-Action Protocol for Personal Injury Claims.[7] **6.04**

(2) Issuing proceedings

A claimant who commences proceedings for damages must state on the claim form how much they expect to recover.[8] When estimating that sum, the effect of the contributory negligence doctrine should be disregarded.[9] The courts are not required to accept the value that the claimant places on their case for the purposes of determining the track to which the case should be allocated. If the court considers that the claimant has placed too high a value on the claim, the court can estimate its value. In exercising this power, contributory negligence will not be taken into account.[10] **6.05**

(3) Pleading

The defendant must specifically plead contributory negligence before the court can apportion responsibility. *Dann v Hamilton*[11] is a striking illustration of the rule. The facts clearly engaged the contributory negligence doctrine (the claimant had accepted a ride from a driver she knew was intoxicated despite being warned of the dangers of doing so by a third party) and the judge even specifically encouraged counsel for the defendant to allege contributory negligence but he 'would not be drawn'.[12] The court considered that it could not address the issue of contributory negligence in these circumstances. More recently, in *UCB Bank plc v David J Pinder plc*, HHJ Hicks QC said that the 'authorities establish the necessity of pleading contributory negligence before it can be considered'.[13] The judge went on to hold that, once pleaded, the court is required to address the doctrine even though the defendant declines to participate further in the proceedings and does not appear at the trial. Conversely, in *Taylor v Simon Carves Ltd*,[14] it was held that where **6.06**

[6] ibid, para 6.21(5)(b).

[7] Pre-Action Protocol for Personal Injury Claims, para 1.3.2(a). See also the Pre-Action Protocol for Low Value Personal Injury Claims in Road Traffic Accidents, para 6.15(1) and the Pre-Action Protocol for Low Value Personal Injury (Employers' Liability and Public Liability) Claims, para 6.13(1).

[8] CPR 16.3(2)(a).

[9] CPR 16.3(6)(b).

[10] CPR 26.8(2)(d).

[11] [1939] 1 KB 509 (KBD).

[12] C Asquith, 'Note' (1953) 69 LQR 317, 317.

[13] [1998] CLC 1262 (QBD) [17]. See also *Fookes v Slaytor* [1978] 1 WLR 1293 (CA); *Taylor v Simon Carves Ltd* 1958 SLT (Sh Ct) 23, 23 (William Garrett QC) ('if contributory negligence is not in issue between the parties then, in my opinion, the Act cannot apply').

[14] 1958 SLT (Sh Ct) 23, 23.

the defendant has raised but not pursued a plea of contributory negligence, it would be inappropriate for it to be considered further.

6.07 It is not, of course, enough for a defendant simply to allege in their defence that the claimant was contributorily negligent in order to discharge their obligations regarding pleading. They must specify with precision in what respect or respects the claimant is said to have fallen short of the relevant standard of care. Particularity is required in order that the claimant can know what the case is that they need to answer, and the position is *a fortiori* where the allegation of contributory negligence rests on serious misconduct by the claimant or criminality. It follows that a judge cannot properly find a claimant contributorily negligent on a basis that is different from that alleged by the defendant.[15]

(4) Amendments to pleadings

6.08 In deciding whether to permit the defendant to amend their pleadings so as to allege contributory negligence or to run a different case on contributory negligence from that which has already been advanced, the court must consider all of the relevant factors. Material considerations include the strength of the case as to contributory negligence, the extent to which an order for costs would adequately compensate the claimant for any prejudice that allowing the amendment would cause, the stage of the proceedings at which the application for permission to amend was made, whether allowing the application would cause the trial date to be lost and the defendant's excuse for not applying for permission earlier or, indeed, for failing to deal with the issue when it served its defence.[16]

(5) Proof

6.09 The defendant carries the burden of proving that the claimant was contributorily negligent.[17] Proof to the civil standard is required to discharge that onus.[18] Thus, establishing merely that it is a 'strong possibility'[19] that the claimant was contributorily negligent is not enough. The defendant does not necessarily need to lead any evidence in order to discharge their burden. Contributory negligence can be established on the basis of evidence adduced by the claimant.[20] It can also be proven by inference. In some cases, expert evidence might need to be led (for which permission must be sought[21]). This is perhaps particularly so where the claimant is a professional and there is a conventional practice that they could reasonably have been expected to follow.

---

[15] *CTO Gesellschaft Fur Containertransport MBH and Co v Dziennik* [2006] EWCA Civ 1456.

[16] *Lenton v Abrahams* [2003] EWHC 1104 (QB) [9]–[10]; *Willmott Dixon Construction Ltd v Robert West Consulting Ltd* [2016] EWHC 3291 (TCC), [2017] PNLR 17.

[17] *Wakelin v London & South Western Railway Co* (1886) 12 App Cas 41 (HL) 47 (Lord Watson) ('I am of opinion that the onus of proving affirmatively that there was contributory negligence on the part of the person injured rests, in the first instance, upon the defendants, and that in the absence of evidence tending to that conclusion, the plaintiff is not bound to prove the negative in order to entitle her to a verdict in her favour').

[18] This is subject to the exception mentioned in 3.48.

[19] *Dawes v Aldis* [2007] EWHC 1831 (QB) [33] (Eady J).

[20] *Morrison v Gardiner* [2005] CSOH 156 [7].

[21] For a case in which the court refused to give permission to adduce expert evidence on issues relevant to contributory negligence, see *Domeney v Rees* [2020] EWHC 2115 (QB).

(6) Contingent consideration of the doctrine of contributory negligence

Where the doctrine of contributory negligence has been pleaded, the court should only consider it after it has addressed the elements of the claimant's cause of action.[22] If the court decides that the ingredients of the claim have not been established, it is usually appropriate nevertheless to address the issue of contributory negligence in case the finding regarding the defendant's liability is set aside on appeal.[23] For the same reason, if it is determined that the claimant was not contributorily negligent, it may be appropriate for the court to consider how responsibility would have been apportioned regardless. However, there will be occasions where making contingent findings is unjustified. Thus, there are numerous cases in which judges who have absolved the defendant of liability have expressly refused to address the issue of contributory negligence, sometimes on the basis that their findings regarding liability made it impossible sensibly to consider the criteria of relative blameworthiness and causal potency.[24] Similarly, it may be difficult for a judge who has absolved a claimant of contributory negligence to engage in a hypothetical apportionment exercise premised on a contrary conclusion. **6.10**

(7) Effect of entry of judgment regarding liability

Because the doctrine of contributory negligence is an issue relating to quantum rather than to liability,[25] the fact that it has been established that the defendant is liable to the claimant, whether on the basis of default judgment, summary judgment, or judgment entered following a trial, does not prevent the defendant from arguing in connection with the assessment of damages that the claimant was contributorily negligent. The doctrine can therefore be raised for the first time upon quantum being addressed provided that any 'judgment [on liability has] not settled any issue on which an allegation of contributory negligence would depend'.[26] Glanville Williams considered that if X obtains judgment against Y in Case 1 in which X's damages are reduced for contributory negligence and Y subsequently sues X in Case 2 in respect of damage suffered in the same accident, the parties' respective shares of responsibility for the damage as determined in Case 1 should also be determinative in Case 2, so that the parties should not be able to reopen the question.[27] However, Williams thought that X ought to be able to say in Case 2 that Y's **6.11**

---

[22] *Griffiths v Vauxhall Motors Ltd* [2003] EWCA Civ 412 [24]. See also 1.28.

[23] Consider Lady Paton's exhortation to trial judges in *Little v Glen* [2014] CSIH 99 [35]. In *Cameron v Swan* [2021] CSIH 30, 2022 SC 1 [86] it was accepted that the judge below had erred in not making a contingent finding as to apportionment for contributory negligence, having absolved the defendant of blame. However, there is much force in the observation of Basten J in *Bevan v Coolahan* [2019] NSWCA 217, 101 NSWLR 86 [35] that it may be 'artificial, if not incoherent, to assess contributory negligence on the hypothesis of error in dismissing the claim on the ground that the defendant was not negligent'.

[24] See, eg, *Norman v Theodore Goddard* [1992] BCC 14 (Ch D) 27; *Gorham v British Telecommunications plc* [2000] 1 WLR 2129 (CA) 2144; *Webster v Ridgeway Foundation School* [2010] EWHC 157 (QB) [196]; *Probert v Moore* [2012] EWHC 2324 (QB) [51]; *Seery v Leathes Prior (a firm)* [2017] EWHC 80 (QB) [68]. Consider also the remarks in *HIH Casualty and General Insurance Ltd v JLT Risk Solutions Ltd* [2007] EWCA Civ 710, [2008] Bus LR 180 [111], where it was said that the first instance judge was wrong to have ventured a contingent view regarding contributory negligence.

[25] See 1.28.

[26] *Maes Finance Ltd v AL Phillips & Co (a firm)* The Times, 25 March 1997 (Ch D) (Sir Richard Scott VC). See also *Pankhurst v White* [2006] EWHC 2093 (QB) [1]; *Lunnun v Singh*, The Times, 19 July 1999 (CA); *Sowerby v Charlton* [2005] EWCA Civ 1610, [2006] 1 WLR 568.

[27] *Williams*, 469.

responsibility for the damage was such that X's conduct was not a cause thereof in law. Williams's position appears sound although there seems to be no authority that is directly on point.

(8) Findings required by the apportionment legislation

6.12 When contributory negligence is established, both the total damages to which the claimant would have been entitled had there been no contributory negligence and the extent to which the damages are to be discounted must be specified.[28] The purpose of this requirement is evidently to avoid the need for a retrial if either the finding of contributory negligence or that concerning the apportionment of responsibility is disturbed on appeal.

(9) Courts of limited jurisdiction

6.13 Where the quantum of the claimant's claim exceeds the jurisdiction of the court seized of the proceedings, the jurisdictional cap applies first and any discount to the claimant's damages for contributory negligence falls to be made thereafter.[29] For example, if the claim is worth £10,000 and the jurisdictional limit is £5,000, the claimant will be entitled to recover only £2,500 if their responsibility for the damage is assessed at 50 per cent.

(10) Interim payments

6.14 A court cannot order an interim payment that exceeds a reasonable proportion of the likely amount of the final award.[30] The purpose of this restriction is to safeguard the defendant from the risk of being required to pay on an interim basis a sum greater than that for which they might ultimately be adjudged liable. Accordingly, the court is required when ordering the defendant to make an interim payment to take account of any discount to the damages that would likely be made for contributory negligence.[31] However, in order to benefit from this rule, a defendant faced with an application for an interim payment must adduce evidence raising contributory negligence as an issue.[32] Absent such evidence, the court will usually be justified in assuming that no discount will be made.[33]

(11) Periodical payments

6.15 In a personal injury case, the court is required to consider and indicate to the parties whether periodical payments are likely to be a more appropriate form for the damages award to take than a lump sum.[34] In considering its indication, the court must take account, among other factors, of any discount that has been made for contributory negligence.[35] The relevance of contributory negligence in this regard is that the smaller the award the less compelling the case will be for making a periodical payment order since the claimant

---

[28] Law Reform (Contributory Negligence) Act 1945, s 1(2) and (6).
[29] See 4.10.
[30] CPR 25.7(4).
[31] CPR 25.7(5)(a).
[32] *Smith v Bailey* [2014] EWHC 2569 (QB), [2015] RTR 6 [8].
[33] ibid.
[34] CPR 41.6.
[35] PD 41, r 1(1).

might require a lump sum in order to meet costs incurred because of the tort.[36] It follows that the fact that a significant discount has been made will often preclude a periodical payment order.[37]

(12) Costs

Where a claimant establishes a right to a remedy but the damages are discounted for contributory negligence, they will generally still be entitled to a costs order in their favour.[38] There is no rule that a claimant is entitled to recover costs only in proportion to the defendant's share of responsibility for the damage. In *Onay v Brown*, where the parties had agreed a 25 per cent discount, Goldring LJ held that 'it [would be] wholly artificial to describe the claimant as other than the winner'.[39] In *Sonmez v Kebabery Wholesale Ltd*, the claimant did not concede that he was contributorily negligent and that question was tried as a preliminary issue. It was found that the claimant had been contributorily negligent and that a discount of 20 per cent should be made. *Onay* was regarded as indistinguishable (perhaps surprisingly as the parties agreed the issues of contributory negligence in *Onay*) and it was held that the claimant was entitled to his costs in connection with the preliminary issue.[40] Conversely, if the discount is very high, such as in the order of 90 per cent, it might be that the claimant would be required to bear the defendant's costs.[41] Ultimately, the issue 'is a question of degree'.[42] It appears that it would ordinarily be inappropriate for the court to make an issues-based costs order as regards the question of contributory negligence.[43] **6.16**

Where a defendant fails on or abandons an allegation of contributory negligence, such failure or abandonment may be taken into account in connection with costs pursuant to the jurisdiction to award costs based on the extent to which the parties succeeded on various issues,[44] and in light of the reasonableness of raising particular allegations.[45] However, the courts will generally analyse the invocation of the contributory negligence doctrine holistically and will not deprive a victorious defendant of an order in respect of the costs incurred simply because certain allegations of contributory negligence were withdrawn or were unsuccessful. In *Governors and Company of the Bank of Ireland v Watts Group plc*, Coulson J said:[46] **6.17**

---

36 *Gillard v McManus* [2013] NIQB 127 [12].

37 Consider ibid [28]–[30].

38 CPR 44.2(2)(a) ('If the court decides to make an order about costs—(a) the general rule is that the unsuccessful party will be ordered to pay the costs of the successful party . . .').

39 [2009] EWCA Civ 775, [2010] 1 Costs LR 29 [29]. Consider also *'KRYSIA' Maritime Inc v Intership Ltd* [2008] EWHC 1880 (Admlty), [2009] 1 All ER (Comm) 292 [29] (30 per cent discount did not preclude the claimant from recovering its costs).

40 [2009] EWCA Civ 1386 [22].

41 *Western Neptune (Owners) v Philadelphia Express (Owners)* [2009] EWHC 1522 (Admlty), [2010] 1 Lloyd's Rep 172 [11].

42 ibid (Steel J).

43 *Sonmez v Kebabery Wholesale Ltd* [2009] EWCA Civ 1386 [22] (Ward LJ) ('In a fully contested trial of liability I would not ordinarily expect that contributory negligence would be treated as a separate issue which one party won and the other party lost').

44 CPR 44.2(4)(b).

45 CPR 44.2(5)(b).

46 [2017] EWHC 2472 (TCC), [2017] 5 Costs LR 899 [12].

> [Counsel for the claimant] argued that, because [the defendant] abandoned a number of contributory negligence allegations at the start of trial, the [claimant] should have the costs of those abandoned allegations. I do not accept that submission. I consider that it is important for the court to look at the costs in the round. The contributory negligence case was successful. The fact that some of the individual allegations of contributory negligence were deleted at the start of the trial is, in my view, simply part of the rough and tumble of the trial process. It is not a matter that should be marked by an adverse order as to costs.

6.18 An offer by the claimant to settle subject to a very small discount for contributory negligence, such as 5 per cent, is still a genuine attempt to settle the proceedings for the purposes of Civil Procedure Rules (CPR) 36.[47] That is so even if the defendant had not alleged contributory negligence with the result that there was never any prospect of damages being discounted.[48] Specialist works on costs should be consulted as regards the complex interplay between CPR 36 and the system governing the recoupment of state benefits where the claimant is contributorily negligent.[49]

6.19 The maximum recoverable trial costs in cases allocated to the fast track are capped by reference to the claim's value.[50] For the purposes of valuing the claim, any discount for contributory negligence is disregarded.[51]

(13) Recoupment of state benefits

6.20 Legislation[52] provides for the deduction of certain state benefits from damages awards (and their subsequent recoupment from the defendant) subject to a variety of conditions.[53] The statutory arrangements make no allowance for the deduction to be reduced where the claimant's damages are discounted for contributory negligence. Accordingly, two claimants who are identically positioned in terms of the quantum of their claim and benefits received save that one is contributorily negligent and the other is not will be liable to have the same sums deducted from their compensation. A different regime applies in relation to certain NHS charges, where the recovery by the government from the defendant of prescribed NHS charges will be diminished in line with the extent to which, if at all, the claimant's compensation has been discounted for contributory negligence.[54]

(14) Counterclaims and setoff

6.21 In some other jurisdictions, the intersection between counterclaims and contributory negligence, particularly in so far as it raises issues regarding setoff, appears to have given rise

---

[47] *Jockey Club Racecourse Ltd v Willmott Dixon Construction Ltd* [2016] EWHC 167 (TCC), [2016] 4 WLR 43 [37]–[38].

[48] ibid [34].

[49] Although see *Williams v Devon County Council* [2003] EWCA Civ 365, [2003] CP Rep 47; *Crooks v Hendricks Lovell Ltd* [2016] EWCA Civ 8, [2016] 1 Costs LO 103.

[50] CPR 45.38.

[51] CPR 45.38(3)(a)(ii).

[52] Social Security (Recovery of Benefits) Act 1997.

[53] For discussion, see R Lewis, *Deducting Benefits from Damages for Personal Injury* (OUP 1999); P Cane and J Goudkamp, *Atiyah's Accidents, Compensation and the Law* (9th edn, CUP 2018) 360–65; *R (Aviva Insurance Ltd) v Secretary of State for Work and Pensions* [2022] EWCA Civ 15, [2022] 1 WLR 2753.

[54] Health and Social Care (Community Health Standards) Act 2003, Pt 3.

to very significant procedural complications.[55] For one reason or another, such difficulties have apparently not arisen in the United Kingdom.[56] The general rule is that were C and D to sue each other, any judgment that D obtains will be set off against C's judgment, and it will usually be appropriate for D to take this point in their defence, although it seems that there is no obligation to do so.[57] It is only in relatively unusual cases, such as where one of the parties is bankrupt, that the setoff rules will become particularly significant. The issues here are not, however, specific to the contributory negligence context, with the result that it is unnecessary to engage further with them.

(15) Applicable law

Treatment of applicable law must be sought in specialist works. For present purposes, it suffices to say that the general rule is that, in the case of claims for breach of non-contractual obligations, the law applicable to the claim will apply also to the issue of contributory negligence.[58] Thus, if German law applies to a claim in respect of damage resulting from a road accident, the issue of contributory negligence will also be governed by German law.[59] If the applicable law provides that contributory negligence is to be presumed to exist in particular circumstances, effect will be given to that presumption.[60] **6.22**

2. Appeals

(1) Permission to appeal

In the case of England and Wales, permission is needed for all first appeals subject to presently irrelevant exceptions.[61] Permission will be given only where the court from which it is sought considers that the appeal would have a 'real prospect of success' or 'there is some other compelling reason for the appeal to be heard'.[62] An appeal will have 'a real prospect of success' when the prospect is realistic as opposed to fanciful.[63] In Scotland, a litigant can appeal against the order of a sheriff to the Sheriff Appeal Court without permission.[64] **6.23**

---

[55] See *Restatement (Third) of Torts: Apportionment of Responsibility* (2000) § 9; VE Schwartz, *Comparative Negligence* (5th edn, LexisNexis 2010) ch 5.

[56] Williams expended considerable energy addressing some of the procedural tangles that might arise in this regard: see *Williams*, ch 19. Despite the amount of time that has passed since he wrote his book, the esoteric complications that he envisaged might occur seem not to have caused any difficulty in practice, and to a very considerable extent appear simply not to have arisen at all. As a result, we pass over them for now.

[57] See CPR 16.6.

[58] See Regulation (EC) No 846/2007 on the law applicable to non-contractual obligations ('Rome II'), art 15(b), which continues to apply in the United Kingdom post-Brexit by virtue of the Law Applicable to Contractual Obligations and Non-Contractual Obligations (Amendment etc) (EU Exit) Regulations 2019, SI 2019/834, subject to certain amendments.

[59] See eg, *Evans v R & V Allgemeine Verischerung AG* [2022] EWHC 2436 (QB) [8]. Consider also *The Soldiers, Sailors, Airmen and Families Association—Forces Help v Allgemeines Krankenhaus Viersen GmbH* [2022] UKSC 29, [2023] AC 597 [77].

[60] See Rome II, art 22(1) and the discussion in L Collins et al, *Dicey, Morris and Collins on the Conflict of Laws* (16th edn, Sweet & Maxwell 2022) para 34.068.

[61] CPR 52.3.

[62] CPR 52.6(1).

[63] *Tanfern Ltd v Cameron-MacDonald* [2000] 1 WLR 1311 (CA) [21] (Brooke LJ).

[64] Courts Reform (Scotland) Act 2014, s 110.

However, appeals lie from the Sheriff Appeal Court to the Court of Session only with permission.[65] Permission will be granted only where the appeal would 'raise an important point of principle or practice' or 'there is some other compelling reason for the Court of Session to hear the appeal'.[66] Conversely, permission is not required to appeal from the Outer House to the Inner House.[67] In Northern Ireland, permission is required to appeal to the Court of Appeal save in relation to issues that are presently irrelevant.[68]

6.24 Permission to appeal to the Supreme Court will not be granted unless the case 'raise[s] an arguable point of law of general public importance'.[69] Accordingly, permission to appeal will rarely be given to challenge an apportionment of responsibility for contributory negligence.[70] However, where permission to appeal has been given, the Supreme Court will only disturb an apportionment of responsibility in the same circumstances as would any other appellate court.[71] The same is presumably also true in relation to an appeal regarding the existence of contributory negligence.

(2) The circumstances in which appellate intervention is permissible

6.25 In *Jackson v Murray*, Lord Reed said, with reference to appeals generally, that intervention is appropriate only where there is 'an identifiable error, such as an error of law, or the taking into account of an irrelevant matter, or the failure to take account of a relevant matter', or where the trial court's conclusion 'was not one which was reasonably open to it'.[72] The circumstances in which a first instance judge will be found to have erred as regards a conclusion on the facts depends on the extent of the advantage that they enjoyed by reason of having seen the witnesses. It is well established that '[t]he greater that advantage, the more reluctant the appellate court should be to interfere'.[73] These general principles are fully applicable to contributory negligence appeals (of which, in fact, *Jackson v Murray* was one). Thus, if the trial judge reached their findings on issues relevant to the contributory negligence doctrine solely on the basis of written evidence, appellate intervention will be justified more readily than where the judge heard oral evidence.

6.26 Because apportioning responsibility involves exercising a discretion,[74] an appeal in relation to apportionment will not be allowed 'merely on the basis of a disagreement as to the precise figure'[75] by which damages should be discounted. Nor will the bare fact that the discount is 'unusual' justify allowing an appeal.[76] Rather, appellate intervention will be warranted only 'in very exceptional circumstances'[77] and where the apportionment of

---

[65] ibid s 113(1).
[66] ibid s 113(2).
[67] Court of Session Rules, r 38.2.
[68] Judicature (Northern Ireland) Act 1978, s 35.
[69] PD 3, r 3.3.3.
[70] *Jackson v Murray* [2015] UKSC 5, [2015] 2 All ER 805 [30].
[71] ibid.
[72] [2015] UKSC 5, [2015] 2 All ER 805 [35].
[73] *Desir v Alcide* [2015] UKPC 24 [25] (Lord Clarke).
[74] See 4.22–4.23.
[75] *Jackson v Murray* [2015] UKSC 5, [2015] 2 All ER 805 [38] (Lord Reed).
[76] *Gul v McDonagh* [2021] EWCA Civ 1503, [2022] RTR 9 [43] (Nugee LJ).
[77] *British Fame (Owners) v Macgregor (Owners)* [1943] AC 197 (HL) 201 (Lord Wright). See also *Quintas v National Smelting Co Ltd* [1961] 1 WLR 401 (CA) 418 (Willmer LJ) ('exceptional'); *Cooke v Thorne* [2001]

responsibility fell beyond the 'acceptable range'.[78] The reasons for appellate restraint in this connection were well explained by Kirby J in *Roads and Traffic Authority of New South Wales v Dederer* as follows:[79]

> This Court has said many times that appellate courts must show restraint in disturbing the apportionment ordered for contributory negligence as between a plaintiff and a defendant, having regard to their respective shares of responsibility for the damage. The point is self-evident. Involved in such an apportionment is a comparative examination of the whole conduct of each negligent party in relation to the circumstances of the accident and an evaluation of the comparative importance of the respective acts and omissions of the parties in causing the damage. Such decisions are evaluative and multi-factorial. Generally speaking, a trial judge, who has full knowledge of all of the evidence, will be in a better position to make such an apportionment correctly. An appellate court, even if it would have reached a different conclusion, will usually be hard pressed to identify an error that warrants disturbance of the primary judge's conclusion on such an issue. Tinkering with apportionments is to be discouraged.

The reluctance of appellate courts to intervene as regards the apportionment of responsibility is such that they may dismiss an appeal in this regard even where the trial judge gave no reasons for their conclusions,[80] although the absence of any reasoning may of course incline the appeal court to interfere more readily than would otherwise be the case.[81]

However, despite the need for restraint in appeals in relation to contributory negligence, and particularly in relation to the apportionment of responsibility, where an error 'is clearly discernible' the appellate court 'must ... interfere'.[82] In such circumstances, there is not merely a power to intervene but a duty to do so.[83] If an appeal is allowed and further **6.27**

EWCA Civ 81 [10] (Longmore LJ) ('extremely reluctant to interfere'); *Curran v Derbyshire and Lancashire Gliding Club* [2004] EWCA Civ 955 [15] (Pill LJ) ('rare'); *Wells v Mutchmeats Ltd* [2006] EWCA Civ 963 [19] (Moses LJ) ('appeals must be restricted').

[78] *Pride Valley Foods Ltd v Hall & Partners* 2001 WL 676719 (CA) [53] (Dyson LJ). See also *Brown v Thompson* [1968] 1 WLR 1003 (CA).

[79] [2007] HCA 42, (2007) 234 CLR 330 [168] (footnote omitted). See also *Joslyn v Berryman* [2003] HCA 34, (2003) 214 CLR 552 [119].

[80] See, eg, *Pride Valley Foods Ltd v Hall & Partners* 2001 WL 676719 (CA) [53]; cf *Starks v Chief Constable of Hertfordshire* [2013] EWCA Civ 782, [2014] RTR 4 [16] (Underhill LJ) ('I have less compunction in differing from [the trial judge's apportionment] because she did not give any reason for her apportionment: she simply referred to the relevant legal principles and announced her conclusion').

[81] See, eg, *Johnson v Greater London Council* [1985] Lexis Citation 2068 (CA) (Ralph Gibson LJ) ('On looking at the judgment, the judge does not explain why he attributed the major responsibility to the plaintiff, and in those circumstances it seems to me that this court is free to substitute for his view the court's own considered view as to what the proportion of contributory negligence ought to be'); *Starks v Chief Constable of Hertfordshire* [2013] EWCA Civ 782, [2014] RTR 4 [16] (Underhill LJ) ('I have less compunction in differing from [the trial judge's apportionment] because she did not give any reason for her apportionment: she simply referred to the relevant legal principles and announced her conclusion').

[82] *Smith v Chief Constable of Nottinghamshire Police* [2012] EWCA Civ 161, [2012] RTR 23 [36] (Ward LJ).

[83] *Hicks v British Transport Commission* [1958] 1 WLR 493 (CA) 507. See also *Kerry v Carter* [1969] 1 WLR 1372 (CA) 1376 (Lord Denning MR) ('the function of this court is to be a Court of Appeal. We are here to put right that which has gone wrong. If we think that the judge below was wrong, then we ought to say so, and alter the apportionment accordingly'); *Jennings v Norman Collision (Contractors) Ltd* [1970] 1 All ER 1121 (CA) 1126 (Salmon LJ) ('It is very unusual for this court to interfere with an apportionment, and we are slow to do so. But we are entitled—indeed, I think it is our duty—to do so if we come to the conclusion that the apportionment is seriously wrong').

facts need to be found before a conclusion on the issue of contributory negligence can be reached, the proceedings will need to be remitted to the first instance judge. Alternatively, if the appellate court feels that it can dispose of the proceedings without further facts being found, it may make the necessary determinations itself.[84] An appellate court will generally not consider the issue of contributory negligence where it was not addressed by the court or courts below. These circumstances obtained in *Corr v IBC Vehicles Ltd* and a majority of the House of Lords considered that it would be inappropriate to deal with the question of contributory negligence as a result.[85]

(3) Empirical data

6.28 According to a study of 129 claims that came before appellate courts in the United Kingdom between 2000 and 2016 concerning contributory negligence,[86] appeals as to the existence of contributory negligence were allowed in 39 per cent of cases and as to the apportionment of responsibility in 33 per cent. The overall rate of appellate intervention was 35 per cent. The lower incidence of intervention in relation to the discount made is consistent with the principle that judges should be particularly reluctant to disturb determinations regarding the apportionment of responsibility.[87] Despite this, it is interesting to observe that there were more appeals in relation to the discount (56 per cent of the total) than in relation to whether the claimant was contributorily negligent (44 per cent). Appeals were particularly unlikely to succeed in occupiers' liability cases (14 per cent), with appellate judges being more willing to interfere in road accident (47 per cent) and employers' liability (41 per cent) cases.

6.29 In the claims that were the subject of the empirical study, claimants brought 44 per cent of the appeals and defendants 56 per cent. Forty per cent of the appeals in relation to the existence of contributory negligence were by claimants and 60 per cent by defendants, whereas claimants brought 47 per cent of the appeals concerning the size of the discount and defendants 53 per cent. Claimants succeeded in 44 per cent of appeals overall, with a success rate of 57 per cent regarding the existence of contributory negligence and 35 per cent in relation to the discount. By contrast, defendants won only 29 per cent of their appeals overall, with the success rates in appeals with regards to the existence of contributory negligence (26 per cent) and as to the discount (31 per cent) being similar. Hence, while the chances of a successful appeal on the apportionment of responsibility were roughly equivalent for claimants and defendants, claimants were almost twice as likely to win appeals concerning the existence of contributory negligence as defendants.

6.30 When an appeal was allowed in relation to the discount, which occurred in 24 of the 129 claims studied, the discount was reduced in 12 of these claims and increased in the other 12. The average reduction in the discount (32 per cent) was considerably larger than the average increase in the discount (20 per cent). Similarly, both the smallest reduction (20 per cent) and the largest reduction (50 per cent) were greater than the equivalent figures

[84] *Heaton v Herzog* [2008] EWCA Civ 1636, [2009] RTR 30 [15]. Consider also *Raybould v T & N Gilmartin (Contractors) Ltd* [2018] SAC (Civ) 31, 2019 SLT (Sh Ct) 1 [36].

[85] [2008] UKHL 13, [2008] 1 AC 884; cf *Cameron v Swan* [2021] CSIH 30, 2022 SC 1 [86].

[86] *Goudkamp and Nolan*, ch 5.

[87] See 6.26.

for increases in the discount (8 per cent and 30 per cent respectively). Hence, it seems that when appellate courts reduce the discount, they tend to do so by larger amounts than when they increase it. The discount was rarely changed in either direction by a small amount. In only one claim was the change in the discount less than 10 per cent, and in only four claims was it less than 20 per cent. These results are consistent with the principle that appellate intervention in connection with the discount is justified only where the appellate court concludes that the decision at first instance was manifestly wrong.[88]

In the appeals studied, children brought 13 per cent of the claims where it was possible to tell whether a human claimant was an adult or child. The youngest claimant was aged nine. There were too few appeals by child claimants concerning the existence of contributory negligence for us to be able to comment usefully regarding them. In relation to appeals against the discount by child claimants, the rate of intervention was much higher where the claimant was a child (80 per cent) than an adult (28 per cent). However, when the discount was disturbed, it was increased as often as it was decreased. It thus appears that although appellate courts are more likely to differ from a first instance court on the appropriate discount where the claimant is a child, this does not translate into any clear tendency to lean either in favour of or against child claimants on the apportionment question. **6.31**

[88] See 6.27.

APPENDIX 1

Apportionment in Frequently Recurring Situations

1. Introduction

(1) The importance of knowing how contributory negligence works in practice

Glanville Williams appreciated that a full understanding of the law of contributory negligence requires ascertaining how the courts apply it in practice. He therefore compiled a list of discounts that had been imposed under the then recently enacted apportionment legislation.[1] However, the novelty of the apportionment regime meant that Williams had virtually no data with which to work. His list was thus very short. Furthermore, the interpretation of the legislation was then rather unsettled in important respects, with it having been said that the courts were at the time 'feeling [their] way in difficult country',[2] which meant that there was reason to doubt the consistency with which the legislation was being applied. The scanty materials on which Williams was able to draw, coupled with the fact that his analysis is now very dated, means his work is of limited usefulness when it comes to understanding how judges apply the law of contributory negligence in the twenty-first century. One of the aims of this volume is, therefore, to provide data regarding how damages are apportioned for contributory negligence in a range of frequently recurring legislation. This is done in this appendix. **A1.01**

It is important to understand how the contributory negligence doctrine operates in practice for two main reasons. The first of these reasons concerns the principle of consistent treatment. It is a fundamental principle of justice that like cases should be treated alike and that different cases should be treated differently. There is a distinct danger that this principle will not be observed as closely as it should be in relation to (in particular) the way in which damages are discounted for contributory negligence unless sufficient information as to the apportionment exercise is readily to hand. In the absence of adequate information in this connection, very different discounts may be imposed in materially equivalent cases[3] and similar discounts in cases that are different from each other in relevant respects. Such outcomes are unjust and, thus, tend to bring the law into disrepute. One practitioner describes the problem as follows:[4] **A1.02**

> Deductions for contributory negligence seem to vary to an extent that often gives the impression that the level of deduction is totally arbitrary. That should not be the case. I believe that the problem often stems from advocates simply not assisting the court to reach the correct level of reduction, if any, by producing the relevant authorities to ensure that the judge does not go wrong.

---

[1] *Williams*, 391.

[2] *Jones v Livox Quarries Ltd* [1952] 2 QB 608 (CA) 615 (Denning LJ).

[3] This difficulty is not merely speculative. There are ample illustrations available of different judges reaching significantly divergent conclusions as to the discount that should be imposed in a given case: see 4.22.

[4] N Tomkins, 'Getting Contributory Negligence Right' [2008] JPIL 196, 197.

By significantly increasing the amount of information that is conveniently available about how judges apply the law of contributory negligence, and especially about how they discount damages, this volume aims to reduce the risk of injustice in this regard.

A1.03 The other reason why it is important to understand how the contributory negligence doctrine operates in practice is that this should promote the settlement of disputes in which contributory negligence is an issue. As Tony Weir pointed out, in connection with discounts for contributory negligence, '[i]f litigants are quite unable to predict what damages may be awarded, they can hardly settle their differences'.[5] For example, our study reveals that, in certain recurrent situations, judges tend to opt for discounts that fall within a relatively small range. In such scenarios, actual and potential litigants and their advisers can be reasonably confident of the extent to which damages will be reduced for contributory negligence if the case reaches court, and this should help them to settle their dispute.

A1.04 It is of course true that the issue of the appropriate discount turns on the individual facts of any given case and that limited weight can, therefore, be placed on discounts imposed on other occasions.[6] At the same time, however, other discounts imposed are far from irrelevant.[7] They offer some guidance, especially reductions made in cases that are factually similar to those with which one is dealing or where an established pattern is clearly discernible. As Kirby J observed in *Joslyn v Berryman*:[8]

> [A]s more decisions upon [the issue of the discount] fall to be made by judges rather than by juries as they once were, and as judicial reasons are examined on appeal, it is probably inevitable and in the interests of judicial consistency (which is a hallmark of justice), that trial judges and appellate courts should look to the way earlier decision-makers have resolved like factual questions. Those decisions do not yield binding principles of law. However, they do provide some guidance as to the approach that has been taken to the solution of problems, the recurring features of which take on a monotonous similarity when different cases are compared.

(2) Methodology

A1.05 As we have said, this appendix explores the discounts imposed for contributory negligence in frequently recurring situations. It is necessary to begin by describing the methodology adopted. The appendix is concerned with the period from 1 January 1998 to 31 July 2022, that is, a period of almost twenty-five years. It thus concentrates on the contemporary operation of the law of contributory negligence. It is likely that the way in which judges reduce damages for contributory negligence has varied over time, given that major social changes have taken place since the apportionment legislation was enacted (such as the introduction of laws making the use of seat belts mandatory).[9] By looking only to cases

---

[5] T Weir, *An Introduction to Tort Law* (2nd edn, OUP 2006) 125.

[6] See 4.24.

[7] ibid.

[8] [2003] HCA 34, (2003) 214 CLR 552 [100]. See also *Walsh v CP Hart & Sons Ltd* [2020] EWHC 37 (QB) [52] (Martin Spencer J) ('Different cases do, of course, turn on their own facts and findings of other judges in other cases are of limited use, but they help to identify the "ballpark" level of contributory negligence'). It is unfortunate that in this case the judge was not referred to the first edition of this work, which provided a systematic analysis of recent cases involving falls from height (see A1.69–A1.74 for an updated account).

[9] But see 4.62.

decided since 1998, there is a reduced risk that different approaches that may have prevailed in earlier times will undermine attempts to understand how judges discount damages for contributory negligence in the present day.

It is commonplace for a case to involve more than one claim, such as when two claimants sue a single defendant in the same proceedings. Where a case involves more than one claim and the claimant (or claimants) is guilty of contributory negligence, the court may reduce damages by different amounts in each claim. For example, if C1 and C2 sue D, the discount for contributory negligence in the claim by C1 may be 30 per cent, whereas the discount in the claim by C2 may be 50 per cent. In order to capture such differences, the analysis that follows concentrates on claims rather than cases. This approach means that a given case often features more than once in a particular sample of claims. **A1.06**

The claims on which the analysis below is based were identified by searching each of the major legal databases (ie Westlaw, LexisNexis and Lawtel). Our search terms, which were entered in the full text dialogue box, were 'Law Reform (Contributory Negligence) Act 1945' and 'contributory negligence'. All of the search results were reviewed and claims were included in the dataset where the court considered how to apportion responsibility for the claimant's damage following a finding of contributory negligence. Where the facts of a given claim fell within a particular category of recurrent act, the claim was included within that category even if it was a 'complex' case in that it involved more than one instance of contributory negligence. All claims within a particular category are listed at the end of the discussion of the category concerned and are sequenced in ascending order of the discount imposed. **A1.07**

Certain types of claim were excluded from the analysis. The most important of these were claims in respect of which the court made a merely contingent determination regarding the appropriate discount for contributory negligence. It is routine for trial judges who find for the defendant on liability, or who hold that the claimant was not guilty of contributory negligence, to nevertheless consider the issue of apportionment and make a hypothetical finding in this connection, although the practice in this regard is not uniform.[10] Trial judges generally proceed in this way in case their decision on liability or the existence of contributory negligence is reversed on appeal. Where this occurs, the previously contingent finding regarding contributory negligence will morph into a finding that has substantive effect, and the need for a retrial on the issue of contributory negligence will thereby be avoided. Claims involving contingent determinations have been excluded from the analysis because trial judges who consider the issue of contributory negligence contingently sometimes treat that issue somewhat cursorily, and so we took the view that these claims were less valuable as a guide to judicial decision-making on the apportionment issue. Other disregarded types of claim include professional negligence claims in which the existence of contributory negligence was in issue only in the underlying proceedings;[11] claims in which the issue was whether the doctrine of contributory negligence applied to the cause of action in question, and not how the doctrine, if it did apply, affected the outcome of the **A1.08**

[10] See 6.10.

[11] See, eg, *Hunter v Earnshaw* [2001] PNLR 42 (QBD).

case on the facts;[12] and claims in which foreign law was applied on the issue of contributory negligence.[13]

A1.09 The appendix is concerned only with the discount that was ultimately imposed in the proceedings. Thus, where an appellate court interfered with a discount for contributory negligence that was made at first instance, only data from the appellate decision have been included, although we sometimes mention the finding at first instance and note that it was overturned. Where an appellate court set aside a finding of contributory negligence, the apportionment decision at first instance has been disregarded.

A1.10 Some of the techniques that are employed to describe the data will be familiar to readers, whereas others may be alien. It is necessary to explain those concepts with which not all readers may be acquainted along with some less well-known aspects of otherwise familiar concepts. It is convenient to start with the average, which is an everyday way of conveying meaning in relation to data. However, several features of that concept merit some brief remarks. The average is a measure of central tendency, that is to say, it is an attempt to identify the typical value in a given sample. It is calculated by dividing all values by the number of values. As a concept, the idea of the average is easy to grasp and it often conveys a significant amount of information. However, an average should be interpreted cautiously when the amount of data from which it has been calculated is limited, because in such cases it is more prone to being distorted by outliers (ie atypical data). When a given sample that is treated in this appendix contains outliers, the average is reported both with and without the outlier(s) in order that the effect of the outlier(s) on the average can be seen by the reader.

A1.11 The mode is another frequently used measure of central tendency. It refers to the value that appears most commonly in a given sample. Suppose that the following discounts for contributory negligence are imposed: 10, 10, 20, 20, 20, 40, 45, 60, 75, 75, 80, 80. In this instance, the mode would be 20. Unlike the average, the mode is not influenced by outliers. However, the mode, in contrast with the average, ignores all of the data save for the most frequently occurring value. The mode will sometimes be the same as (or close to) the average but this will not necessarily be the case. A given sample may have more than one mode, and if no values recur, no mode at all.

A1.12 The standard deviation is a measure of the variability of data. In other words, it reveals whether the data concerned are homogeneous or, conversely, heterogeneous. More specifically, the standard deviation is the average amount by which data diverge from the average. Suppose, for example, that the standard deviation for a given sample of discounts imposed for contributory negligence is 25 per cent. That would mean that, on average, the discount imposed in each claim within the sample is 25 per cent higher or lower than the average discount. A standard deviation of 25 per cent is relatively large in the context of discounts for contributory negligence. It suggests that the data are reasonably dispersed from each other. Conversely, a standard deviation of, say, 10 per cent would mean that most data points are clustered within a reasonably confined bracket.

---

[12] See, eg, *Standard Chartered Bank v Pakistan National Shipping Corp (Nos 2 and 4)* [2003] UKHL 43, [2003] 1 AC 959.

[13] See, eg, *Barings plc (in liq) v Coopers & Lybrand (No 7)* [2003] EWHC 1319 (Ch), [2003] PNLR 34; *Vann v Ocidental-Companhia De Seguros SA* [2015] EWCA Civ 572; *Lambert v Motor Insurers' Bureau* [2022] EWHC 583 (QB).

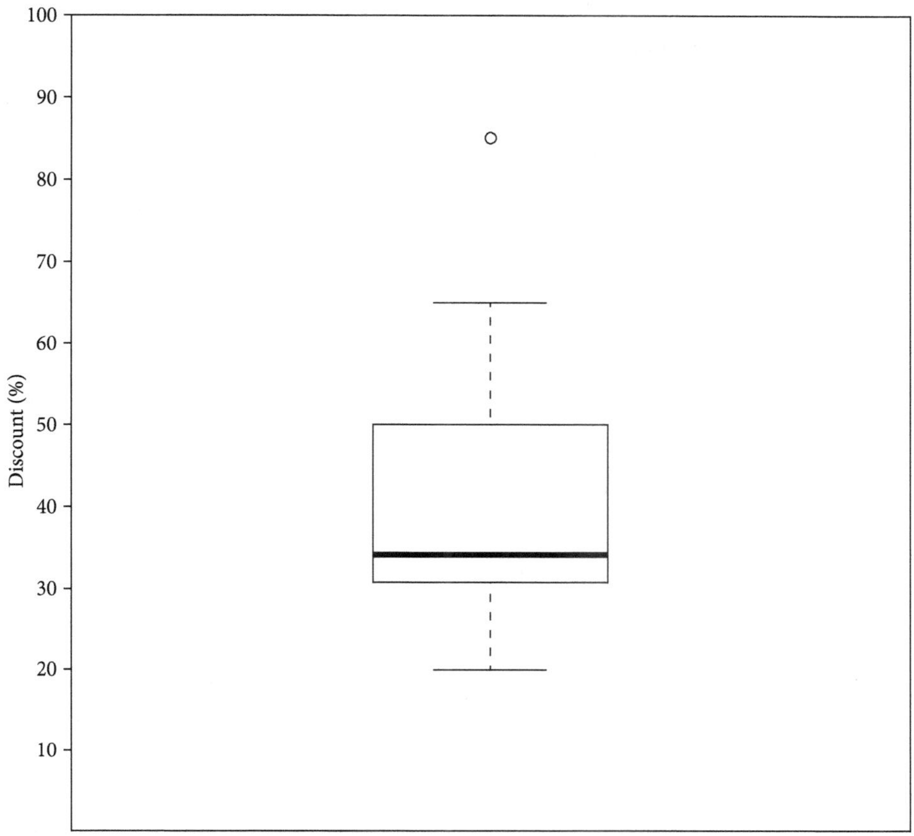

Figure 1 ***Illustration of a boxplot***

The range refers to the difference between the highest and lowest value within a given sample. For example, if the highest discount for contributory negligence in a sample of claims is 80 per cent and the lowest is 20 per cent, the range would be 60 per cent. Like the standard deviation, the range is a widely used measure of the variability of data. However, it is generally much less meaningful than the standard deviation because, unlike the standard deviation, it ignores most of the data. The range concentrates only on the most extreme values in the sample. **A1.13**

Boxplots that show the distribution of discounts for recurrent acts of contributory negligence are provided. An example of a boxplot can be seen in Figure 1. The thick black line indicates the median, that is to say, the value that represents the midpoint in terms of the data.[14] The median, together with the average and mode, is another measure of central tendency. Fifty per cent of the data always falls above the median and 50 per cent below it. The bottom of the box represents the first quartile (ie the number below which a quarter of the data points lie), the top of the box the third quartile (ie the number above which a quarter of the data points lie), and the whiskers show the full range of values disregarding outliers, which are shown as dots. An outlier is a value that falls below the first quartile or **A1.14**

[14] When there are an even number of claims, the median is the average of the centremost values.

above the third quartile by more than 1.5 times the interquartile range (ie the difference between the top and bottom of the box).

2. Intoxicated Pedestrian Injured by Motorist

(1) Scope

A1.15 This section concerns reductions in the damages that intoxicated pedestrians recovered from negligent motorists.

(2) Descriptive statistics

Number of claims	18
Average discount	41.8%
Mode	33.3%
Highest discount	85%
Lowest discount	20%
Standard deviation	16.1%

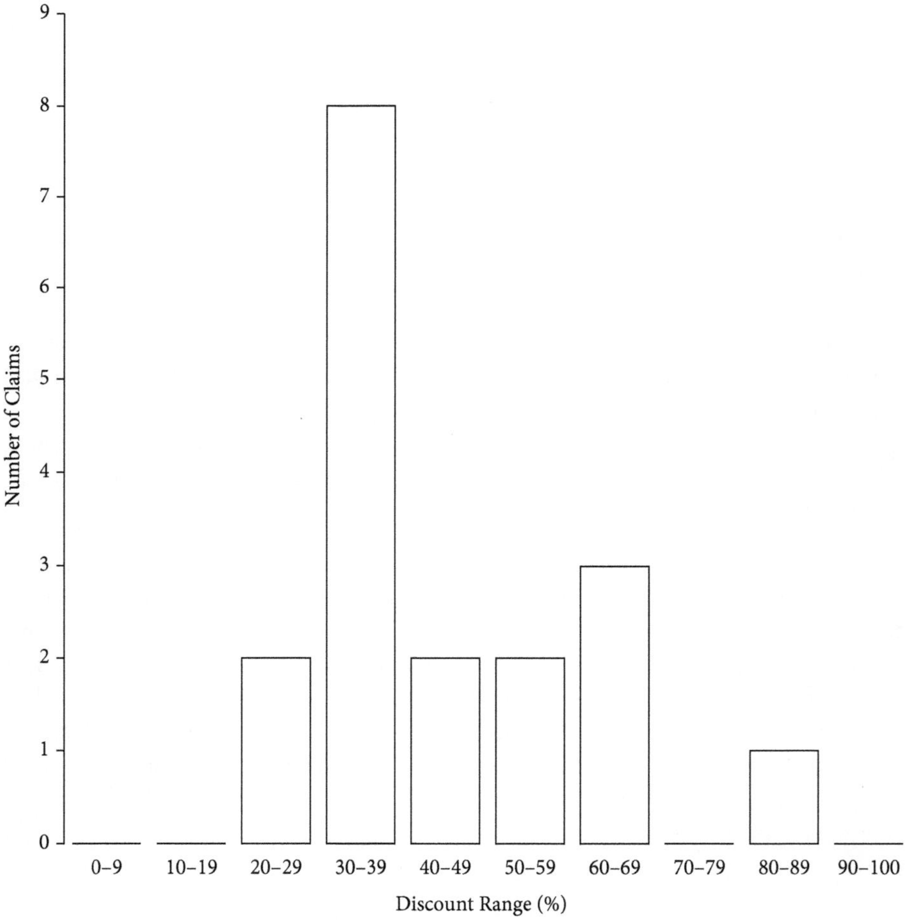

Figure 2 ***Intoxicated pedestrian injured by motorist***

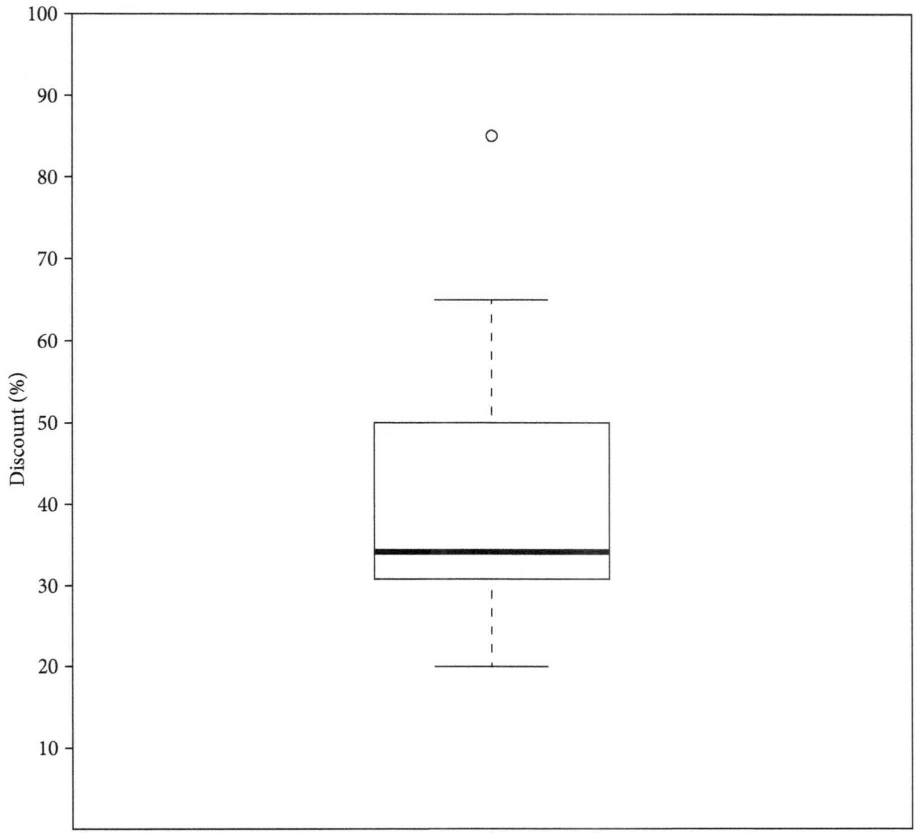

Figure 3 *Intoxicated pedestrian injured by motorist*

(3) Remarks

The discounts imposed exhibit relatively little variability. Nearly all the discounts fell between 20 per cent and 40 per cent. Two discounts of 60 per cent and discounts of 65 per cent and 85 per cent are abnormal. There were no discounts below 20 per cent, which suggests that that is the minimum discount that an intoxicated pedestrian who is contributorily negligent can realistically expect in a claim against a negligent motorist. It might be thought that the claim involving a discount of 85 per cent exerts a significant influence on the average discount. However, this is not so, as the average discount falls only to 39.3 per cent if that claim is excluded from consideration. **A1.16**

(4) Illustration of case involving a discount near the average

In *Lightfoot v Go-Ahead Group plc*,[15] the claimant, then aged fifty-two, was struck by the defendant's bus. The accident happened at night-time on an unlit rural road. The bus was travelling at between 23 and 25 mph at the time of impact, with the applicable speed limit **A1.17**

[15] [2011] EWHC 89 (QB), [2001] RTR 27.

for buses being 50 mph. The claimant was 'very drunk'. He had proceeded diagonally into the carriageway and attempted to flag down the bus. The bus driver had been reading a laminated timetable with the cabin light activated at the time of the accident. Further, he was driving with dipped headlights. A 40 per cent discount was imposed.

(5) Illustration of case involving a high discount

A1.18 In *Smith v Bluebird Buses Ltd*,[16] the pursuer, who was intoxicated, entered the carriageway in order to argue with a passenger in a vehicle that had stopped at the traffic lights. The pursuer turned away from that vehicle and walked a few steps without looking for oncoming traffic. At that point, the pursuer was struck by the defender's bus. The bus had been travelling at between 5 and 10 mph at the time. The court found that '[t]he driver had little opportunity to avoid the collision', although his view of the pursuer was unobstructed. An 85 per cent discount was imposed.

(6) Illustration of case involving a low discount

A1.19 The accident in *Ayres v Odedra*[17] occurred just after midnight on a one-way street within a pedestrianized zone in the centre of a city and close to a pedestrian crossing. The claimant, who was then aged twenty-four, was drunk and unsteady on his feet. He placed himself in front of the defendant's vehicle, which had stopped at traffic lights, dropped his trousers, and remained on the road after the traffic lights had turned green. The claimant was struck when the defendant proceeded to drive forward. A 20 per cent discount was imposed.

(7) Claims in the sample

A1.20 (1) *Ayres v Odedra* [2013] EWHC 40 (QB) (20 per cent); (2) *Sedge v Prime* [2011] EWHC 820 (QB) (25 per cent); (3) *Cook v Thorne* [2001] EWCA Civ 81 (30 per cent); (4) *Cook v Thorne* [2001] EWCA Civ 81 (30 per cent); (5) *Wooldridge v George* (QBD, 23 January 2017) (30 per cent); (6) *Adams v Gibson* [2016] EWHC 3209 (QB) (33.3 per cent); (7) *Griffiths v Brown* [1999] PIQR P131 (QBD) (33.3 per cent); (8) *Lunt v Khelifa* [2001] All ER (D) 428 (QBD) (33.3 per cent); (9) *Smith v Chief Constable of Nottinghamshire Police* [2012] EWCA Civ 161, [2012] RTR 23 (33.3 per cent); (10) *Parkinson v Chief Constable of Dyfed Powys* [2004] EWCA Civ 802 (35 per cent); (11) *Lightfoot v Go-Ahead Group plc* [2011] EWHC 89 (QB), [2011] RTR 27 (40 per cent); (12) *Eagle v Chambers (No 1)* [2003] EWCA Civ 1107, [2004] RTR 9 (40 per cent); (13) *Forbes v Ferguson* [2009] 3 WLUK 343 (Tayside, Central and Fife Sheriff Court) (50 per cent); (14) *Warsama v London Fire Brigade* [2020] EWHC 718 (QB) (50 per cent); (15) *Green v Bannister* [2003] EWCA Civ 1819 (60 per cent); (16) *McCaughey v Mullan* [2014] NIQB 132 (60 per cent); (17) *Cameron v Swan* [2021] CSIH 30 (65 per cent); (18) *Smith v Bluebird Buses Ltd* [2014] CSOH 75, 2014 Rep LR 91 (85 per cent).

[16] [2014] CSOH 75, 2014 Rep LR 91.
[17] [2013] EWHC 40 (QB).

3. Non-intoxicated Pedestrian Injured by Motorist: Adult Pedestrian

(1) Scope

This section concerns reductions in the damages that non-intoxicated adult pedestrians recovered from negligent motorists. **A1.21**

(2) Descriptive statistics

Number of claims	36
Average discount	39%
Mode	50%
Highest discount	80%
Lowest discount	10%
Standard deviation	18.9%

(3) Remarks

The majority of the discounts were concentrated between 30 per cent and 50 per cent. It is striking that the average discount in the case of *non*-intoxicated adult pedestrians who were injured by a motorist (39 per cent) is only marginally lower than the average discount **A1.22**

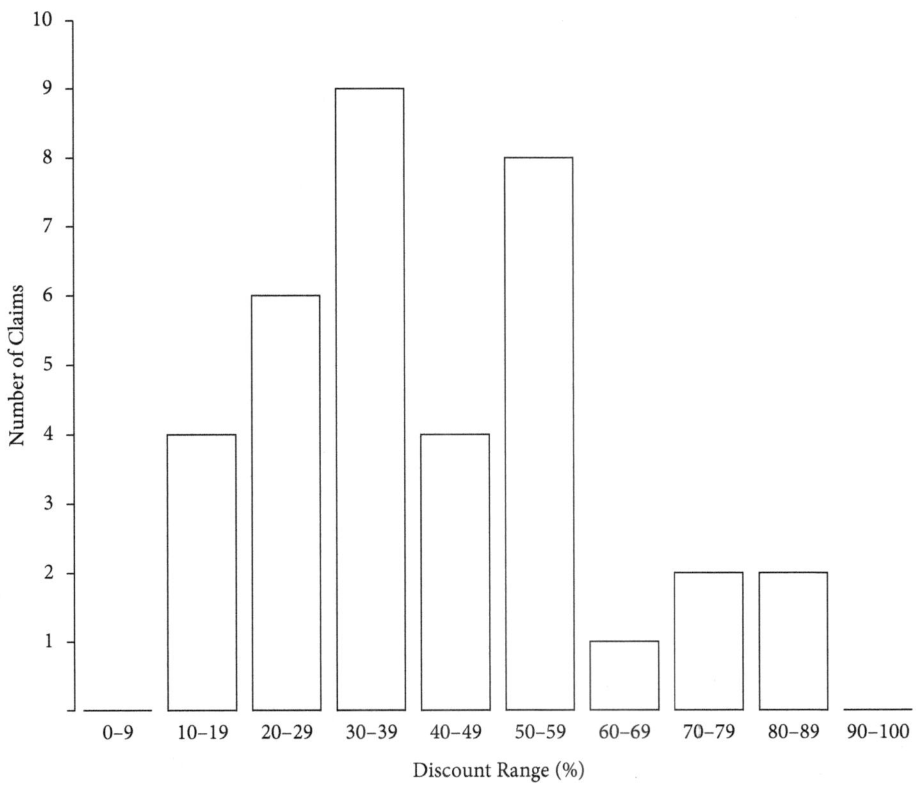

Figure 4 *Non-intoxicated pedestrian injured by motorist: adult pedestrian*

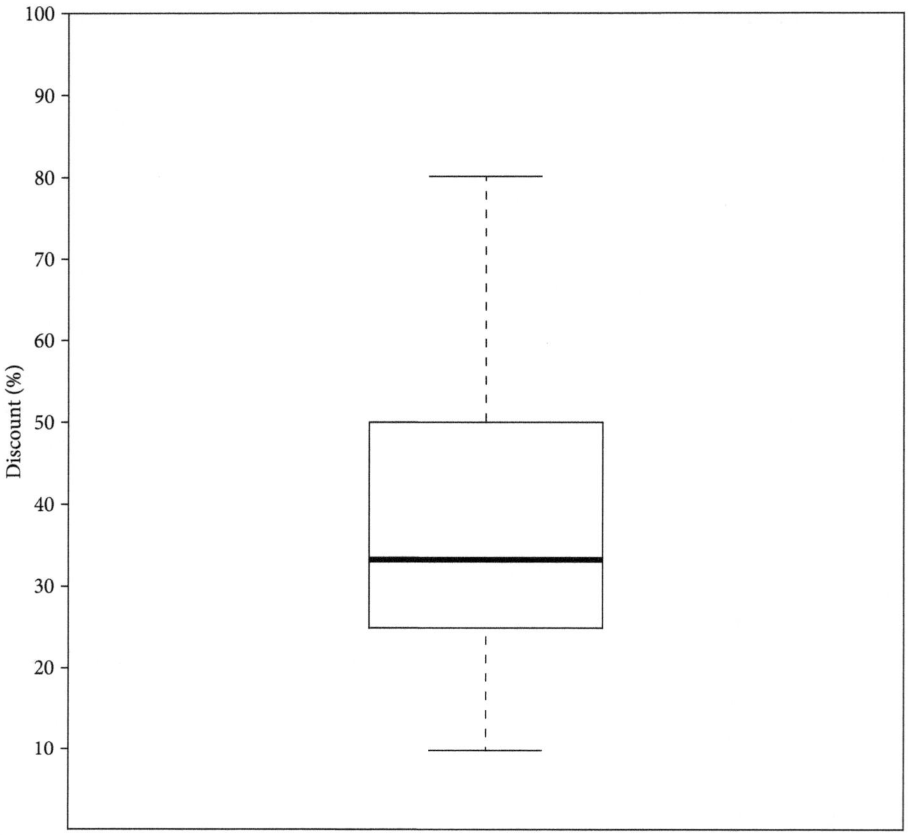

Figure 5 ***Non-intoxicated pedestrian injured by motorist: adult pedestrian***

in claims by intoxicated pedestrians (41.8 per cent).[18] The reason why the averages in these two datasets substantially converge is not immediately clear, although it does not appear to be due to the impact of outliers. One possible explanation lies in the idea that motorists are expected to take particular care when driving in areas where it is known that intoxicated pedestrians are likely to be present.

(4) Illustration of case involving a discount near the average

A1.23 In *McDonald v Chambers*,[19] the pursuer stepped from a traffic island into a road before establishing that there were no oncoming vehicles, although she had pushed the control button to bring up the walk signal. The defender motorist had seen the pursuer and had also noticed that she had pushed the control button. However, the defender drove through an amber light and struck the pursuer. Lord McCluskey said: 'A pedestrian who is using a set of traffic lights, with signals for both traffic and pedestrians, to cross a busy road can hardly escape a charge of carelessness if she steps into a roadway when the roadway is not

[18] See A1.15.
[19] 2000 SLT 454 (OH).

clear or when there is traffic which is still moving towards the place where the pedestrians are to cross.'[20] Damages were reduced by 33.3 per cent.

(5) Illustration of case involving a high discount

Watson v Skuse[21] involves an unusually high discount for a pedestrian case. The claimant was trying to cross a road at a pelican crossing. He checked the traffic lights, which he noted were red, and started to cross the road. However, he did not look at the pedestrian light, which was also red, and should have realized that the traffic lights were about to turn green. Upon entering the roadway, the claimant passed so close to the front of a large lorry with a sheer bonnet that its driver was unable to see him. When the traffic lights turned green, the lorry moved forward and struck the claimant. The claimant had been drinking but was not intoxicated. The trial judge held that the driver should have seen the claimant as he started to move into the road and ought to have anticipated that the claimant would act as he did. The Court of Appeal increased the discount of 50 per cent that had been imposed at first instance to 80 per cent. Sedley LJ described the claimant as being 'the principal author of his own misfortune' and added '[i]t was the claimant who [sought to cross the road] at a moment when he could and should have seen that the red pedestrian light was against him, so that the lights were about to change in the defendant's favour'.[22] Arden LJ referred to the claimant as having taken 'a foolish gamble'.[23] **A1.24**

(6) Illustration of case involving a low discount

In *McDermott v Pettit*,[24] the claimant was struck by the defendant's car as he sought to cross a major arterial road in the early hours of the morning. The trial judge found that the defendant had a blood–alcohol content greater than the permitted limit and had been driving significantly in excess of the speed limit. The claimant was found guilty of contributory negligence on the basis that he should have used a pedestrian crossing that was located just 10 metres from where he had entered the road. The judge also emphasized that the road comprised a three-lane carriageway and that nearby traffic lights were showing green in favour of oncoming traffic. A 10 per cent discount was imposed. **A1.25**

(7) Claims in the sample

(1) *McDermott v Pettit* [2011] EWHC 3074 (QB) (10 per cent); (2) *Sklair v Haycock* [2009] EWHC 3328 (QB) (10 per cent); (3) *Douglas v O'Neill* [2011] EWHC 601 (QB) (12.5 per cent); (4) *Bright v Bourn* [2018] EWHC 1948 (QB) (15 per cent); (5) *Bruma v Hassan* [2017] EWHC 3209 (QB) (20 per cent); (6) *Carpenter v Lunnon* [2004] EWHC 3079 (QB) (20 per cent); (7) *Neill v Moore* [2019] NIQB 46 (20 per cent); (8) *White v Chapman* 2001 WL 825325 (QBD) (20 per cent); (9) *Sabir v Osei-Kwabena* [2015] EWCA Civ 1213 (25 per cent); (10) *Sedge v Prime* [2011] EWHC 820 (QB) (25 per cent); (11) *Cameron v Nwankwo* [2022] CSOH 7 (30 per cent); (12) *Cassells v Allan* [2019] **A1.26**

[20] ibid 455.
[21] [2001] EWCA Civ 1158.
[22] ibid [27].
[23] ibid [33].
[24] [2011] EWHC 3074 (QB).

CSOH 14 (30 per cent); (13) *Podesta v Akhtar* [2018] EWHC 1245 (QB) (30 per cent); (14) *Greenwood v Cummings* (QBD, 9 April 2008) (33.3 per cent); (15) *Lenord v First Manchester Ltd* [2020] EWHC 982 (QB) (33.3 per cent); (16) *Markowski v Elson* [2001] CLY 4477 (Weymouth CC) (33.3 per cent); (17) *McDonald v Chambers* 2000 SLT 454 (OH) (33.3 per cent); (18) *McKeever v Redmond* [2021] NIQB 30 (33.3 per cent); (19) *Rooke v Liston* 1999 WL 477713 (CA) (33.3 per cent); (20) *Brownlow v Knight* [2003] NIQB 71 (40 per cent); (21) *George v Stagecoach South-East London* 2001 WL 513089 (QBD) (40 per cent); (22) *Hickman v London Central Bus Company Ltd* [2013] EWHC 1703 (QB) (40 per cent); (23) *Hughes-Jukes v Etti* [2006] EWHC 2493 (QB), [2007] RTR 2 (40 per cent); (24) *Gonzalez-Ramirez v First Eastern Counties Buses Ltd* (QBD, 26 October 2017) (50 per cent); (25) *Hill v Master Concrete Northern Ltd* [2010] EWHC 3613 (QB) (50 per cent); (26) *McCreery v Letson* [2015] CSOH 153 (50 per cent); (27) *Rehill v Rider Holdings Ltd* [2012] EWCA Civ 628, [2013] RTR 5 (50 per cent); (28) *Parker v McClaren* [2021] EWHC 2828 (QB) (50 per cent); (29) *Rose v South East London and Kent Bus Company Ltd* [2004] EWHC 1106 (QB) (50 per cent); (30) *Sahakian v McDonnell* [2007] EWHC 3242 (QB), [2008] RTR 19 (50 per cent); (31) *Smeed v Sparrow* 1999 WL 477490 (CA) (50 per cent); (32) *Belka v Prosperini* [2011] EWCA Civ 623 (66.6 per cent); (33) *Bryce v McKirdy* 1999 SLT 988 (OH) (75 per cent); (34) *Pritchard v Ralph* 2000 WL 1791426 (CA) (75 per cent); (35) *Maughan v Boylan* [2006] NIQB 38 (80 per cent); (36) *Watson v Skuse* [2001] EWCA Civ 1158 (80 per cent).

4. Non-intoxicated Pedestrian Injured by Motorist: Child Pedestrian

(1) Scope

A1.27 This section is concerned with child pedestrians who were injured after moving into the path of oncoming traffic and who were not intoxicated at the time.

(2) Descriptive statistics

Number of claims	15
Average discount	37.6%
Mode	20%
Highest discount	75%
Lowest discount	10%
Standard deviation	21.1%

(3) Remarks

A1.28 Slightly more than one-third of the claims on which this section is based involved discounts between 10 per cent and 20 per cent. The rest of the discounts were spread more or less evenly over most of the rest of the spectrum. The average discount in the claims on which this section is based (37.6 per cent) is only fractionally below the average discount in the case of sober adult pedestrians who were injured by motorists (39 per cent).[25]

[25] See A1.21.

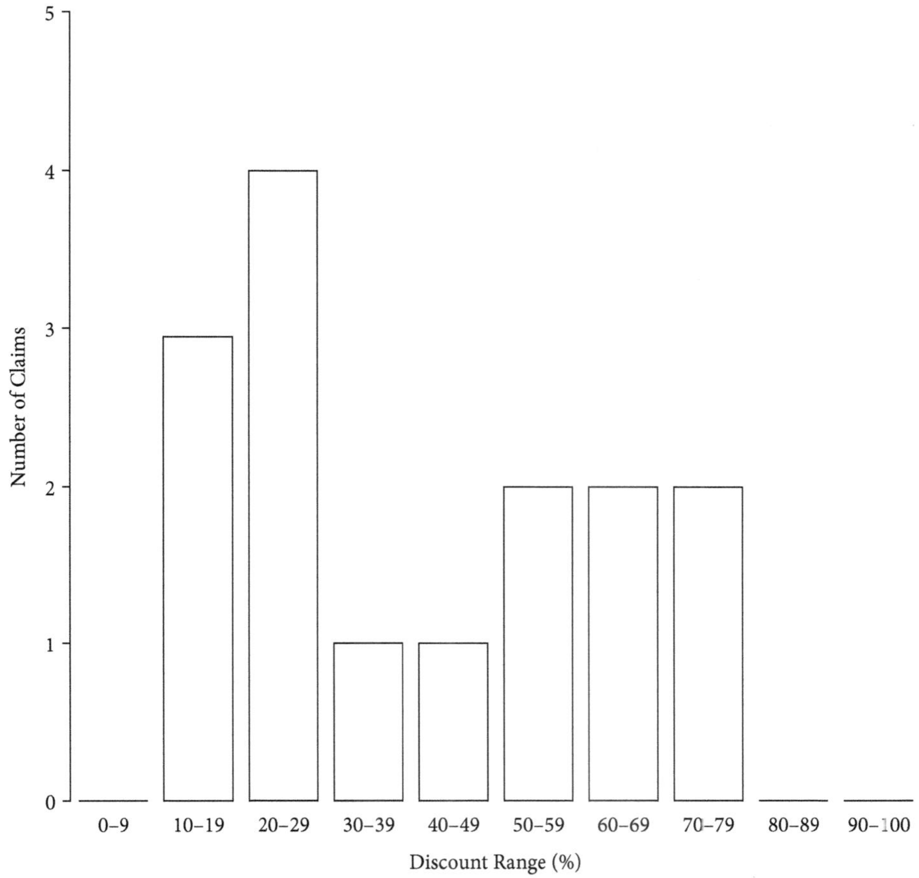

Figure 6 ***Non-intoxicated pedestrian injured by motorist: child pedestrian***

(4) Illustration of case involving a discount near the average

Eagle v Chambers[26] is a well-known and important decision of the Court of Appeal. The claimant was aged seventeen at the time of the accident, which occurred on a dual carriageway at night-time in good driving conditions. She had entered and was walking along the roadway in a distressed state and had failed to heed at least two warnings that had been given to her by persons concerned for her safety. The defendant motorist, who had been driving at approximately 30–35 mph, collided with the claimant. An event had recently finished near the scene of the accident, and several pedestrians were walking on the footpath in the vicinity. The defendant had been drinking prior to the accident and admitted that he had drunk enough to impair his driving ability. He failed a roadside alcohol breath test but was found to be just below the limit when tested again at a police station. At first instance, damages were reduced by 60 per cent. On appeal, the discount was reduced to 40 per cent, with the Court of Appeal apparently finding that there was **A1.29**

[26] [2003] EWCA Civ 1107, [2004] RTR 9.

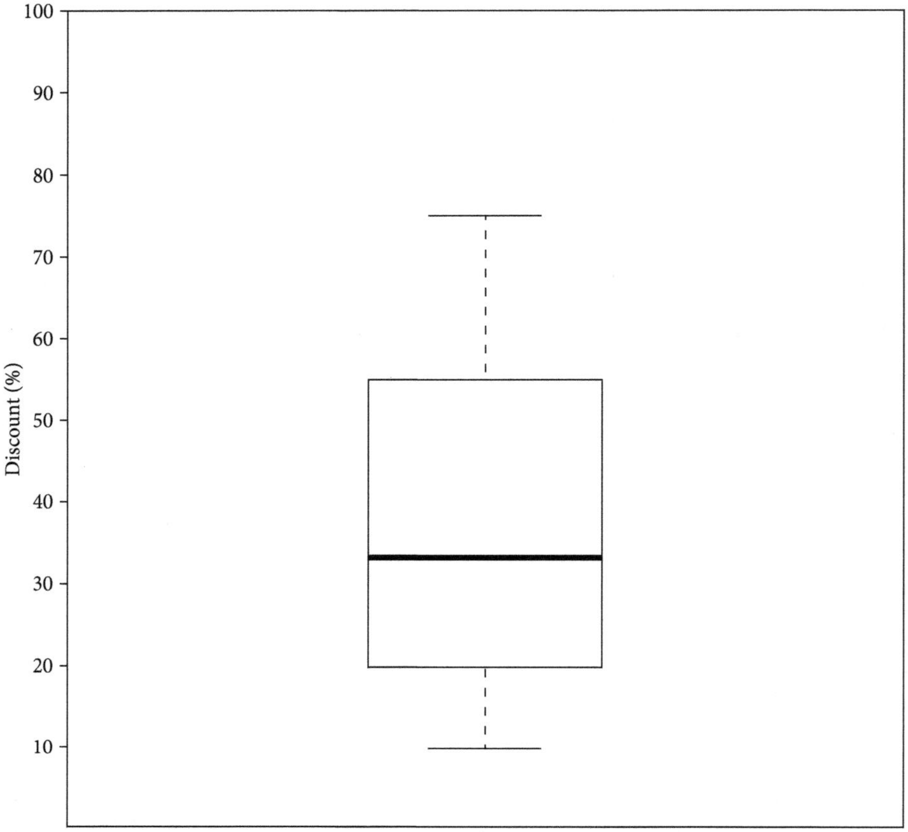

Figure 7 *Non-intoxicated pedestrian injured by motorist: child pedestrian*

insufficient evidence to support the trial judge's conclusion that the claimant had been intoxicated.

(5) Illustration of case involving a high discount

A1.30 In *Paramasivan v Wicks*,[27] the claimant, who was then aged thirteen, was struck by the defendant's vehicle. The claimant had been standing outside a shop with several of his friends and had suddenly run into the road after throwing an ice cream at one of the group's members, apparently in order to avoid the consequences of having done so. The claimant passed between two parked cars. The defendant was found to have been driving too fast and to have been paying insufficient attention. The accident occurred at night-time. Hughes LJ said that the claimant was 'quite old enough to understand roads' and that it was he 'who created the hazard and he did it by doing something entirely unexpected and ... very careless'.[28] Damages had been reduced by 50 per cent at first instance. The discount was increased to 75 per cent on appeal.

[27] [2013] EWCA Civ 262.
[28] ibid [17].

(6) Illustration of case involving a low discount

In *AB v Main*,[29] the claimant suffered catastrophic brain injuries when, aged eight years and ten months, he was struck by the defendant's vehicle. The accident occurred in the afternoon. The road concerned had a single lane running in each direction and was a relatively busy one, with a speed limit of 40 mph. The claimant had been playing nearby and jogged into the road to fetch a bottle that was lying on the far side of it. The claimant was 'completely unaware' of the defendant's vehicle prior to its striking him. The trial judge found that the defendant had seen the claimant before he had entered the roadway, should have realized that the claimant was playing, should have reduced her speed, and should have moved into the centre of the road. The trial judge also found that the defendant had been driving at about 30 mph at the time of the impact. Damages were reduced by 20 per cent. **A1.31**

(7) Claims in the sample

(1) *Gul v McDonagh* [2021] EWCA Civ 1503 (10 per cent); (2) *Joyce v Bradbury* [2019] NIQB 82 (15 per cent); (3) *SH v Farrell* [2007] NIQB 42 (15 per cent); (4) *AB v Main* [2015] EWHC 3183 (QB) (20 per cent); (5) *Honnor v Lewis* [2005] EWHC 747 (QB) (20 per cent); (6) *McCluskey v Wallace* 1998 SLT 1357 (IH) (20 per cent); (7) *Scutts v Keyse* 2000 WL 33201536 (QBD) (25 per cent); (8) *Toropdar v D* [2009] EWHC 2997 (TCC) (33.3 per cent); (9) *Eagle v Chambers* [2003] EWCA Civ 1107, [2004] RTR 9 (40 per cent); (10) *Jackson v Murray* [2015] UKSC 5, [2015] 2 All ER 805 (50 per cent); (11) *Rainford v Lawrenson* [2014] EWHC 1188 (QB) (50 per cent); (12) *Breslin v McCarron* [2018] NIQB 101 (60 per cent); (13) *Futter v Bryceland* 2000 GWD 9-339 (OH) (60 per cent); (14) *Ehrari v Curry* [2006] EWHC 1319 (QB) (70 per cent); (15) *Paramasivan v Wicks* [2013] EWCA Civ 262 (75 per cent). **A1.32**

5. Failure to Wear a Seat Belt

(1) Scope

This section concerns claims that involve either a failure to wear a seat belt or a failure to use a seat belt properly. **A1.33**

(2) Descriptive statistics

Number of claims	14
Average discount	21.7%
Mode	15%
Highest discount	50%
Lowest discount	10%
Standard deviation	10.5%

[29] [2015] EWHC 3183 (QB).

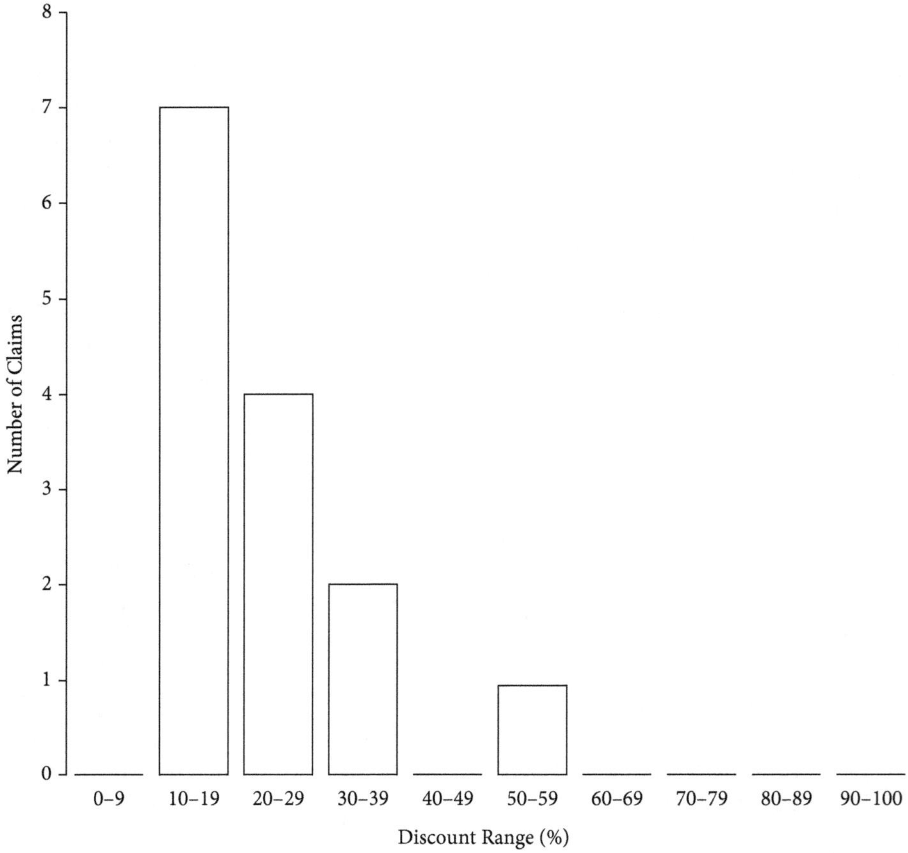

Figure 8 ***Failure to wear a seat belt***

(3) Remarks

A1.34 The discounts imposed in the claims that are addressed in this section are relatively homogenous with most being clustered around the average (21.7 per cent). The concentration of claims within this narrow band is undoubtedly due to the guidelines that were established in *Froom v Butcher*[30] for apportionment in seat-belt cases. In *Froom*, Lord Denning MR, with whom the other members of the Court of Appeal agreed, held that, in the ordinary course of things, a discount of 25 per cent for contributory negligence is appropriate if wearing a seat belt would have avoided the injury altogether, and a discount of 15 per cent is appropriate where the injury would have been less serious had a seat belt been used. It is therefore unsurprising that the most common discount in this type of case was 15 per cent. Another explanation for the low average discount (around half of the overall average) may lie in the fact that in virtually all (if not all) seat-belt cases the contributory negligence contributes only to the claimant's injuries and not to the accident that causes them.

[30] [1976] QB 286 (CA). See 4.60–4.66.

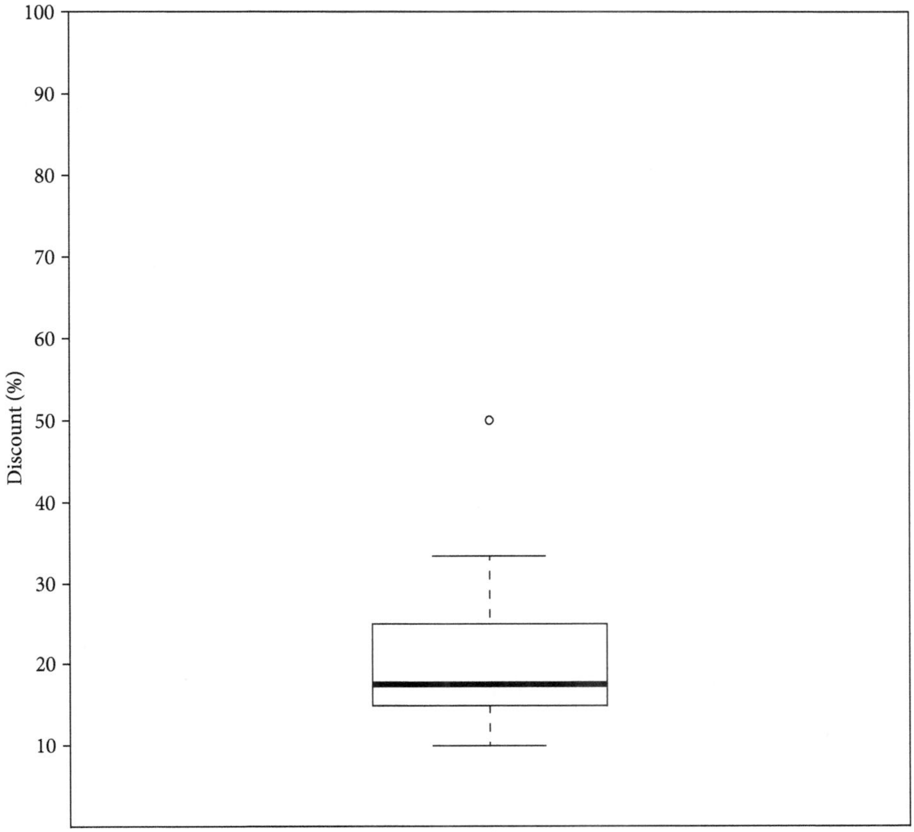

Figure 9 ***Failure to wear a seat belt***

(4) Illustration of case involving a discount near the average

In *Hazlett v Robinson*,[31] the claimant suffered fractures of the leg, arm, and spine in an accident caused by the defendant's negligence. The claimant had been sitting in the rear of a vehicle being driven by the defendant. The judge found that his injuries 'would have been very [much] less severe had he been wearing a seatbelt'.[32] In reaching that conclusion, the judge accepted the evidence of two expert witnesses who had testified that fractures to the bones concerned were very unlikely to occur when a seat belt was used. A 20 per cent discount was imposed. **A1.35**

(5) Illustration of case involving a high discount

In *Eyres v Atkinsons Kitchens and Bedrooms Ltd*,[33] the claimant driver suffered severe spinal injuries when he fell asleep and his vehicle overturned. He sued his employer alleging negligence in permitting him to drive when he was too tired to do so safely. At first instance a discount of 25 per cent was imposed only on the basis that the claimant had not been **A1.36**

31 [2014] NIQB 17.
32 ibid [53].
33 [2007] EWCA Civ 365.

wearing a seat belt. The Court of Appeal increased the discount to 33.3 per cent on the ground that the claimant's contributory negligence had been aggravated by the fact that he drove while tired. Ward LJ remarked that the employer did 'nothing to guard against the very risk of injury from which he ought to have been saving his employee' and hence bore the bulk of the responsibility for the damage.

(6) Illustration of case involving a low discount

A1.37 In *Mattar v Shenouda*,[34] the deceased, a fifty-one-year-old man who had been sitting in the front passenger seat of the defendant's vehicle at the relevant time, suffered fatal injuries due to the defendant's negligence. Buckley J held that had he been wearing a seat belt he 'would not have been killed but would nevertheless have sustained multiple and fairly serious injury'. A 15 per cent discount was imposed.

(7) Claims in the sample

A1.38 (1) *Corbett v Cumbria Kart Racing Club* [2013] EWHC 1362 (QB) (10 per cent); (2) *Corbett v Cumbria Kart Racing Club* [2013] EWHC 1362 (QB) (10 per cent); (3) *Garth v Grant* (QBD, 25 May 2007) (15 per cent); (4) *Edwards v Martin* [2010] EWHC 570 (QB) (15 per cent); (5) *Mattar v Shenouda* 2001 WL 606384 (QBD) (15 per cent); (6) *Palmer v Kitley* [2008] EWHC 2819 (QB) (15 per cent); (7) *W v Hardman* [2001] CLY 4452 (Leeds CC) (15 per cent); (8) *Hazlett v Robinson* [2014] NIQB 17 (20 per cent); (9) *Al Gouri v Achkar* [2007] CLY 3079 (QBD) (25 per cent); (10) *Gawler v Raettig* [2007] EWHC 373 (QB) (25 per cent); (11) *Pearson v Anwar* [2015] EWCA Civ 1011 (25 per cent); (12) *Steele v WH Malcolm Ltd* 2013 GWD 25-511 (North Strathclyde Sheriff Court) (30 per cent); (13) *Eyres v Atkinsons Kitchens & Bedrooms Ltd* [2007] EWCA Civ 365 (33.3 per cent); (14) *Taylor v Leslie* 1998 SLT 1248 (OH) (50 per cent).

6. Speeding

(1) Scope

A1.39 This section concerns claims made by motorists or motorcyclists who suffered injury while driving or riding too quickly. It includes cases in which the claimant, although travelling below the speed limit, was held to have been travelling too fast in the circumstances.[35]

(2) Descriptive statistics

Number of claims	28
Average discount	49%
Mode	50%
Highest discount	90%
Lowest discount	20%
Standard deviation	21.8%

[34] 2001 WL 606384 (QBD).

[35] See, eg, *Edwards v Jerman* [2004] CLY 2743 (Liverpool CC) (25 per cent); *Russell v West Sussex CC* [2009] EWHC 1063 (QB) (50 per cent).

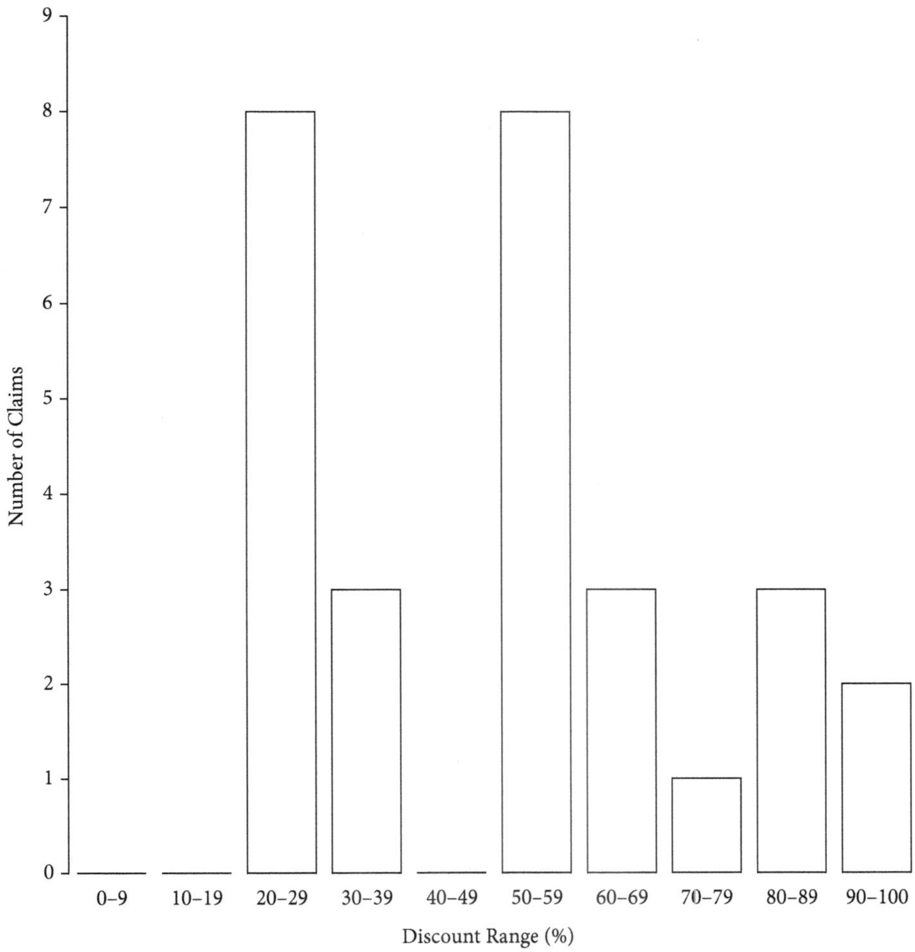

Figure 10 *Speeding*

(3) Remarks

The most notable feature of the statistics is the high average discount of 49 per cent. It seems that the courts tend to regard speeding as conduct that involves greater culpability or causal potency than many other types of contributory negligence.[36] **A1.40**

(4) Illustration of case involving a discount near the average

In *Russell v West Sussex CC*,[37] the claimant's vehicle skidded off the road and struck a tree. **A1.41**
The claimant suffered severe injuries. The accident might not have happened if the road had been level with the verge. The verge was some 6 inches lower than the road at the point at which the vehicle left the road, and the drop resulted in the claimant needing to

[36] See 4.42.
[37] [2009] EWHC 1063 (QB).

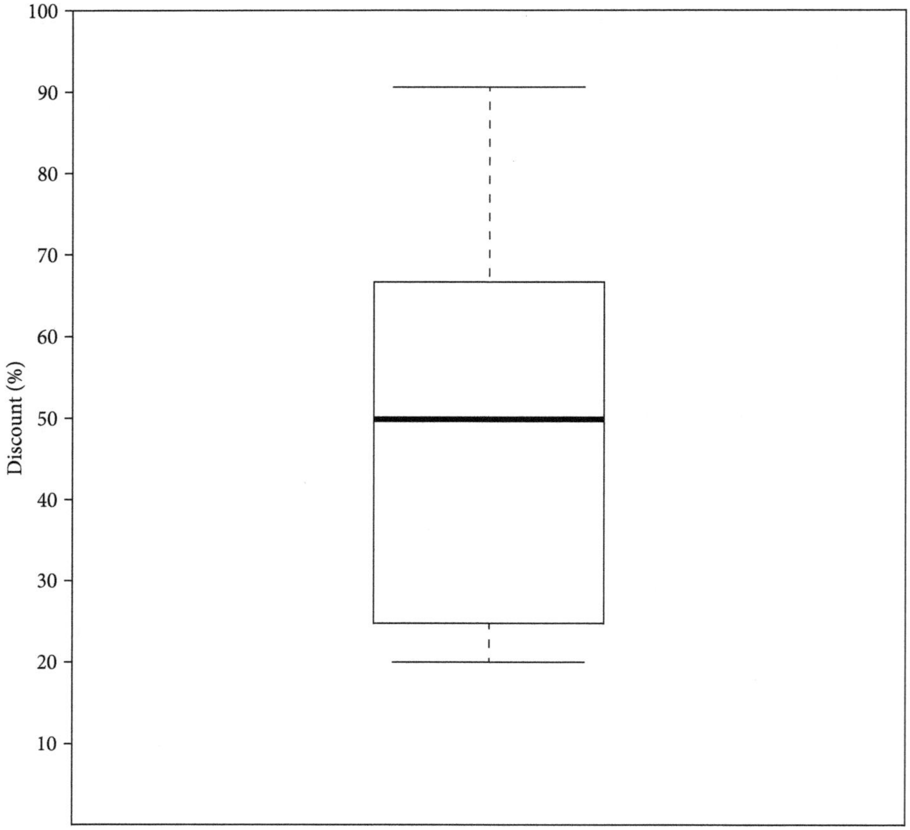

Figure 11 *Speeding*

make a violent correction, which contributed to the vehicle slewing off the road. The speed limit was 60 mph and the claimant was found to have been driving at 45 mph at the time. However, the judge found that 45 mph was too fast given that it was a frosty morning and there was ice on the road. Damages were reduced by 50 per cent.

(5) Illustration of case involving a high discount

A1.42 In *Train v Secretary of State for Defence*,[38] the defendant, who was driving a minibus, turned in front of the deceased motorcyclist. The deceased braked but was unable to avoid the impact and was fatally injured. It was found that the defendant, who had seen the deceased, had negligently concluded that it was safe for him to turn across his path, having underestimated the speed at which the deceased was travelling. Although no precise finding was made as to the deceased's speed at the time of the accident, the judge said that he was travelling at 'a very high speed'[39] and 'probably in excess of 40mph',[40] even though the speed limit was 20 mph. An 80 per cent discount was imposed.

[38] [2014] EWHC 1928 (QB), [2014] RTR 28.
[39] ibid [33].
[40] ibid [24].

(6) Illustration of case involving a low discount

In *Day v Suffolk CC*,[41] the claimant suffered injury when his vehicle ran into a pothole on a rural, single-lane road near his home. The claimant, who had been driving at about 25 mph, sued the highway authority that was responsible for maintaining the road, which owed him a duty under section 41 of the Highways Act 1980. The first instance judge held that he had been driving too quickly given the road's condition, of which the claimant was aware, and in view of the need to keep a proper lookout for potholes. Damages were reduced by 25 per cent, which discount the Court of Appeal reluctantly declined to increase. **A1.43**

(7) Claims in the sample

(1) *Ellis v Lokat* (QBD, 6 October 2011) (20 per cent); (2) *Powell v Hansen* 2001 WL 753470 (QBD) (20 per cent); (3) *Day v Suffolk CC* [2007] EWCA Civ 1436 (25 per cent); (4) *Edwards v Jerman* [2004] CLY 2743 (Liverpool CC) (25 per cent); (5) *Everett v Dyer* [2019] EWHC 2049 (QB) (25 per cent); (6) *McKee v Tough* 2022 GWD 6-104 (Sheriff Personal Injury Court) (25 per cent); (7) *Morrison v Gardiner* [2005] CSOH 156 (25 per cent); (8) *Shevlin v European Metal Recycling Ltd* [2018] EWHC 1695 (QB) (25 per cent); (9) *Jones v Lawton* [2013] EWHC 4108 (QB) (33.3 per cent); (10) *MacKenzie v Perth & Kinross Council* (OH, 22 January 2003) (33.3 per cent); (11) *Nicolson v Willis* [2006] EWHC 2402 (QB) (33.3 per cent); (12) *Buchan v Whiting* [2008] EWHC 2951 (QB) (50 per cent); (13) *Daly v Heeps* 2018 GWD 2-45 (Lothian and Borders Sheriff Court) (50 per cent); (14) *Gilfillan v Barbour* 2003 SLT 1127 (OH) (50 per cent); (15) *Grace v Tanner* [2003] EWCA Civ 354 (50 per cent); (16) *Jenkins v Holt* [1999] RTR 411 (CA) (50 per cent); (17) *Russell v West Sussex CC* [2009] EWHC 1063 (QB) (50 per cent); (18) *Woodham v M Turner (t/a Turners of Great Barton)* [2012] EWCA Civ 375 (50 per cent); (19) *Wheeler v Chief Constable of Gloucestershire Constabulary* [2013] EWCA Civ 1791 (50 per cent); (20) *Wallett v Vickers* [2018] EWHC 3088 (QB) (60 per cent); (21) *Buswell v Symes* [2015] EWHC 1379 (QB) (66.6 per cent); (22) *McPherson v Smith* [2018] EWHC 1433 (QB) (66.6 per cent); (23) *Stark v Lyddon* [2019] EWHC 2076 (QB) (70 per cent); (24) *Burton v Evitt* [2011] EWCA Civ 1378 (80 per cent); (25) *Ringe v Eden Springs (UK) Ltd* [2012] EWHC 14 (QB) (80 per cent); (26) *Train v Secretary of State for Defence* [2014] EWHC 1928 (QB), [2014] RTR 28 (80 per cent); (27) *Kyriacou v Finch* [2021] EWHC 3791 (QB) (90 per cent); (28) *Stephen v Peter* 2005 Rep LR 53 (OH) (90 per cent). **A1.44**

7. Slip-and-fall Accidents: Workplace

(1) Scope

This section concerns slip-and-fall accidents that occurred while the claimant was at work. It extends to all claims in which the claimant failed to pay attention to their footing or to dangers on the ground. It is not confined to cases in which the claimant fell when on their employer's premises. **A1.45**

[41] [2007] EWCA Civ 1436.

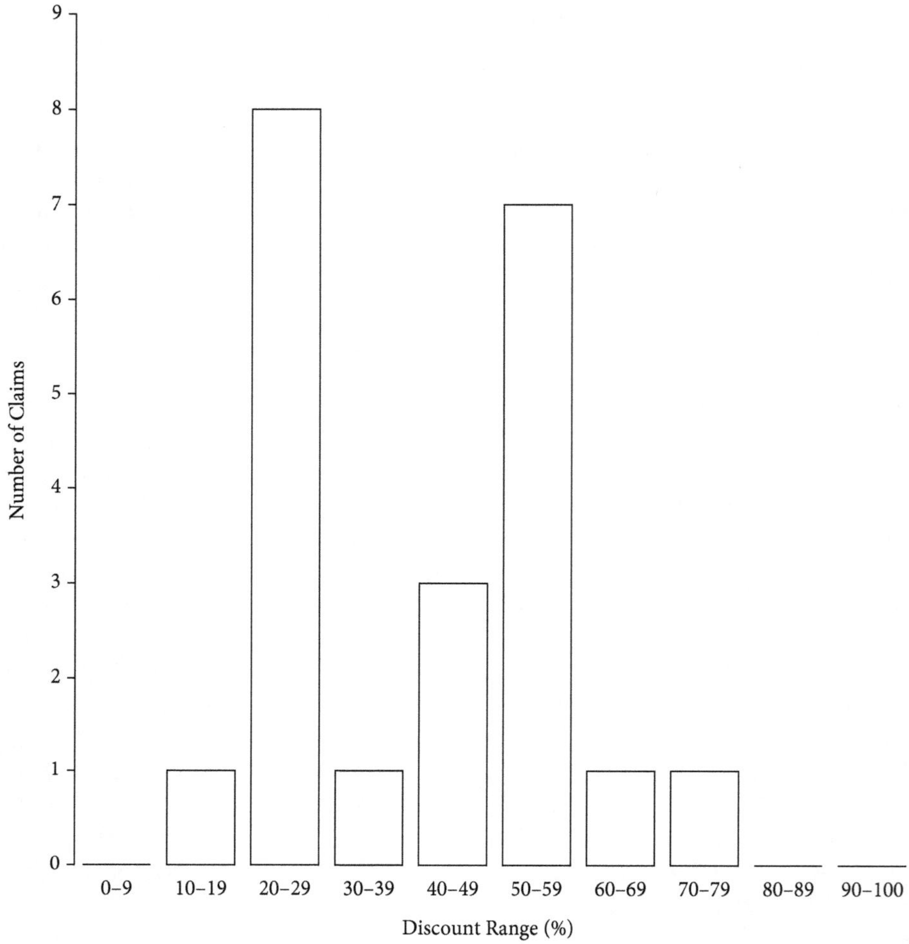

Figure 12 ***Slip-and-fall accidents: workplace***

(2) Descriptive statistics

Number of claims	22
Average discount	38.4%
Mode	50%
Highest discount	75%
Lowest discount	15%
Standard deviation	15.9%

(3) Remarks

A1.46 The discounts in cases of this type exhibit quite a high degree of variability. Nevertheless, in all but two claims, the discount was 50 per cent or less. The average discount was 38.4 per cent.

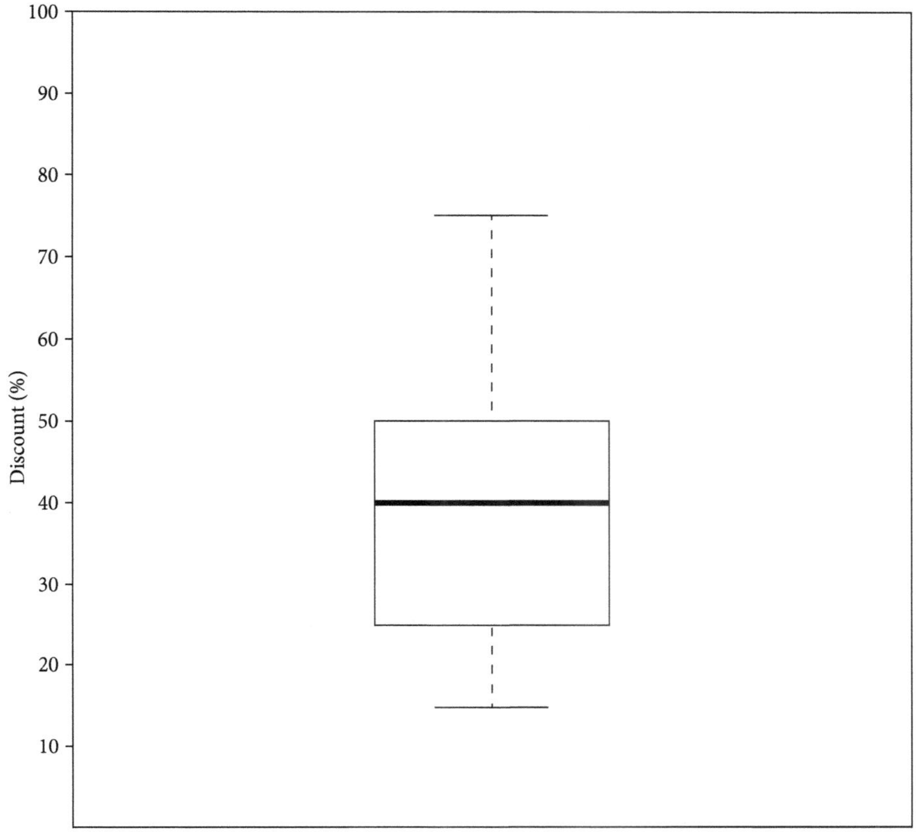

Figure 13 *Slip-and-fall accidents: workplace*

(4) Illustration of case involving a discount near the average

In *Ellis v Bristol City Council*,[42] the claimant was employed by the defendant council to provide nursing care at a home for elderly and infirm persons. While working, the claimant slipped and fell in a pool of urine which had been left by one of the residents in the main corridor of the home. The floor was made from vinyl and slippery when wet. The claimant was found guilty of contributory negligence due to her failure to keep a proper lookout. The defendant had placed a warning sign regarding the slipping hazard in the staff room and near where the claimant fell. Non-slip mats had been placed in the vicinity but they did not cover the section of floor where the accident happened. A 33.3 per cent discount was imposed. **A1.47**

(5) Illustration of case involving a high discount

In *McEwan v Lothian Buses plc*,[43] the pursuer was an experienced motor mechanic. While repairing a bus at the defender's depot, the pursuer slipped on coolant that he had spilled. **A1.48**

[42] [2007] EWCA Civ 685, [2007] ICR 1614.
[43] [2006] CSOH 56, 2006 SCLR 592 (OH).

The pursuer was contributorily negligent in spilling the coolant, failing to clean it up, and proceeding over the area in question when he had no reason to do so. The defender was held to have been negligent in failing to provide receptacles that would have caught some of the coolant, failing to provide cleaning equipment sufficient to deal with spillages, and failing to provide cleaning staff on the weekend, which was when the accident happened. A discount of 75 per cent was imposed.

(6) Illustration of case involving a low discount

A1.49 In *Cheung v Zhu (t/a Yang Sing Fish & Chip)*,[44] the claimant, who was then aged fifty-three, was employed by the defendant to work in her fish-and-chip shop. As the claimant was leaving work at the end of a long shift, she slipped on rainwater that had accumulated on the tiled floor of the premises and fell over. The rainwater had been able to accumulate as the door to the shop had been left open and nothing had been laid on the floor to absorb it. The claimant either knew or ought to have known that the floor was wet. It was not the claimant's job to clean up the water. A 15 per cent discount was imposed.

(7) Claims in the sample

A1.50 (1) *Cheung v Zhu (t/a Yang Sing Fish & Chip)* [2011] EWHC 2913 (QB) (15 per cent); (2) *Caerphilly CBC v Button* [2010] EWCA Civ 1311, [2011] ICR D3 (20 per cent); (3) *Campbell v Elliot Group Ltd* [2009] CSOH 63 (20 per cent); (4) *Craigie v Lanarkshire Health Board* [2005] CSOH 118 (20 per cent); (5) *Bailey v Command Security Services Ltd* 2001 WL 1535385 (QBD) (25 per cent); (6) *Bailey v Command Security Services Ltd* 2001 WL 1535385 (QBD) (25 per cent); (7) *Coates v Jaguar Cars Ltd* [2004] EWCA Civ 337 (25 per cent); (8) *Parkinson v Northern Ireland Fire and Rescue Service* [2009] NIQB 87 (25 per cent); (9) *James v H Buxton & Sons Ltd* 1999 WL 851957 (CA) (25 per cent); (10) *Ellis v Bristol CC* [2007] EWCA Civ 685, [2007] ICR 1614 (33.3 per cent); (11) *Johnstone v AMEC Constructions Ltd* [2010] CSIH 57 (40 per cent); (12) *MacKenzie v Co-Operative Group (CWS) Ltd* 2007 Scot (D) 14/6 (Dingwall Sheriff Court) (40 per cent); (13) *Wells v Mutchmeats Ltd* [2006] EWCA Civ 963 (40 per cent); (14) *Anderson v Newham College for Further Education* [2002] EWCA Civ 505, [2003] ICR 212 (50 per cent); (15) *Burgess v Plymouth CC* [2005] EWCA Civ 1659, [2006] ICR 579 (50 per cent); (16) *Home Office v Lowles* [2004] EWCA Civ 985 (50 per cent); (17) *King v Rco Support Services Ltd* [2001] ICR 608 (CA) (50 per cent); (18) *Parker v PFC Flooring Supplies Ltd* [2001] EWCA Civ 1533 (50 per cent); (19) *Taylor v Wincanton Group Ltd* [2009] EWCA Civ 1581 (50 per cent); (20) *Walsh v CP Hart & Sons Ltd* [2020] EWHC 37 (QB) (50 per cent); (21) *Willows v Craggs (t/a Wellingore Garages)* [1999] CLY 2855 (Lincoln CC) (66.6 per cent) (22) *McEwan v Lothian Buses plc* [2006] CSOH 56, 2006 SCLR 592 (75 per cent).

8. Slip-and-fall Accidents: Public Place

(1) Scope

A1.51 This section concerns claims arising from slip-and-fall accidents that occurred in a public place.

[44] [2011] EWHC 2913 (QB).

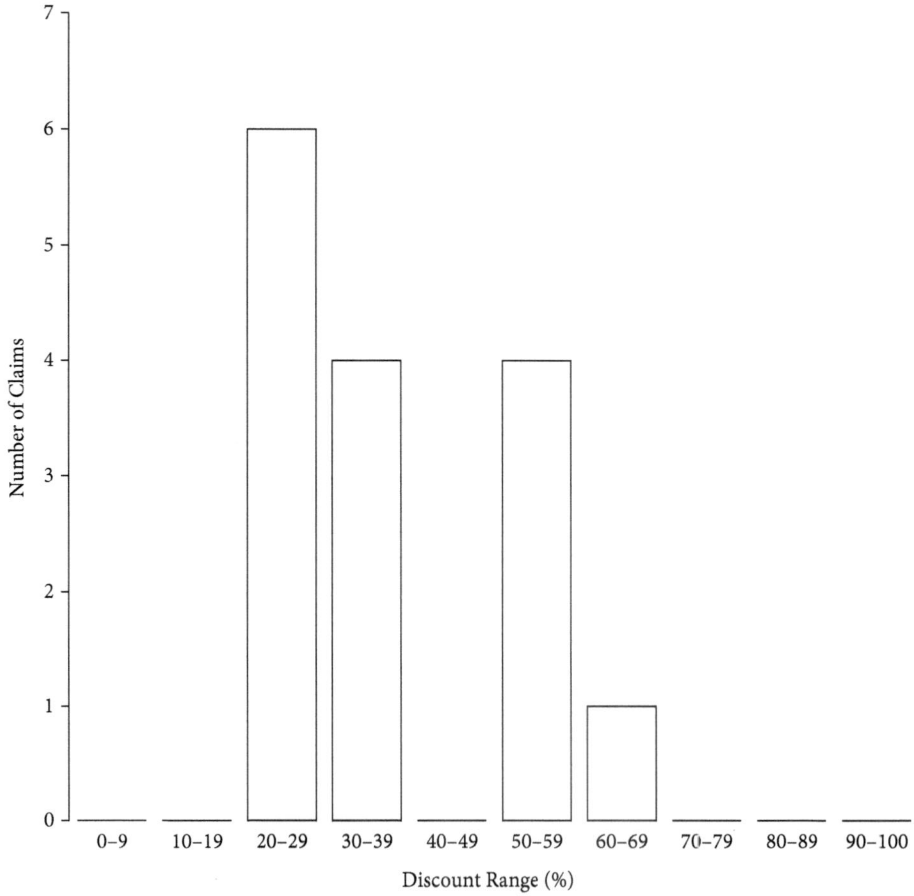

Figure 14 ***Slip-and-fall accidents: public place***

(2) Descriptive statistics

Number of claims	15
Average discount	36%
Mode	25%
Highest discount	60%
Lowest discount	25%
Standard deviation	12%

(3) Remarks

The discounts in cases of this type exhibit a low degree of variability, so that the courts rarely imposed discounts that strayed far from the average of 36 per cent, which is slightly lower than the average discount in claims involving a slip-and-fall accident that occurred in the workplace (38.4 per cent).[45] In nearly half of the claims, a discount of 25 per cent was imposed. **A1.52**

[45] See A1.45.

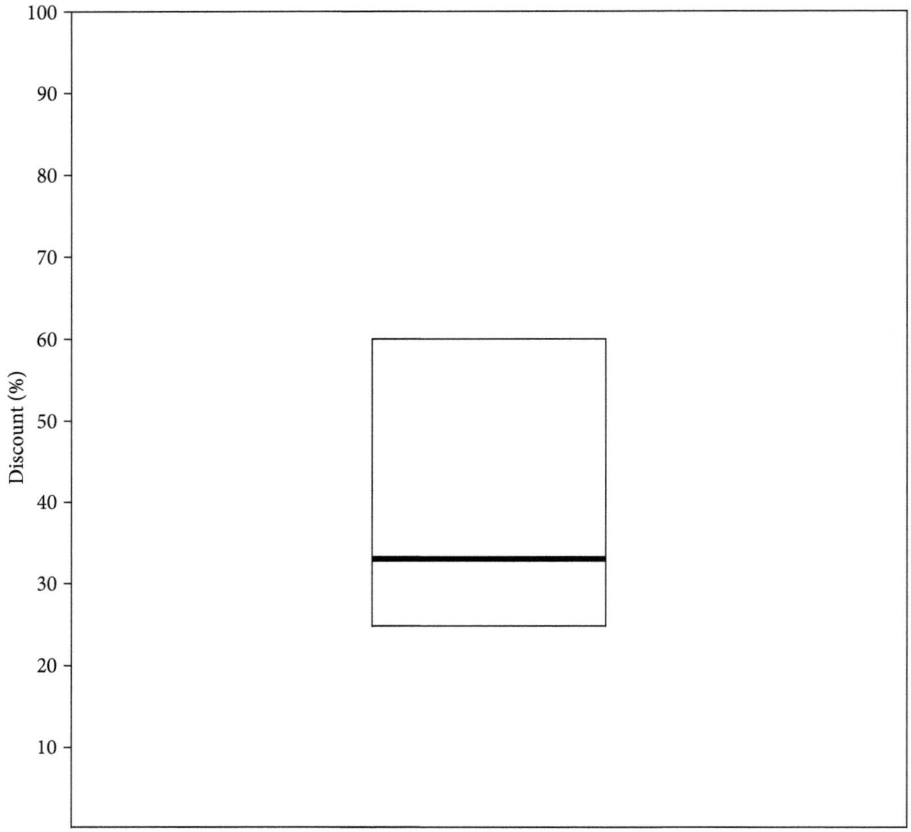

Figure 15 *Slip-and-fall accidents: public place*

(4) Illustration of case involving a discount near the average

A1.53 In *Walker v Newham LBC*,[46] the claimant had fallen and suffered injury when he placed his foot into a gap between two paving stones on a flight of steps outside his home. The gap had been present for at least eight or nine months prior to the accident and an employee of the defendant local authority who had inspected the steps prior to the accident had failed to notice it. The claimant knew of the danger (he passed up and down the steps approximately five times a week), had failed to report it to the defendant, and had fallen previously as a result of it. A 33.3 per cent discount was imposed.

(5) Illustration of case involving a high discount

A1.54 In *Maynard v Wigan MBC*,[47] the claimant, who had been carrying her youngest child at the time, fell over when her foot entered a depression in the grass outside her house. The claimant had previously complained to the council about the depression, which was 'considerably more than 2 inches deep'.[48] A 50 per cent discount was imposed.

[46] [2002] CLY 3256 (Central London CC).
[47] [2011] EWCA Civ 1694.
[48] ibid [29].

(6) Illustration of case involving a low discount

In *Dingley v Bromley LBC*,[49] the claimant had parked her car in a disabled parking space on a busy road. Upon exiting the vehicle, her foot entered a pothole in the parking space, causing her to fall and suffer injury. The defendant had checked for potholes on Sunday mornings, when fewer vehicles were present. However, the court found that it should have arranged for its inspectors to check for potholes hidden by parked cars. The claimant was held to be contributorily negligent on the ground that she knew of the pothole's existence. A 25 per cent discount was imposed. **A1.55**

(7) Claims in the sample

(1) *Brown v City of Edinburgh Council* 1999 SLT (Sh Ct) 43 (Lothian and Borders Sheriff Court) (25 per cent); (2) *Dingley v Bromley LBC* [2000] CLY 4244 (Bromley CC) (25 per cent); (3) *Swain v Geoffrey Osborne Ltd* [2010] EWHC 1108 (QB) (25 per cent); (4) *Swain v Geoffrey Osborne Ltd* [2010] EWHC 1108 (QB) (25 per cent); (5) *Thorpe v Aberdeen CC* 2007 Rep LR 105 (Grampian, Highland and Islands Sheriff Court) (25 per cent); (6) *Wilson v Glasgow CC* [2007] CSOH 143 (25 per cent); (7) *Prentice v Hereward Housing Association Ltd* 1999 Lexis Citation 3165 (QBD) (30 per cent); (8) *Bell v Havering LBC* [2010] EWCA Civ 689 (33.3 per cent); (9) *Kemp v Secretary of State for Scotland* 2000 SLT 471 (OH) (33.3 per cent); (10) *Walker v Newham LBC* [2002] CLY 3256 (Central London CC) (33.3 per cent); (11) *Hogarth v Marstons plc* [2021] 3 WLUK 229 (Torquay and Newton Abbott CC) (50 per cent); (12) *Maynard v Wigan MBC* [2011] EWCA Civ 1694 (50 per cent); (13) *Nixon v Thames Water Utilities Ltd* [2006] CLY 2913 (Romford CC) (50 per cent); (14) *Raybould v T & N Gilmartin (Contractors) Ltd* [2018] SAC (Civ) 31, 2019 SLT (Sh Ct) 1 (50 per cent); (15) *Varney v Fife Scottish Omnibuses Ltd* 2020 Rep LR 34 (Sheriff Personal Injury Court) (60 per cent). **A1.56**

9. Slip-and-fall Accidents: Occupiers' Liability

(1) Scope

This section concerns claims arising out of slip-and-fall accidents where the defendant was sued as an occupier. **A1.57**

(2) Descriptive statistics

Number of claims	17
Average discount	37%
Mode	25%
Highest discount	75%
Lowest discount	10%
Standard deviation	19.2%

[49] [2000] CLY 4244 (Bromley CC).

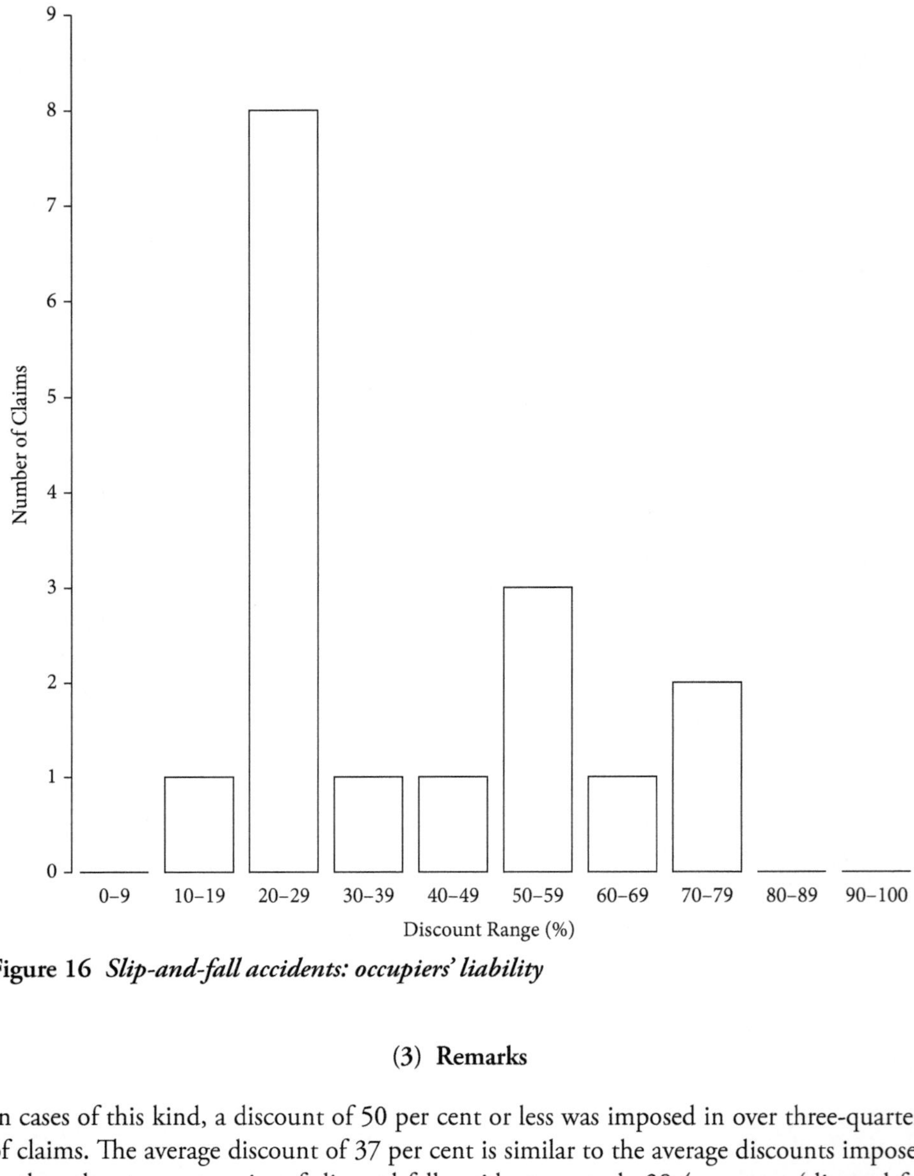

Figure 16 ***Slip-and-fall accidents: occupiers' liability***

(3) Remarks

A1.58 In cases of this kind, a discount of 50 per cent or less was imposed in over three-quarters of claims. The average discount of 37 per cent is similar to the average discounts imposed in the other two categories of slip-and-fall accidents, namely 38.4 per cent (slip-and-fall accidents in the workplace[50]) and 36 per cent (slip-and-fall accidents in public places[51]).

(4) Illustration of case involving a discount near the average

A1.59 A 33.3 per cent discount was imposed in *Wells v Mutchmeats Ltd*.[52] The claimant was a meat inspector who had attended the first defendant's abattoir. A plastic tray had been placed by the first defendant in the doorway between two rooms in its premises. The tray

[50] See A1.45.
[51] See A1.51.
[52] [2006] EWCA Civ 963.

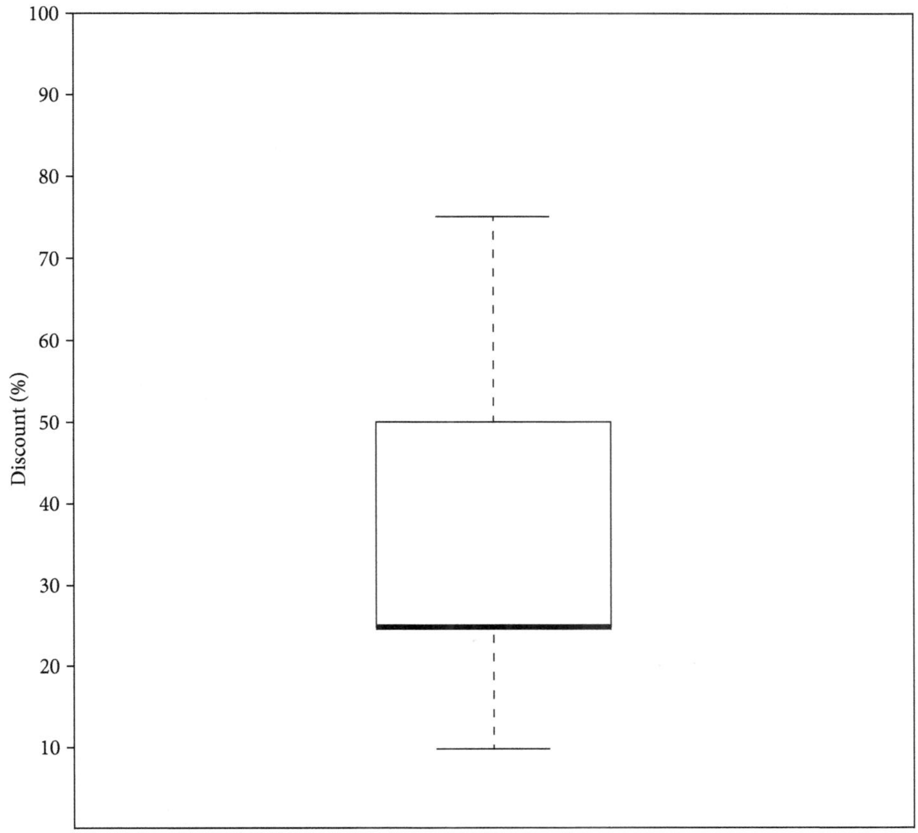

Figure 17 *Slip-and-fall accidents: occupiers' liability*

was usually filled with disinfectant liquid, the weight of which would prevent the tray from moving when persons stepped into it. On the day in question, however, the tray was nearly empty. The claimant placed one foot in the tray and it slid away from him, causing him to fall and sustain injury. The trial judge held that the claimant was guilty of contributory negligence in stepping in the tray or, alternatively, in failing to move it. An appeal by the claimant to the Court of Appeal was dismissed. However, the Court of Appeal suggested that a lower discount might have been imposed had the matter been considered *de novo*.[53]

(5) Illustration of case involving a high discount

In *Harvey v Plymouth CC*,[54] the intoxicated claimant, who was twenty-one years old at the time, fled from a taxi without paying and entered land owned by the defendant. He ran through some bushes and tripped over a chain link fence, which had been pushed down to **A1.60**

[53] ibid [17] (Gage LJ), [19] (Moses LJ).

[54] [2010] EWCA Civ 860, [2010] PIQR P18.

a height of about 14 inches, and then fell almost 6 metres onto the adjoining plot of land. A 75 per cent discount was imposed.

(6) Illustration of case involving a low discount

A1.61 In *Lawson v The Broomfield Holiday Park*,[55] the pursuer was walking along a private road at a camping and caravan site after dark. She tripped over a speed hump and fell to the ground. The lighting provided was insufficient to allow pedestrians to see the speed hump in the dark. No signs warning of the hump had been placed next to it and a warning that had been written on the hump itself had not been painted in reflective paint. The pursuer was found guilty of contributory negligence on the basis that she was aware of the presence of two speed humps on the road in question, having driven along the road earlier in the day. She had also failed to take reasonable care for her own safety by not carrying a torch. A 20 per cent discount was imposed.

(7) Claims in the sample

A1.62 (1) *Craig v Strathclyde Regional Council* 1998 Hous LR 104 (Glasgow and Strathkelvin Sheriff Court) (10 per cent); (2) *Lawson v The Broomfield Holiday Park* 2007 Scot (D) 9/7 (Dingwall Sheriff Court) (20 per cent); (3) *Palfrey v VM Morrisons Supermarkets plc* [2012] EWCA Civ 1917 (20 per cent); (4) *Dean and Chapter of Rochester Cathedral v Debell* [2016] EWCA Civ 1094 (20 per cent); (5) *Forrest v Iceland Foods Ltd* 2021 Rep LR 74 (Sheriff Personal Injury Court) (25 per cent); (6) *Lawrence v NCL (Bahamas) Ltd (t/a Norwegian Cruise Line)* [2016] EWHC (Admlty) (25 per cent); (7) *Lowe v Cairnstar Ltd* 2020 SLT (Sh Ct) 151 (Sheriff Personal Injury Court) (25 per cent); (8) *Morgan v Twyford Tots Nursery Ltd* [2006] CLY 2912 (Telford CC) (25 per cent); (9) *Wright v National Galleries of Scotland* [2020] SAC (Civ) 6, 2020 SLT (Sh Ct) 175 (25 per cent); (10) *Spencer v Wincanton Holdings Ltd* [2009] EWCA Civ 1404 (33.3 per cent); (11) *Wells v Mutchmeats Ltd* [2006] EWCA Civ 963 (40 per cent); (12) *Butcher v Southend-on-Sea BC* [2014] EWCA Civ 1556 (50 per cent); (13) *Burgess v Plymouth CC* [2005] EWCA Civ 1659, [2006] ICR 579 (50 per cent); (14) *English Heritage v Taylor* [2016] EWCA Civ 448 (50 per cent); (15) *The White Lion Hotel v James* [2021] EWCA Civ 31 (60 per cent); (16) *Buyukardicli v Hammerson UK Properties plc* [2002] EWCA Civ 683 (75 per cent); (17) *Harvey v Plymouth CC* [2010] EWCA Civ 860 (75 per cent).

10. Carelessness in Connection with Work Equipment

(1) Scope

A1.63 This section concerns claims in which the claimant was found guilty of contributory negligence in the manner in which work equipment was used. It does not include claims where the claimant was working at height and injured in a fall, which are the subject of the next section.

[55] 2007 Scot (D) 9/7 (Dingwall Sheriff Court).

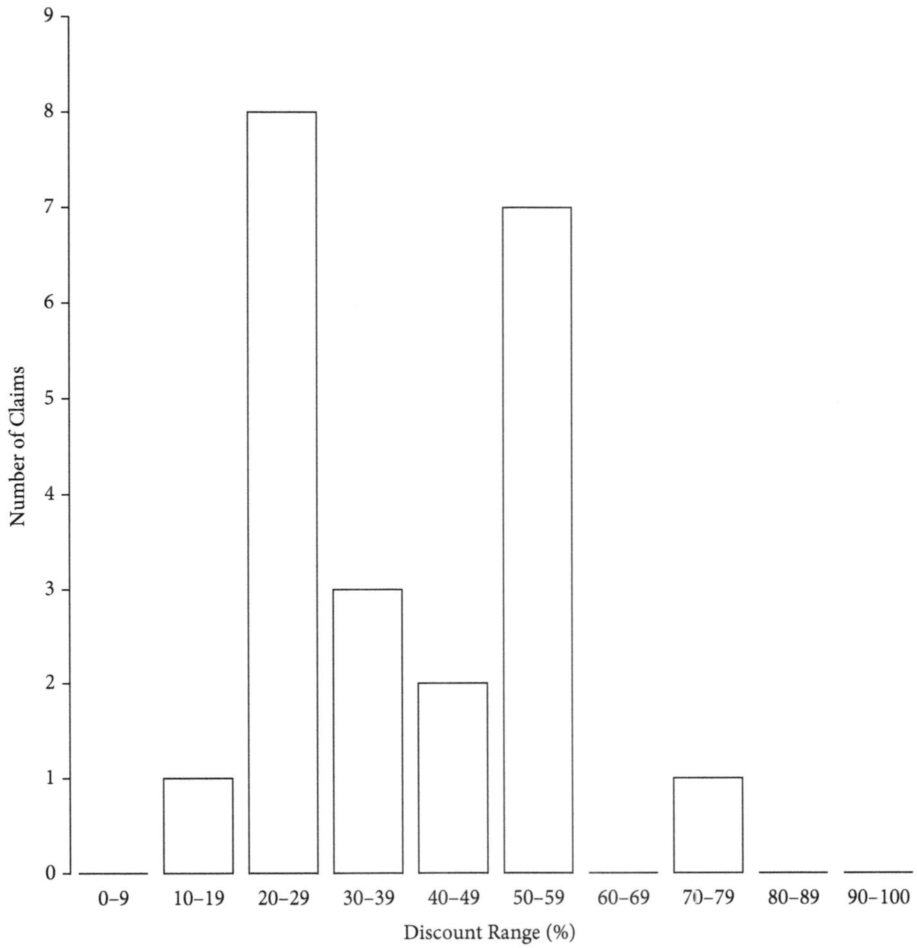

Figure 18 ***Carelessness in connection with work equipment***

(2) Descriptive statistics

Number of claims	22
Average discount	35.9%
Mode	50%
Highest discount	70%
Lowest discount	15%
Standard deviation	14.6%

(3) Remarks

The distribution of discounts is skewed towards the lower end of the spectrum. By some margin, the most common discount was 50 per cent, and there was only a single discount in excess of that figure. **A1.64**

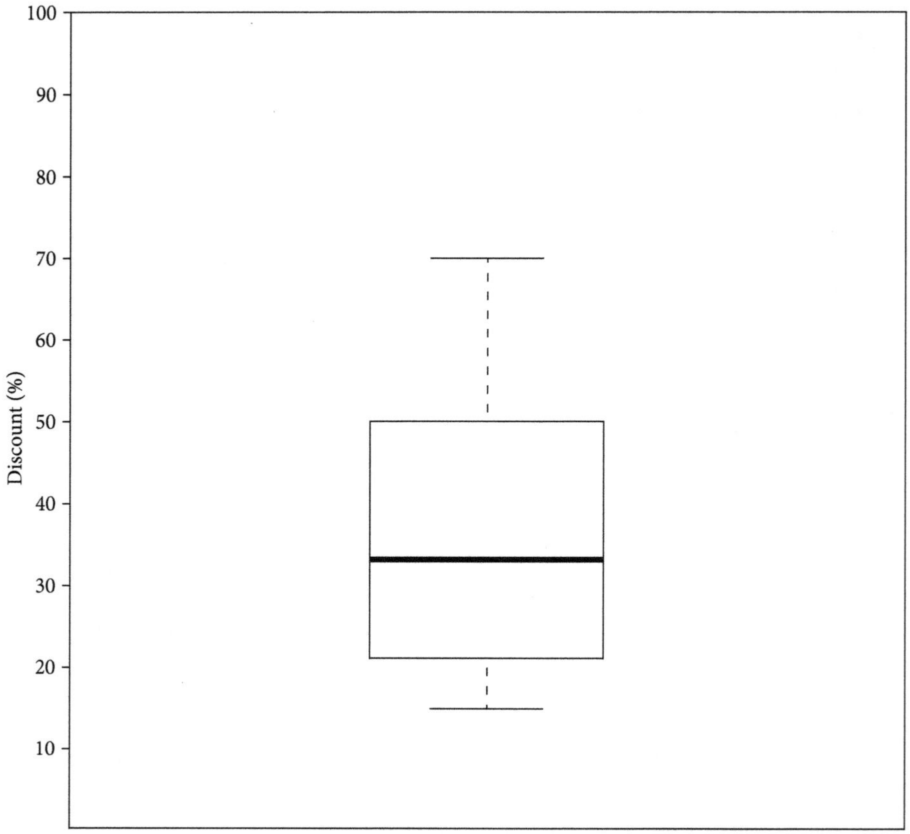

Figure 19 ***Carelessness in connection with workplace equipment***

(4) Illustration of case involving a discount near the average

A1.65 In *Milroy v British Telecommunications plc*,[56] the claimant engineer had been employed by the defendant to work on elevated mobile platforms. While working on a raised platform, he came into contact with high-voltage powerlines and suffered serious injury. The defendant was found to have breached its common law duty of care and various statutory duties by giving the claimant inadequate training. It was also held to be vicariously liable for the negligence of another of its employees, who had failed to consider a method of work that did not involve using the mobile platform in proximity to the powerlines. The trial judge held, however, that the claimant had been guilty of contributory negligence in driving the mobile platform in a manner that led to the accident when he knew that the powerlines were nearby, and in failing to keep a proper lookout. Damages were reduced by 33.3 per cent.

[56] [2015] EWHC 532 (QB).

(5) Illustration of case involving a high discount

In *Woods v Police Service of Northern Ireland*,[57] the claimant police officer, who was employed as a senior armourer, accidentally shot himself in the hand while dismantling a gun. The gun concerned had been presented to him by another police officer as being defective. The claimant alleged that his employer had breached various statutory duties regarding the provision of safe work equipment. The claimant had extensive experience and training with guns, including in relation to the type of gun in issue. The trial judge held that the employer had wrongfully failed to ensure that a 'range officer' was present to check that the weapon was safe to handle. For his part, the claimant was found guilty of contributory negligence in various respects, including in firing the weapon before dismantling it, failing to point it in a safe direction, and failing to devise and follow a risk assessment in connection with the test firing and dismantling of the weapon. The damages were reduced by 50 per cent. **A1.66**

(6) Illustration of case involving a low discount

In *McLellan v Dundee CC*,[58] the pursuer was a gardener employed by the defender. He was using a motorized lawnmower when the blades became clogged by wet grass. The pursuer used a crowbar, with which he had been supplied by the defender, to remove the grass. Once the grass had been extracted, the mower's blades started moving again even though the mower had been switched off, on account of energy that had been retained in the mower's hydraulic system. The pursuer's hand came into contact with the blades whereupon he suffered serious injury. In addition to acting negligently, the defender was found to have breached statutory duties that required it to conduct proper risk assessments and to provide the pursuer with adequate health and safety information about the operation of the mower. The pursuer had, however, also been at fault in putting his hand in proximity to the blades while trying to clear the blockage, despite having been instructed to keep his hands well clear of the blades at all times. The damages were reduced by 20 per cent. **A1.67**

(7) Claims in the sample

(1) *Kern v Bridgend CBC* (Bridgend CC, 17 October 2008) (15 per cent); (2) *Hyndman v Brown* [2012] NICA 3 (20 per cent); (3) *McFarlane v Corus Construction & Industrial* 2006 SLT 375 (OH) (20 per cent); (4) *McLellan v Dundee CC* [2009] CSOH 9, 2009 Rep LR 61 (20 per cent); (5) *McLellan v Mitie Group plc* [2015] CSOH 151, 2015 SLT 861 (20 per cent); (6) *Sowmez v Kebaberry Wholesale Ltd* [2008] EWHC 3366 (QB) (20 per cent); (7) *Berry v Star Autos Ltd* [2013] 7 WLUK 871 (QBD) (25 per cent); (8) *Chisholm v D&R Hankins (Manea) Ltd* [2018] EWHC 340 (QB) (25 per cent); (9) *Drinnan v The Bone Group Ltd* 2005 SLT (Sh Ct) 119 (South Strathclyde, Dumfries, and Galloway Sheriff Court) (25 per cent); (10) *Causby v Seagoe Technologies Ltd* [2009] NIQB 24 (33.3 per cent); (11) *Fraser v Winchester Health Authority* 1999 WL 477756 (CA) (33.3 per cent); (12) *Milroy v British Telecommunications plc* [2015] EWHC 532 (QB) (33.3 per cent); (13) *Marsden v Ministry of Defence* (QBD, 11 November 1998) (40 per cent); (14) *Wilson v* **A1.68**

[57] [2009] NIQB 35.
[58] [2009] CSOH 9, 2009 Rep LR 61.

North Star Shipping (Aberdeen) Ltd [2014] CSOH 156 (40 per cent); (15 *Ashbridge v Christian Salvesen plc* [2006] CSOH 79, 2006 SLT 697 (50 per cent); (16) *Chapman v Tangmere Airfield Nurseries Ltd* 1998 WL 1042616 (CA) (50 per cent); (17) *Ellis v William Cook Leeds Ltd* [2007] EWCA Civ 1232 (50 per cent); (18) *Griffiths v Vauxhall Motors Ltd* [2003] EWCA Civ 412 (50 per cent); (19) *Mcfarlane v Scottish Borders Council* 2005 SLT 359 (IH) (50 per cent); (20) *Robertson v Glasgow CC* [2007] CSOH 89 (50 per cent); (21) *Woods v Police Service of Northern Ireland* [2009] NIQB 35 (50 per cent); (22) *Cox v Superior Forklift Services Ltd* (CA, 18 December 1998) (70 per cent).

11. Carelessness in or while Working at Height

(1) Scope

A1.69 This section concerns claims in which the claimant was injured in a fall while working at height.

(2) Descriptive statistics

Number of claims	16
Average discount	38.3%
Mode	50%
Highest discount	60%
Lowest discount	20%
Standard deviation	12.3%

(3) Remarks

A1.70 All the discounts in this category of claims with one exception were below 60 per cent, with 50 per cent being the most popular discount. The discounts were relatively uniform and the average was 38.3 per cent.

(4) Illustration of case involving a discount near the average

A1.71 In *Smith v Wilgar (t/a Wilgar Contracts)*,[59] the deceased, a diabetic, suffered a hypoglycaemic attack while working on a 20-foot ladder and fell to the ground. The defendant employer had breached statutory duties on account of its having failed to select appropriate equipment and in negligently failing to ensure a suitable system of work. The damages were reduced by 33.3 per cent due to the claimant having failed to draw sufficiently clearly to the defendant's attention his history of suffering such attacks.

(5) Illustration of case involving a high discount

A1.72 In *Warke v British Telecommunications plc*,[60] the claimant engineer was injured when a ladder that he was descending fell away from a telegraph pole on which he had been

[59] [2011] NIQB 67.
[60] [2004] NIQB 60.

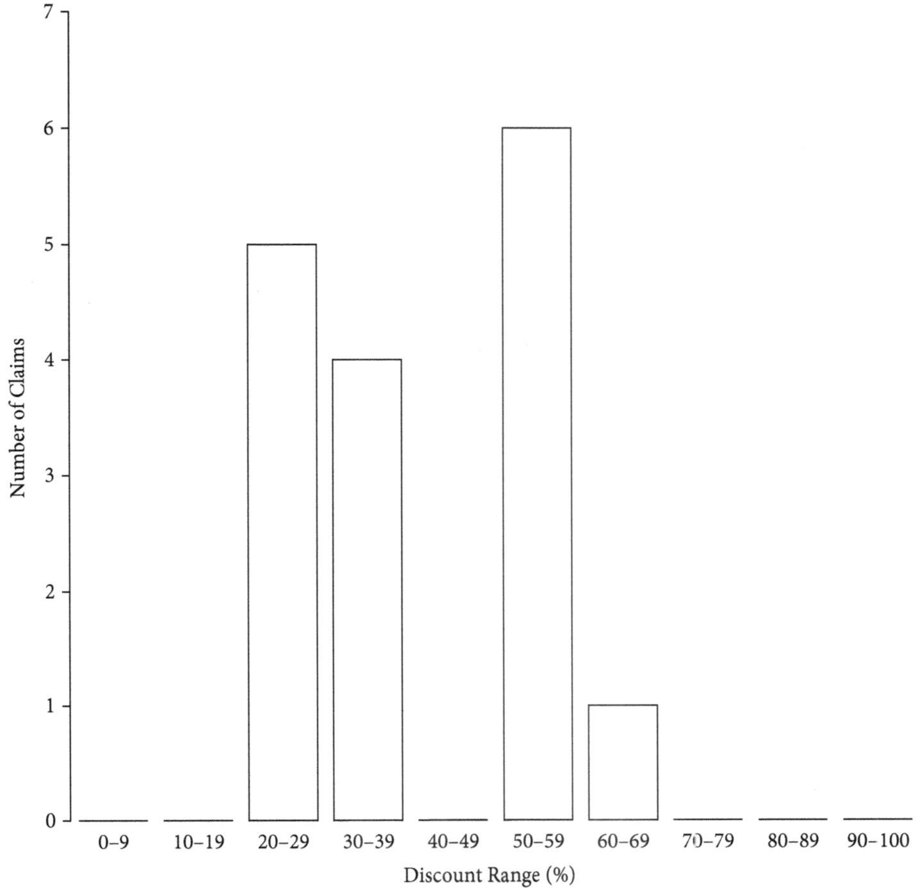

Figure 20 ***Carelessness in or while working at height***

working. His employer had been negligent in failing to provide him with proper training in the use of ladders and had breached various statutory duties regarding the use of workplace equipment. The claimant was contributorily negligent in failing to ensure that the stiles of the ladder were level before he ascended it and in failing to lash the bottom of the ladder to a nearby fence. The damages were reduced by 50 per cent.

(6) Illustration of case involving a low discount

In *Hill v Norside Ltd*,[61] the pursuer, an experienced roofer, fell approximately 10 feet while **A1.73**
descending from scaffolding and broke his neck. The fall occurred when the ladder that he was using fell away from the structure. The defender employer was found to have breached various statutory duties: it had failed to give any thought as to how its employees were to access the scaffolding and could easily have provided a safe system of work by installing

[61] [2012] CSOH 187, 2013 Rep LR 22.

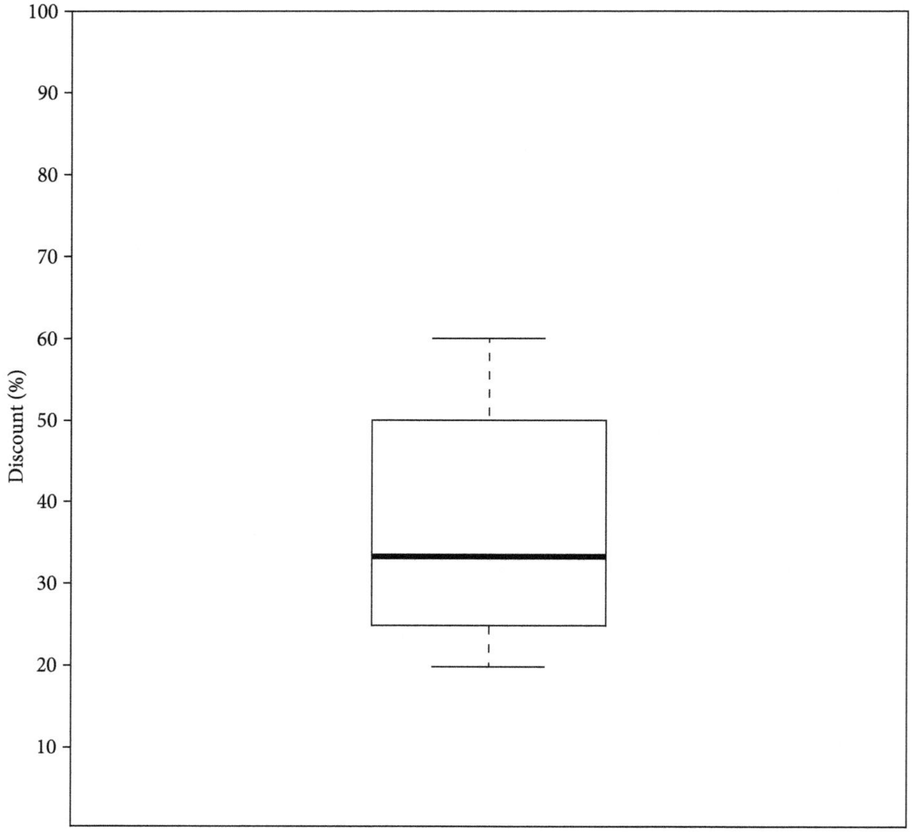

Figure 21 ***Carelessness in or while working at height***

a fixed ladder. However, the pursuer was contributorily negligent in failing to tie off the ladder. Damages were reduced by 20 per cent. Lady Dorrian said:[62]

> For reasons relating to the much greater degree of control which they had over the site, and in particular, the scaffolding ... I consider that the blameworthiness of the defenders is of a very different degree to that of the pursuer. The fault of the defenders is not coextensive with that of the pursuer; it goes beyond, and is independent of it. The pursuer quite simply should not have been put in the position he was by the defenders. Inattention on the part of a workman is precisely one of the risks which the statutory duty is there to guard against.

(7) Claims in the sample

A1.74 (1) *Hill v Norside Ltd* [2012] CSOH 187, 2013 Rep LR 22 (20 per cent); (2) *Gower-Smith v Hampshire CC* (Southampton CC, 27 June 2008) (25 per cent); (3) *McLachlan v Early Learning Centre Ltd* [2011] CSOH 25, 2011 Rep LR 30 (25 per cent); (4) *Donaldson v Brighton & Hove Council* 2001 WL 1743237 (Lewes CC) (25 per cent); (5) *Donaldson v Brighton & Hove Council* 2001 WL 1743237 (Lewes CC) (25 per cent); (6) *Bhatt v Fontain Motors Ltd* [2010] EWCA Civ 863, [2010] PIQR P17 (33.3 per cent); (7) *Proctor v City*

62 ibid [29].

Facilities Management Ltd [2012] NIQB 99 (33.3 per cent); (8) *Smith v Wilgar (t/a Wilgar Contracts)* [2011] NIQB 67 (33.3 per cent); (9) *Wallace v Stewart Homes (Scotland)* [2013] CSOH 30 (33.3 per cent); (10) *Leitch v Reid* [2003] NIQB 45 (50 per cent); (11) *Neil v East Ayrshire Council* 2005 Rep LR 18 (OH) (50 per cent); (12) *Robb v Salamis (M&I) Ltd* [2006] UKHL 56, [2007] ICR 175 (50 per cent); (13) *Toner v George Morison Builders* [2010] CSOH 125, 2011 Rep LR 18 (50 per cent); (14) *Warke v British Telecommunications plc* [2004] NIQB 60 (50 per cent); (15) *Wharf v Bildwell Insulations Ltd* [1999] CLY 2047 (QBD) (50 per cent); (16) *Brown v Farmview Dairies Ltd* (QBD, 18 December 1998) (60 per cent).

12. Children Injured while Playing

(1) Scope

This section concerns claims in which a child suffered injury while playing. **A1.75**

(2) Descriptive statistics

Number of claims	12
Average discount	36.4%
Mode	25% and 50%
Highest discount	60%
Lowest discount	15%
Standard deviation	14.2%

(3) Remarks

The highest discount imposed in this category was 60 per cent. Most of the discounts fell between 25 per cent and 50 per cent. **A1.76**

(4) Illustration of case involving a discount near the average

In *DE v S Garages Ltd*,[63] the claimant, who was then aged thirteen years (but a few days short of his fourteenth birthday), suffered serious burns when petrol with which he had been playing ignited. Together with a friend (also aged thirteen), he had purchased the petrol from the defendant's garage and had been sniffing it. The trial judge found that the claimant's friend had thrown something down, whether a match or a cigarette, which caused the petrol to ignite. Damages were reduced by 33.3 per cent. The judge said: **A1.77**

> [T]he defendants put the petrol into circulation when clearly they ought not to have. What happened, namely, ignition, was an obvious risk. The claimant knew that it was wrong for him to buy petrol and to sniff petrol, and that petrol was inflammable. I am not satisfied that he knew of its volatility. The claimant was at fault in acquiring the petrol. I am not satisfied that he turned his mind to the fact that anyone sniffing petrol might do something dangerous, nor do I think the reasonable 13-year-old would have thought in those terms. I accept ... the claimant's statement

63 2000 WL 33281292 (QBD).

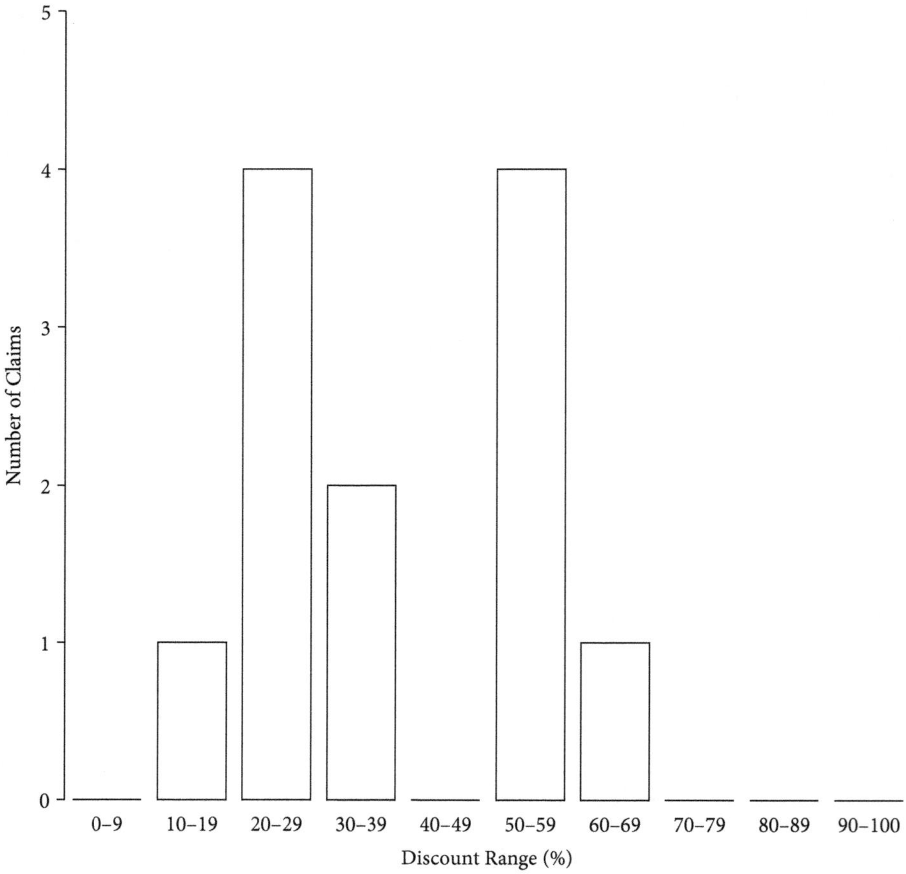

Figure 22 ***Children injured while playing***

> that he saw the sniffing as something which might raise a laugh. At the same time, by the sniffing, which was a joint venture by the claimant and [his friend], they both became less responsible, which I suspect played some part in what happened.

(5) Illustration of case involving a high discount

A1.78 In *Young v Kent CC*,[64] the claimant, who was then aged twelve and a half, was playing football unsupervised with friends at a school after school hours. The football ended up on the roof of one of the school's buildings. The claimant climbed onto the roof concerned with a view to retrieving it but fell through a skylight and suffered serious injury. The defendant knew that children sometimes climbed onto the roof in question, and that they had 'easy, ready access to the roof'[65] via a passageway. It could have eliminated the danger by the 'low-cost solution'[66] of installing two short fences at either end of the passageway. The claimant 'ha[d] a complicated medical history with learning difficulties' and, the trial

64 [2005] EWHC 1342 (QB).
65 ibid [33] (Morrison J).
66 ibid.

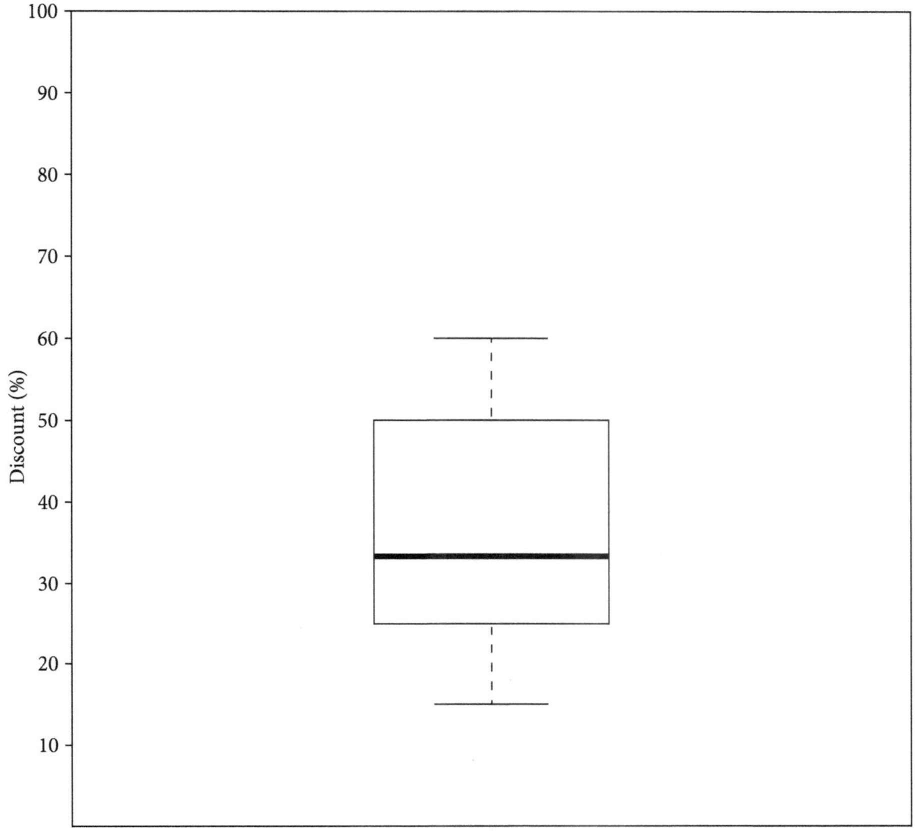

Figure 23 ***Children injured while playing***

judge found, was thus 'more vulnerable than most other children to understanding the concepts of risk and danger'.[67] Damages were reduced by 50 per cent.

(6) Illustration of case involving a low discount

In *Re Kelly v Nugent*,[68] the claimant, who was then aged nine years and eight months, was playing on a tricycle. He cycled out onto a narrow country road whereupon he was hit by the defendant's vehicle. The trial judge found that the defendant had not kept a proper lookout, and had been driving too quickly, at around 20 mph, given the nature of the road. The claimant 'did acknowledge that whilst he had had no road traffic safety lessons in school until aged about 10 or 11, he did know it was dangerous to go out on to the road at this age and that his mother and father would not let him take his tricycle on to the road'. Damages were reduced by 15 per cent. **A1.79**

[67] ibid [11].
[68] [2011] NIQB 79.

(7) Claims in the sample

A1.80 (1) *Re Kelly v Nugent* [2011] NIQB 79 (15 per cent); (2) *McLeod v British Railways Board* 2001 SLT 238 (IH) (20 per cent); (3) *Anderson v Imrie* [2016] CSOH 171, 2017 Rep LR 21 (25 per cent); (4) *Jolley v Sutton LBC* [2000] 1 WLR 1082 (HL) (25 per cent); (5) *Morton v Glasgow CC* 2007 SLT (Sh Ct) 81 (Glasgow and Strathkelvin Sheriff Court) (25 per cent); (6) *Dawson v Scottish Power plc* 1999 SLT 672 (OH) (33.3 per cent); (7) *DE v S Garages Ltd* 2000 WL 33281292 (QBD) (33.3 per cent); (8) *C v Imperial Design Ltd* [2001] Env LR 33 (CA) (50 per cent) (9) *Dynes v Transport NI Department of Infrastructure* [2019] NIQB 81 (50 per cent); (10) *Wardle v Scottish Borders Council* 2011 SLT (Sh Ct) 199 (Lothian and Borders Sheriff Court) (50 per cent); (11) *Young v Kent CC* [2005] EWHC 1342 (QB) (50 per cent); (12) *N (a child) v Newham LBC* [2007] CLY 2931 (Central London CC) (60 per cent).

13. Other Recurrent Situations

A1.81 Other recurrent situations were observed where the number of claims was lower than in the situations outlined above. These recurrent situations are set out below, along with the claims in the relevant category and the discounts imposed.

(1) Accepting ride from an intoxicated driver

A1.82 (1) *W v Hardman* [2001] CLY 4452 (Leeds CC) (15 per cent); (2) *Campbell v Advantage Insurance Co Ltd* [2021] EWCA Civ 1698 (20 per cent); (3) *Green v The Estate of Raymond Gaymer* 1999 WL 33232687 (QBD) (20 per cent); (4) *Gleeson v Court* [2007] EWHC 2397 (QB), [2008] RTR 10 (30 per cent); (5) *Currie v Clamp* 2002 SLT 196 (OH) (33.3 per cent).

(2) Unsafe overtaking

A1.83 (1) *AC v TR* [2013] EWCA Civ 418, [2014] RTR 1 (50 per cent); (2) *Woodham v M Turner (t/a Turners of Great Barton)* [2012] EWCA Civ 375 (50 per cent); (3) *Moseley v Pell* [2003] EWCA Civ 1533 (50 per cent); (4) *Deller v King* [2021] EWHC 3398 (QB) (60 per cent); (5) *Wallett v Vickers* [2018] EWHC 3088 (QB) (60 per cent); (6) *Ringe v Eden Springs (UK) Ltd* [2012] EWHC 14 (QB) (80 per cent); (7) *Burton v Evitt* [2011] EWCA Civ 1378 (80 per cent).

(3) Failure to wear helmet

A1.84 (1) *Kirby v Ageas Ltd* [2021] 6 WLUK 413 (QBD) (10 per cent); (2) *McCracken v Smith* [2015] EWCA Civ 380, [2015] PIQR P19 (15 per cent);[69] (3) *Perrin v Ministry of Defence*

[69] But the overall deduction was 65 per cent. In this case, the defendant minibus driver had collided with a motorbike on which the claimant was a passenger. At the time, the claimant was participating in a criminal joint enterprise (riding a stolen motorbike dangerously on an adjacent cycle path). The participation was said to be a cause of his own injuries, and his participation should not be minimized. As such, there was a 50 per cent discount.

[2001] EWCA Civ 1310 (20 per cent); (4) *Clark v Farley* [2018] EWHC 1007 (QB) (40 per cent); (5) *Reynolds v Strutt & Parker LLP* [2011] EWHC 2263 (QB) (66.6 per cent).

(4) Diving cases

(1) *McCarrick v Park Resorts Ltd* (QBD, 26 October 2012) (33.3 per cent); (2) *Ministry of Defence v Radclyffe* [2009] EWCA Civ 635 (40 per cent); (3) *Evans v Kosmar Villa Holiday plc* [2007] EWCA Civ 1003, [2008] 1 WLR 297 (50 per cent); (4) *Hurst v Thomson Holidays Ltd* [2004] CLY 1879 (Cambridge CC) (50 per cent); (5) *Donoghue v Folkestone Properties Ltd* [2003] EWCA Civ 231 (75 per cent). **A1.85**

(5) Smoking (asbestos exposure cases)

(1) *Shortell v BICAL Construction Ltd* (QBD, 16 May 2008) (15 per cent); (2) *Badger v Ministry of Defence* [2005] EWHC 2941 (QB), [2006] 3 All ER 173 (20 per cent); (3) *Hanbury v Hugh James Solicitors (a firm)* [2019] EWHC 1074 (QB) (20 per cent); (5) *Horsley v Cascade Insulation Services Ltd* [2009] EWHC 2945 (QB) (20 per cent); (6) *Blackmore v Department for Communities and Local Government* [2017] EWCA Civ 1136, [2018] QB 471 (30 per cent). **A1.86**

(6) Dangerous lifting

(1) *Goodchild v Organon Laboratories Ltd* [2004] EWHC 2341 (QB) (10 per cent); (2) *Magee v Kenneth and Stewart* [2019] NIQB 93 (25 per cent); (3) *Tibbatts v British Airways plc* [2009] EWHC 815 (QB) (33.3 per cent); (4) *Costa v Imperial London Hotels Ltd* [2012] EWCA Civ 672 (35 per cent); (5) *Quinn v Keenan* [2013] NIQB 55 (50 per cent); (6) *Egan v Central Manchester and Manchester Children's University Hospital NHS Trust* [2008] EWCA Civ 1424, [2009] ICR 585 (50 per cent); (7) *Lips v Older* [2004] EWHC 1686 (QB), [2005] PIQR P14 (66.6 per cent). **A1.87**

APPENDIX 2

Law Reform (Contributory Negligence) Act 1945

An Act to amend the law relating to contributory negligence and for purposes connected therewith.

1. Apportionment of liability in case of contributory negligence

(1) Where any person suffers damage as the result partly of his own fault and partly of the fault of any other person or persons, a claim in respect of that damage shall not be defeated by reason of the fault of the person suffering the damage, but the damages recoverable in respect thereof shall be reduced to such extent as the court thinks just and equitable having regard to the claimant's share in the responsibility for the damage:

Provided that—

(a) this subsection shall not operate to defeat any defence arising under a contract;

(b) where any contract or enactment providing for the limitation of liability is applicable to the claim, the amount of damages recoverable by the claimant by virtue of this subsection shall not exceed the maximum limit so applicable.

(2) Where damages are recoverable by any person by virtue of the foregoing subsection subject to such reduction as is therein mentioned, the court shall find and record the total damages which would have been recoverable if the claimant had not been at fault.

(3) ...

(4) ...

(5) Where, in any case to which subsection (1) of this section applies, one of the persons at fault avoids liability to any other such person or his personal representative by pleading the Limitation Act 1939, or any other enactment limiting the time within which proceedings may be taken, he shall not be entitled to recover any damages from that other person or representative by virtue of the said subsection.[1]

(6) Where any case to which subsection (1) of this section applies is tried with a jury, the jury shall determine the total damages which would have been recoverable if the claimant had not been at fault and the extent to which those damages are to be reduced.

(7) ...

2. ...

3. Saving for Maritime Conventions Act 1911, and past cases

(1) This Act shall not apply to any claim to which section one of the Maritime Conventions Act, 1911, applies and that Act shall have effect as if this Act had not passed.

---

[1] In the case of Scotland, subsection 1(5) provides: 'Where, in any case to which subsection (1) of this section applies, one of the persons at fault avoids liability to any other such person or his personal representative by pleading the Limitation Act 1939, or any other enactment limiting the time within which proceedings may be taken, he shall not be entitled to recover any damages or contributions from that other person or representative by virtue of the said subsection.'

(2) This Act shall not apply to any case where the acts or omissions giving rise to the claim occurred before the passing of this Act.

4. Interpretation

The following expressions have the meanings hereby respectively assigned to them, that is to say—

'court' means, in relation to any claim, the court or arbitrator by or before whom the claim falls to be determined;

'damage' includes loss of life and personal injury;

. . .

'fault' means negligence, breach of statutory duty or other act or omission which gives rise to a liability in tort or would, apart from this Act, give rise to the defence of contributory negligence.

5. Application to Scotland

In the application of this Act to Scotland—

(a) the expression *'dependant'* means, in relation to any person, any person who would in the event of such first mentioned person's death through the fault of a third party be entitled to sue that third party for damages or solatium; and the expression *'fault'* means wrongful act, breach of statutory duty or negligent act or omission which gives rise to liability in damages, or would apart from this Act, give rise to the defence of contributory negligence;

(b) . . .

(c) for subsection (4) of section one the following subsection shall be substituted—

> '(4) Where any person dies as the result partly of his own fault and partly of the fault of any other person or persons, a claim by any dependant of the first mentioned person for damages or solatium in respect of that person's death shall not be defeated by reason of his fault, but the damages or solatium recoverable shall be reduced to such extent as the court thinks just and equitable having regard to the share of the said person in the responsibility for his death.'

6. Provisions as to Northern Ireland

(1) . . .

(2) This Act shall not extend to Northern Ireland.

7. Short title and extent

This Act may be cited as the Law Reform (Contributory Negligence) Act 1945.

APPENDIX 3

Law Reform (Miscellaneous Provisions) Act (Northern Ireland) 1948

An Act to abolish the defence of common employment; to amend the law relating to contributory negligence and the measure of damages for personal injury or death; and for purposes connected with the matters aforesaid.

1. ...

2. Apportionment of liability in tort where more than one person is at fault

(1) Where any person suffers damage as the result partly of his own fault and partly of the fault of any other person or persons, a claim in respect of that damage shall not be defeated by reason of the fault of the person suffering the damage, but the damages recoverable in respect thereof shall be reduced to such extent as the court thinks just and equitable having regard to the claimant's share in the responsibility for the damage:

Provided that—

(a) this sub-section shall not operate to defeat any defence arising under a contract;

(b) where any contract or enactment providing for the limitation of liability is applicable to the claim, the amount of damages recoverable by the claimant by virtue of this sub-section shall not exceed the maximum limit so applicable.

(2) Where damages are recoverable by any person by virtue of the preceding sub-section subject to such reduction as is therein mentioned, the court shall find and record the total damages which would have been recoverable if the claimant had not been at fault.

(3) ...

(4) ...

(5) Where, in any case to which sub-section (1) of this section applies, one of the persons at fault or his personal representative avoids liability to any other such person or his personal representative by pleading any enactment limiting the time within which proceedings may be taken, he shall not be entitled to recover any damages ... from that other person or representative by virtue of the said sub-section.

(6) Where any case to which sub-section (1) of this section applies is tried with a jury, the jury shall determine the total damages which would have been recoverable if the claimant had not been at fault and the extent to which those damages are to be reduced.

3. ...

4. Operation of Act and saving for Maritime Conventions Act, 1911

(1) Sections one, two and sub-section (1) of section three of this Act shall apply only where the cause of action accrues after the passing of this Act; but sub-sections (4) and (5) of the said section three shall apply whether the cause of action accrued or the proceedings were commenced before or after such passing.

(2) Section two of this Act shall not apply to any case to which section 187 of the Merchant Shipping Act 1995, applies.

5. …

6. Interpretation

(1) In this Act the following expressions have the meanings hereby respectively assigned to them, that is to say—

'court' means, in relation to any claim, the court or arbitrator by or before whom the claim falls to be determined;

'damage' includes loss of life and personal injury;

'fault' means negligence, breach of statutory duty or other act or omission which gives rise to a liability in tort or would, but for this Act, give rise to the defence of contributory negligence;

'personal injury' includes any disease and any impairment of a person's physical or mental condition, and the expression 'injured' shall be construed accordingly.

7. Short title

This Act may be cited as the Law Reform (Miscellaneous Provisions) Act (Northern Ireland), 1948.

APPENDIX 4

Merchant Shipping Act 1995

. . .

187. Damage or loss: apportionment of liability

(1) Where, by the fault of two or more ships, damage or loss is caused to one or more of those ships, to their cargoes or freight, or to any property on board, the liability to make good the damage or loss shall be in proportion to the degree in which each ship was in fault.

(2) If, in any such case, having regard to all the circumstances, it is not possible to establish different degrees of fault, the liability shall be apportioned equally.

(3) This section applies to persons other than the owners of a ship who are responsible for the fault of the ships, as well as to the owners of a ship and where, by virtue of any charter or demise, or for any other reason, the owners are not responsible for the navigation and management of the ship, this section applies to the charterers or other persons for the time being so responsible instead of the owners.

(4) Nothing in this section shall operate so as to render any ship liable for any loss or damage to which the fault of the ship has not contributed.

(5) Nothing in this section shall affect the liability of any person under a contract of carriage or any contract, or shall be construed as imposing any liability upon any person from which he is exempted by any contract or by any provision of law, or as affecting the right of any person to limit his liability in the manner provided by law.

(6) In this section 'freight' includes passage money and hire.

(7) In this section references to damage or loss caused by the fault of a ship include references to any salvage or other expenses, consequent upon that fault, recoverable at law by way of damages.

APPENDIX 5

Civil Liability Act 1961 (Ire)

...

34. Apportionment of liability in case of contributory negligence

(1) Where, in any action brought by one person in respect of a wrong committed by any other person, it is proved that the damage suffered by the plaintiff was caused partly by the negligence or want of care of the plaintiff or of one for whose acts he is responsible (in this Part called contributory negligence) and partly by the wrong of the defendant, the damages recoverable in respect of the said wrong shall be reduced by such amount as the court thinks just and equitable having regard to the degrees of fault of the plaintiff and defendant: provided that—

(a) if, having regard to all the circumstances of the case, it is not possible to establish different degrees of fault, the liability shall be apportioned equally;

(b) this subsection shall not operate to defeat any defence arising under a contract or the defence that the plaintiff before the act complained of agreed to waive his legal rights in respect of it, whether or not for value; but, subject as aforesaid, the provisions of this subsection shall apply notwithstanding that the defendant might, apart from this subsection, have the defence of voluntary assumption of risk;

(c) where any contract or enactment providing for the limitation of liability is applicable to the claim, the amount of damages awarded to the plaintiff by virtue of this subsection shall not exceed the maximum limit so applicable.

(2) For the purpose of subsection (1) of this section—

(a) damage suffered by the plaintiff may include damages paid by the plaintiff to a third person who has suffered damage owing to the concurrent wrongs of the plaintiff and the defendant, and the period of limitation for claiming such damages shall be the same as is provided by section 31 for actions for contribution;

(b) a negligent or careless failure to mitigate damage shall be deemed to be contributory negligence in respect of the amount by which such damage exceeds the damage that would otherwise have occurred;

(c) the plaintiff's failure to exercise reasonable care for his own protection shall not amount to contributory negligence in respect of damage unless that damage results from the particular risk to which his conduct has exposed him, and the plaintiff's breach of statutory duty shall not amount to contributory negligence unless the damage of which he complains is damage that the statute was designed to prevent;

(d) the plaintiff's failure to exercise reasonable care in the protection of his own property shall, except to the extent that the defendant has been unjustly enriched, be deemed to be contributory negligence in an action for conversion of the property;

(e) damage may be held to be caused by the wrong of the defendant notwithstanding any rule of law by which the scope of the defendant's duty is limited to cases where the plaintiff has not been guilty of contributory negligence: but this paragraph shall not render the defendant liable for any damage in respect of which he or a person for whose acts he is responsible has not been careless in fact;

(f) where an action is brought for negligence in respect of a thing that has caused damage, the fact that there was a reasonable possibility or probability of examination after the thing had left the hands of the defendant shall not, by itself, exclude the defendant's duty, but may be taken as evidence that he was not in the circumstances negligent in parting with the thing in its dangerous state.

(3) ...

35. Identification

(1) For the purpose of determining contributory negligence—

(a) a plaintiff shall be responsible for the acts of a person for whom he is, in the particular circumstances, vicariously liable;

(b) a plaintiff in an action brought for the benefit of the dependants of a deceased person under Part IV (whether such plaintiff is the personal representative or a dependant of the deceased) shall be deemed to be responsible for the acts of the deceased;

(c) a plaintiff suing as personal representative of the person suffering the damage shall be deemed to be responsible for the acts of such person;

(d) a plaintiff suing on behalf of another (in this section called a nominal plaintiff) shall be deemed to be responsible for the acts of that other (in this section called the beneficiary) and, in particular, a person suing as personal representative of a deceased person shall be deemed to be responsible for the acts of those who would profit by success in the action, including the dependants of the deceased where the action is brought under Part IV: provided that—

(i) where a nominal plaintiff is suing on behalf of more than one beneficiary and one beneficiary has been guilty of contributory negligence while another beneficiary has not, the provisions of subsection (1) of section 34 shall apply only in respect of the share of the beneficiary guilty of contributory negligence; and the provisions of section 21 shall apply in favour of the defendant against the beneficiary so guilty of contributory negligence, in respect of the sum payable by the defendant for the benefit of the beneficiary not guilty of contributory negligence;

(ii) where it is found to be more convenient, the court may allow a nominal plaintiff to recover in full notwithstanding the contributory negligence of a beneficiary, and the provisions of section 21 shall then apply in favour of the defendant against the beneficiary so guilty of contributory negligence;

(e) a plaintiff suing as assignee of another, whether by operation of law or otherwise, shall be deemed to be responsible for the acts of that other;

(f) where the plaintiff's damage was caused by two or more persons and such persons would have been concurrent wrongdoers were it not for a contract by the plaintiff with one of such persons before the occurrence of the damage exempting that person from liability, the plaintiff shall be deemed to be responsible for the acts of that person;

(g) where the plaintiff's damage was caused by concurrent wrongdoers and before the occurrence of the damage the liability of one of such wrongdoers was limited by contract with the plaintiff to a sum less than that wrongdoer's just share of liability between himself and the other wrongdoer as determined under section 21 apart from such contract, the plaintiff shall be deemed to be responsible for the acts of that wrongdoer;

(h) where the plaintiff's damage was caused by concurrent wrongdoers and after the occurrence of the damage the liability of one of such wrongdoers is discharged by release or accord made with him by the plaintiff, while the liability of the other wrongdoers remains, the plaintiff shall be deemed to be responsible for the acts of the wrongdoer whose liability is so discharged;

(i) where the plaintiff's damage was caused by concurrent wrongdoers and the plaintiff's claim against one wrongdoer has become barred by the Statute of Limitations or any other limitation enactment, the plaintiff shall be deemed to be responsible for the acts of such wrongdoer;

(j) where the plaintiff's damage was caused by concurrent wrongdoers and, in an action against one of such wrongdoers, judgment is given for the defendant and the plaintiff then brings an action against another of such wrongdoers, the plaintiff shall be deemed to be responsible for the acts of the successful defendant if the defendant now sued can prove that he and the successful defendant were in fact concurrent wrongdoers;

(k) a plaintiff who is responsible for the acts of another under paragraphs (a) to (j) of this subsection shall be responsible also for the acts of any other persons for whose acts the said other person would be responsible under the said paragraphs if he were plaintiff in the action.

(2) For the purpose of subsection (1) of section 34, the contributory negligence—

(a) of a nominal plaintiff, or

(b) (where the action is brought for the loss of the consortium or services of a wife or for the loss of the services of a child or servant) of a wife, child or servant, shall neither bar recovery nor reduce the damages awarded; but the provisions of section 21 shall apply in favour of the defendant against the said nominal plaintiff, wife, child or servant,

as the case may be.

(3) Nothing in subsection (1) of this section shall affect the rights of the plaintiff against, or render the plaintiff liable in damages for the acts of, a person for whose acts he is deemed by the said subsection to be responsible.

(4) Where a plaintiff is held to be responsible for the acts of another under this section and his damages are accordingly reduced under subsection (1) of section 34, the defendant shall not be entitled to contribution under section 21 from the person for whose acts the plaintiff is responsible.

36. Set-off and claims

(1) When judgment is given for the plaintiff on a claim and for the defendant on a counterclaim under subsection (1) of section 34, the one judgment shall be set off against the other and only the balance found owing shall be recoverable.

(2) This section shall apply notwithstanding that one party is a bankrupt or (where a personal representative is party to an action) that the estate administered by him is insolvent.

(3) This section, and also section 251 of the Irish Bankrupt and Insolvent Act, 1857, in so far as it applies to a set-off of judgment debts owing by and to a bankrupt, shall operate only in relation to the satisfaction of debts, and, for all purposes (including

the construction of policies of insurance) other than that aforesaid, a judgment shall be treated as creating a debt, duty, obligation and liability for the full amount of the judgment as if there were no set-off, and for such other purposes a debt (whether by judgment or otherwise) shall be deemed to be paid by the judgment debtor to the extent of a debt set off against it.

(4) Notwithstanding anything in section 62, where a claim is made against a person who is insured in respect of a liability alleged in that claim and the claim is paid by the insurer with a deduction in respect of a sum owed to the insured by the person making such claim, the insured or any person representing or deriving title under him shall be entitled to recover from the insurers the amount of the said deduction.

37. Estoppel in case of contributory negligence

(1) Where a plaintiff has his damages reduced under subsection (1) of section 34 on account of contributory negligence and the defendant subsequently brings an action against the plaintiff in respect of damage arising out of the same facts, the determination of liability and the apportionment of fault in the first action shall be binding between the parties in the second action.

(2) Subsection (1) of this section shall apply between two parties notwithstanding that one of them is party to the two actions in different capacities.

38. Liability of concurrent wrongdoers where plaintiff guilty of contributory negligence

(1) Where an action is brought against one or more of concurrent wrongdoers by an injured person who is found in such action to have been guilty of contributory negligence and it is held to be just and equitable that the plaintiff's damages should be reduced under subsection (1) of section 34 having regard to his contributory negligence, the judgment against one wrongdoer shall not be for the whole of the plaintiff's recoverable damages but the court shall determine the respective degrees of fault of the plaintiff and of all the defendants to the plaintiff's claim at the time of judgment, leaving out of account the degrees of fault of persons who are not such defendants, and shall give the plaintiff a several judgment against each defendant for such apportioned part of his total damages as the court thinks just and equitable having regard to that defendant's degree of fault determined as aforesaid.

(2) The plaintiff, at any time within the period limited by law for the enforcement of judgments and upon proof that, after taking reasonable steps, he has failed to obtain satisfaction of any judgment in whole or in part, shall have liberty to apply for secondary judgments having the effect of distributing the deficiency among the other defendants in such proportions as may be just and equitable.

(3) This section shall not apply where one of the defendant wrongdoers is responsible for the acts of another; such wrongdoers shall, subject to subsection (1) of section 34, be liable to the plaintiff for a single portion of his damages.

(4) After judgment has been given in accordance with subsection (1) of this section, the plaintiff shall not be entitled to bring a second or subsequent action against a concurrent wrongdoer against whom judgment has not been given, unless he satisfies the court in such action that it was not reasonably possible for him to join such wrongdoer as co-defendant in the first action.

(5) The plaintiff, when commencing such second or subsequent action, shall be under a duty to the wrongdoers already successfully sued who have a right of contribution against the wrongdoer now sued or proposed to be sued to take reasonable steps to notify them of such second or subsequent action at least fourteen days before the institution of proceedings in such action or as soon as is reasonably possible after the commencement of such period.

(6) A wrongdoer receiving such notice shall have the right to become co-plaintiff in the action if the proceedings have not been instituted and otherwise to apply to the court for leave to be joined as co-plaintiff or for consolidation of actions; and a wrongdoer who unreasonably fails to take any of those steps as aforesaid shall be barred from his right of contribution.

(7) If the plaintiff is successful in such second or subsequent action, he shall be entitled to the difference between the total of the damages awarded to him in the previous judgment or judgments and the total of damages that in the view of the court would have been awarded if the said wrongdoer had been joined with the previous defendant or defendants as co-defendant in the earlier action or actions; and he shall be entitled in addition to the provision mentioned in subsection (2) of this section: provided that—

(a) nothing in this subsection shall entitle a plaintiff to recover from such wrongdoer more than he could have recovered had he not brought such previous action or actions;

(b) nothing in this subsection shall preclude such wrongdoer from disputing any issue that he is otherwise entitled to dispute and, if the plaintiff's damages are found to be less than they were held to be by the court in the earlier action or actions, such wrongdoer shall not be liable for more than his due proportion as between himself, the plaintiff and the previous defendant or defendants of the damages so found;

(c) such wrongdoer may at his option avail himself of any matter decided against the plaintiff in such previous action or actions as though such matter were res judicata between them.

(8) Where damages are awarded against a wrongdoer in accordance with the provisions of this section, such wrongdoer may recover contribution from any other wrongdoer not sued at the same time where such recovery is just and equitable subject to the provisions of Chapter II of this Part.

(9) A wrongdoer, when commencing such action for contribution, shall be under a duty to the injured person who has a right of action against the contributor and to the other wrongdoers already successfully sued by the injured person who have a right of contribution against the contributor to take reasonable steps to notify them of such action for contribution at least fourteen days before the institution of proceedings in such action or as soon as is reasonably possible after the commencement of such period.

(10) The injured person or a wrongdoer receiving such notice shall have the rights specified in subsection (6) of this section, and if he unreasonably fails to take advantage of his rights he shall be barred from his right of action for damages or for contribution as the case may be.

(11) Where the injured person brings a second or subsequent action in accordance with the provisions of this section, and where a wrongdoer brings an action for contribution as provided in subsection (8) of this section, the parties to the action shall be bound by the

apportionment of fault made in the earlier action or actions: but the defendant shall not be bound by such apportionment if provision comes to be made for distributing any deficiency caused by the failure to obtain satisfaction of any judgment in whole or in part from one of the wrongdoers already sued.

(12) Where—

(a) the plaintiff sues one wrongdoer and either because he obtains judgment by default or because the court negatives contributory negligence the plaintiff recovers judgment in respect of the whole of his damages against such wrongdoer, and

(b) the plaintiff subsequently sues another wrongdoer who is held to have been a concurrent wrongdoer with the first, the plaintiff also being held to have been guilty of contributory negligence as regards both wrongdoers,

the defendant secondly sued shall be entitled to credit for the same proportion of the sum received from the defendant first sued as the proportion of the damage adjudged to be borne by the plaintiff as between himself and the defendant secondly sued, and in the event of overpayment shall be entitled to repayment.

39. Bankruptcy of one wrongdoer

Where it is made to appear to the court that—

(a) one wrongdoer in whose favour judgment is given is or may become a bankrupt, or

(b) the estate of one wrongdoer for the benefit of which judgment is given is or may be insolvent,

provision shall be made to ensure that such first-mentioned wrongdoer or such estate, as the case may be, shall be deprived of recovery to the extent that the wrongdoer or estate is liable to another party or in the aggregate to other parties as a result of the same accident, occurrence or transaction; and for that purpose judgment in favour of the wrongdoer or for the benefit of the estate shall, where necessary, be attached in whole or in part for the benefit of another party in whose favour judgment is given.

40. Special findings

(1) Where damages are awarded to any person by virtue of subsection (1) of section 34, the jury or if there is no jury then the judge or arbitrator shall find and record—

(a) the total damages that would have been awarded if there had not been contributory negligence;

(b) where the plaintiff's damages are reduced under the said subsection, the proportion of such damages that shall not be awarded to the plaintiff and the proportion that shall be payable by the defendant, or the respective proportions that shall be payable by each of the defendants if more than one, expressed in each case in percentage of the total fault of the plaintiff and defendant or defendants;

(c) whose negligence, want of care or caution, or wrong contributed to whose or what damage, and in what respects.

(2) It shall be the duty of the judge or arbitrator to make the requisite calculations following upon such findings.

41. Courts of limited jurisdiction

Where an action is brought in a court of limited jurisdiction, the court may award damages up to the limit of its jurisdiction, even though such damages have first been reduced under subsection (1) of section 34 on account of the plaintiff's contributory negligence.

42. Costs in cases of contributory negligence

As a general principle, but not so as to limit the judge in the exercise of his discretion, where damages are awarded on claim and counterclaim subject in each case to a reduction for contributory negligence under subsection (1) of section 34, costs shall be awarded in the same proportions as damages.

43. Application to breaches of strict duty

In determining the amount of contribution or of reduction of damages under subsection (1) of section 34 for contributory negligence the court may take account of the fact that the negligence or wrong of one person consisted only in a breach of strict statutory or common-law duty without fault, and may accordingly hold that it is not just and equitable to cast any part of the damage upon such person.

44. One-sided periods of limitation

Where, in any claim for contribution between wrongdoers, or in any case to which subsection (1) of section 34 applies, the defendant avoids liability to the plaintiff by pleading the Statute of Limitations or any other limitation enactment, neither he nor any other person responsible for his acts shall be entitled to recover any damages or contribution from the plaintiff.

INDEX